# Pre-Confederation Canada:

# The Structure of Canadian History to 1867

J. L. Finlay
University of Manitoba

Prentice-Hall Canada Inc., Scarborough, Ontario

## Canadian Cataloguing in Publication Data

Finlay, John L., 1939-
    Pre-Confederation Canada

Includes bibliographical references and index.
ISBN 0-13-692476-X

1. Canada — History — To 1763 (New France).
2. Canada — History — 1763-1867.
3. Canada — Politics and government — To 1763.
4. Canada — Politics and government — 1763-1867. I. Title.

FC161.F56 1989        971      C88-095338-1
F1032.F56 1989

©1990 Prentice-Hall Canada Inc., Scarborough, Ontario

Prentice-Hall, Inc., Englewood Cliffs, New Jersey
Prentice-Hall International, Inc., London
Prentice-Hall of Australia, Pty., Ltd., Sydney
Prentice-Hall of India Pvt., Ltd., New Delhi
Prentice-Hall of Japan, Inc., Tokyo
Prentice-Hall of Southeast Asia (Pte.) Ltd., Singapore
Editora Prentice-Hall do Brasil Ltda., Rio de Janeiro
Prentice-Hall Hispanoamericana, S.A., Mexico

ISBN 0-13-692476-X

Production Editors: Peter Buck and Jamie Bush
Map Research: Margaret Conrad
Cartographers: Geoffrey A. Lester and Rod Dunphy
Designer: Deborah-Anne Bailey
Production Coordinator: Sandra Paige
Typesetting: Labelle Typesetting — Oakville

    2   3   4   5   IG   94   93   92   91

Printed and bound in Canada by Gagné Printing Ltd.

# Contents

# Illustrations

## Maps

## Diagrams

# Preface

*Pre-Confederation Canada* is based, for the most part, on published materials, especially monographs and articles that have appeared within the last twenty years. The main sources are acknowledged at the end of each chapter, under the headings "Suggested Reading." These references, although intended to give the reader an appreciation of the wider debate on the many issues covered in the main body of the text, cannot possibly describe the various interpretations in all their complexity and detail. Nor can they adequately acknowledge the full debt owed to my colleagues, past and present, without whose meticulous archival research the present volume would have been quite impossible.

Among the many people who have made this work possible, there are, however, certain individuals whom I would like to single out. Professors R. Hall (University of Western Ontario), G. Panting (Memorial University), and W. Turner (Brock University) read the typescript thoroughly and made valuable suggestions; I hope that I have done them justice. The staff of Prentice-Hall, above all Peter Buck, together with Margaret Conrad of Acadia University, who researched the maps, have been patient and supportive. A special thank-you goes to Pat Buchanan, Blanche Miller, and Jeannine Watson for their cheerful and efficient transformation of the original manuscript.

# CHAPTER 1

# THE INVENTION OF AMERICA

## — 1. European Push —

The town is now only recognizable by its edifices and magnificent houses and no longer by its teeming population, the decrease and destruction of which is constantly augmented by the piled-up corpses, of which 60 000 were burned . . . , 170 000 have further been buried in huge trenches . . . .The air is always so thick and misty, and is further obscured by multitudes of birds enticed by the carrion of the corpses, the stench of which is overwhelming. The dead are no longer counted. Misery and grief are great and general.

Only the reference to surviving edifices and magnificent houses indicates that this description does not deal with a twentieth-century holocaust, such as the firebombing of Dresden or the atomic destruction of Hiroshima. In fact, the description predates modern horrors by hundreds of years; it is about the impact of the plague upon Naples, merely one episode in the Black Death that ravaged Europe between 1347 and its last visitation in 1720.

Of the many cycles that occurred during this pandemic, the original, of 1347-51, was the most devastating. In those few short years a third of the population was wiped out. In certain areas mortality was total. Nothing had prepared medieval humanity for this shattering experience; it had no means of comprehending such a disaster. The Black Death, then, was a calamity on such a scale that it effectively divides the solidity and prosperity of the High Middle Ages from the gloom and despair of the ensuing century.

In that hundred years, roughly from 1350 to 1450, Europe was no friendly setting. Something of the magnitude of the tensions that gripped society may be judged from the outburst of flagellants that followed the Black Death. Bands of zealots, sometimes hundreds strong, travelling from town to town, would ceremonially scourge themselves in a frenzied attempt to expiate the guilt they irrationally but helplessly felt. The contemporary Henry of Hereford observed,

> Each scourge was a kind of stick from which three tails with large knots hung down. Through the knots were thrust iron spikes as sharp as needles which projected about the length of a grain of wheat, or sometimes a little more. With such scourges they lashed themselves on their naked bodies so that they became swollen and blue, the blood ran down to the ground and bespattered the walls of the chambers in which they scourged themselves. Occasionally they drove the spikes so deep into the flesh that they could only be pulled out by a second wrench.

The flagellant example was intense, but short-lived. A rather longer lasting example of psychopathology was the witchcraft craze. The fifteenth and sixteenth centuries, not the Dark Ages, marked the peak of this belief system. Particularly striking was the widespread opinion that Anti-Christ was imminent; the signs of a collapsing civilization could only herald the coming of Satan. That the Muslims were expanding at the expense of Christendom was seized upon to confirm this: Adrianople, guarding the flank of Europe, fell to the Islamic Turks in 1361; the capital of Orthodox Christianity, Constantinople, fell in 1453; in 1480 Turkish raiders landed in Southern Italy; in 1529 they besieged Vienna. Europe was on the defensive, and physically shrinking. It had become a hostile and threatening environment, and there were those who wanted out.

This was especially true of one section of society. In the aftermath of the Black Death a major reordering of relationships took place. A loss of working population on such a scale meant a vastly increased bargaining power for the survivors. The move away from the fixity of feudal bonds was

## Map 1.1: Europe in 1600

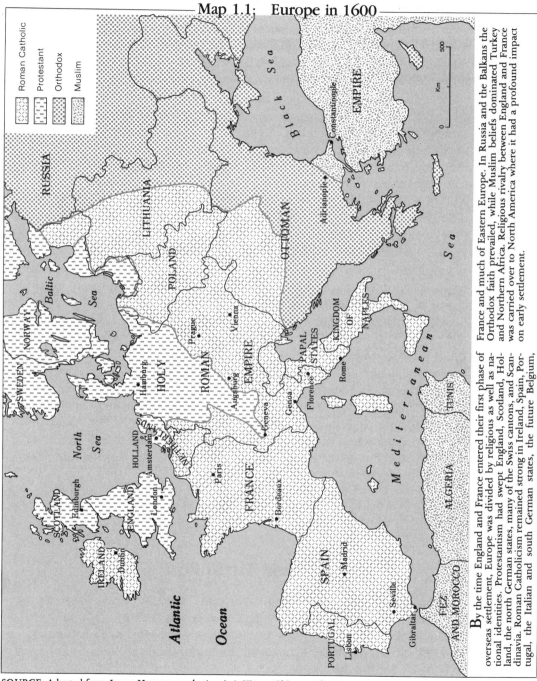

By the time England and France entered their first phase of overseas settlement, Europe was divided by religious as well as national identities. Protestantism had swept England, Scotland, Holland, the north German states, many of the Swiss cantons, and Scandinavia. Roman Catholicism remained strong in Ireland, Spain, Portugal, the Italian and south German states, the future Belgium, France and much of Eastern Europe. In Russia and the Balkans the Orthodox faith prevailed, while Muslim beliefs dominated Turkey and Northern Africa. Religious rivalry between England and France was carried over to North America where it had a profound impact on early settlement.

SOURCE: Adapted from James Henretta et al., *America's History* (Chicago: The Dorsey Press, 1987), p. 25.

speeded up, and the ability of the lord of the manor to control his tenants was significantly diminished. A series of peasant risings in this period served to keep the changing reality constantly before the ruling élite, and to make them hanker after the "good old days" when the lower orders knew their place.

The traditional ruling class was also under pressure from another source. Indeed, it was being ground between the upper and nether mill-stones, for in this period there emerged a new phenomenon: the State. In the Middle Ages the state had barely existed. Power, rather than being concentrated in any one locus, had been diffused, split up among the nobles who insisted upon their equality with the king — was not their collective name for themselves the *peers* of the realm? With power too broken up, the disintegrating tensions of 1350-1450 had gone to their extremes. Most of Europe had degenerated into civil war: in England, the War of the Roses; in France, the struggle between the Valois rulers and the House of Burgundy; in Italy and Germany, the anarchy of princely particularism. This very disintegration nevertheless produced its own antidote. If countries were to survive at all, it was to be thanks to the ruthless mobilization of all resources behind the idea of the state. Ambitious individuals would thrust themselves into power and speak for a centralized state so efficient that no feudal noble could hope to maintain a claim to equality.

Examples of such new states and their rulers were Florence under the Medici, England under the Tudors, France under the Valois, or (thanks to splendid marriage coups) the Hapsburgs of Austria, Spain, and the Netherlands. Rulers such as these both terrified and fascinated the feudal knightly class, threatening to diminish their power and status on the one hand, but on the other shining forth as instances of what the successful condottiere could become.

# — 2. New World Pull —

It is salutary to stress the importance of "push," the reasons why inhabitants of old countries felt obliged to get out. Too often it is assumed (especially in a land of immigrants) that the attractive qualities of the new lured people away from the old. In many cases, however, the impossibility of the old has been responsible for the uprooting.

This is not to deny, of course, that "pull" factors were operating. Two in particular may be mentioned. The first was the economic. The Black Death may have caused savage setbacks in some directions, but in others and in the longer haul its results were quite otherwise. In time the population decline was halted and eventually, in about 1450, reversed, and spectacularly, too: the population of England doubled between 1450 and 1600. An expanding population is itself a cause of an economic boom. The growing population provides increased demand; at the same time, the availability of workers prevents wage rates from rising too rapidly; and the population is composed disproportionately of the productive young and lacks the unproductive old who might impose a welfare drag upon the economy.

Even more important than mere technical causes of economic expansion was the changed psychology that marked European society at this time. The Black Death had intensified a new approach to trading. It was as if the survivors agreed on a new beginning, quite free of the traditional way of doing business. Indeed, in some cases this was literally true: the authorities accepted a sweeping away of the existing, restrictive trade guilds, throwing open careers to those who would seize the opportunities. If this was a time of new monarchs, it was also a time of new merchants. There was about the fifteenth-century trader a new ruthlessness every bit as savage as that of the new rulers. Typical in this regard was Jacob Fugger (1459-1525). His grandfather founded the family business (in textiles) in the very early years of the fifteenth century, but Jacob, wheeling and dealing on a princely scale, diversified into gold and silver mining, copper mining, mercury production, moneylending to Emperor and to Pope, and amassed lands that yielded wheat, wool, and all manner of products. The Fugger empire spread from Spain to Hungary, from the Baltic to the Mediterranean. Some idea of the increased scale of business may be divined by comparing the Fuggers' fortunes: in the grandfather's day the firm was worth only 3000 gulden; by Jacob's it had risen to over two million; in the 1540s, at the peak, it was over five million. It is hardly surprising that this was the time when the story of Dick Whittington (an actual Lord Mayor of London in about 1400) caught the public fancy.

Expansion in trade and commerce went hand in glove with that of the state, as the example of Jacob Fugger bankrolling the Emperor makes plain. For both individuals and states, expansion was self-fuelling. The build-up of power, whether economic or judicial, could not pause, for increasingly powerful neighbours were standing threats to any notion of complacency. Thus, each would-be leader was compelled on a course that could lead to the war of each against the others. Given such a dynamic, the pull of distant territories was immense. If one did not take advantage of their possibilities, then a rival would. Rulers and merchants, separately and in conjunction, were drawn irresistibly beyond the known world.

## — 3. The Religious Imperative —

The pull of the unknown was not restricted to economic-strategic considerations, however. There was in addition a more venerable reason for being attracted to strange lands, the age-old Christian imperative to "go forth and convert the heathen." The last major manifestation of this missionary enterprise had been the Crusades, a series of initiatives to win the Holy Land for Christianity. By the eve of the Black Death, however, that movement had petered out, and since then Christendom had been retreating. The sense of defeat was such that by the mid-fifteenth century both Dominicans and Franciscans, the leading missionaries, had disbanded their special missionary organizations.

Yet the imperative remained, and the fantastic late medieval world was an ideal setting for the legend of Prester John. He was believed to be a Christian king ruling an empire embedded in the hostile world of Islam; at various times this empire had been variously located, now in India, now in Africa. In the fifteenth century, whatever its location, it tugged at the imagination, suggesting that if contact could be made then the Muslim flank might be turned.

Alongside this preoccupation, the older, more general imperative slumbered on. It awaited the birth of some suitable focus for the Church's missionary energies. Meanwhile, intellectuals were preparing the ground by altering the basis of missionary activity. Whereas previously brute force had loomed large, now the emphasis was increasingly placed upon convincing non-Christians of the superiority of the Christian faith, so leading to a voluntary and genuine conversion.

## — 4. The Portuguese End-Run —

The first to take advantage of widening horizons were the Portuguese. Beginning early in the fifteenth century, they slowly but inexorably extended their knowledge of the world. In 1415 they captured Ceuta, an Islamic city opposite Gibraltar; in the next generation the Madeiras, Canary, and Azores islands were settled; by 1460 present-day Sierra Leone had been reached; by 1475 the Cameroons; by 1482 Angola. The great breakthroughs followed quickly. In 1487-88 Bartholomew Diaz rounded the Cape of Good Hope into the Indian Ocean, and just ten years later Vasco da Gama landed in India. The king of Portugal signalled this triumph by adding to his royal title "Lord of the Conquest, Navigation and Commerce of Ethiopia, Arabia, Persia and India."

In carrying through such a spectacular enterprise, the Portuguese brought together most of the elements touched on above. In the early crucial days the backing of the royal family was vital. Prince Henry (*d.* 1460) was so committed to exploration that he earned the title "the Navigator." His successors kept up the royal commitment. Very quickly, however, the merchants took up the costs of exploration; thus, in 1470 the West African trade was granted to the Lisbon merchant Fernâo Gomes in return for his undertaking annually to explore a hundred leagues of *terra incognita.*

Well might both king and traders be interested. There was gold to be had in Africa, and also "black gold," *i.e.,* slaves. The great lure, however, was the spice trade. European agriculture was a subsistence agriculture. Meat was always in short supply and, in the absence of refrigeration, that available by winter's end was more often than not putrid. Simply to mask the stench of high meat and to add variety to a monotonously bland diet, Europeans craved spices, and were willing to pay exorbitant prices for them. Thus, India and the Spice Islands (The Moluccas) immediately overshadowed Africa as regions of interest.

Present, too, was the element of the spiritual mission. The Navigator constantly required his captains to search out news of Prester John: in 1486 ambassadors were dispatched overland to Ethiopia and India to this end. And da Gama, on landing in India, was delighted to find what he considered Christian groups among the Muslims of the Malabar Coast.

The only element missing was colonization. The Portuguese were content to trade. A series of forts was built to police the long route to the East, and pitched battles were fought to secure control of key staging posts, for example, at Ormuz in 1515 to give control of the Persian Gulf. However, the notion of sending out appreciable numbers of Portuguese to settle foreign soil was not then part of the Portuguese endeavour. Why should it have been? There were fortunes to be made in mere trade.

# — 5. Spanish Empire by Conquest —

Hard on the heels of the Portuguese came the Spaniards, and their experience was to be crucially different. To understand this difference it is necessary to grasp the unique quality of later medieval Spain.

Amid the disintegration of the fifteenth century, Spain stood out as the exception. Where others were in danger of fragmenting, Spain was coming together; the marriage of Ferdinand of Aragon and Isabella of Castile in 1469 laid the basis of a potent unity. Its dynamic was underlined when Spanish forces completed in 1492 the centuries-old *Reconquista* by driving the Moors from their last stronghold, Granada.

This triumph was at once military and religious. It blended the medieval chivalric ideals in a striking fashion, but in a more mundane way it left Spain with a surplus of unsatisfied energies. The knightly class had been mobilized for war and trained in its arts. Yet in the moment of seeming fulfillment that class had to recognize that the fruits would be meagre, for the Spanish monarchy was every bit as centralizing as its European counterparts. It was the same in religious terms. The spiritual energies of the time were not adequately discharged, for the defeated Muslims were handled as a political question, required to convert *en masse* and outwardly.

Thus, when the Spanish had to face the imminent Portuguese breakthrough, they were ready to respond in bold ways. In 1492 Columbus was fitted out with a flotilla of three ships with which to find a way to the East — not by trespassing on Portuguese preserves, but by sailing westward across the Atlantic. When Columbus made landfall in the Caribbean he was convinced he had accomplished his task, and the very name, the West Indies, commemorates this historical blunder. Not for several years did Europe realize that a new continent barred the route to the Indies.

From the very first, Spanish ventures differed from the Portuguese. Already Columbus's second expedition was to colonize. It is clear that in the case of Spain the "push" factors outweighed the "pulls." The drive of Spain was to be fulfilled in New Spain. Brave men could gain great wealth and status and save literally millions of souls; as Bernal Diaz, the warrior chronicler of New Spain, put it, the *conquistadores* were to be honoured, for "they died in the service of God and His Majesty, and to give light to those who sat in darkness, and also to acquire that wealth which most men covet." It was a combination to be seen to perfection in the conquest of Mexico (1519-21) by Cortés.

Cortés fitted out an expedition that at no time numbered more than 1000

Europeans. He had, however, several crucial advantages when he took on an Aztec empire of millions. To begin with there was technological superiority. Cortés had with him horses, metal armour and swords, and guns, with which to overawe opponents who knew nothing of such things. More important was his ability to exploit structural weaknesses in the Mexican state, for the Aztec empire was poised on a knife edge. An all-powerful warrior caste maintained an elaborate and sophisticated civilization on the basis of an abject slave population. Public order was kept against a background of human sacrifice practised on a terrible scale; in one four-day period on the eve of the Spanish onslaught some 80 000 were slain. The temples were found to be crusted with blood six inches thick in places. Given such terrorism, there were Indian tribes with reason to back the Spaniards rather than the Aztecs, and Cortés had the support of tens of thousands of Indian allies at key junctures. Above all, Mexican mythology had spoken of a benevolent god, Quetzalcoatl, who would return one day to resume his rightful place as emperor and put an end to human sacrifice. Quetzalcoatl was pictured as bearded and pale skinned. Thus, as reports of Spaniards began to filter through to the Aztecs, there was a mood of fatalistic resignation, a willingness to accept the fulfillment of prophecy. The Aztec leader, Montezuma, abdicated and paved the way for his people's conquest.

The outcome was the total replacement of Aztec power by Cortés's. This is a crucial point as, in the initial phase, it was not Spanish power that had triumphed so much as Cortés's own personal power. Cortés, a second son who in the normal way could not have expected much from late medieval Spanish society, had seized for himself, in defiance of properly constituted authority, a vast feudal kingdom. By slotting himself into the place of his defeated rival, he had become the instant feudal noble complete with thousands if not millions of subservient peasants. Beneath him other Spanish *arrivistes* were made *encomanderos*, that is, were given lordship over Indians. In New Spain was recreated a way of life rapidly vanishing in Spain itself.

The magnitude of Cortés's achievement has to be grasped. In one sense the New World was a vast embarrassment, an obstacle that stood in the way of the real goal. Today it is difficult to appreciate this devaluation of the Americas. Perhaps two observations will drive home this truth. It must not be forgotten that Columbus did not discover America; rather he rediscovered it. Europeans had known of that continent much earlier. Whoever was the first European to visit America is not important, but it is certain that about 1000 A.D. the Vikings knew of Labrador, Newfoundland, and perhaps Maine. This knowledge disappeared from general currency and became fabulous, for at that date Europe simply had no *use* for these lands. The second observation is the following from a school principal's introduction to a geography textbook; significantly, it was written in 1512, *i.e.,* after Columbus but before Cortés:

> In our life time, Amerigo Vespucci is said to have discovered that New World. . . . He says . . . that this New World is quite distinct from (Africa) and bigger than our Europe. Whether this is true or a lie, it has nothing . . . to do with the Cosmography and the knowledge of History. For the people and places of that continent are unknown and unnamed to us and sailings are only made there with the greatest dangers. Therefore it is of no interest to geographers at all.

Cortés had done more than discover new lands and cultures. He had invented a new world, had shown that something useful might be made out of a blunder. When in 1530 Pizarro with even fewer Europeans conquered the Inca empire of Peru, the imagination of the Old World had been seized by the Spanish variant of overseas expansion.

# — 6. French Emulation —

The Portuguese and the Spaniards, having been well poised to take advantage of these possibilities, seemed by the early sixteenth century to control the expanding world. Their dominance was made all the stronger because they had papal warrant for their division of the new-found spoils. Soon after Columbus's discovery, the Pope of the day, the Spaniard Alexander VI, granted Ferdinand and Isabella all rights to islands discovered to the west of the Azores. When the Portuguese protested that this infringed on rights granted them by a previous Pope, negotiations pushed the dividing line further west (so giving Portugal Brazil). This agreement, cemented by the Treaty of Tordesillas in 1494, seemed to validate under papal auspices an Iberian claim to the entire New World.

It was not to be expected, however, that other European powers would agree to such a monopoly. France in particular was likely to challenge such claims. From 1515, the French king was Francis I, a ruler who saw himself as the leading figure of Europe and who challenged the Hapsburgs even to the point of contesting their claim to the Holy Roman Empire. He was fearful of Spanish and Hapsburg growth, and wished to have his own overseas empire to maintain his due splendour. In turning his gaze to America he had something of a precedent to guide him and to give weight to any claim he might advance. For a generation or more French fishermen had been voyaging to the Grand Banks of Newfoundland to fish for cod alongside Portuguese, Basques, and Englishmen. By this time the "green" fishery (whereby the cod was salted down in the ship's hold while the fishing proceeded) was being superseded by the "dry" (whereby the cod was dried on land before being loaded for the voyage home) and so a minimal occupation of the coast was already underway. In this tenuous fashion, the French had the basis for an interest in a portion of North America.

The first attempt to translate theory into practice took place in 1524. In that year the French sent an expedition under the Italian, Verrazano, to survey the coast north of the Spanish sphere of influence. He sailed from Florida to Newfoundland, but failed to find the hoped-for Northwest Passage to the Indies. In this sense the voyage was a failure, and it was not immediately followed up. However, there was one consequence; Verrazano applied the name Arcadia to North America, an allusion to the classical world's name for a rural paradise; in time this designation migrated from the original Virginia to Nova Scotia and in so doing its name changed to Acadia.

A more serious initiative was begun ten years later. In 1534 Jacques Cartier made the first of his voyages to North America. It amounted to no more than a brief survey of the Newfoundland region during two summer months. Two Indians were taken back to France with the intention they become interpreters, but otherwise little was accomplished. The following year Cartier was back. This time the St. Lawrence was discovered and penetrated far upstream. The French party visited Stadacona (present-day Quebec City), and then some ascended to Hochelaga (present-day Montreal). There Cartier was made aware of the rapids that, he thought, barred his way to China (hence their name to this day — Lachine). Despite this disappointment, the voyage seemed to be a success. Contact was made with the Indians (for Stadacona was the home of the two taken to France the year previously) and their stories convinced Cartier that they were on the border of the Kingdom of the Saguenay, an advanced state on the lines of the Aztec empire, rich in gold and slaves and ripe for the taking. It was a prospect to buoy their spirits through an arduous winter spent at Stadacona, and to make meaningful a sojourn in a land otherwise described by Cartier as the "land God gave to Cain." When the spring break-up occurred, the survivors returned in high fettle to Francis I, taking with them the Indian chief, Donnacona, and several of his "subjects."

European entanglements prevented Francis from capitalizing on these beginnings until 1541. Cartier's third voyage was then mounted to search for the "large city called Sagana where there are many mines of gold and silver . . . and there is abundance of clove, nutmeg, and pepper" — evidently Donnacona had been telling his hosts what they wanted to hear. When the expedition was finalized, there were two novel features. The first was the additional stipulation that Cartier undertake missionary work. This afterthought was added presumably to strengthen French right of entry to territory otherwise ceded to Spain by the papacy; certainly this aspect was not taken seriously, but it is important since it became part of the myth of French colonization that religion was always of prime importance. The second novelty was the replacement of Cartier as commander by Jean-François de la Roque, Sieur de Roberval. Socially superior to Cartier, he was also the military leader of the force that was to replicate on the Saguenay the Spanish exploits in South America. The fitting out of this army taking time, Cartier was sent on ahead. Not until a year later in 1542 was Roberval ready to sail.

Both parties wintered on the St. Lawrence, a year apart. For both the expedition was a failure. Cartier's relations with the Indians were no longer good, perhaps because not a single one of those taken to France had lived to make the return journey. He did find "certaine leaves of fine gold as thicke as a man's nail" and a "good store of stones, which we esteemed to be Diamants," and with these he set sail for France. Not even Roberval's express command to return to Canada, given when the two flotillas bumped into each other off Newfoundland, could induce him to spend more time in such an inhospitable setting. Within the year Roberval too had learned to his cost what a Canadian winter could mean: over half his force was dead of scurvy. He too trailed back to France defeated, to discover that Cartier's jewels had turned out to be worthless. Henceforth they served to designate anything worthless — *voilà un diamant de Canada*.

## — 7. The English Variant —

English initiatives in the New World were even more tentative than those of the French. It is true that before the fifteenth century was out Henry VII, first of the Tudor kings, had commissioned John Cabot, an Italian, to search for a passage to the East. Thanks to this voyage England had established a claim to Newfoundland, but since that beginning little had been done. The reason in part was the diversion of English energies into Ireland.

English involvement in Ireland dated all the way back to 1152, but the conquest had never been complete, and Ireland was for England a constant drain. Moreover, its position meant that it was always a potential backdoor into England for its enemies, France and Spain. Thus, England's rulers were compelled to seek solutions to the problem, and this was especially true of the centralizing Tudors. In the sixteenth century, then, determined efforts were made to force Ireland into submission.

A watershed in these attempts marked the 1560s. In that decade a novel approach was championed by Sir Henry Sidney, a diplomat who had served several years in Spain and undoubtedly knew at first hand the success of the *conquistadores*; later he was to be active in transatlantic ventures. His plan was to colonize Ireland, planting Englishmen in key areas and driving out the natives. In this way Irish resistance would be worn down, and English ways would permeate the land. The prospectuses he issued to attract participants explicitly appealed to younger, landless sons and held out the prospect of their becoming squires controlling a tenantry.

Over the next generation and more this policy was pursued in Ireland. Two points need to be stressed. The first is that the method was rooted in a notion of cultural superiority. The colonizers were appalled by the Gaelic-speaking tribal society they found, and setting it against their increasingly modern, efficient style deemed it nothing short of barbaric; as one observer put it, if the Irish "were suffered to possess the whole country . . . they would never . . . build houses, make townships or villages, or manure or improve the land as it ought to be; therefore it stands neither with Christian policy nor conscience to suffer so good and fruitful a country to lie waste like a wilderness." Within a few short years older views of the Irish were replaced by a stereotype that saw them as less than human, a stereotype that was psychologically valuable to colonists intent on dispossessing the rightful owners. English treatment of the Irish became brutal in the extreme. One official boasted that in April 1573 alone he had "kylled and hanged . . . of the rebels and their ayders about the number of eight hundred persons." Two years later the English massacred over 600 hundred men, women and children on Rathlin Island, a good example of "government" by terror.

The second point to be made is that in all this the Catholic-Protestant clash was very much in evidence. When the Protestant Tudors began to tighten their control of Ireland, the native people turned increasingly to Catholicism as a badge of identity, nationality, and resistance. On the other hand the colonists, overwhelmingly from Devon and the Southwest of England, were aggressively Protestant. Prominent backers of Sidney included Humphrey Gilbert, Richard Grenville, and Francis Drake (the last, incidentally, a perpetrator of the Rathlin Island massacre). These men were leading anti-Catholic, anti-Spanish activists, eager to spread the Protestant evangel and to break into the Spanish monopoly in the New World.

For them, and for an influential body of English opinion, the Irish experience was crucial. It merged the notions of cultural and religious superiority, and forged an early notion of the white man's (or WASP's) burden. As one Irish colonizer put it, "how godly a deede it is to overthrowe so wicked a race the world may judge: for my part I thinke there cannot be a greater sacrifice to God." When the Elizabethans exported the technical expertise gained in Ireland to America, they also exported this potent ideology. There it was to be directed against Indians, and against French Catholics.

That export began in 1584 with a series of experiments that led first to the failure of Roanoke and then to the ultimate success of Jamestown, both in Virginia. The leading light in the early stages was Sir Walter Ralegh, half brother to Gilbert, cousin to Grenville, and distantly related to Drake, and himself a confirmed Protestant and veteran of the Irish wars. Later, Ralegh having been pushed aside, the Virginia Company was chartered in 1606, and this company founded Jamestown in 1607. It is important to note that this initiative, unlike those of the Spanish and French, was a private one without direct state participation. After coming perilously close to failure, the colony was bullied through its "Starving Time" by the military rule of Sir Thomas Dale, and kept alive long enough to hit upon the means of its deliverance.

That discovery was made in 1614 when John Rolfe shipped to England the first cargo of tobacco from an English colony. Previously Englishmen had learned to enjoy tobacco imported from Spanish colonies, and although King James had presciently condemned the practice of smoking as "a custome lothsome to the eye, hateful to the nose, harmfulle to the braine, dangerous to the lungs, and in the blacke stinking fume thereof, neerest resembling the horrible Stigian smoke of the pit that is bottomless," the habit grew apace. Thus Rolfe's experiment proved extremely successful, and Virginian exports shot up — to 2300 pounds in 1616 and to almost 50 000 pounds in 1618. Jamestown became North America's first boom-town, so given over to the cultivation of tobacco that "streets and all other spare places [are] planted with tobacco . . . , the Colony dispersed all about, planting tobacco." When Indian land got in the way, its owners were simply poisoned.

Those involved with the Virginia company recognized that they had failed to emulate the Spaniards and the Portuguese. As William Simmonds put it in 1612, their experience was not

> delightful, because not stuffed with relations of heaps and mines of gold and
> silver, nor such rare commodities as the Portugals and Spaniards found in the

East and West Indies. The want whereof hath begot us . . . no lesse scorne and contempt, than their noble conquests and valiant adventures . . . praise and honor . . . . It was the Spaniards good hap to happen in those parts where were infinite numbers of people, whoe had manured the ground . . . and time had brought them to that perfection [that] they had the use of gold and silver . . . so that what the Spaniard got was only the spoile and pileage. . . . But had these fruitful Countries beene as savage, as barbarous, as ill-peopled, as little planted, laboured and manured, as Virginia, their proper labours, it is likely would have produced as small profit as ours . . . . But we chanced in a lande, even as God made it. Where we found only an idle, improvident, scattered people, ignorant of the knowledge of gold and silver . . . and careless of anything but from hand to mouth . . . .

Thus it was that, driven by necessity and succeeding almost by inadvertence, England had invented another America, that of the cash crop. It was possible thanks to the southern climate, to that temperate setting that had justified its original title, Arcadia. Meanwhile, the more northerly parts of North America, the more recent Acadia, were slowly responding to renewed European contacts. In their climate a tobacco boom was out of the question. It remained to be seen if anything else could be made out of the "land God gave to Cain."

## Suggested Reading

Before mentioning books specific to this chapter, it would be well to make certain general observations. Considerable help may be obtained from the following: D.A. Muise, *A Reader's Guide to Canadian History: 1. Beginnings to Confederation* (1982), which is usefully annotated. *The Dictionary of Canadian Biography* is vital not only for its stated purpose: it also contains overviews of the more significant contexts. The standard survey of Canadian history is the Centenary Series, the individual volumes of which will be noted at the appropriate points; readers may also benefit from the very full bibliographies that they contain. Readers should also be aware of D.G.G. Kerr, *A Historical Atlas of Canada* (1975); G. Matthews (ed.), *Historical Atlas of Canada* (in progress); and M.C. Urquhart and K.A.H. Buckley (eds.), *Historical Statistics of Canada* (1965).

Since it is assumed that readers will be working systematically through this text, books mentioned in the bibliographical notes at the end of each chapter will in general be noted once only.

Two books that describe the European setting are P. Ziegler, *The Black Death* (1969) and J. Huizinga, *The Waning of the Middle Ages* (1924). For more detailed coverage of this setting the *New Cambridge Modern History* (several volumes) may be consulted. Information on the Portuguese and Spanish exploits is contained in, respectively, C.R.V. Bell, *Portugal and the Quest for the Indies* (1974) and E. Wolf, *Sons of the Shaking Earth* (1959). On Cortés, R.C. Padden's *The Hummingbird and the Hawk: Conquest and Sovereignty in the Valley of Mexico* (1967) is essential.

For French and English endeavours the older J.B. Brebner, *The Explorers of North America* (1933) is still useful. Also to be recommended are J.M. Elliott, *The Old World and the New* (1972) and S.E. Morison, *The European Discovery of America* (1971); E. O'Gorman's, *The Invention of America* (1961) is difficult and provocative.

The distinctive impress of Ireland on English development may be traced in K. R. Andrews *et al.*, *The Westward Enterprise: English Activities in Ireland, the Atlantic, and America* (1979). The Virginia invention is treated in E.S. Morgan, "The Labour Problem at Jamestown, 1607-18," *American Historical Review* (1971).

The relevant volume of the Centenary Series is T.J. Oleson, *Early Voyages and Northern Approaches* (1959). It must be pointed out that the author's central thesis on the origin of the Inuit peoples is not accepted by most scholars.

# CHAPTER 2

## INTEREST REVIVED

## — 1. Tentative Connections —

Since Cartier's voyages of the mid-sixteenth century, European interest in northern America had languished. It is true that some contact with the area was kept up. Fishing was important, and the search for the Northwest Passage to Cathay was not forgotten. In this search the English were particularly persistent. Martin Frobisher mounted expeditions in three successive years, from 1576 to 1578, with the Passage in mind. John Davis did likewise between 1585 and 1587, penetrating into high arctic latitudes. To look a little further ahead there were the voyages of Henry Hudson. At first in Dutch employ, but at the end sailing for English companies, he gave his name to two mighty entrances into the northern continent, the Hudson River and Hudson Bay; but since neither led to the East he had, despite his magnificent achievements, failed. His murder in the Bay in 1611 was a tragic end to a long line of endeavour.

Meanwhile, the age-old search for gold and other minerals was not wholly given up. Frobisher was soon seduced from the search for a Northwest Passage by the lure of gold, but assays in England showed that he had returned as empty-handed as Cartier and Roberval before him. All told there was a fair amount of English contact in northern America, so it was not surprising when in 1583, building on memories of John Cabot's original discovery of 1497, Humphrey Gilbert formally took possession of Newfoundland in the name of Queen Elizabeth — but since Gilbert was drowned on the return voyage the Beothuk Indians never experienced the Irish lesson from the master's own hand.

Already by the latter part of the sixteenth century there was a tacit understanding that the St. Lawrence and its approaches were a French sphere of influence. Only in the 1590s did the English, attracted mainly by the fisheries, attempt to intrude. It was an initiative capped in 1597 by a colonizing expedition to the Magdalen Islands by a party of left-wing Protestants, until then in jail in London. Their entry was stoutly resisted by the Bretons and Basques already "in possession" of the area, and their repulse marked the end of an aberration.

French interest in the St. Lawrence was signalled in 1588. In that year belated recognition was given to Cartier when his nephew, Jacques Noël, was granted a trading monopoly for twelve years. He was not to enjoy his grant for long, as it turned out, but that it was given at all points to a quickening of interest on the part of the French. Even so, the French were not yet able to identify a consistent course, as the bizarre story of Sable Island indicated. On this treeless speck of sand (it is only 32 kilometres long and little more than a kilometre wide) over 160 kilometres off shore, was established in 1598 a fishing and whaling enterprise. Despite the presence of extensive animal life on the island, left there by a Portuguese expedition of 1520, the inhabitants were dependent on supplies from France. When in 1602 these supplies failed to arrive they mutinied. Such a course of action was perhaps to be expected, since the island was peopled by hardened criminals, and ought more properly to be looked upon as a penal colony. The climax of what had always been a weird undertaking came when the surviving murderers were taken back to France and there rewarded by the king from the profits of the trade!

So this activity, both French and English, was desultory. Only with the coming of the new century was there a more sustained interest in northern America, for it was still true that the fortunes of the New World depended more upon the "push" of the old than upon its own inherent attractive powers.

# — 2. European Volte-Face —

Politically there were reasons why Europe should turn to the New World with greater energies than previously. The sixteenth century had been marked for much of its course by dynastic war, as the previous chapter indicated. The scope and scale of conflict was to increase in the seventeenth and eighteenth. For a few short years around 1600, however, a lull appeared in the fighting, and it looked for a while as if a new era of peace might dawn.

In France the reigns of the latter Valois had been disasters. For a generation and more the country had been wracked by religious turmoil. War had been fought between Catholics and Huguenots, as the French Calvinists were called. The conflict was savage indeed; for example, in 1572 there occurred the St. Bartholomew's Day massacre, in which the Catholics assassinated thousands of Huguenots who had assembled in Paris for the wedding alliance of two leading Protestant families. But in 1589 the last of the Valois was succeeded by Henry IV, first of the Bourbons. A Calvinist, he was enough of a realist to recognize that the country would accept only a Catholic king, and with the cynical aside that "Paris is worth a mass" he converted to the faith of the majority. At the same time he saw the need to conciliate a powerful minority, and in 1598 the Edict of Nantes was issued, which conceded a tolerated, second-class citizenship to the Huguenots. Destructive passions within France began to abate, and energies became available for new directions.

In the same year as the Edict of Nantes, the king of Spain, Philip II, died. Throughout his long reign (he became king in 1556) he had been the champion of the Counter-Reformation. He had mobilized his people and the fortunes of the Indies in the service of Catholicism, in particular to defeat the Dutch attempt to break free from the Hapsburg system, and to defeat the English by the dispatch of the Armada in 1588. Now, with Spain on the brink of bankruptcy, his successor drew back from war. In 1598 Spain and France agreed to the Peace of Vervins; the Treaty of London in 1604 brought peace between Spain and England; and in 1609 a truce was made with the Dutch.

In England, too, the new century brought a new beginning. In 1603 Elizabeth, last of the Tudors, died and was succeeded by her cousin, James Stuart, king of Scotland. The Puritan hatred of Spain which was noted in the last chapter and which reached its apotheosis in the defeat of the Armada, could now be allowed to fade way. James, an intelligent man, saw that his new kingdom could gain from a period of peace and especially from a pro-Spanish policy. Those who longed for the older ways were in trouble; nowhere was

## Map 2.1: European Explorations in North America, 1492–1632

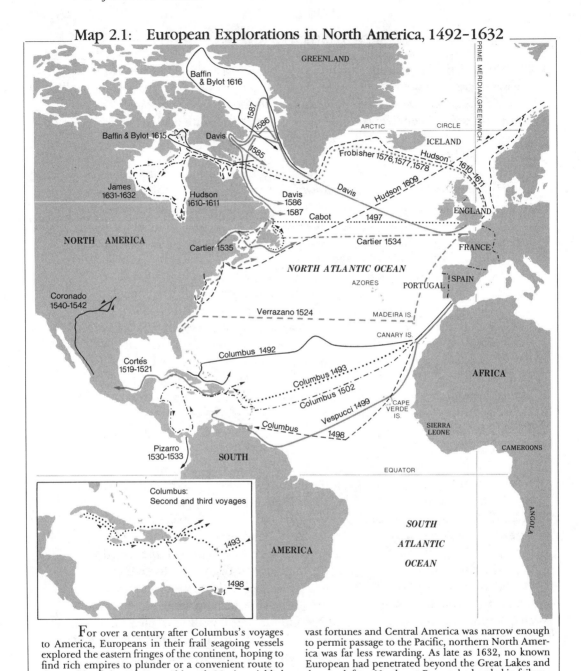

For over a century after Columbus's voyages to America, Europeans in their frail seagoing vessels explored the eastern fringes of the continent, hoping to find rich empires to plunder or a convenient route to the wealth of the Far East. Although Mexico yielded vast fortunes and Central America was narrow enough to permit passage to the Pacific, northern North America was far less rewarding. As late as 1632, no known European had penetrated beyond the Great Lakes and the search for a Northwest Passage had ended in failure.

SOURCES: Mary Beth Norton et al., *A People and a Nation: A History of the United States* (Boston: Houghton Mifflin, 1982); D. G. G. Kerr, *Historical Atlas of Canada*, 3rd rev. ed. (Toronto: Nelson, 1975), pp. 8, 14.

this more clearly shown than in the case of Ralegh. This too aggressive symbol of Puritan anti-Spanish sentiment was arrested, jailed in the Tower of London, and finally beheaded in 1618. At all costs peace and quiet were to prevail.

Thus, at the opening of the seventeenth century the maritime nations of Europe provided themselves with a breathing space. It was a setting conducive to renewed involvement in overseas adventure.

## — 3. Spain Eclipsed —

Important though these political developments were, they were overshadowed by other factors. At long last Europe had awakened to the fact that there were limits to the Spanish monopoly. Very revealing in this respect were the negotiations leading up to the Treaty of London. The Spanish very naturally wanted the English to agree to respect their New World monopoly. James was agreeable, so long as the monopoly was founded on effective occupation as opposed to abstract legalism. In the end an explicit statement of the English position did not find its way into the Treaty, but in practice the Spaniards conceded the point. It is this that distinguishes James's protest from that of Francis I's over 70 years before: when the French king slyly brought in the Bible and asked to see Adam's will that purportedly had given such a vast inheritance to the Spaniards alone he had shocked his fellow-ruler, but now the truth of Francis' sally was being admitted.

When it came to effective occupation it was clear that the Spanish were not prepared to move into northern America; indeed, in the mood of retrenchment after Philip II's death they even contemplated withdrawing from Florida. Thus, James could charter the Virginia Company and Jamestown could be founded in the first decade of the new century.

Spanish hegemony was also passing in another way. It was no longer possible to believe in the *conquistador*. It was not simply that the Spanish experience had shown the inevitability of state power's reasserting itself over the *conquistadores* and bringing them to heel. Rather, it was the unavoidable realization that there were no more Aztec or Inca civilizations left to appropriate. The great expedition of Coronado in 1540 had failed to replicate those of Cortés and Pizzaro, for the Indians of the Plains were too poor and unsophisticated to form the basis of an instant empire. This is why Ralegh is such a crucial figure. He was himself one of the last believers in the *conquistador* tradition, but the Roanoke expedition that he inspired was that and something more. In that undertaking, and even more clearly in the Virginia

21

company that sprang from it, a new motive for European expansion becomes apparent. Overseas possessions had a role to play in mercantilist thinking.

# — 4. Mercantilism —

Economic theorizing was jolted into intensified activity in the opening years of the seventeenth century. The long period of prosperity that had begun in the late fifteenth century had now come to an end. From about 1590, the European economy soured. Harvests were poor, if they did not fail altogether; plague reappeared; the population began to stagnate where it did not actually decline. As rulers and merchants strove to stabilize a declining situation, the theorists elaborated a doctrine known as mercantilism.

Medieval economic notions might have been fading away, but they did not disappear overnight. It might be true that at the level of the individual a dynamic outlook was taking the place of the static, and something of this explosion in making wealth has been touched upon in connection with the Fuggers, but at the national and international level this change had not yet occurred. The overall framework within which the Fuggers and their competitors operated was still a static one, for it was firmly believed that the world's wealth was finite. It was a cake whose portions could be variously shared out, but whose size could not be increased.

From this it followed that for any one person or nation to get rich someone had to become poor. Wealth could be transferred but not created. Thus, by an act of piracy, say by Drake's seizing a Spanish galleon, the English could become that much more wealthy; but by the same token the Spanish would be poorer by an identical amount. Given such thinking it is easy to see how trade was to be seen as war carried on by other means. Each nation's aim was to obtain from its rivals as much as it could and to deny them as much as possible.

To this end, countries were eager to intervene in the economy; it was simply too important to be left to mere traders. For example, a country would prohibit entirely the import of certain goods: if its subjects were permitted to buy these goods then money would be flowing out of the country and going to swell the wealth of a competitor. If it were felt impolitic to ban an import altogether, then a heavy import duty could be levied to keep trade down to a reasonable level. This would have the useful side effect of bringing in much-needed revenue to the government. Similarly, countries would try to maximize exports, as every sale abroad meant money flowing out of the competitor's economy and flooding into one's own. To encourage this state of affairs governments would pay bounties to exporters.

Mercantilism went further yet. From time to time a government might have to allow the import of foreign goods. For instance, in times of bad harvest England might reluctantly have to buy Baltic grain to head off possible bread riots. The thought of paying out English gold to the foreigner for grain was bad enough, but there was also the freight to pay for. If the freight had been put up to competitive bid in the early seventeenth century, the odds were overwhelming that a Dutch firm would have landed the contract — their ships were superior, they operated with smaller crews, their insurance coverage was much cheaper, their commercial intelligence so much more extensive. However, to give the contract to the Dutch would have meant the loss of additional specie. Therefore, at mid-century the government passed the first of the Navigation Acts, requiring that goods coming into England come in English "bottoms" (or in ships of the goods' country of origin — the Acts were directed against the carrying trade of the Dutch). It did not matter that the freight costs would be higher. Let them be twice those of the Dutch! The all-important point was that the freight charges stayed in England and out of the hands of a rival.

Against such a background the renewed interest in overseas possessions is perfectly understandable. Expanding the trading area would bring the mother country and her dependencies closer to the goal of self-sufficiency (but one where the mother country carried on the industries, the colonies supplied the raw materials). In a perfectly arranged mercantilist world each empire would be able to find all possible goods and there would simply be no need to go to one's competitor. If such perfection was too much to hope for, at least the strategic goods could be cornered; in this way in time of war a country would have an assured supply of war goods, would not be dependent on the good will of others, but rather in a position to deny those goods to any potential enemy.

This is why the Virginia Company represents the transition. The desire for empire by conquest was disappearing, even as Ralegh himself was. The Prospectus of 1610 began by announcing as the first aim "to preach and baptize into Christian Religion, and by propagation of the Gospell, to recover out of the Armes of the Divell, a number of poore and miserable soules, wrapt up unto death, in almost invincible ignorance . . . ." But this, too, smacked more of the past than of the future. Much more significant was the last reason given by the promoters: "by recovering and possessing to themselves a fruitful land . . . they may furnish and provide this Kingdome, with all such necessities and defects [copper, iron, steel, timber for ships, yards, masts, cordage, soap ashes] under which we labour, and are now enforced to buy, and receive at the curtesie of other Princes . . . ." Prominence was given here to strategic goods, but the quest for others was also to play a part in the expansion of empire; thus, the Caribbean islands became a bone of contention on account of their sugar.

## — 5. Colonists Take the Stage —

Around 1600, then, northern Europe rekindled its interest in northern America. There was an evolving awareness of the need to lay claim to as large a portion of the New World as possible. There was, however, a divergence when it came to the best way to make that claim. It will be remembered that at the very outset of European expansion there had been two models: the Portuguese had initially stressed the primacy of trade, while the Spaniards had from the first emphasized settlement. Now, with a new round of imperial expansion, which model would prevail?

Once again, the Virginia Company Prospectus is revealing. Sandwiched between the religious and mercantilist imperatives came yet another, the "transplanting [of] the ranknesse and multitude of increase in our people; of which there is left no vent, but age; and evident danger that the number and infinitenesse of them will out-grow the matter whereon to worke for their life and sustenation . . . ." Its inclusion draws attention to deep-seated tensions within English society.

The post-Black Death recovery of the population in England (as indeed in Europe generally) was by now very advanced. In place of a dearth of labourers there was now a dearth of land, so much so that the pressure of population on resources was to bring a halt to the population increase about the mid-seventeenth century and in certain areas an actual decline. Nevertheless, for the first thirty or so years of that century the population pressure was certainly making itself felt in England. The problem was intensified by the incredible price rise of the sixteenth century. In that hundred years the average inflation was five-fold, and if to modern ears this seems modest it must be remembered that it was taking place in a still-traditional setting unaccustomed to rapid change. Then there was the Reformation. When Henry VIII broke from Rome he seized the property of the Church, around 25% of all the land in the kingdom. Large amounts were disposed of, and a buoyant speculative land market developed.

All this was taking place against the new attitude to making money noted in the last chapter. Some rack-rented their tenants simply to maintain their traditional standard of living in shifting times; some did so because they wished to amass wealth on a scale they had never before enjoyed. It did not matter. Whatever the individual motivation the trend was toward a more efficient, harsher exploitation of resources. The most salient aspect of this trend was what was known and denounced as "enclosure." It meant either of two things. It could mean taking mixed farm land out of commission and giving it over entirely to sheep. The aim here was not simply to cash in on the strong demand for English wool but to cut down the wage bill, since vast numbers of sheep over huge tracts of land could be managed by a shepherd and a couple of dogs. It could also mean the break-up of the old, inefficient farming whereby an individual's holding was split up into small parcels and scattered among those of his neighbours, and its replacement by a system whereby individual farms were formed of contiguous fields. In theory of benefit to all, in practice it meant gain for the better-off and loss for the poorest, especially the loss of common grazing rights for which they could show no written deed, merely immemorial custom. Either way, enclosure meant that many were forced off the land and contributed to the growing number of "sturdy beggars" who wandered the countryside and at times terrorized it.

To complicate an already desperate situation, the welfare system, such as it was, collapsed. In medieval times welfare was in the hands of the Church, especially the monasteries. With their disappearance in the Reformation there was a void. The Tudors sought to fill it by evolving a Poor Law, the various elements of which were consolidated in the last years of Elizabeth, 1597 and 1601. Its harshness indicated the novelty of the problem, with government lashing out because it had not had the time to learn any better. That the authorities were barely able to hold down popular disturbances was shown in 1607 when the Midland peasantry revolted.

Finally, to add to the list of those for whom emigration was becoming attractive, there were the Puritans. Their hopes were briefly raised when James came down from Presbyterian Scotland, but quickly evaporated when he showed himself very taken with Anglicanism. Indeed, he made life so unbearable for them that increasing numbers chose to get out. The Stuarts had no objection to their going to English possessions overseas.

For all these reasons, then, there was an outpouring of people from England in the early seventeenth century. By 1629 it is estimated that in North America (including the Caribbean) there were almost 10 000 English colonists.

# — 6. Traders Maintain Primacy —

In France the situation was different. The pressure of the population on land, while real, was not so pressing. There had been less upheaval in land tenure and less of a break in traditional social arrangements. The mania for enclosure and improvement was not nearly so marked. The Huguenots were to lose ground after 1598, it is true, but the French kings were not open to the idea of their settling in other parts of the realm; when Huguenots were lost to France they went into exile in other European countries. Above all, the French in this period seem to have lacked the urge to uproot themselves and try fortune in distant lands.

In the absence of a strong colonizing impulse the traders found it relatively easy to dictate the pattern of French expansion. As early as 1588 this could be seen. In that year, when Jacques Noël spoke of colonizing and missionary activity as part of his grant, the Breton merchants were able to protest so effectively that the king cancelled the grant. In this the merchants were aided by the nature of the trade they intended to carry on (how it militated against settlement will be explained in a subsequent chapter). Had the colonizing push from France been sufficient, this trading emphasis might have been less pronounced. As it was, settlers were few and late in coming. Louis Hébert, the first *habitant*, was an isolated curiosity in 1617. In 1629 the French in the New World amounted to barely more than 100. Even the trading Dutch had twice that in New Holland on the Hudson! This early pattern foreshadowed Louis XIV's later view, expressed in 1666 via his minister, that "it would not be prudent to depopulate [this] kingdom . . . to populate Canada." It was a pattern that persisted until the passing of New France.

## Suggested Reading

In addition to the references at the end of the previous chapter, the following will be useful: D. Quinn, *North America from Earliest Discovery to First Settlements: The Norse Voyages to 1612* (1977) and K.G. Davies, *The North Atlantic World in the Seventeenth Century* (1974). The Basque whaling connection is covered in R. Bélanger, *Les Basques dans l'estuaire du Saint-Laurent, 1535-1665* (1971).

The English seventeenth-century background is well approached via C. Hill, *The Century of Revolution* (1961). A more specific work on the English outpouring is C. Bridenbaugh, *Vexed and Troubled Englishmen* (1968).

The classic treatment of mercantilism is E. Hekscher, *Mercantilism* (1935); beginning students will do well with the "problem" approach of D.C. Coleman, *Revisions in Mercantilism* (1969) and W.E. Minchinton, *Mercantilism* (1969). It is also useful for students to realize that for topics like this, a good source is the *International Encyclopedia of the Social Sciences*.

The Centenary Series volume dealing with this period is M. Trudel, *New France 1534-1661* (1973).

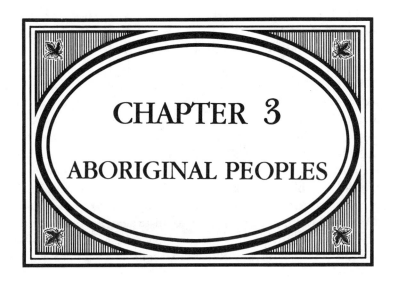

# CHAPTER 3

## ABORIGINAL PEOPLES

## 1. "For their days are all nothing but pastime"

In the history of a people as colonial as the Canadians it is fitting to dwell upon the European background; but such background would be overdone if it led to a neglect of the aboriginal peoples of northern America.

Immediately one seeks to sketch the nature of Indian society at the time of contact, however, the difficulties became apparent. To begin with, the problem of sources is a major one. The Indian culture was oral, not literate, so the Indian side of the story has to be read through the medium of the Europeans. One snag is that a main source is the *Jesuit Relations*, a long series of almost annual reports made by the priests in Canada for a European readership. One function of these *Relations* was to impress upon Europeans some notion of their own decadence, and a useful device was to highlight the Indian as the "noble savage," whose innocence and lack of guile would contrast sharply with European duplicity. Thus, despite themselves, the Jesuits' observations would be coloured by what they wished to see. On the other hand and paradoxically, these same Jesuits were keen to spread an interest in their work, to encourage vocations to their Order, and to raise funds for their missions; to this end they built up the stories of Indian ferocity and cruelty, and delighted in retailing the minutiae of martyrdom. This again dictated the subconscious choice of material and its interpretation.

Moreover, it is clear that in a more general way early European observers, for all their interest, intelligence, and honesty (though of course these qualities were not always present), brought their European preoccupations to the task of recording unfamiliar ways. In many instances they were simply unable to grasp what they were actually observing. To take one example, the chroniclers, who were accustomed to sophisticated European political arrangements, wrote of the Iroquois *nation*. They were aware that in the seventeenth century it was composed of five distinct tribal groupings — Mohawks, Oneidas, Onondagas, Cayugas, and Senecas — and concluded from this that there must be a formal confederacy binding them together in a systematic way. In fact, the Iroquois were bound together by the loosest of ties, and there were many occasions when the Mohawks in particular would pursue an independent course, even to the point of working against the other tribes. For the Europeans, however, who assumed that because they had formed an understanding with one tribe they had therefore an understanding with them all, the real situation could easily lead to an accusation of treachery.

In addition to the problem of contaminated European records is the more basic one of contamination itself. European-Indian interaction was perhaps unique: in other situations the clash of cultures had been mediated, either over time or in other ways, and it was possible for observers to gain an understanding of the other's way of life as it was in its purity. In this instance, however, mediation was scarcely possible. Here, a technologically superior people encountered a technologically inferior. Virtually overnight, as will be explained later in this chapter, the Indians came to depend upon European goods. The objects of European penetration, hides and furs, were products that individual hunters could trap and deliver, so that the contact was broad and "democratic" rather than narrow and elitist. The result was a rapid, almost instantaneous erosion of Indian ways, with a consequent difficulty of observing what pre-contact Indian life was like.

These difficulties are theoretical. It should be possible to go beyond them, either by making corrections to the written record in the light of anthropological, archaeological, ethnographic, or other data, or else simply by accepting that what will be studied will be not so much pristine Indian culture as Europeanized Indian culture as it existed at any particular date. There remains a third difficulty, however, a more pragmatic one in a book such as this. Put candidly it is that there is no such thing as a single Indian culture. One may talk of the culture of a specific Indian band, but the attempt to speak of a Pan-Indian culture is absurd.

Early observers knew something of the diversity of Indian groupings. In the mid-seventeenth century one wrote: "These people number as many as forty nations speaking diverse languages, living under different laws and diverse customs." Even this did not go far enough. There was about Indian society a fluidity that Europeans found difficult to grasp. In the seventeenth century the Iroquois were the Five Nations; in the eighteenth they were more properly to be known as the Six Nations, for by that time they had been joined by the Tuscarora. Who were these newcomers to present-day upper New York State? They were the remnant of a tribe defeated by English colonists in the Tuscarora War of 1711-13 in North Carolina. This was not merely an isolated example of tribal movement. In 1535 Cartier had encountered Iroquois in the St. Lawrence valley. When the French returned about 1600 there was no trace of them in that region. A rather different example is furnished by the Blackfoot of the Rockies; although separated by over 3000 kilometres they are very closely related to the Micmac of the Atlantic seaboard. A vast flux and reflux was constantly taking place across a continent, tribe merging with tribe, losing an old identity, taking on a new. To this day scholarly debate rages over tribal identification.

Accompanying diversity was hostility. The aboriginal peoples of northern America were not aware of themselves as culturally one, differing over inessentials but fundamentally united. They could not imagine themselves as *Indians* at all; that was something that emerged only out of the interaction with Europeans, and only recently at that. Each group was prepared to treat every other on the basis of self-interest. If that meant peace, so be it. If it meant war, then war it was. In the time of initial French contact, the Inuit still maintained themselves on the north shore of the St. Lawrence, but soon thereafter they were pushed headlong into the far north. However, it was not the French that drove them, but the Montagnais Indians. Not only did they do this, but they gave the Inuit the name by which they are still sometimes known today, Eskimo, which is a term of abuse meaning "eaters of raw meat." Even where conclusions were not so bloody there was the same limited self-interest analogous to European national rivalries. Cartier had discovered this when Donnacona placed obstacles in the way of his going up river to Hochelaga, the people of Stadacona wanting to keep French trade to themselves.

Beyond these differences were those of varying tribal response to varying conditions. Some were nomadic, wandering in pursuit of food and having no settled abode; such were the tribes the French encountered first in about 1600. Others were more sedentary, the best example being the Huron, who cultivated fields of corn near the shores of Georgian Bay. Even in this case the exhaustion of the soil dictated the removal of villages every eight to twelve years or so.

Even within the broad distinctions of nomadic and sedentary there was room for difference. The Huron built up a large trading network, the basis of which was their corn and their mastery of the birch-bark canoe. Their empire was spread over an immense territory; their trading journeys annually took

**Map 3.1:   First Nations on the Eve of European Contact**

7  Huron-Petun
8  Neutral-Erie
9  St. Lawrence Iroquois
10  New York Iroquois
11  Beothuk
12  Micmac/Maliseet/ Passamaquody

1  Thule-Inuit
2  Athapaskan
3  Northwest Coast
4  Salishan
5  Plains
6  Algonkian/ Ojibwa/Cree

When the Europeans arrived in North America, they were confronted with aboriginal people as varied in culture as were the Europeans themselves. A variety of cultural groups, each with its own languages, territorial boundaries, and customs occupied the northern half of the continent.

SOURCE: Adapted from R. Cole Harris, ed., *Historical Atlas of Canada*, Vol. I, *From the Beginning to 1800* (Toronto: University of Toronto Press, 1987), plate 9.

them as far as Tadoussac via a great northern arc through Lake Matagami, with the return journey made by the Ottawa River. From their centre they acted as middlemen to the tribes to the west and south. So dominant were they that they had no need to learn other languages but their own, all neighbouring Indians being obliged to learn Huron, the *lingua franca* of the region.

If the Huron went on to build such an intricate system, the nearby Neutrals of the Niagara Peninsula, who cultivated corn and theoretically were in a position to emulate the Huron, carried on little trade; in fact, they did not know how to make or manage canoes! Here were truly sedentary Indians. So just as the Indians were like the Europeans in their rivalries, so too were they like the Europeans in their differing adaptations to their settings.

Yet, ultimately, just as there is a common quality to European life, so too there is something that distinguishes the Indians as a whole. Sufficient caveats having been given, it is now possible to attempt a sketch of these qualities.

## Map 3.2: Ecological Regions and the Seasonal Activities of Four Indigenous Societies on the Eve of European Contact

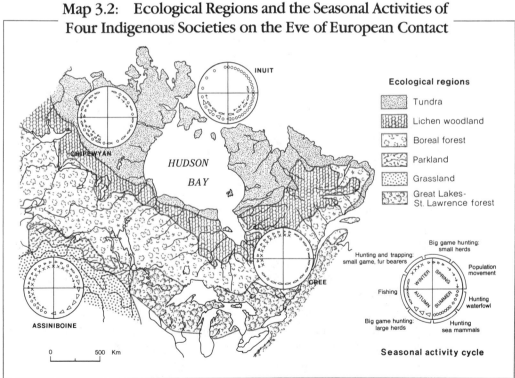

SOURCE: R. Cole Harris, ed., *Historical Atlas of Canada*, Vol. I, *From the Beginning to 1800* (Toronto: University of Toronto Press, 1987), plate 57. Copyright © University of Toronto Press. Reprinted by permission of University of Toronto Press.

At the time of contact, some quarter million aboriginals were scattered over the territory that would eventually be Canada. In certain areas the people were rather more densely concentrated than this average would indicate; the Huron are acknowledged to have had the densest population — about 20 000 lived in an area of approximately 900 square kilometres. This is a density of only 20-odd per square kilometre, which pales against the contemporary European figures. Italy was the most densely populated of the European countries, at 45 per square kilometre, and when it is remembered that this was an average for an entire country many, many times larger than Huronia, it will be seen how slight the average peopling of northern America was.

Here is the first pointer to the nature of Indian society. They were, from the European perspective, unable to tame nature. Europeans, who knew how to alter the countryside by clearing land and ploughing, by dyking the seashore or by draining marshes, who could harness the power of stream and air for mills, and who could maintain roads for the passage of wheeled traffic, saw the Indians as dominated by their world. By European standards they were a poor people. Simmonds, remember, had characterized them as "an idle, improvident, scattered people," and in so doing was merely echoing Cartier's sentiment from more than 70 years earlier. On his first voyage, Cartier noted the Indians of the Bay of Chaleur region: "they can with truth be called savages," he wrote, "as there are no people poorer than these in the world, and I believe they do not possess anything to the value of five pennies apart from their canoes and nets. Their whole clothing consists of a small skin . . . . Their dwellings are their canoes which they turn upside down and lie down under them on the bare ground . . . ."

It was still a Stone Age culture that Cartier and the other Europeans found. Axes were made of stone. Warfare and hunting were carried on with bow and arrows tipped with stone. No metal was employed, except a little copper, and since the means of smelting was unknown it was used cold-hammered for jewellery only. Cooking was done by heating stones and placing them in containers that were too brittle to stand being placed directly over a fire. The wheel was unknown. The only domesticated animal was the dog, which certain tribes kept like sheep for meat.

Despite this apparently unprepossessing inventory, however, the Indian had come to terms with a savage land. The sedentary Indians, especially the Huron about whom much is known, enjoyed a vigorous existence. The endless fare of corn mush, the notorious *sagamité*, flavoured with whatever was to hand (not excepting bugs and insects), was monotonous and to Europeans foul-tasting. Nevertheless, it was healthy, and together with the meat and even more so with the fish that was eaten, the Huron in an average year received a more than adequate diet from a caloric and nutritional point of view. The clothing that Cartier so looked down upon and the beaver-skin robes that were worn in winter were, it has been argued, much more hygienic than the European woollens of the day. It is no surprise, then, that the new-comers were impressed by the size, comeliness, and strength of the Indians, nor that they in their turn looked down upon the pale European weaklings, so many of whom were disfigured by crooked limbs, defective vision, and the like. As a European himself admitted in the 1630s, "they are as handsome young men and beautiful young women as may be seen in France. They are great runners and swimmers, and the women too have a marvellous disposition. They are usually more slim and nimbler than we and one finds none who are paunchy, hunchbacked, deformed, niggardly, gouty, or stony among them." Indian medicine was, in its own compass, effective and, at a time when European medical science was little advanced, compared favourably. Certainly when Cartier's men were dying of scurvy it was the Indians who provided the necessary antidote in an infusion made of cedar bark.

Only in two particulars did the Indians' physical well-being show deficiencies, at least as regards post-contact interaction. They had no re-sistance to European disease, and epidemics were to cause horrendous losses. They also had no tolerance of alcohol, which likewise wreaked untold harm over the years.

Besides the physical adaptation in the matter of food, there was the suc-cessful adaptation to the terrain. Most Indian bands in the region of the birch were skilled in the use of the canoe, a means of transport ideally suited to long journeys over turbulent streams and frequent portages. In winter they used the snowshoe, and were therefore able to pursue large game that bogged down in the deep drifts. Both in summer and winter they were at home on the land, almost to the point of being at one with it.

To European eyes the Indian life was a bare existence, but what is striking is the persistent failure of the Europeans to convert the Indians to a Europe-an style of existence. Attempts to bring them into reservations or to make them practise Old World farming amounted to little, and that only when some disaster obliged the Indians to tolerate the shift. Attempts to get Indian children to attend French schools were failures, the children sickening and eventually running away. Rather more successful was the conversion, by ex-ample and opportunity, of French youth to a "savage" life. The "going na-tive" of Etienne Brûlé, who joined the Indians as a sixteen-year-old in 1610, is the best known example, but by no means the only one.

Early in the contact experience the Jesuit Father Biard observed that "[the Indian canoe] is so light that you can easily pick it up and carry it away with

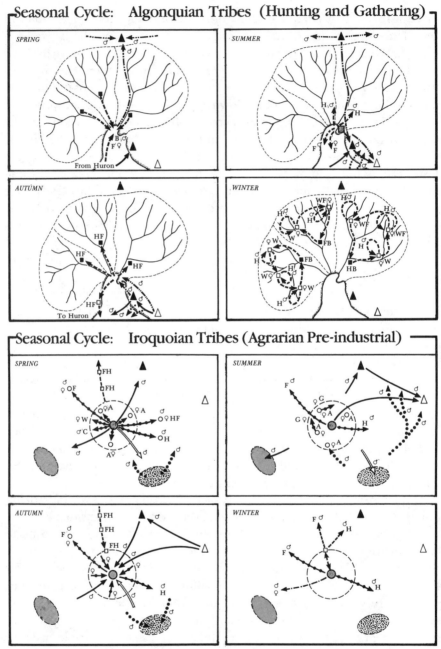

**Seasonal Cycle:   Algonquian Tribes (Hunting and Gathering)**

**Seasonal Cycle:   Iroquoian Tribes (Agrarian Pre-industrial)**

SOURCE: R. Cole Harris, ed., *Historical Atlas of Canada*, Vol. I, *From the Beginning to 1800* (Toronto: University of Toronto Press, 1987), plate 34. Copyright © University of Toronto Press. Reprinted by permission of University of Toronto Press.

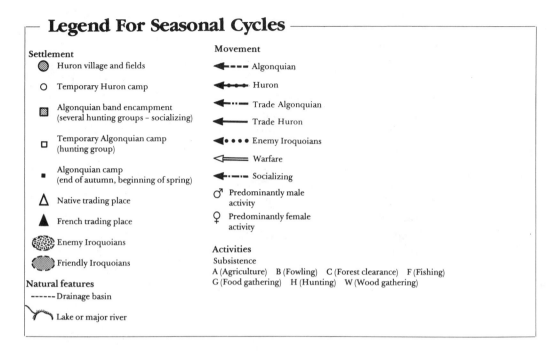

## Legend For Seasonal Cycles

**Settlement**

- ⊛ Huron village and fields
- ○ Temporary Huron camp
- ▨ Algonquian band encampment (several hunting groups – socializing)
- ▢ Temporary Algonquian camp (hunting group)
- ▪ Algonquian camp (end of autumn, beginning of spring)
- △ Native trading place
- ▲ French trading place
- Enemy Iroquoians
- Friendly Iroquoians

**Natural features**

- ------ Drainage basin
- Lake or major river

**Movement**

- ◄---- Algonquian
- ◄-•-•- Huron
- ◄-••-- Trade Algonquian
- ◄——— Trade Huron
- ◄•••• Enemy Iroquoians
- ◄═══ Warfare
- ◄-•--•-- Socializing
- ♂ Predominantly male activity
- ♀ Predominantly female activity

**Activities**

Subsistence

A (Agriculture)   B (Fowling)   C (Forest clearance)   F (Fishing)
G (Food gathering)   H (Hunting)   W (Wood gathering)

your left hand; so rapidly sculled that, without any effort, in good weather you can make thirty or forty leagues a day; nevertheless," he went on, "we scarcely see these savages posting along at this rate, for their days are all nothing but pastime. They are never in a hurry." Father Biard was not wholly correct, for appearance to the contrary there was much that the Indians had to do. Even so, he was more right than wrong in his judgment; he had put his finger on a basic difference in outlook that made the Indian, from that day to this, look with suspicion on the European style. They sensed that Biard was correct when he rounded out his observation with the following: "we can never do anything without hurry and worry; worry, I say, because our desire tyrannizes over us and banishes peace from our action." The full force of this statement, and the reason why the Indian could accept technological inferiority without giving up his notion of general superiority over the European, will become clearer when Indian social relationships have been set out.

## — 2. A Clash of Cultures —

This last statement by Father Biard is at first sight surprising when set alongside the earlier comment that the Indian was as self-seeking as any European. Certainly they showed that they were keen to acquire European goods, and as cheaply as possible; indeed, they showed from the outset that they could haggle with the best, learning to wait at Tadoussac until several European ships had arrived, knowing that the competition of the traders would drive up the price of Indian goods. Does this suggest that Biard was wrong, that he had been deceived by surface appearances, and that deep down there was no difference between Indian and European motivation?

What is important is not so much the pursuit of wealth as the ends to which that wealth is put, though the use of wealth in turn will dictate limits to the pursuit. Salient in the Indian tradition is the potlatch. This term is in its technical sense restricted to the West Coast Indians, with whom in its extreme manifestation it took the form of periodic festive gatherings at which bands would engage in ceremonial gift-giving, and which might culminate in the destruction of the luxury goods of a band. So threatening did European society find this ceremony, so outlandish and destructive of what it considered true civility, that in the late nineteenth century the British Columbia government passed an act outlawing the practice. If this was the most developed form of potlatch, it was known in more subdued forms in many other Indian tribes. Ceremonial feasting at great cost was common. Gift-giving was practised extensively. Gambling was always a feature of Indian life, sometimes carried to a point where an Indian would lose his entire possessions, including his family.

These are all related practices, and they draw attention to two traits basic to Indian culture. The first is the importance of community solidarity. This quality was particularly significant at times of instability when existing patterns were crumbling. Thus, whether it was for Indians a question of taking in a group of people as new members of the village, or tribe, or confederacy, or a question of reordering society after obtaining a supply of European goods, the ceremony of the potlatch (in the widest sense of that term) had a vital role to play. The circulation of goods bound giver and receiver together and, by slowing down the emergence of rich and poor, cemented the essential oneness of the band. The second quality is the refusal to become attached to something to the point of being enslaved to it.

These two traits are well illustrated by the living arrangements of Indians, even of the sedentary tribes. It has been noted that Huron villages were not permanent settlements, but moved every decade or so. Within these villages, clans lived in longhouses, which differed widely in size, but an average of some 30 metres by 8 metres has been established. Built lightly of saplings and bark, they must frequently have been destroyed by fire, storm, and other accidents. They were divided down the long axis by a line of fires, the number depending on the number of families occupying the house. Each family had "individual" quarters notionally marked off from the rest, which measured about three and a half metres long (from the rim of the central fire to the outer long wall) by four and a half metres wide. Thus, the average longhouse would contain (after making allowances for corn storage bins at either end of the long axis) some ten families, five on each side, and thus five central fires. These fires were for warmth, and the cooking was done on smaller fires in the individual quarters.

In all this there was no privacy as Europeans knew it, and given the smoke, the dust from the floor, the dogs, to say nothing of the children and adults, the fleas, the smell of fish and of urine, it is not surprising that the missionaries always insisted on having their own cabin apart. Father Jérôme Lalemant described the longhouse as "a miniature picture of hell." Nevertheless, for the Huron this close, claustrophobic living was desirable. In the longhouse they could indulge their feelings of group solidarity, keeping their corn in communal bins, sharing the central fires for warmth, caring for their young and old and sick. In this arrangement, none were abandoned, none were destitute, and those Indians who had been to France returned with horror stories of the want and beggary that plagued that kingdom.

Their political arrangements were congruent with the rest of their culture. Something has already been said of tribal fluidity; the lack of permanent commitment set against a countervailing communal solidarity was well seen in the ease with which individuals could be strangers one minute and firm members of the clan the next. A good example of this possibility is provided by the case of Father Jogues; after torturing him, the Mohawk adopted him into the tribe, not an uncommon practice. At the village level politics was vibrant, with council meetings taking place almost daily; above the village level political activity and effectiveness fell off rapidly, tribal councils meeting sporadically and the confederacy only once a year. When councils were held, procedure was directed toward finding a consensus; there was no place for the more atomized method of counting heads and having the majority prevail.

At the same time, the Indians did not have an advanced political structure, at least by European standards. Cartier expressed surprise that their chief "was in no way better dressed than the other Indians," and a century later the French were still puzzled by the absence of an abstractly defined hierarchy of power. "There is nothing so difficult," ran the complaint, "as to control the tribes of America. All these barbarians have the law of wild asses — they are born, live, and die in a liberty without restraint; they do not know what is meant by bridle and bit.'' This was not to say that the Indians did not have their prohibitions, their codes, and their taboos. They did, and they were enforced by communally transmitted feelings of shame. What they did not have was the European sense of permanence that gave rise to long-term, future goals requiring an elaborate political machinery.

The two cultures were poles apart. Neither was right, neither was wrong; they simply *were*. But because they were so far apart, bridging was extremely difficult. The tragedy of incomprehension persists to this day.

# — 3. Patterns of Interaction —

The grounds for European-Indian interaction were various. One reason was simple curiosity, the wish to explore a way of life so different from one's own, but till then quite unknown. A few Indians approached the Europeans on this basis, though it has to be stressed that they very quickly formed the opinion that European ways were beneath their dignity. As has been mentioned already, the lure of curiosity operated much more powerfully in the opposite direction. Another reason was the missionary impulse; this is so important that it will warrant a separate chapter to itself (Chapter 5). Yet another was the wish to form alliances with which to pursue rivalries that predated European-Indian contact. But overwhelmingly, there was the desire to trade.

The Indians may have felt a generalized sense of superiority over the Europeans, but in one area they had to admit they compared poorly with the newcomer. When it came to technology Europeans were massively superior. All manner of goods were sought by the Indians. Early items of trade were, in the Old World inventory, cheap trinkets. The established measure of Indian wealth and status was wampum, belts and collars made out of shell fragments that had been traded from coastal tribes over long distances. The Europeans could provide the equivalent in glass and metal beads in prodigious quantities, measuring them out by the fathom. European food became a much sought-after luxury for some Indians, and those that Cartier had taken to France developed a craving for wheat bread. Cloth was wanted, as were other textiles. Soon European architectural items appeared in Indian settings, and by the 1630s doors with hinges were already to be found in Mohawk houses. Indian demand became so sophisticated that native tobacco was given up — and only choice Brazilian would do.

By far the greatest desire, however, was for alcohol and metal goods. At a time before the vitiation of the Indian, alcohol was prized because it confirmed and intensified certain aspects of that culture well established before the contact period. In most Indian societies great reliance was placed upon dreams. It was thought that commands received in the dream state were of overriding importance and had to be carried out — even to the point of murder. No shame attached to a person carrying out such an imperative, for it was believed that the dreamer had been drawn into a higher realm where the spirits spoke directly to him. Thus, whatever was done in accordance with the dream's dictate was sacred. Alcohol fitted into this pattern, for the drunken state paralleled the dream; in both, the individual was taken out of himself or herself and given over to a greater and truer power. The results were appalling. Some headmen recognized the ill effects, and begged the Europeans to stop making liquor available to the Indians. Some Europeans, the missionaries in particular, wanted to stamp out the traffic. On one occasion the authorities of New France debated the question at the so-called Brandy Parliament of 1678. In the end, however, the reality of the imperial trading rivalry prevailed; that being the issue, the outcome was a foregone conclusion. Despite the king's wish to limit the liquor trade, it proved impossible to prevent brandy from reaching the Indians.

The demand for metal goods was enormous. The Indians wanted iron heads for arrows, iron and steel tomahawks, and hatchets, the use of which halved the time and effort required to fell a tree. Iron awls, pins, nails, and a host of similar goods were always coveted. Above all, there was the attraction of metal kettles. The native method of boiling by hot rocks was difficult; iron and, especially, copper kettles were much more convenient. So wonderful were these articles that when an Indian visited Paris he delighted in "the Rue Aubry-bouché, where there were then many coppersmiths," and he went in to ask "his interpreter if they were not relatives of the King, and if this was not the trade of the grandest Seignors of the Kingdom." Little wonder that the Huron name for the French was *Agnoulia* — "Iron People."

An especial form of metal work that appealed to the Indians was firearms. The various colonial powers were initially firm in withholding guns from the Indians, but in about 1620 they began to find their way into native hands through illegal traders in the St. Lawrence. Somewhat later they began to filter through from Dutch traders on the Hudson and from the English on the Connecticut and from the Swedes on the Delaware. In time the authorities, bowing to the same logic that had dictated the liquor trade, were obliged to follow suit. At first the French tried to restrict the sale of guns to Christian Indians, but eventually this halfway position had to be given up. Firearms became general among the tribes.

Inevitably, trade of this scope had a profound impact upon Indian culture. The old skills were quickly lost; within a generation knowledge of the intricate art of making stone arrowheads disappeared. Thus, dependence upon a continuing supply of trade goods could easily set in. Once the taste had been acquired, it had constantly to be slaked, as there was an exceedingly rapid turnover of goods. Kettles, for instance, were often punctured from the harsh treatment they inevitably received — if they were not deliberately cut up for trinkets; many items were lost in rapids or in tribal skirmishes; many were buried as a part of funeral rites; others were needed to maintain trading and diplomatic ties with tribes still farther to the west. All this meant the need for a continuous flow of goods from Europeans to Indians.

As the dependence increased, so the impact grew. To obtain these goods, more and more furs had to be traded. To increase the supply of fur meant changes in traditional patterns. The men had to devote more and more time to trapping; consequently, they were away from home for longer and longer periods, and the tendency to matriarchy in the Iroquois and Huron tribes that had predated the contact period was intensified. Among the sedentary tribes the amount of time and effort that could be given to clearing and planting the soil diminished. The nature of intertribal war also changed. Previously it had been a limited affair, partly because of the primitive equipment available, and partly because it existed to validate the prowess of the braves and to supply a quota of captives. Now Indians were armed with superior weapons, and at stake were not merely a few captives and a handful of scalps, but access to vital trade goods. Indian warfare now approximated the European; it was for the control of economic resources and moved closer to total war.

The effect of all this was that Europeans did not endear themselves to the Indians. Intercultural contact frequently leads to bad feelings because neither side understands the other. In this case Indians antagonized Europeans by their inability to grasp the meaning of private property in the full European sense: what the Indians considered "borrowing" the Europeans considered "stealing." On the other hand, Europeans confronted by Indian sexual permissiveness were not able to appreciate that sexual conduct among the Indians was nevertheless governed by a code, and in transgressing the code they earned the enmity of the Indians. To this inevitable mutual hostility, trading dependence added a further measure of unpleasantness. Within a generation the Huron, for instance, were aware that they had lost true autonomy. Their resentment found concrete expression in the 1630s when European disease struck in a series of epidemics that killed half the population (other tribes in the St. Lawrence and Hudson valleys and on the Atlantic sea-board were similarly affected). Under such an impact the Indian tendency to ascribe French power, especially technological superiority, to black magic found full play. With remorseless logic one tribal elder, a woman, concluded

> It is [the Jesuits] who make us die by their spells; listen to me, I prove it by the reasons you are going to recognize as true. They lodged in a certain village where everyone was well, as soon as they established themselves there, every-one died except for three or four persons. They changed location and the same thing happened. They went to visit the cabins of the other villages, and only those they did not enter were exempted from mortality and sickness. Do you not see that when they move their lips, what they call prayers, those are so many spells that come forth from their mouths? It is the same when they read in their books . . . . If they are not promptly put to death, they will complete their ruin of the country, so that there will remain neither small nor great.

Yet so great was Indian dependence upon the Europeans, so massive had been the realignment of traditional patterns, any attempt to carry out her prescription would have been impossible. To drive the missionaries out would be to break with the French, the "Iron People," and this simply was not feasible. The Huron found, as the Algonkin had before them, that, once it was established, trade was an irreversible stream.

The inescapable reality was the continuance of contact, yet a limited choice remained. Would contact be with the French or with the English? (The Dutch and Swedish alternatives may be disregarded; the former took over the latter's settlements in 1655 and together they passed to the English in 1664. The old Dutch fur-trading capital of Fort Orange continued, re-named Albany.)

There were tribes who gravitated to an alliance with the English. For this there were often good political reasons. To take the best example, the Iroquois had long been at odds with the Huron. When the latter came to an understanding with the French and carried on trade along the St. Lawrence and Ottawa valleys, it was almost inevitable that the Iroquois would adopt an anti-French orientation. From their base south of Lake Ontario they aligned themselves first with the Dutch and subsequently with the English and traded via Albany and the Hudson River. Putting aside such political accidents, and ignoring the fact that very often the cheapness and superiority of English trade goods over French dictated alliances, it is fair to say that more Indians turned to the French than to the English.

In part this was due to the difference in the means by which the two countries exploited northern America. The French were always over-whelmingly interested in the fur trade, and for this reason required good relations with the tribes. Therefore they worked at pleasing the Indians, hoping thereby to attract them to Quebec and Montreal. The English on the other hand were farmers to a much greater extent. They wanted extensive acres, they wanted clear title, and they wanted the Indians cleared off. As Governor Thomas Power of Massachusetts put it in the eighteenth century,

> an insatiable thirst after landed possessions . . . is the sole ground for the loss and alienation of the Indians from the English interest, and this is the ground that the French work upon; on the contrary the French possessions interfere not with the Indian's Rights, but aid and assist their interest and become a means of their support.

Power was wrong to claim this as the "*sole* ground" for superior French-Indian relations. Equally important was the fact that the French were always much closer to the Indian mentality than were the English. If all northern Europeans tended to be contemptuous of outsiders, this was much truer of the English than of the French. One goes back to the Irish experience. There, a rapidly modernizing English nation had confronted its prototypical "sav-ages" and recoiling from them had learned to value all the more its own rationality and efficiency. In the New World these identifications were con-firmed. The English considered themselves the wave of the future; those who lacked the modern virtues of thrift, sobriety, acquisitiveness, retentiveness, and long-range planning were to be swept aside. When the contrast is put in these terms, it is clear that the French had broken from the old ways to a less-er extent than had the English, and accordingly were better placed to appre-ciate the Indians, and to be appreciated by them.

To understand this last point fully, we must wait until more has been said about France and New France. For now, in the context of the Indian trading wants discussed in this chapter, we may consider the European side of the bargain.

## Suggested Reading

While it contains only passing references to North American Indians, M. Harris, *Cannibals and Kings: The Origins of Cultures* (1977) should be read for its impressive championing of hunter-gatherer cultures. More specifically on the North American tribes are the works of the leading scholar, B.G. Trigger: *The Huron: Farmers of the North* (1969), *The Children of Aataentsic* (1976), and *Natives and Newcomers* (1985). The contact experience may be studied in J. Axtell, *The Invasion Within* (1985); A.G. Bailey, *The Conflict of European and Eastern Algonkian Cultures* (1969); C.J. Jaenen, *Friend and Foe* (1976); and O.P. Dickason, *The Myth of the Savage and the Beginnings of French Colonialism in the Americas* (1973). For the Indians and the liquor trade see A. Vachon, "L'eau de vie dans la société indienne," *Canadian Historical Association Report* (1960).

The impact of European trade is a vexed topic. G.T. Hunt, *The Wars of the Iroquois* (1970) should be set alongside C. Martin, *Keepers of the Game* (1978); the latter is particularly provocative and produced the critique in S. Keach (ed.), *Indians, Animals, and the Fur Trade* (1981). C. Heidenrich, *Huronia* (1971), should be also read.

The relevant volume in the Centenary Series is M. Trudel, *The Beginnings of New France* (1973).

# CHAPTER 4

## THE FUR RUSH

## — 1. European Uses for Northern America —

Europe's original use for northern America was as a shore from which to take fish — a very pressing use, indeed. Given the backwardness of European agriculture at that time, meat was always a luxury in short supply, so people were eager for a protein substitute. Moreover, in southern Europe, where Catholicism had maintained itself, the religious requirements of fasting and abstinence meant a heavy reliance upon fish: on Fridays and Saturdays year-round no meat might be eaten, and during the whole of Lent, Sundays excepted, as well as at other liturgically significant times, the same prohibition applied. Even in Protestant countries something of this pattern prevailed. Elizabethan England, moved more by mercantilist than religious thinking, knew the "political lent." Here the aim was to foster a large fishing community by encouraging the eating of fish. The fishing community was in turn required for the health of the navy; in those days a standing navy was the exception, and in wartime a naval force was built up using the merchant marine as a reservoir of trained personnel. This policy applied to all countries that aspired to the first rank, and was to dictate imperial strategy well beyond the sixteenth century. The eighteenth century accepted as "a certain maxim that all states are powerful at sea as they flourish in the fishing trade."

With the enormous demand for fish and for fishing, the attraction of the Grand Banks was understandable. The prodigal quantities of fish in these waters never failed to impress. Sebastian Cabot, son of the discoverer of Newfoundland, claimed that "fyshes somtymes stayed his shyppes." Fishermen from Europe began to congregate in large numbers, and when Roberval put into St. John's, Newfoundland, in 1542, he encountered 17 vessels in the harbour. Although the records are sketchy for the sixteenth century it may safely be assumed that no year passed without the gathering off Newfoundland of Portuguese, Spanish, Basque, French, and English ships. Certainly by the last quarter of the century, fleets were growing impressively in size, so that the 75 ships a year of the 1570s had risen to perhaps 600 by 1600. A few of them would be engaged in whaling and in hunting for walrus; the oil they yielded was needed in an age that knew no petroleum, and the walrus also provided hides and ivory ("as soveraigne against poyson as any Unicornes horne"). The vast majority, however, were there for the cod.

At first the cod fishery had been what was known as "green" fishing. The early seventeenth-century writer Lescarbot described it as follows:

> Fifteen or twenty sailors have each a line of from forty to fifty yards in length, at the end of which is a large baited hook and a sinker of three pounds weight to carry it down. By means of this they fish for the cod, which are so greedy that no sooner is the bait down than they are caught, anywhere at least where the fishing is good. When the cod have been hauled on board they are prepared on benches in the form of narrow tables which run along the sides of the vessels. One man cuts off the heads and throws them overboard; another cuts the fish open and takes out the entrails, passing it on to the next who removes the greater part of the bones. This done, they put it in the salting barrel for four and twenty hours when at length it is pressed; and in this way they work continuously (not even stopping on Sunday) for the space of about three months, with sails down until the cargo is complete.

To carry on the "green" fishery a supply of inexpensive salt was necessary. The Portuguese and French, who owned coastal salt pans where the heat of the sun evaporated the water from brine, had such supplies, but others, especially the English, did not. Therefore, an alternative curing method was developed which required only a little salt — the "dry" fishery. Since it gave a superior product it eventually prevailed. Again, Lescarbot has provided a description:

> For the dry cod the fishermen go ashore. There are harbours in great numbers both in Newfoundland and at Cape Breton where the ships remain at anchor for three months. At daybreak the sailors row out to sea and fill their boats with cod, which takes until about one or two o'clock in the afternoon. They then return to the harbour and throw the fish on a platform built at the water's edge. Here on a large table they are prepared as by the deep-sea fishermen. When the fish has been salted they are dried on rocks exposed to the wind or on the pebbles of the beach. At the end of six hours they are turned, and this is done several times until they are quite dry. They are then pressed. To dry them well, however, the weather must not be foggy or they will rot, not too hot or they will perspire, but the temperature must be moderate with plenty of wind.

The shift from "green" to "dry" was a crucial one, for it meant occupation and knowledge of the land. This was, it is true, minimal; the coastal strip was used, that was all, and the exploitation of the resources was sketchy. Wood was needed for drying platforms, for fuel, and for building crude cabins for a transient work force, and some food was taken. There were early complaints about the unthinking destruction of resources; "the woods along the coasts are so spoyled by the fishermen that it is a pity to behold them, and without redresse undoubtedly [it] will be the ruine of this good land. For they wastefully barke, fell and leave more wood behinde them to rot than they use about their stages although they imploy a world of wood upon them." When complainants added that "5000 acres of wood [were] burned maliciously by the fishers in the bay of Conception Anno 1619 with many more thousands of acres burned and destroyed by them within these 20 years" the foreshadowing of a pattern that later marked the timber trade was very clear.

If the impact on the land was minimal and negative, that of the "dry" fishery on the people was rather different. It brought together Europeans and Indians and laid the faint groundwork of the fur trade. That these initial barterings were "accidental" rather than systematic is indicated by the earliest European artifacts found in the region; they are clearly sailors' everyday goods hurriedly pressed into service as chance presented itself.

This coming together of European and Indian occurred at an opportune time. The fur trade was old and established in Europe, and the fact that the Skinners' Company stood sixth in precedence among the guilds of London testified to the importance of fur in the medieval economy. At that time, fur was not merely a matter of fashion and status, though of course the rich and powerful did spend extravagantly on sable and marten. Rather, in the wretchedly ill-heated houses of the day, rich and poor alike depended on fur to keep warm, and the humbler fur of squirrel and even dormouse was widely used: as a sour Venetian languishing in England observed in 1513, "in England it is always windy, and however warm the weather the natives invariably wear furs."

Within 50 years of this comment, however, the demand for fur had collapsed. The early Tudors had commonly been portrayed in furs, but such pictures of Elizabeth are the exception. In part this was due to changing fashion, but more significantly it probably reflected a rise in living standards, with rebuilt houses graced with glass windows, an increased use of coal fires, wainscotted halls in place of bare stone or tapestry, and a richer ambiance in general. But whatever the reason, the result was unambiguous; except when used as decorative trimming, or as part of the traditional costume of state dignitaries, fur declined in importance.

Thus, the luxury furs of Canada never bulked large in trade; but just as this market declined, another rose to take its place. In the sixteenth century the felt hat became all the rage. Tradition gives 1510 as the date of the introduction of felting to England for hat-making, and over the next 100 years the trade grew, quite forcing out the previously prevalent woollen caps, so much so that Act after Act was passed to regulate the competition. However, attempts to stem the tide were unavailing, and in 1604 the feltmakers were recognized as a separate company, distinct from their former masters, the Haberdashers.

Felt-making consists in matting together wool fibers with the aid of heat, moisture, and friction; legend has it that it was invented by St. Clement (patron saint of hatters) who, on pilgrimage and with torn feet, wrapped them in lambs wool, only to find on taking off his shoes that he had discovered a new textile. Almost any wool could be used, but when it came to hats one type stood out as superior. Most felts lacked firmness, and when fashion decreed a broad-brimmed hat the usual rabbit felt was found to droop despondently. Beaver, however, was perfect. The wool hairs were barbed, and so when matted together clung tenaciously and firmly. As a result, the beaver trade grew rapidly, and already by 1638 King Charles I hived off the Beavermakers' Company to police the new trade, and to yield an additional revenue to the Crown. With the beaver extinct in England since 1526, and quickly being depleted in Europe, including Russia, the attraction of New World supplies was obvious. There the supply seemed inexhaustible. Certainly beaver pelts were cheap. When Bellenger fitted out a fur-trading expedition from France in 1583 he spent 40 crowns on trinkets and other trade goods; he sold the furs they bought for 400 crowns.

Suddenly a revolution took place. A fitful trade had existed for years. When Cartier had entered the Gulf he and his crew had been met by Indians who, he noted, "made frequent signs to us to come on shore, holding up to us some furs on sticks. They bartered all they had to such an extent that they went back naked without anything on them; and they made signs to us that they would return on the morrow with more furs." However, since these same Indians had large supplies on hand, and since they sent the women into the woods when they went forward to trade, it is evident that dealing with Europeans predated this encounter. Yet then and for years to come Cartier's verdict that fur was "a thing of little value" remained true, but beginning in the 1580s it was realized that the profits could be enormous. Traders tried to keep the new-found wealth a secret. In the closing years of the sixteenth century, a French syndicate resorted to chartering a ship in the Channel Islands (which were English) and manning it with a Breton crew (who were barely French). Their very success was their undoing; with a profit of 1500 percent the secret could not be contained. An intense scramble for fur resulted, and the great Canadian fur rush was on.

## — 2. Empire at a Distance —

The object of this furious activity was an animal "of the biggness of a water-spaniel," weighing some 20 kilogrammes, and yielding a pelt of about half to three quarters of a kilogramme. It was found in almost every part of North America where water and trees were available, and an estimate of their number at the time of contact puts the figure at 60 million. The more northern regions were the home of prime beaver, for the animal's preferred habitat was that combination of lake, stream, and timber that characterizes the Canadian Shield. Moreover, the more northerly the setting the better from the trapper's point of view, since the colder the winter the more luxuriant the fur; thus, those skins taken in winter yielded the greatest returns, and *castor d'hiver* was highly prized.

It bears repeating that the Indians were vital to this trade: without their cooperation the fur rush could never have taken place. They trapped the animal and brought it in to the Europeans at their bases on the Atlantic or in the St. Lawrence. More importantly, the Indians wore the beaver skins as cloth-

and it was their cast-offs that so appealed to the trader. An Indian's beaver robe consisted of six to eight skins sewn together, and was worn with the fur against the body. After a year to a year and a half's wear, two critical alterations would have taken place. Excellent though beaver was for felting, in its original state it was not suitable for working. The fur was "double," consisting in Lahontan's words of "two lays of hair; one is long and of a shining black colour, with a grain as big as that of a Man's Hair; the other is fine and smooth, and in winter fifteen lines long. In a word, the last is the finest Down in the World." It was this down, or *duvet*, that the felter wanted, and lacking the knowledge of how to separate it from the long guard hairs he had to have it shipped by the Dutch to Russia for processing, all of which offended not merely mercantilist susceptibilities but also a merchant's notion of profitability. Once the fur had been worn by an Indian, however, the guard hairs were loosened, enabling the *duvet* to be obtained without the need for specialized treatment. The second alteration was the greasing of the fur from constant contact with the human body. This left the skin very supple and easy to work, and when the *duvet* had been shaved off a useful leather was a welcome by-product. Thanks to this second alteration such fur was known as *castor gras* (coat beaver as opposed to parchment beaver in English parlance) and *castor gras d'hiver* was the top of the line. For all these reasons, then, the Indian was essential to the trade, and it was largely for these reasons that men like Etienne Brûlé were sent out to live with the tribes. He and his fellow *coureurs de bois* were expected to encourage their hosts to trap and to bring in their furs, and to this end Brûlé was on an annual retainer of 100 *pistoles*.

The logic of the fur rush very quickly dictated one change, however. It was not possible for long to remain tied to the Atlantic, waiting for the furs to be brought to ship. From earliest days the tendency was irresistible to move ever deeper into the interior. About 1600 the original fur trading rendezvous was Tadoussac. Then Quebec was seized upon as the *entrepôt*. But already by 1611 plans were afoot to make the site of the future Montreal (not to be founded for over a generation) the centre for fur trading, for there, at the confluence of the St. Lawrence with the Ottawa, was an excellent site. Nor did the shift stop there.

The reasons for this development were several. Fur in the regions adjacent to tidewater was soon exhausted. The beaver is a sedentary animal; a pair having set up house in a particular pond will remain there for years at a time, and in their foraging will not venture too far afield. Taking the animals was thus relatively easy, especially after European tools had been obtained. Lahontan's account shows how easy it was to trap beaver:

When the hunting season comes, each [Indian] family pitches its tents in the neighbourhood of its chosen district, and having reconnoitered the paths taken by the beavers to their feeding ground, the traps are made in the following manner. They make a sort of barrier by means of stakes driven into the ground on either side of the path, close to the pond, leaving only enough space for the passage of the beaver . . . .There, they arrange two large levers of about the thickness of an arm, and from eight to ten feet long, called "saumier." They make a snare to the end of which is attached a piece of the beaver's favorite food. To give sufficient weight to the raised "saumier," they cross over it two or more logs. When the animal starts to eat the bait, which it can only do by passing between the levers, the "saumier" falls on its body, and holds it. . . . The winter hunting is more cruel. The Indians break the ice opposite the spot where the beavers come out of their huts, and surround it with stakes driven into the ground. They leave a small opening which a hunter covers with a net, which is swiftly pulled across the ice, and the hunter kills it with a blow on the head. . . . The spring hunting is the most destructive. The hunters break the dams so as to drain the ponds. As the water runs off, they make entrenchments with stakes in the water, where the animals are caught.

Accordingly, reports of overtrapping were early recorded. It was said of the Micmac of the Atlantic coast as early as the mid-seventeenth century that "they would take all. The disposition of the Indians is not to spare the little ones any more than the big ones. They killed all of each kind of animal that there was when they could capture it." Even earlier, by 1635, it was claimed that the Huron had exhausted their region of beaver. Whatever interpretation is adopted to explain this is immaterial to the point being made here: fur-bearing regions were rapidly exhausted, and a move into the untapped interior became necessary.

Furthermore, it was always the dream of the trader to bypass the Indian middleman, who merely traded fur, and make contact with those who actually did the trapping. In this way middleman profits could be cut out, and beaver obtained for the best possible price. Nor was it possible to depend upon Indian initiative to bring in the furs. The European presence rested on the fur trade, and without it there would be expense with no possibility of profit. When, for whatever reason, trading did not take place disaster loomed. Significantly, the first occasion on which the *coureurs de bois* systematically went out to bring in the fur rather than wait on the Indians was 1653, the year immediately after the total failure of any Indians to trade furs at Montreal. Finally, it must not be forgotten that the vision of a Northwest Passage had not totally faded; when Jean Nicolet left in 1634 on an expedition that took him into present-day Wisconsin he packed what was thought to be an outfit of Mandarin clothing, just in case; and as late as 1717 de la Noue was active at Kaministikwia (Thunder Bay) in the search.

In the years after 1653 a whole way of life grew up, a subculture of the fur trade. As the logic of the trade opened up more and more remote areas, and as the volume of furs began to mount, the organization became more and more sophisticated. To protect the long and vulnerable routes, and to serve as centres for trade, a series of forts was established, and to look ahead to the eighteenth century is to see the prairies as far as the Rockies dotted with islands of the European presence.

By this time the trading empire was so far flung that it was impossible to make the trip within one summer. A staging post was needed, and in 1731 it was decided to make Grand Portage, at the head of Lake Superior, the break between the two "halves." To this point, the journey from the St. Lawrence was made by *canôts du maître*, some 12 metres long, taking up to four tonnes of freight, and paddled by up to ten *voyageurs*. Beyond this point the smaller *canôts du nord*, with only three men and a tonne and a half of trade goods, were used. Even to make this "half" journey and return in a season was backbreaking work. Interminable days of 15 hours of paddling were the norm, cramped among the bales without movement since the least knock could spring the gum-sealed birch bark. Constant portages, some of them several kilometres long, were the rule (there were over 130 between Grand Portage and The Pas) where the 40-kilogramme bales had to be carried, several at a time, to say nothing of the canoe itself. It was a gruelling test of stamina, and yet there was never any shortage of recruits. For some it was a lifelong commitment, for others an adventure that lasted only as long as the indenture, usually three years. But there were hundreds in the *pays d'en haut* in any given year by the eighteenth century and any attempt to restrict the outflow by a licensing system failed completely; thus, in 1693 there were 25 *congés* issued, but 187 canoes were out trading. In the space of a century and a half, then, the entire northern portion of a continent east of the Rockies had been taken in fief, and such was the logic and drive of the fur rush that even that barrier was to fall soon after. Laconically the conqueror of the Rockies announced his triumph in vermilion and grease on a rock at the mouth of the Bella Coola: "Alexander Mackenzie from Canada by land, the twenty second of July, one thousand seven hundred and ninety three. Lat. 52° 20' 48"N."

The logic had unfolded, yet not without its discontinuities. That the Pacific victory had gone to a Scot by way of New York and not, say, to one from

Trois Rivières, is a reminder that the fur-trading empire had grown amid the clash of wider imperial conflicts. This is not the place to describe the grand climacteric whereby British replaced French as the fur masters, but something must be said of earlier struggles in the seventeenth century.

# — 3. Fur Trading Rivalries —

Rivalry was endemic to the fur trade from the first. Yet the initial contention was not that of nation against nation, but the more limited struggle to establish orderly trading in any given area. The experience of the French, the first into the fur trade, well exemplified the problem.

A new beginning took place in 1603. It was not that that dreary series of trading grants and revocations, of high promises and lesser accomplishments that had characterized the last years of the sixteenth century, came to an end with the opening of the new. Far from it; a bewildering succession of monopoly holders crowded the next quarter century. Nor was it that the French had hit upon the key to success in northern America; the expedition mounted in 1604 by Pierre du Gua, Sieur de Monts, could not escape the spell cast earlier by Sable Island, and it settled on St. Croix Island in Acadia. It became apparent immediately that such an area could not be policed from such a site. Not only were the Dutch successful interlopers, but members of de Monts' syndicate itself competed against each other. Rather it was that in 1604 Samuel de Champlain made his first appearance in northern America in an official capacity. He had visited America before, but now he came as geographer to de Monts. His worth was plain, his rise to positions of power rapid, and soon he was lieutenant to the viceroy of New France, in effect the business and site manager. It was Champlain's participation that gave continuity and a sense of purpose to the French presence. Now in the New World, now back in France, now in the field concluding Indian alliances or becoming the first European to descend the Lachine Rapids, now at court memorializing the king, publishing, mapping, coaxing, bullying, he was the ever tireless animator of French hopes until the day he died, in Quebec City, in 1635.

On his advice Acadia was abandoned for a return to the St. Lawrence. The river, he argued, would be sufficiently self-contained so that a well regulated fur trade would be possible. His first attempt was not propitious, however. On arriving at Tadoussac in 1608 he found the Basques already "in possession," unwilling to abide by his royal commission, and he was obliged to proceed up stream. There, at the site where Cartier and Roberval had wintered so long before, he rediscovered what he believed to be the ideal centre for French power. In 1608, and again in 1612, and yet again in 1620, he established Quebec *Habitation*; as he wrote to his king in 1618 he proposed

> to build at Quebec . . . at a narrow part of the said river . . . a town . . . which shall be called . . . Ludovica [the King was Louis XIII] . . . . A fort with five bastions will be built alongside the said town . . . which will command the said town and the narrows of the said river. On the other side of the river and directly opposite will be built a fort of the same dimensions in order to bar completely the passage of the said river, as being the entrance and gateway of the said country. . . .

Champlain's initiative placed the French fur trade on a firm footing. It took time, however, and in 1621 civil war was all but raging in New France between competing groups of merchants. It was not without its violence, for in 1608 Quebec was almost sold out by a traitor and Champlain felt justified in hanging the ringleader of the conspiracy. Nor was the site as perfect as Champlain believed, for Quebec was a flawed jewel. It was always vulnerable to a naval force that commanded the Gulf. As early as 1629 this was made plain when the British privateers, the Kirke brothers, sailed up to capture the city and with it the whole of New France without a shot being fired.

While Champlain was laying the foundations of New France he was also helping to lay down the lines of a wider rivalry. Within months of founding Quebec he had cemented a trading alliance with one group of Indian tribes and alienated another, thereby setting a pattern that was to endure for over a century and a half. The allies were the Huron who in 1609 prevailed upon a not unwilling Champlain to accompany them on one of their traditional raids against their enemies, the Iroquois. The two Indian bands encountered each other by Lake Champlain. The three Frenchmen who were part of the Huron force had arquebuses, and against the unsuspecting Iroquois they were deadly. The three Iroquois chiefs were killed in the first salvo, and in the panic that followed a quarter of the Iroquois force was slain; others were captured as torture victims. When a similar skirmish with similar results took place the following year the ties between French and Huron were drawn tighter yet — and the gap between French and Iroquois grew wider.

The French paid dearly for Iroquois hostility. When just a few years later the Dutch moved into the Hudson River valley the Iroquois had a European alternative to set against the French. When the Dutch gave way to the English, the Iroquois transferred their loyalty to them. Even long before that happened, the Iroquois showed how they could disrupt French trade. Beginning in the early 1640s they harassed Huronia. In 1649 they broke with traditional methods by moving into position over the winter so as to be able to fall upon the Huron villages as early as March. Disoriented and helpless before Iroquois impetuosity, the Huron fled in panic. Some tried to find refuge on Christian Island, but food was so lacking that those who did not starve were reduced to cannibalism. Finally, a remnant, a mere 300 or so out of an original population of 20 000, managed to find shelter at Quebec where after a series of false starts they settled down at Lorette. No wonder no furs at all reached the French in 1652!

Nor did the Iroquois attacks on the Huron's allies end there. Iroquois haunted the very environs of Quebec, and in 1652 the Governor of Trois Rivières himself was killed. By 1658 outlying farms were being abandoned as settlers took refuge in Quebec. In 1660 Dollard des Ormeaux and his party of French and Huron were wiped out at the battle of the Long Sault, and if it has lived in myth as a noble sacrifice it was in reality a costly defeat. Only the sending from France of large numbers of regular troops contained the Iroquois, and only in 1701 was a lasting peace with the Iroquois completed.

## Suggested Reading

The cod fisheries are treated in H. Innis, *The Cod Fisheries* (1954). Innis was the leading economic historian of his day (and to this day?), and his *The Fur Trade in Canada* (1956), is equally valuable. Some readers may want to go on to read his study which grew out of these monographs, *Empire and Communications* (1972), in which he reflected upon the wider implications of economic structure.

Those interested in the fur trade would do well to read W.J. Eccles, "A Belated Review of . . . *The Fur Trade in Canada*," in the *Canadian Historical Review* (1979). Although in a sense they belong in Chapter 8, there may be added here A.J. Ray, *Indians in the Fur Trade* (1974), and E.E. Rich, *The Fur Trade and the Northwest* (1967). On the general question there is "Early Staples" in W.L. Marr and D.G. Patterson, *Canada: An Economic History* (1980).

M. Bishop provides a descriptive account of the early French presence in the St. Lawrence and an heroic approach in his *Champlain* (1948). The meaning of the incident at the Long Sault is examined in J. Chevalier, "Myth and Ideology in 'Traditional' French Canada: Dollard, the Martyred Warrior, " *Anthropologica* (1979).

# CHAPTER 5

# RELIGIOUS FRONTIER

## — 1. Tridentine Roots —

When in 1618 Champlain set forth his vision of New France he wrote of

> Ludovica, in the centre of which will be built a fair temple dedicated to the Redeemer, and called the Church of the Redeemer, as a memorial and commemoration of the good that it shall please God to do to these poor people, who have no knowledge of His holy name, to incline the King to bring them to the knowledge of the holy Christian faith and to the bosom of our holy mother Church.

In so stressing religion he was taking up a theme announced by Cartier and Roberval and contemporaneously set forth by the Virginia Company. In his case it had the added force of an increasingly ardent Catholicism. His formulation of 1618 nicely balanced reference to Huguenot "temple" with that to Catholic "holy mother Church" and is a reminder that Champlain, who may have been born a Protestant, was always close to the Huguenots like de Monts who were prominent in the early days of New France. By the end of his life, however, he was a committed Catholic, and had turned Quebec into something of a monastery: pride of place was given to Notre Dame de la Recouvrance, named for the recovery of New France from the Kirke brothers in 1632 by the Treaty of Saint-Germain-en-Laye; the Angelus was rung thrice daily; edifying readings accompanied the communal meals; and the day ended with prayer read by Champlain himself. In this development Champlain was giving witness to the Counter-Reformation, that massive outpouring of Catholic religiosity that took place from the mid-sixteenth century on.

The Council of Trent met between 1545 and 1563. The stirrings of reform that had been noticeable since the beginning of the century were galvanized by the shock of the Reformation, and now the Church was responding, impressively if belatedly, to the challenge. By the time the council ended, it was hard to find an aspect of Church life that had not been touched. Dogma is not of concern here, though it may be noted in passing that in this area there was little attempt to accommodate Protestant viewpoints; rather, the stress was upon clearer, harder definitions of traditional Catholicism. What is of concern here are those areas that more directly affected the evolution of societies, and the common thread is the practical measures taken for the good of the faith. This is not to deny that there was a welling-up of mysticism associated with the post-Tridentine Church; that current was very powerful and references will be made to it at the appropriate place. When set against the totality of Trent, however, it plays a minor role.

Much more striking, for instance, were the steps taken to improve the quality of the priesthood. Trent had concluded that a major reason for the falling away of the early sixteenth century had been the deplorable level of the average priest. Even where he was well-meaning he was often ignorant and hence ineffectual. A requirement of Trent was the founding in each diocese of a seminary for the up-to-date training of priests. Similarly, there was a stress upon missions, and those not only to non-European countries. It was recognized that vast areas of Christendom itself were little better than pagan deserts, and that missionary activity to them would be necessary. Orders and societies were founded which worked out new techniques of conversion and retention. It was a new emphasis eventually recognized in Rome itself when the Papal Curia set up the Congregation for the Propagation of the Faith in 1622 and the College of Propaganda in 1627.

Paradigmatic of this post-Tridentine Catholicism was the Society of Jesus, known as the Jesuits. It had been founded just before Trent, was already significant in guiding the workings of the council, and flowered in its full splendour in about 1600. Its founder was the Spanish ex-soldier Ignatius Loyola, converted while recovering from wounds received in a siege. Like any good soldier, Loyola emphasized the power of the will — "I can find God whenever I will," he remarked, indicating how, despite certain tendencies towards mysticism, his rule would not tolerate anything that smacked of quietism. Similarly military was the long and disciplined period of training that each Jesuit had to undergo. The result was a body of priests who were extremely well prepared and capable of being employed to good effect. Two areas in particular where they showed their abilities were education and foreign missions; in both fields a flexible approach, an understanding of other points of view, and a grasp of what may be appropriate at different stages of growth, stood them in good stead. By the first quarter of the seventeenth century they had over 400 colleges (mainly secondary schools, though they also operated some universities), 50 seminaries, and 40 training houses for their own order, and no continent remained unpenetrated, even China and Japan being opened to them.

Especially noteworthy was Jesuit obedience. The ex-soldier always stressed this quality, and Jesuits stood out on account of their special and extra vow of direct obedience to the Pope. Indeed, the head of the order was known as the General. This draws attention to another crucial fact about Trent: its Roman-centredness. Trent was a vindication of the concept of papal monarch, and a defeat for an earlier tradition of a conciliar Church run by co-equal bishops of whom the Pope, the Bishop of Rome, was merely one, a tradition that surfaced again only with Vatican II in the 1960s. Trent was the apotheosis of what is known as ultramontanism, the view that all Christendom should look for leadership beyond or over the mountains (the Alps) to Rome.

The spirit of the post-Tridentine reform infused the whole Church, but nowhere was it more felt than in France. The first half of the seventeenth century was a period when the French Church set the pace for the rest of Europe. There were pockets of resistance, of course, as that great mystic, seminarian, and future cardinal, Bérulle was to find to his cost when, exercising his rights of visitation at an Augustinian house, he was pelted with stones by the canons who seized the candlesticks from the altar with which to beat him. The pouring forth of spirituality was astounding, even so. In France the Jesuits were particularly strong; a succession of them were confessors to the Bourbon kings; their college at La Flèche was widely held to be the very best in all of Europe. In France the training of priests, and even training the trainers, was most advanced; here Jean-Jacques Olier, who founded the Sulpicians in Paris in 1642, was the outstanding leader. But the best gauge of the all-pervasiveness of piety in France is the *Compagnie du Saint-Sacrement*, a society of laymen, begun in 1627 by the Duc du Ventadour (who briefly had been one of the controllers of New France and Champlain's superior). It drew together some of the greatest in the land, and operated in secret. In addition to weekly meetings for prayer, its members saw to charitable works and the support of religious endeavours: the Jesuits, for instance, were among the beneficiaries of their alms-giving. A less acceptable side of their activities became apparent, however, when they began to act as a puritanical "police force," bringing pressure to bear against those they considered to be leading unedifying lives and reserving positions for those whom they judged good Catholics. Eventually the authorities moved against the *Compagnie du Saint-Sacrement* by clamping down on secret societies, and by 1666 it had ceased to play a significant part. Nevertheless, while it lasted it was a power in the land, and an indication of the tempo of the time.

France's prominent position in the Counter-Reformation did cause one problem, however. The Counter-Reformation tradition as codified by Trent was ultramontane, but France had an even older tradition of independence from Rome which, in deference to the old name for the country, was known as Gallicanism. Before the Reformation the French king, Francis I, had secured legal recognition of his independent standing when he concluded with the Papal Curia the Concordat of Bologna, 1516. By that document was admitted his ability to control the Catholic Church in France, even to the point of selecting its bishops. Given this tradition it is not surprising that France never formally accepted the decrees of the Council of Trent. The conflict between Gallican and ultramontane viewpoints was to be a source of great tension in the years ahead, though at the opening of the seventeenth century the ultramontane cause was in the ascendant and seemingly carrying all before it.

# — 2. Recollet and Jesuit —

Although the first priest to work in New France after the revival of French interest in the seventeenth century was a secular, Father Jessé Flesché, and although he scored a notable success in baptizing the Micmac chieftain, Membertou, who all agreed made an exemplary Christian, it was clear that the missionary enterprise was more than any individual priest could manage and that it would call for that coordinated effort that only an order could provide. As might be expected, the Jesuits were keen to take part, and in 1611 Biard arrived in Acadia where, despite Champlain's removal to Quebec, a French presence was still maintained. However, this beginning was cut short when Samuel Argall sailed up from Virginia and attacked what he considered to be trespassers against the English Crown. He razed the buildings, killing a Jesuit in the bombardment, and took the remainder captive. When the next missionaries went out it was not Jesuits but Recollets who accompanied Champlain, and they went not to Acadia but to the St. Lawrence.

The three Recollet priests who arrived at Quebec in 1615 were members of a branch of the Franciscans, an order that had been the first to accompany the Spaniards to the New World. What distinguished Franciscan religiosity was the stress placed upon poverty, and this quality stood them in good stead among the Indians; their repudiation of property, which contrasted so markedly with the outlook of the fur traders, was something that the Indians could understand and respond to. However, this was about the only quality that the Recollets had in their favour. In other respects they were not suited for such a mission. Their very poverty meant that they lacked the resources adequately to mount a mission in a land that, unlike Mexico, did not possess surplus wealth on which to draw. At the same time their authorities at home could not afford to support them either, and at no time in this initial period on the St. Lawrence did they number more than four. It was the same in Acadia, where a tiny presence came to an end in 1624 with the transfer of the Recollets there to Quebec. Moreover, they antagonized the trading companies that were in control of the fortunes of New France. For instance, in 1621 one of their number, Father Le Baillif, published in France a violent attack upon the Huguenots who were so prominent in New France; that he resorted to forged evidence made his crime all the greater. Equally serious was the question of Recollet strategy. Upon arriving in 1615 they had immediately split up, one going to the Montagnais around Tadoussac, one to the Abenaki to the south-east, and one to the Huron. The following year, discouraged by what they had found and especially by the first two tribes, which were nomadic, they met in Quebec and after discussion laid down the lines for future work. Absolutely necessary in their view was a method for first civilizing the Indians, that is, turning them into French people. Only then could they be made Catholic. To make this possible French colonists would be brought out in significant numbers, and the Indians would be encouraged to live among them, learn their ways, and become settled. No doubt the Recollets were driven to this paradoxical conclusion by their own worship of poverty: only when the Indians had become Europeans, they reasoned, and had lost their *innocent* poverty would it be possible to teach them a *conscious* repudiation of property — only in this way would the Franciscans *qua* Franciscans preserve their *raison d'être*. However, such a program of Europeanization was anathema to the fur traders. They did not want the expense and the trouble of settlers. Nor could they abide the notion of too many sedentary Indians, for who would carry on the fur trade? For that matter, the Recollet strategy did not work; Indian distaste for French ways has been alluded to already, and certainly the Recollect experiment of sending Indians to France to be civilized was a failure; of six who went only one returned a "success."

Above everything else, the Recollect Order was not right for the time or the place. The Franciscan movement had begun as far back as 1210 and the Recollets were merely one of several reform movements (this one dating from 1570) that had grown up as the original Franciscan message became diluted. The order was simply not attracting the best minds and most committed souls in Counter-Reformation Europe. A similar pattern marked the Capuchins, another reformed Franciscan order, this one dating from 1525, and their mission in Acadia from 1632 to 1655 had very little to show for itself. What captured the mood of Christendom at this time were the Jesuits, so it was fitting that in 1624, when the Recollets admitted the need for reinforcements, they invited the Society of Jesus to return to New France. Once returned, they were to stay until the order was suppressed in 1773, by a Franciscan Pope. The Recollets did not remain; when the Kirke brothers took Quebec missionary activity was interrupted, and when it was resumed in 1632 the decision was taken not to allow the Recollets to return. Not until 1670 were they allowed to come back to New France, and they always blamed the Jesuits for keeping them out.

On their arrival at Quebec in 1625 the Jesuits quickly agreed with the Recollets that the prospects of conversion among the nomadic tribes were nonexistent, and that Huronia offered the best chance of success. In one crucial particular they parted company from the Recollets: the Jesuit belief that Hurons as Hurons could become good Catholics, that they did not have to become French first. Indeed, rather than run the risk of being debauched by the Europeans, they should be kept segregated. In this, the Jesuits were profiting from the lesson that their confreres had learnt in Paraguay. There, beginning in 1609, a vast system of reductions, states within the state, had grown up with, at its peak, some 100 000 Guarani Indians living in some 30 missions. In these ghettoes, cut off from the Spanish state as well as from the

Spanish society, native economies of some sophistication had been built up, and conversion went on impressively.

The Jesuits wanted this approach to be repeated in Huronia. To this end, efforts were made to expel the *coureurs de bois*. Ordinary lay workers, whom they needed but over whom they would have too little control, were replaced where possible by *donnés*, lay members of the order who worked for their keep. Given the appreciable funds that the order could draw upon, the fruit of pious response in France to the *Relations*, they were able to build up a sizable European community in the villages of Huronia. Mission chapels were established, including one in the European architectural style, and there were thirteen priests to staff them by the end of the 1630s. Despite this effort, however, the results were meagre. There were conversions, and since Christian traders received preferential treatment and higher prices for beaver there was always a disproportionate element among the Huron traders who had been baptized.

The onset of epidemics, which coincided with the resumption of missionary activity among the Huron in 1634, provided another opportunity for conversion. The priests feared to receive someone into the Church who was not a genuine convert, for the scandal associated with apostasy was great; for this reason the work of Father Flesché, despite his conversion of Membertou, had been looked at askance. But converts close to death were not likely to have an opportunity to apostasize, so baptism could be performed safely. In this light the epidemics were looked upon by the missionaries as blessings, all the more so if the baptized Huron recovered, showing that the Catholic priest was more powerful a shaman than the Huron. This route to conversion was to be a major one by the end of 1640s as Huronia was destroyed, but the 1630s, despite the virulence of the epidemics, did not yield a large harvest of souls.

By the close of the 1630s the number of professing Huron Christians was not more than 100. This paucity may have caused Father Jérôme Lalement, appointed superior of the Jesuits in Huronia in 1638, to change the approach. An organizer rather than a preacher, Lalement concluded that some permanent centralized base was needed, that is, one that would not have to be refounded every ten years or so as the Huron rebuilt their village some distance from the old. Such a headquarters would provide continuity, and would be a centre from which Jesuits could radiate and to which they could regularly return to pool ideas. Accordingly, near the present-day town of Midland was built Sainte Marie. There, in a spot previously unoccupied by the Huron, was established a very European-style mission, where punctuality and the correct discharge of the liturgical offices were insisted upon. It was a most un-Jesuit-like turn to take, and a retreat in fact to the earlier Recollet style.

Just how the Lalement method would have worked must remain conjecture. It never had a chance to develop under normal conditions, for no sooner was it under way than the Iroquois attacks began to disrupt Huronia. With their culmination in 1649 in the destruction of an entire people went the destruction of Sainte Marie and the Jesuit mission on Georgian Bay. The Jesuits themselves burnt Sainte Marie to the ground and the diaspora recounted in an earlier chapter took place. It was as if, from the point of view of the Indians, the work of 15 or more years had never been. Yet it was not without its consequences, for its impact upon the evolving *mythos* of New France was profound.

# — 3. Martyrdom and Montreal —

Like any other movement of renewal, the Counter-Reformation produced its quota of zeal bordering on fanaticism. That mystical strain so characteristic of the period frequently took the form of a longing for immolation, for martyrdom. Inevitably this longing was found to a marked degree among the Jesuits, those who had responded most ardently to the spirit of the times. As one member put it, reflecting on their experiences among the Indians, "We can say that we are like perpetual victims among them, since there is not a day when we are not in danger of being massacred; but it is that also which makes the pinnacle of our joy and the source of our purest consolations." That it was an attitude widely shared is indicated by the following opinion: "Crosses and sufferings are more agreeable to me than all the delights of the world; let them send me to the depths of the most cruel Barbarism, there will be my delights. . . . I go gladly to follow my dear Jesus and suffer all he will require for his love." This was written in France following a reading of the *Jesuit Relations*; the writer was a woman, Marie de l'Incarnation, who later did follow Jesus, in Canada, and although any wish for martyrdom was not granted her she showed, by her refusal to leave in the face of Iroquois attacks, that she was prepared to practise what she preached.

This pervasive longing for martyrdom, now conscious, now subconscious, found in the Indian missions an ideal setting. In all, the order was to have 22 of its members killed in Canada. The best known are the six priests and two *donnés* martyred by the Iroquois and their allies, and of these Fathers

Brébeuf and Gabriel Lalement stand out. The former was granted his wish, expressed on hearing of the death a year before of a fellow Jesuit, when he "begged God to grant him the same token of love."

The fortitude of such men has continued to mould opinion down to the present day. At the time it heightened still more the salience of the Jesuits in the all but formless colony. Their ability to command the allegiance not only of the infant community but also of the metropolitan authorities was enhanced by such evident signs of piety. In a wider and more lasting sense that fortitude has contributed to the impression that New France (even in its later prairie avatar) had been set aside for some providential mission. That the martyrs were Jesuits has served only to intensify the feeling that New France's commitment to the Church was to its widest, most ultramontane sense. The notion even developed that New France was to provide a refuge for the papacy when its enemies in the Old World proved too much for it. The idea of *Catholic* New France had many roots, but one of the most tenacious and nourishing was the earliest.

Even at this early date, however, the Jesuits did not have a monopoly on mystical piety and self-abnegation. At the very time when events in Huronia were moving toward their climax another example of a similar fortitude was unfolding in New France. In it the Jesuits played a significant if tangential role, though, paradoxically, it was to work against them in the end.

In 1636 at La Flèche a vision came to Jérôme Le Royer de la Dauversière, a pious ex-pupil of the Jesuit Collège; he was commanded to found a religious colony on the island of Montreal. His lack of means meant that nothing could be done at once to implement his vision, but three years later he met Jean-Jacques Olier, another ex-pupil of the Jesuits and later the founder of Saint Sulpice, and learnt that on that very day Olier too had heard the call to the selfsame task. It could no longer be evaded. Olier and La Dauversière were both members of the *Compagnie du Saint-Sacrement* and drawing on its resources and personnel they formed themselves into *Messieurs et Dames de la Société de Notre Dame pour la conversion des Sauvages de la Nouvelle France*, a subsociety within the parent body. By 1641 they had completed the negotiations by which they came to possess the Île de Montréal and had fitted out their ships for the expedition.

The arrival of these colonists, a mere 45 of them, caused consternation in Quebec. In part it was the very mundane realization that any settlement upstream would be in a position to intercept fur traders, a fear that was borne out when, in conformity with Champlain's prediction as far back as 1611, Montreal became the centre of that trade. It was also in part a recognition of the fact that any settlement so far out on the frontier would be one in the lion's den; the Iroquois were already on the warpath and menacing Huronia. That the settlers were accompanied by women, notably the nurse and social worker Jeanne Mance, only made matters worse.

Nevertheless, the governor of the mission state, Paul de Chomédy, Sieur de Maisonneuve, was not one to turn back. An ex-soldier, but pious, he had been "converted" by a reading of the *Jesuit Relations*, and going to see Father Charles Lalement (brother of Jérôme and uncle of Gabriel) was sent by him to La Dauversière. Immediately the Société de Notre Dame recognized him as the man they needed, and they were not disappointed. In Quebec, when they sought to persuade him to exchange the Île d'Orléans for the Île de Montréal he expressed his determination to carry out his orders "even if all the trees in that island were to change into so many Iroquois."

Québécois forebodings seemed all too accurate. Within the year of Montreal's founding in 1642 six settlers had been lost to the Iroquois; they were only the first of many to follow. However, Maisonneuve, by a combination of piety and military firmness, held the little outpost together under siege conditions; their first mill was provided with gun ports to double as a fort. Reinforcements followed, including brides. By 1660 it was clear that if New France survived at all, then Montreal would, for with its 300 inhabitants it was well on the way to surpassing Quebec in size.

The religious tone to Quebec was to become diluted in the years ahead, especially as the fur trade grew ever larger. Nevertheless, it could never be entirely forgotten that Montreal's original name had been Ville-Marie, or that Blessed Marguerite Bourgeoys had worked there from 1653 with her Company of the Sisters of Notre Dame. Montreal, too, contributed to that religious aura that was always to mark New France.

# — 4. A Church for New France —

It may have been noticed that of late references to "colony," "settlers" and "inhabitants" have crept in. The aim of establishing a French *colony* in North America had been announced by Cartier, Champlain, and many others, but the resistance of traders and the reluctance of French individuals to put themselves forward had held back the attempt. By the 1650s, however, a genuine French colonial presence could not be denied; by then there were 1700 inhabitants in the St. Lawrence valley and some 300 or so in Acadia.

The community was growing not only in size but in sophistication as well.

In 1639 the Hospitalières of Dieppe had sent out their first sisters to establish the Hôtel Dieu in Quebec. On the same boat had sailed Marie de l'Incarnation with her Ursuline teaching sisters, and they also had their house in Quebec. In Montreal Jeanne Mance had recruited a tiny band of nursing sisters from La Dauversière's foundation in La Flèche, and Marguerite Bourgeoys had begun working toward her foundation. The Jesuits had begun their *collège* in Quebec in 1635, the seed from which Laval University was eventually to grow. Indeed, so rich was the religious institutional life of the young colony that Francis Parkman, the nineteenth-century American authority on New France, exclaimed "Quebec had a seminary, a hospital, and a convent before it had a population." Thus, when numbers grew in the 1650s it became necessary to organize a Church that would serve not only pagan Indians but also Catholic French.

When the first religious went out early in the century the Indian missions were everything. The Recollets were sent on the word of the papal authorities, and although they reported via the French province of their order (that of Saint Denis in the case of the St. Lawrence brothers, that of Aquitaine for Acadia) any real connection with the French ecclesiastical establishment was minimal. So it was with the Jesuits. As notorious ultramontanes they too looked to Rome, and in particular to their General; only in passing did they consult their French superiors who took their lead from the centre. But as the relative importance of missionary work declined and pastoral work among the settlers rose, a new kind of organization was needed.

There was another reason for changing the institutional framework. Quebec and Montreal had always been at loggerheads, the former insisting upon its status as capital of New France and the latter brandishing royal patents confirming its independent status. In 1656 Maisonneuve thought to underline his autonomy by seeking for his colony priests other than the Jesuits (who had ministered to his flock until this time). Given his ties with Olier it was inevitable that he would ask to have Sulpicians sent out, and equally inevitable that Olier, on his deathbed and thinking back to his commitment to Montreal, should agree. In fact, the Sulpician initiative went further. By this date the original Company of Notre Dame was on its last legs, and was eager to transfer its title to the Île de Montréal to the Sulpician Order. It was the beginning of a long tradition of service; in addition to parish activity the Sulpicians founded the Collège de Montréal in 1767 and the Grand Séminaire in 1840.

Sulpician forwardness did not stop there, however. They raised the question anew, one that had been agitated before, of a bishop for New France, and advanced the candidature of one of their number, the abbé de Queylus. The Jesuits fought back. Able to rely upon highly placed sympathizers in France they beat down the suggestion. Their own candidate was François de Laval. He was not a Jesuit (but then Jesuit regulations were against their becoming Church dignitaries), but he had been educated by them at La Flèche and had since remained in institutions under Jesuit auspices. The king having agreed to his nomination, his name was forwarded to Rome for approval.

At this point, however, the Gallican-Ultramontane dispute began to complicate proceedings. The Archbishop of Rouen had always claimed jurisdiction over New France on the grounds that the great bulk of the settlers there had originated from his archdiocese. Rouen, always a hotbed of Gallicanism, was not happy to see a Jesuit nominee put into territory it considered its own and accordingly was delighted to appoint de Queylus vicar general (that is, the archbishop's delegate) for New France. On their side, Laval, the Jesuits, and the papacy were not keen to have New France raised to the status of a bishopric, for that would mean, by the terms of the Concordat of Bologna, too great a submission to the French Crown. Therefore it was decided that Laval would be appointed bishop of Petrea (an Arabian city once Christian but now *in partibus infidelium* — in the regions of the infidel) and would exercise his jurisdiction in New France as a vicar apostolic; in this way his links would be with Rome and not through France. Further to avoid the implications of Bologna, Laval was consecrated in the Parish Church of St. Germain-des-Prés, which was not under the jurisdiction of the French hierarchy.

In 1657, in this hole-in-a-corner manner, the religious framework of New France was set up. It was several years, however, before de Queylus could be induced to yield his and Rouen's claims, and in the end Laval had to call on the arm of the state to enforce the Sulpician's removal from the colony; it was an earnest of things to come.

The Gallican-Ultramontane quarrel did not end there. Upon arriving in New France in 1659 Laval took steps to set up a parish system, but it was not to be like that of the mother country. There the parish and *curé* were closely identified; the incumbent priest was likely to be a permanent fixture; he was supported by his own parishioners through the tithe, a compulsory levy of one thirteenth of the produce of the earth. Such a system did not appeal to Laval: it was too decentralized, it allowed ecclesiastical control to slip into the hands of the *curé* and his parishioners, and by default it benefited the state at the expense of the Church. His alternative was a centralized seminary at Quebec that would be the headquarters, indeed the home, for all the priests of the diocese. It was to be similar to Lalement's experiment in Huronia, a place from which agents would be sent out and to which they would periodically return. Moreover, the tithe was to be paid to the bishop as trustee for the seminary; in this way he would control a sizable fund that he could apply in a flexible manner as he saw fit. It is easy to see how those of Gallican outlook would be appalled by such an arrangement.

In the formative years of New France, then, certain presuppositions were being built into the fabric. However, they were not unchallenged, for as the next chapter will show a strenuous campaign was mounted against Laval, so effective that on key points he was forced to yield.

## Suggested Reading

A full, standard account of the Counter-Reformation is H. David-Rops, *The Catholic Reformation* (1962); more compact coverage is in M.R. O'Connell, *The Counter-Reformation* (1974). For the Jesuits, see M. Harney, *The Jesuits in History* (1941), and T.A. Hughes, *A History of the Society of Jesus in North America* (1907-17), but J.H. Kennedy, *Jesuit and Savage in New France* (1950), is more acceptable.

Overviews of religion in this period will be found in H.H. Walsh, *The Church in the French Era* (1967), C.J. Jaenen, *The Role of the Church in New France* (1976).

A most useful source on religious terms and ecclesiastical matters in general is *The New Catholic Encyclopedia*. Students will benefit from becoming familiar with it.

More specialized works include J.C. Falardeau, "The Seventeenth-Century Parish in French Canada" in M. Rioux and Y. Martin (eds.), *French Canadian Society* (1964); W.H. Paradis, "L'érection du diocèse de Québec et l'opposition de l'Archevêque de Rouen, 1662-1672," *Revue d'Histoire de l'Amérique Française* (1956); E.R. Adair, "France and the Beginnings of New France," *Canadian Historical Review* (1944).

# CHAPTER 6

## TRADING POST TO ROYAL COLONY

## — 1. Brave Beginnings, Dashed Hopes —

The dominant role of the Church in the early period was due largely to its
intrinsic merits and the very real sacrifices and achievements are worthy to be
remembered. Yet at the same time it is necessary to point out that that dominance was also won by default. The state, which might have been expected to
share in the colonizing endeavour, and which might have challenged the pretensions of the Church (as it was to do after 1660), was simply not able in this
early period to play the part expected of it.

It was not for want of trying. By the 1620s it was becoming increasingly
clear to the French authorities that their country was losing out to the more
aggressive powers of Holland and England. In Europe as in the wider world,
markets were being denied to the French. When in that decade the direction
of France passed to the energetic and able minister Cardinal Armand-Jean
du Plessis de Richelieu, a full-scale overhaul of the economic organization of

the kingdom was undertaken. It was only part of an overhaul that addressed almost every aspect of the government and society.

The seventeenth century was nothing if not comprehensive in its schemes. Richelieu was no exception, and if in the economic sphere his preference was for increased French trade with the Levant, he did not omit to make plans for the rest of the globe. Consciously basing his plans on the models of the Dutch and English trading success, he determined to replace the existing French companies that were undercapitalized and insufficiently organized with new ones adequate to the challenges of a mercantilist world. In this total reordering North America was not overlooked. So it was that existing arrangements were swept aside and, after a false start or two, the Company of One Hundred Associates was set up in 1627.

The very name was an indication of the new régime. No less than 100 backers would join together, each investing at least 3000 livres. The strength of this venture may be judged by comparing its theoretical capital (300 000 livres) with the cost of a year's business in the St. Lawrence, estimated by the previous controller at 46 000 livres. Furthermore, no dividends would be paid for three years; instead, any profits would be plowed back into the business. Withdrawal of capital would be possible only over a three-year spell, thus encouraging members to stick with the venture. In addition, it was arranged that the company should enjoy special privileges: among others, for instance, artisans who practised their skill in New France for six years would on their return to the mother country automatically enjoy the status of "master craftsmen" and with it entry into the exclusive guild system, the controlling ranks of the craft. Also, for the first 15 years of the company's existence, no duties were to be levied on merchandise exported or imported. Moreover, this time a serious attempt was to be made to plant settlers in North America; plans called for 4000 to be there by the end of the initial 15-year period. (All were to be Catholic, Huguenots being barred from the colony.)

The spirit was willing, but the timing was wretched. The first expedition of the new company sailed in 1628, the very year that the Kirke brothers began hostilities in North America. The fleet, with its almost 400 settlers (well above the average needed to meet the stipulated figure), was intercepted and captured, and an investment of 165 000 livres was wiped out at a blow. Even so, the company resolved to try again. In 1629 a second fleet, only slightly less costly than the first, was dispatched. This time the Atlantic conspired with the Kirkes to complete its destruction. Again an investment of over 100 000 livres was lost. Peace returned in 1631 when France and England concluded the Treaty of St. Germain-en-Laye, but it did the company little good. Since 1618 most of Europe had been engulfed in the last of the wars of religion, the Thirty Years' War. So far France had played only a peripheral role, but by the 1630s, fearing to be surrounded by the Spanish-Austrian Hapsburgs, had committed itself fully to the war. Attention could no longer be spared for outlying regions, and Richelieu's drive was no longer felt in North America. The gauge of the failure of the high hopes of 1627 was that in 1641, when there should have been over 3000 settlers in the country, there were only some 200.

The company acknowledged this failure when in 1645 it turned the administration of the colony over to the settlers themselves. The Hundred Associates still owned New France, but its day-to-day running and the expenses involved would be borne by the inhabitants. This appeared to be a brave new beginning, and when shortly afterwards a council was instituted to manage the affairs of the community on a more broadly-based representation it seemed that all was set fairly. The composition of the council was revealing; the members were to be the governors of Quebec, Trois Rivières, and Montreal (to stress the military aspect of the colony), the Superior of the Jesuits (testimony of the Church's leadership, and of the Society of Jesus in particular), the former governor of Quebec (but it was provided that if there should be none available he was to be replaced by an inhabitant, suggesting that the transitory nature of officialdom was taken for granted), and two settlers elected by the councillors and the syndics of the three towns (syndics were representatives elected by the prominent townspeople). Such a system was not democratic by any means, since even the two settlers were elected by indirect means, but it did provide for community input.

Yet this initiative too was unlucky in its timing. The later 1640s saw the destruction of Huronia, the interruption of the fur trade, and the beginning of the full force of the Iroquois onslaught. Soon the colonists' company was in debt, and by 1657 the Hundred Associates had to be allowed back into the colony's administration. But what good could this do? The mood was by now one of deep pessimism, and with reason. Iroquois attacks were scarcely to be withstood: in 1661, when the total European population on the St. Lawrence was about 3000, no fewer than 70 settlers were killed by the Indians.

More than anything else, military defeats such as these reveal the demoralization of the colony. Although it was tiny in comparison both to the projected total and to the numbers of English and Dutch settlers in North America (over 90 000), it compared favourably to the numbers of Iroquois. That confederacy theoretically had some 2300 warriors; in fact, the vast bulk of the Iroquois attacks were mounted by the Mohawk alone, and they totalled only

500. Against them the French should have been able to mobilize about 1000 able-bodied adult males. However, since many settlers were considered to be poor military material, and since they had as yet not mastered the art of guerilla war in the forest (witness the costly loss at the Long Sault), and since above all there was a lack of efficient and coordinated leadership, the French could never make the most of their advantages.

So the French remained at the mercy of the Indians. As an Iroquois chief boasted years later, the Indians so confined the French to their strong points "that they were not able to goe over a door to pisse." The disruption of normal activity was such that agricultural work almost ceased. Grain was in short supply, and by 1660 food had to be imported from France. The colony was plainly unable to manage its own affairs and to provide for its own existence. A series of desperate appeals was launched to France to save the daughter

## Map 6.1:  France in America, 1598-1663

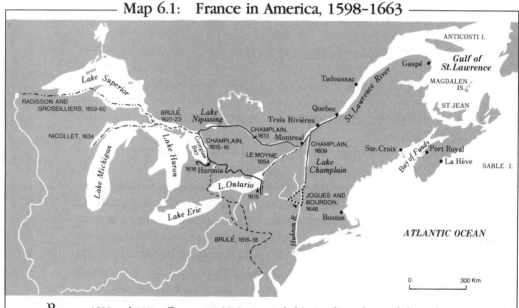

Between 1598 and 1608, efforts to establish a French base in North America were tentative. Sable Island, Ste. Croix, and Port Royal proved disappointing to their founders. In 1629, when Quebec was captured by David Kirke, it was still little more than a trading post. Between 1634 and 1660 the French presence expanded in Acadia and moved down the St. Lawrence River to Montreal. Although a few fur traders and missionaries, and Champlain himself, penetrated the interior by 1663, the French had failed to advance much farther than Cartier had done over a century earlier.

SOURCES: Kerr, *Historical Atlas of Canada* (1975), p. 17; Harris, *Historical Atlas of Canada*, Vol. I, *From the Beginning to 1800* (1987), plate 36.

colony. In 1661 Pierre Boucher, governor of Trois Rivières, was sent to plead with the king. In 1662 the recently arrived Laval saw the hopelessness of the situation and returned to France to add his weight, and that of the Jesuit connection, to the cries for help. Miraculously, the appeals were heard and answered. For once the timing was right. In the 1660s France had the leeway, and above all France had the king, that would make possible the salvation of New France.

# — 2. Modernizing Mother Country —

The time was ripe: at mid-century in France, earlier trends were coming together in the fullness that historians know as absolutism, and were receiving their quintessential expression at the hands of an outstanding king, Louis XIV. Under his guidance France rapidly emerged as *the* European power, the very epitome of the modern, efficient country.

The roots of French Absolutism go back at least to the troubles of the fifteenth century. As the English ravaged the country and set their king on the French throne, the nation recognized that if it were to survive at all it would have to mobilize all its forces and place them in the service of some central authority. Thus, France allowed its kings to maintain a standing army well before the rest of feudal Europe abandoned the view that armies were gatherings of nobles called together for some specific engagement. Since that time the authority of the French had sometimes been eclipsed, notably in the religious wars at the end of the sixteenth century. Nevertheless, the setbacks had never been total, and the accession of the Bourbons had once more signalled a royalist tide; Henry IV and his successors were determined to build upon the earlier monarchical tradition.

This is what Louis XIV did so brilliantly. He had come to the throne as a child of five in 1643, the country being run by Cardinal Mazarin. When that minister died in 1661, Louis announced that henceforth he would have no chief minister but would himself rule. From that moment Louis dominated: his superb self-confidence (when the Pope rebuked Louis because he would not go along with all the other powers in giving up diplomatic extra-territoriality in Rome, Louis replied "God put me here to give example to others, not to be given it") and his extraordinary capacity for detail and hard work (it is said that never once in his reign, which lasted until 1715, did he neglect to go over the papers daily with his ministers) enabled him to impose himself upon his nation and to capitalize upon the political situation and the inherent wealth of his people to inaugurate the splendid century. In 1648 the

Treaty of Westphalia ended the Thirty Years' War, leaving Spain, Austria, and Germany ruined, and France the real winner, a position underlined in 1659 when France won territory from Spain by the Treaty of the Pyrenees. France, enjoying peace, was able to mobilize her almost 20 million people (the largest population of any European country, England having only six million) so as to support great expenditures in the arts, war, and government. In 1661 little stood in the way of Louis as he set forth the full-blown doctrine of absolutism.

The basis for Louis' system was a belief in the divine right of kings. Louis had it preached that he was king because God had made him so. Was this not how he had answered the Pope? Any resistance to his commands was therefore blasphemy. An instance of this conception of kingship was the practice of touching for the king's evil (scrofula), in the belief that the touch of an anointed king was sufficient to cure the disease. Another way in which the divine notion was kept before his subjects was the constantly repeated motif of the sun in architecture, furnishings, and paintings. Louis was the sun-king, the *roi-soleil*, and in this subliminal way people were constantly reminded of his heavenly pre-eminence.

Rhetoric and theory would be empty, of course, unless they could be backed by sanctions, and these Louis could, and would, employ. He made a point of crushing institutions that could conceivably be the focus of opposition to his authority. Thus, no matter how divine the origins of his power, and no matter how seriously he took his title "Most Christian King," he fought against any papal pretension that might impair his independence. In keeping with the words attributed to him "*L'état, c'est moi*," he viewed the Church in France as *his* Church. He was a most extreme Gallican, therefore, and on several occasions led his Church to the brink of schism to uphold his rights against any ultramontane meddling from Rome.

Just as the Church was tamed, so too was the feudal nobility. Louis inherited an entrenched aristocratic outlook, and he was never able to break it completely, but he was able to go a good way towards bringing it under control. The way was prepared for him in part by events which took place during his minority. Throughout the nation, but particularly in Paris, a confused series of rebellions occurred, known collectively as the *Fronde*, 1648-53. Essentially, this was the last kick of an expiring nobility that hated Bourbon centralism and longed to return to a feudal past when they mattered and had enjoyed high office as a right. The mindless selfishness of the *Fronde* was all too apparent, and in the long run it contributed to the triumph of absolutism by exposing the bankruptcy of its opponents. In the short run, too, it contributed; an infant Louis was forced to parade before the *Frondeurs* in Paris, an insult he never forgot and which encouraged him in later life to avoid Paris, its mobs, and its memories.

Once he had become his own master, Louis furthered his attack upon the nobility. Two methods may be singled out. He extended and perfected the use of *intendants*. Previously, control of the provinces had been in the hands of the governors, who were drawn from the nobility and exercised almost hereditary authority in their regions. All too often they were not up to the bureaucratic demands of the office, and their loyalties were less to the state than to their own families. Louis' *intendants* were "new" men, drawn not from the old feudal nobility but from the professional and trading classes. They were picked for their merit, and worked for the king and the good of the state. They rapidly became the real authorities in the provinces, pushing the governors to one side as mere ceremonial figures. Second, Louis built Versailles. This monstrous palace, some twenty kilometres from hated Paris, became the hub of the vast empire. Huge sums of money were spent on its crushing bulk and ornate splendour; at one time over 36 000 workers were busy on it. So huge did it become that a smaller, more personal place in the grounds, the Trianon, became necessary. But even that was too imposing, and yet another, the Petit Trianon, was built. This incredible world was deliberately designed to appeal, to attract, and to ensnare. Anybody who was anyone had to be in residence, and since court etiquette was so intricate as to be a lifetime study, that residence had to be full time. This being so, nobles had to give up their provincial loyalties, and cut off from their roots they were transformed from nobles into courtiers. As a class they were hamstrung.

If Louis broke the power of the *noblesse de l'épée*, he was determined not to allow their rivals, the *noblesse de la robe* (the professional nobility, socially inferior to the former, and recruited from the bourgeois families via bureaucratic office), to rise in their place. The bastion of *robe* power was the *parlements*, the high judicial-administrative courts of the land, about 12 in number. Traditionally they had significant powers by which they could hold up and even nullify royal ordinances by refusing to register the king's edicts. Louis would have none of that. When the *parlement* of Brittany, a notoriously independent province incorporated in the kingdom only in the sixteenth century, attempted to use its right of remonstrance, Louis did not hesitate to act: the troops were sent in, the offending pages in the *parlement* journal were ripped out, and the delinquent members exiled from the provincial capital of Rennes to the backwoods for 15 years.

The Bourbon distrust of nobility, bourgeoisie, and even of the Church, was epitomized by the fact that representative institutions ceased to exist. The French parliament, the *Estates-General*, was composed of those three orders; it had a long history, going back to the High Middle Ages. After 1614, however, it was not summoned, and only the shock of impending revolution in 1789 caused it to be convened once again. During the *ancien régime*, and above all in the heyday of Louis XIV, a representative body could only detract from the majesty of the king, the prime mover of the new state, the efficient cause of what was progressive and up-to-date. Little wonder, then, that the king's writ was law, and that a royally signed *lettre de cachet* could condemn a man to lifelong imprisonment without cause shown or a trial's taking place. The institutions of Bourbon France existed to further the will of the Crown, not to check it.

There remains one other element of absolutism to note. Behind it all was a longing to control, a wish to see uniformity. A hint of this has already been given in reference to Richelieu's economic policy: it was not enough to have a trading company for the Levant; the whole globe had to be provided for. A more significant example of the same drive was to be seen in religious policy. The existence of a Huguenot minority was anathema to the absolutist mind. Already in 1627 Richelieu had moved against them, and his prohibition of Huguenot participation in the Hundred Associates came at the very time that his king was reducing La Rochelle, the last Huguenot citadel, to obedience. Under Louis XIV, however, the urge to uniformity was most nakedly shown. In 1685 the Edict of Nantes was revoked. It was pointless to argue that the Huguenots were among the most loyal of French people. It was useless to urge that they were among the most industrious and inventive workers in the nation, and that their loss would offend against the mercantilist orthodoxy of the day, as indeed against any orthodoxy. As it was some 200 000 went into exile, and enriched other countries at France's expense; for instance, the English paper and silk industries were largely Huguenot, and many took service in the British army and in that capacity later made their mark upon Canada. Such arguments were unavailing. The wish to have 20 million French of one Catholic faith was overwhelming.

This last observation points to a flaw in the Bourbon modernization of France. They wanted an efficient state and were prepared to use a meritocracy to bring it about. In many ways the reign of Louis XIV was the golden age of the bourgeoisie, but its rise was not unfettered. There was too great a residue of pre-modern, aristocratic, totalitarian elements for the full mobilization of resources. The drag that a persistent aristocratic ethos imposed was crushing; it was to be seen in the crippling cost of Versailles itself, and even more so in the wars that Louis and his nobility fought for the sake of their "*gloire.*" More significantly this aristocratic drag was to be seen in connection with *dérogeance* and with venality.

The former refers to the attitude that only the profession of arms was truly noble, and that trade was demeaning. This might have had a certain validity in the Middle Ages, but at a time when modern professional armies paid for by the profits of trade were the order of the day, such a view was counterproductive. The Bourbons were aware of changed conditions, and would have liked to have swept away *dérogeance*, the doctrine whereby one of noble blood taking part in trade lost his noble standing, became a commoner, and condemned his offspring to the same fate. However, the weight of opinion was against such a revolution, and only partial assaults upon it could be made. In conferring benefits on the Hundred Associates, Richelieu included the provision that noble participants would not be liable to *dérogeance*. Such a shilly-shallying attitude contrasted poorly with Dutch and English practice, where the nobles were free to engage in commerce, and where indeed they were often the leading innovators.

Venality is the practice of buying and selling state offices. The meritocratic principle ran into a block from the older ways, according to which an office was looked upon as a personal possesssion, much like real estate, that could be sold for the going price. The attraction this had for the bourgeoisie was that most offices conferred noble status (*robe* as opposed to *épée*, it is true, but noble status nonetheless), if not for the buyer then at least for his descendants. Such was the lure of nobility in *ancien régime* France, and such the disdain for bourgeois status, even by the successful bourgeois themselves, that there was a constant and active market in venal offices. In this way a perpetual hemorrhaging of bourgeois talent into the ranks of nobility took place, draining France of the trading initiative that she would need if she were to compete with the Dutch and English. At the same time a swollen nobility, effectively cut off from mercantile profits, was obliged to resort to an outdated, penny-pinching exploitation of feudal dues as a means of keeping its head above water. In this way the aristocratic tone of French society was intensified, especially as in the eighteenth century *robe* and *épée* tended to intermarry and coalesce.

These were long-term drawbacks. What was striking about Louis XIV in 1661 was that he was eager to take on the vested interests of the past, keen to build an efficient state, and determined to construct in New France the kind of society he would like to have in France but that the dead weight of the past made difficult to implement. Truly, the time was ripe for New France.

## — 3. A Royal Laboratory —

The time was also short. The first years of Louis' personal rule were spent in his finding his feet and preparing the way for his chosen advisors, and not until 1663 were he and the new régime firmly in place. That was the year when the Hundred Associates were required to turn their rights over to the Crown, and when New France was turned into a royal province essentially no different from Normandy or Saintonge. Already by 1672 the time of undiverted attention was over. In that year Louis succumbed to his ever-present temptation, the pursuit of *gloire* by force of arms. He went to war with the power that constantly obsessed him, the Dutch, for they were the very antithesis of all he and his style stood for. The decade of peace that had permitted France to experiment on the St. Lawrence was over. As dispatches of 1673 made brutally clear "I will repeat again to you that his Majesty has not planned on giving any assistance to Canada this year because of the large and prodigious expenses that he has been obliged to make for the raising of . . . 200 000 soldiers presently mobilized . . . and one hundred ships and twenty-five galleys presently at sea." Nevertheless, short though it was, that period was of decisive importance.

During that time the direction of colonial matters (as indeed of so many others in France) was entrusted to Jean-Baptiste Colbert. There was nothing brilliant about the man, no flashes of originality; he was outstanding because his virtues, which were great, were those in demand at the moment. He was a mercantilist and bureaucrat *par excellence*. He had an enormous appetite for paper work, could see clearly how matters dovetailed together, was able to select and motivate able subordinates, and could direct the whole to a new level of efficiency and comprehensiveness. He accepted all the orthodoxies of the economic doctrine of the day, and was determined to build on Richelieu's foundations to make France economically the master of Europe. Naturally, the colonies featured prominently in his schemes, and he lavished attention and resources on the frail colony of New France.

Together Colbert and Louis inspired confidence, and astonishingly quickly the mood of pessimism on the St. Lawrence was dissipated. An early ground for this change of heart was the promise of military aid. In 1662 only a token force of less than 100 could be sent, but the psychological impact was significant. Then in 1665 the Carignan-Salières regiment, veterans of the continental wars and a thousand strong, was committed to New France. So eager were the authorities to try conclusions against the Iroquois that they sallied forth in January 1666 and, as may have been expected, suffered badly in the unfamiliar conditions. However, a repeat performance in the fall had better luck. It did not lead to the conclusive victory on the field of battle that the professional soldiers sought, for the Mohawk melted away before them in the forest, to regroup later. Nevertheless, the Carignan-Salières regiment had shown itself in force, had been able to burn down the Indian settlements and disrupt their economies, and the next year the Iroquois did sue for peace. That a major reason was the state of Indian diplomacy, with the Iroquois barely able to hold their own against hostile tribes, or that Mohawk willingness for peace was largely the result of a raging epidemic, was irrelevant; the colony had been freed from a crushing burden and the perceived cause was the king's generosity in providing massive military resources.

Equally impressive was the boost in the size of the population during this short breathing space. As Colbert wrote in 1688 to an official in New France, "the end and role of all your conduct should be the increase of the colony; on this point you should never be satisfied but labour without ceasing to find every imaginable expedient for preserving the inhabitants, attracting new ones, and multiplying them by marriage." The dispatch of troops had ensured preservation; now Colbert would see to it that the other two points were taken care of.

The French authorities sent out an average of almost 500 men a year, and when the Carignan-Salières regiment was recalled in 1668, attractive severance pay was granted to encourage any soldier who wished to remain in the colony. In this way some 400 desirable settlers were retained. Since the immigration was unbalanced — there were far too many men for the number of women — care was taken to recruit single women. These volunteers were outfitted at the king's expense and given a dowry of 50 livres (more than any colonial woman could hope to have) and once they were married further payments might be made to the couple for several years. In the period from 1663 to 1673, almost 1000 *filles du roi* were sent out in this way. As befitted the *protégées* of the sun-king, they were of exemplary character. Indeed, by and large the same held true of all immigrants in this period. The authorities wanted no questionable material and the unsatisfactory were weeded out before sailing; as Colbert wrote, "in the establishment of a country it is important to sow good seed."

When it came to "multiplying them by marriage" Colbert showed himself the true mercantilist. Both carrot and stick would be used. Bounties for children were paid, just as for any other product; a decree of 1670 ordered that in future all inhabitants of the . . . country who have up to ten legitimate children living . . . will be paid a yearly gratuity of three hundred livres, and those who have twelve, four hundred livres; . . . In addition . . . it is the King's will . . . that all males who marry before the age of twenty, and females below the age of sixteen, will receive on their wedding day twenty livres to be known as the King's gift . . . .

Fines were in force for those whose children did not marry by the recommended ages, and one year the authorities hit upon an ingenious method of coercion to achieve their aim; Colbert commended them, agreeing that "you did well to order that volunteers would be deprived of the right to engage in the fur trade and hunt unless they married within fifteen days of the arrival of the vessels bringing the women."

Actually, such incentives and sanctions were superfluous. Other colonies in North America showed a rate of natural increase every bit as spectacular as the French, a doubling every 20 years. Given the availability of land that permitted earlier marriage, and given the generally higher standard of living for the majority of the people, much greater fertility was to be expected in the New World. A colonial observer put it bluntly when he noted that "women bear almost every year as do animals native to the country." Nevertheless, once again, irrespective of the efficacy of the measures, it is the psychological impact that has to be stressed. The king was seen to care, and to be supporting his children in a tangible fashion. The mere increase in numbers was also psychologically satisfying: by 1673 the settlers numbered almost 7000.

These developments guaranteed Colbert a viable colony on which he and the king could experiment. Its very fragility in 1661 was a token of its formlessness. It was a *tabula rasa*, a clean slate void of the traditional, feudal impediments that obstructed an absolutist reformer in France and clogged the drive toward order and efficiency. On the St. Lawrence, on virgin soil, they could fashion the perfect society according to the blueprint of the future. They set to work with great determination.

A king who was smashing the feudal nobility at home was clearly not going to tolerate such relics in his colonies. On the other hand, given his attachment to the aristocratic ethos, he could not entirely give up his attachment to hierarchy and proper social gradations. Thus, the royal province of New France took over, from the days of the Hundred Associates, the existing form of seigneurial landholding, but took care to deprive it of any genuine feudal content. Large tracts of land were granted to nobles *en seigneurie*; in exchange the noble occupiers swore medieval homage and fealty to the king; in turn, the seigneur made grants to the commoner-settlers, the *habitants*, who rendered loyalty and dues, again in a mediaeval form, to him. That these grants were mere outward form, lacking any real noble power, was made crystal clear in 1669 when the state militia companies were established. The nobility might have expected to command by right of their status — after all, what did nobility mean if it did not mean command in battle? However, the Crown ordained that command should go to *capitaines de milice*, ordinary *habitants*. In New France the nobility enjoyed aristocratic status, but little else.

By the same token, a king who was to take on the *parlementaires* could not be expected to give a toehold to lawyers and *robe* nobility. In fact, lawyers were barred from New France. Litigants were to argue their own cases, and in real estate and similar transactions lowly *notaires*, glorified scriveners, were employed. Above all, venality was not permitted in the colony. The officials were to be given no chance to become a self-perpetuating caste or to escape royal control. In New France offices were not a species of property, and an incumbent holding office at pleasure could be removed on the king's word with no legal right to compensation. In New France status might have been for sale, but never power.

Finally, no inkling of representative institutions was to be allowed. The composition of the sovereign council, the equivalent of the *parlement* of Paris, say, makes this plain. It was to consist of the governor, the intendant, the bishop, and others (the number varied) jointly appointed by these three (the bishop soon lost the right to take part in the appointing). What is striking is the omission of even the modest degree of popular representation that characterized the council in the days of the Habitants' Company, from 1645 to 1657. Nor was this an accident. When Governor Frontenac in 1672 had the effrontery to summon what looked like an *Estates-General*, although its purpose was nothing more than to magnify his own status by providing a suitably magnificent backdrop, Colbert rebuked him, observing,

> The Assembly, and division of all the inhabitants of the country which you called in order that they might swear allegiance may have produced a good effect at the time but it is well that you note that you must always follow in the government and conduct of that country the forms used here. The King has not, for a long time, called together the Estates-General believing this to be beneficial to his service. . . . In order slowly to abolish this ancient form you should rarely, to be more accurate, never, use this form. . . .

Colbert went even further, for in the same dispatch he referred to the still-existing town syndics and warned that "you should suppress the syndic who presents requests in the name of all the people, for it is well that each speak for himself and none for all." If ever even quasi-representative meetings took place in the colony (as happened for instance in the "Brandy Parliament" of 1678 when the views of 20 leading colonists were sought on the propriety of trading liquor to the Indians) it was on the initiative of the Crown, and then for a specific purpose only. Even then, the colonists did not jump at the chance to express their views, and it was not unknown for meetings to be cancelled for want of participants. An efficient absolutism could, and would, get the job done.

In a short but decisive dozen years a rapidly failing invention — that of the fur trading enterprise — had been saved on the brink of disaster. A new invention, that of a laboratory of absolutism, had been superimposed. It now remains to examine the long-term viability of that invention, and to assess the quality of life that it made possible.

## Suggested Reading

In addition to the Trudel volume cited in Chapter 2, there are two useful overviews by W.J. Eccles: *The Canadian Frontier* (1969), and *France in America* (1972). A major older study is H.P. Biggar, *The Early Trading Companies of New France* (1901).

The French background is well treated in D. Parker, *The Making of French Absolutism* (1983) (which has the merit of rooting the account in the sixteenth century) and in the excellent J. Lough, *An Introduction to Seventeenth Century France* (1969). Also to be highly recommended is W.H. Lewis, *The Splendid Century* (1953).

Colbert is exhaustively covered in C.W. Cole, *Colbert and a Century of French Mercantilism* (1939).

Demographic aspects are examined in M. Trudel, *La Population canadienne au début du XVIIIè siècle* (1954). There is also G. Lanctôt's *Filles de Joie ou Filles du Roi* (1954).

Institutions of New France (which are also dealt with in the following chapter) are the subject of R. Cahall, *The Sovereign Council of New France* (1929), and A.G. Reid, "Representative Assemblies in New France," *Canadian Historical Review* (1946). A recent synthesis is A. Vachon, "The Administration of New France," *Dictionary of Canadian Biography II*.

# CHAPTER 7

# THE STYLE OF NEW FRANCE

## 1. The Rulers: Seigneurs, Bishops, Governors, and Intendants

More clearly than in the social theory of most régimes, Bourbon social theory called for a recognition of the gulf that separated rulers and ruled. Indeed, given Louis XIV's values, an almost caste-like division of society was considered the most desirable. This account of French society in North America, then, may usefully begin under these two headings: rulers and ruled.

Immediately, two institutions of great importance in traditional societies such as France may be played down. Already it has been noted that the *seigneurs* were allowed no military power in the colony. Now it may be added that *seigneurial* arrangements were such that as a class they were allowed no economic power, and hence no social power either.

A *seigneur* was one who received a tract of land — usually from the king but sometimes from another *seigneur* — that could vary in size from a few hectares to over a 2500 square kilometres, in return for which he had the right and the duty of settling farmers. Those whom he settled on his fief were obliged to render him various traditional feudal dues. Thus, each farmer paid *cens*, from which they were legally known as *censitaires*, although they always insisted upon being known as *habitants*. The *cens*, however, was a trifling sum, less an economic charge than a legal one to establish non-*seigneurial* status, and so insignificant that many *seigneurs* could not be bothered to collect it. A little more worthwhile was the *rente*, but here too the return was minimal. In addition, the *seigneur* may have had other feudal income, for instance, a percentage of fish caught, or so much per head for animals pastured on the common (if there was any). Certainly there was the *seigneur's* cut of the grain ground at the mill that he was obliged to build and to which all his *censitaires* had to bring their grain. However, this last underlines the precarious state of *seigneurial* economies. The obligation to provide a mill was an onerous one, and one that the *seigneur* tried to avoid. It was the *habitants* who brought pressure to bear to have one built, for a mill was expensive to construct and costly to maintain, and the milling charge, one fourteenth of the grain ground, was often not enough to offset these charges. In the early years, before many settlers had established themselves on the *seigneurie*, appreciable losses would be experienced, and it has been computed that not until some 30 to 40 families lived on the estate would it become even marginally profitable to the *seigneur*. Thus, the great majority of the *seigneurs* could not afford to live off their feudal income and had to work their *seigneurial* domain, their own farm, labouring alongside and in no way differently from their tenants. For the same reason very few bothered to exercise the right to dispense justice to their *censitaires*; there were profits to be made from the administration of law and order, but only if and when the *seigneurie* filled up with a great number of families, and since most *seigneuries* were underpopulated the fixed costs involved would simply be too great.

Nor was it possible for the *seigneur* (or for that matter, the upwardly mobile *censitaire*) to increase his estate by emulating the English to the south and building up a cash-crop business such as tobacco. To begin with there was the *ancien régime* prejudice against trade: it is true that a regulation of 1685 abolished *dérogeance* for colonial nobles engaging in trade, but legislation could not affect deep-seated attitudes overnight. The fur trade persisted, for there was enough of the élan and the physically dangerous about it to make it compatible with the *noblesse* tradition.

Other ventures were not pursued with the same vigour — what crops were possible? Tobacco of the right quality did not seem likely, and anyway, before any possible market could be explored, its exploitation was ended by the mercantilist authorities. In their logical comprehensive fashion, viewing the French empire as one complementary trading bloc, the mercantilists recognized the West Indies as the source of the best tobacco and would not allow the St. Lawrence to compete with second best. In addition, agricultural products, for whose export great hopes had initially been held, did not become a trading staple. The intended market for fish, grain, and barrel staves was the West Indies, but the St. Lawrence was frozen over for half the year, and when sailing was possible it was the hurricane season in the Caribbean. Moreover, the New England merchants already controlled that market (illegal though that was in a mercantilist world) and their lead was not to be overcome. Finally, seigneurialism posed its own technical obstacles to the build-up of large landholdings, the necessary basis for large-scale production for the market. When a *seigneurie* was sold, a tax of one fifth of the purchase price, the *quint*, had to be paid to the feudal superior, usually the king. When the land of a *censitaire* was sold out of the line of direct descent a tax of one twelfth (*lods et ventes*) had to be paid to the *seigneur*. Moreover, land sales, even when seemingly concluded, could be easily upset. The *retrait roturier* permitted the *seigneur* to dispossess a purchaser of a *censitaire's* land by paying the sale price within a stipulated time of the sale. In a similar fashion the *retrait lignager* gave one whose right of succession to the land had been affected the right to buy the land back at the sale price. Then there was the *légitime*, the right of the children to half the original inheritance, and if a land sale denied them this right then the sale could be voided; sometimes years would pass after a sale before such a denial came to light, and this threat was a potent one to dissuade would-be purchasers. The way these rights could act as a brake upon land speculation and land consolidation can be appreciated when the practices of Connecticut are compared with those of New France. In the former colony land on average changed hands at least four times every 20 years. In the latter, concessions stayed within families for generations. In Ste. Famille on the Île d'Orléans, only ten of 70 farms were absorbed by the others in the period from 1670 to 1725.

Until quite recently, a consensus was emerging that seigneurialism had little impact on the lives of the *habitants*. Of late there has been some challenge to this thesis, but as yet it seems proper to retain the older view. There is one revealing piece of evidence. In the Old World the elite's local power was cemented by the close alliance between squire and parson, often achieved by the former's right to choose the latter. The same arrangement was possible in New France. If the *seigneur* built a proper church, that is, one of stone, he would gain the right to choose the priest. It was a right he would have loved. Only a handful had the means to do so, however, so in the vast majority of cases the Church retained the right of presentation.

The *curé*, not the *seigneur*, was the real authority figure in the localities. It was to him the *habitants* turned for advice. This was partly because the *seigneur* lacked the standing he might have enjoyed in the old country, and partly because the village institutions of France had not been transported to the colony. In the formless world of the St. Lawrence the first institution to emerge was the parish, and since it filled the void it became, for want of an alternative, the focal point of local activity. It was here on Sundays and feast days after mass that the *habitants* could meet and socialize. It was here that buying and selling would take place, and here, too, that orders from the centre would be transmitted (by the *capitaine de milice*, remember, not by the *seigneur*). Moreover, the head of the parish, the priest, was literate, and by virtue of his place in the ecclesiastical hierarchy in touch with the wider world. He was the natural leader. When it is remembered that all education, such as it was, came under the Church, and that most welfare and charitable work was done by priests and nuns, it is easy to see why the Church mattered in this grass-roots fashion.

To acknowledge that the Church filled this very important role is not to claim that the Church as an institution was a ruler in New France. As might have been expected, Louis XIV's takeover of the Church in 1663 meant the replacement of the previous ultramontane independence by a thoroughgoing Gallicanism. As Colbert pointed out,

> It is absolutely necessary to hold in just balance the temporal authority, which resides in the person of the King and in those who represent him, and the spiritual authority, which resides in the persons of the . . . Bishop and the Jesuits, in such a manner, nevertheless, that the latter be inferior to the former.

So, although the Church was permitted to have its own courts, appeals lay from them to the sovereign council. Moreover, the erosion of ecclesiastical autonomy was speeded by poor episcopal control. Too often and for too long bishops were absent from the diocese. Laval himself was away for 12 years, his successor, St. Vallier, for 17 (captivity in England was in part responsible for this, but only in part), and Mornay, his successor, never set foot in Canada, although its bishop for six years. Above all, the colonial Church was poor. The basis of its revenue was to be the traditional tithe. In France this had been fixed in the main at one thirteenth of the products of the earth. In New France Laval, despite long and bitter struggles, could never get such a rate accepted. The best that could be managed was one twenty-sixth of the wheat grown, and not even this was always paid. The shortfall in ecclesiastical funds was made good by the state, each year the royal purse providing one third or so of the revenue spent by the Church. Its client status was all too plain and it could not be said to have any significant power. It was, as an institution, no ruler in New France.

There remained the state, represented by the governor and the intendant. The same line of development which in France was pushing the former to the side and was bringing the latter to the fore was to be seen in the colony too, but with the added advantage that personalities provided a lurid illumination for the clash of principles.

In 1672, at a crucial period in the colony's development when the undivided attention previously given was ending, the Comte de Frontenac was chosen to be governor. The representative of the sun-king, he was, like every other governor of New France bar one, a member of the *noblesse d'épée*. That, seemingly, was his only qualification; he was, in fact, quite unfit for office. Nevertheless, his psychotic personality did drive him to make claims that could not be ignored. Always quick to promote his own *gloire* (remember his creation of a provincial estates to witness his investiture) he was a stickler for his own rights and privileges. He was a quarreller, and was not above taking the law into his own hands when challenged, imprisoning enemies and threatening to dismiss councillors who would not blindly back his actions. In all this, however, he took good care to couch his conduct in terms of upholding the royal dignity, suggesting that the viceroy of an absolutist monarch should himself be untrammelled in his own bailiwick. Quickly complaints reached Colbert, along with Frontenac's side of the story transmitted by his secretary.

When in 1675 the royal response reached Quebec it was seen that Frontenac's pretensions had been struck a series of heavy blows. While his precedence in the colony was confirmed (after all, he was still the king's representative) it was ordered that the intendant (who ranked third, after governor and bishop) was to preside over meetings of the council. Furthermore, the councillors were henceforth to hold their commissions from the minister of marine and not from the governor; in this way they were to be free from his threats of dismissal. It was explained that the governor should confine himself to the business of war and foreign affairs, with only a general supervising brief over the rest of the colony's affairs.

If the governor had had his wings clipped, by the same royal dispatch the intendant had been placed on the road to continued growth. He quickly became the animator of the colony. His authority was aided by the fact that in the sovereign council votes were not taken, but rather the sense of the meeting; this enabled a skillful official to have his way unless there was substantial and well-articulated opposition. Moreover, the intendant enjoyed wide powers that were his alone, not to be exercised with and through the council. For example, the intendant communicated directly with the metropolitan authorities, and in this way not only played a major role in framing royal policy for the colony but also received in return the power to implement that policy. He had the oversight of the judicial process, and furthermore possessed original jurisdiction himself, notably in cases affecting royal rights (trade, *seigneurial* dues). He could issue policy and other regulations, seeing to weights and measures, laying down fire regulations, checking on the conduct of inns, prohibiting straying cattle and barking dogs, and a host of similar rulings; no subject was too trivial for his attention.

Here is intendant Jacques Raudot in 1706:

> We order that there will be but two tanners in Montreal, to wit, Launay and Barsalot. So that each may have an equal amount of work, the city's five butchers will divide among them equally, as to quantity and quality, the skins of all the animals they will slaughter. In processing these skins the tanners will make use of all the methods that are necessary and required to provide the public with good merchandise, and thus under pain of a fine of three livres for each item which our inspectors will consider below the standards set down in our *ordonnance*.
>
> We forbid the butchers to make French shoes, . . . but we do authorize them to make mocassins. . . . We also forbid the butchers to engage in the traffic of animal skins with the *habitants* and order the latter to bring all said skins to the market established in Montreal. Thus they will place them on display and sell them only to the tanners.

The intendant was to foster industry. The supervision of the colony's finances was his responsibility. There was, in truth, scarcely an aspect of life in New France that his activities did not touch. Even war, theoretically the preserve of the governor, fell to him — his control of the financial side, of supplies and expenses, of the building and repair of fortifications, could and did affect military matters profoundly. The wonder is that France could find bureaucrats capable of bearing such a burden. But it did: all eleven of the intendants who served in New France down to 1760 were able men, and if Bigot, the last, was a scoundrel and a thief, he was like the others a more than competent man of affairs.

## — 2. The Ruled: *Habitants* —

In Bourbon New France the *habitant* was the ruled. Recently it has been stressed that the towns of Quebec, Trois Rivières, and Montreal contained a sizable proportion of the population, with some 20 to 25 percent of the people lodged in them. The urban concentration of New France was greater than any other in North America at that time, and in many instances in the Old World, too. The fact remains, however, that the vast bulk lived on the land.

Establishing themselves on the land had been a hard struggle for the *habitants*. The work of clearing the dense forest that greeted them everywhere was arduous. It was all that 20 people could do working for a whole year to clear some thirty *arpents* (say, 10 hectares). Even with a few hectares cleared, the difficulties were not over. Long after the Carrignan-Salières regiment had helped to break the Iroquois power, the threat that the Indians represented remained real. In 1689 the Iroquois burst upon the settlements around Lachine and killed 24 on the spot; a further 42 were carried off never to return. If it was not Indian attacks, it was English assaults, as the colony was drawn into European wars that raged at the turn of the century.

Nevertheless, the population continued to increase and the settlement to expand. Eventually, the shores of the St. Lawrence and some of the leading tributaries were lined by a scarely broken row of *rotures*, as the *habitants'* farms were called. By the eighteenth century a second row of settlement behind and parallel to the first was becoming general. In time this second *rang* filled up, too, and by the end of the French régime in 1760 a third *rang* was beginning to make its appearance. Even so, some 90% of the population lived within one and a half kilometres of the St. Lawrence.

The obvious advantage of farms along the river exercised a compulsion over settlement patterns and dictated the general shape of *rotures* that persisted even when the *rangs* extended away from the St. Lawrence. Although the size and shape of *rotures* varied almost as much as did the *seigneuries* from which they were carved, the norm was some one to two *arpents* of frontage (the linear *arpent* was about 60 metres) by some 30 to 40 *arpents* deep, giving a holding of some 30 hectares. Such a shape had its disadvantages; settlement was diffuse, so protection against attack was not easily arranged, and the narrow strip meant that time was lost in making long journeys to farm the outer limits. For these reasons, the intendants from time to time called for the abandonment of the conventional pattern and decreed the formation of consolidated villages with fields encircling a compact huddle of houses. A few were built to this model, but such was the *habitant's* attachment to the linear pattern, the village pattern was allowed to lapse. Indeed, so keen was the *habitant* to maintain his strip farm, he was prepared to go to absurd lengths. Division of *rotures* among heirs was normal: in 1723 the point was reached when a farm emerged that was 4 metres wide. It was still a fair size — about six kilometres deep — but its impracticality was such that some time later the authorities laid down a minimum frontage; even so, this was no more than one and a half *arpents*.

Once established on his *roture* a *habitant* enjoyed a satisfactory economic existence. The corollary of an impoverished *seigneurial* class was a well-to-do peasantry; the feudal dues that were paid were, as has been seen, trifling. At the same time, the low tithe has been noted. Moreover in New France, unlike the mother country, there was no direct taxation. Indeed, the only indirect taxes, until almost the end of the French régime were the *quint* (a tax of one fifth on the value of beaver pelts sold), the *dix* (one tenth on moose hides), and a 10 percent duty on imported wines and liquor. All in all, the average *habitants* could not have been taxed more than about 10 percent of their income.

In France, on the other hand, taxation was onerous. There the nobility was exempt from direct taxation (they paid by giving their blood on the battlefield) and the *don gratuit* paid by the Church was far less than its fair share of the burden, with the result that the weight of taxation fell on the *paysan*. The *taille* and *capitation* were heavy direct taxes. In addition there were those like the *gabelle* (the salt tax) that fell, as do all indirect taxes, with disproportionate effect on the lower classes. What with one tax and another, it has been reckoned that the average French people were paying between a third and a half of their income to the state. Finally, it may be pointed out that in New France the *corvée* and billeting, two institutions that could be crushing in France, were known only in attenuated form; the former, obligatory days of work on the *seigneur*'s land, was all but a dead letter, while the second, necessary in an age when barracks were unknown, was less a charge upon the settlers than a source of additional revenue. Little wonder, then, that a French officer at the end of the French régime could marvel at the silverware made from melted-down coins that the *habitants* possessed. At that date their French cousins would in many cases have been using wooden plates and bowls. (At the same time, it is well to bear in mind that despite this wealth New France attracted few immigrants; in its entire history only 500 French left France for the colony on their own initiative.)

The *habitants* enjoyed other advantages over their French counterparts besides the straightforwardly economic. A good example is the justice system.

Here the superiority of their régime comes out, not only *vis-à-vis* that of France, but even more clearly when set against that of England and her colonies. Both the French and the English régimes were cumbersome systems, for they had fallen under the control of lawyers who, charging fees for each separate piece of business in a case, found ways of dragging out the proceedings to an interminable length. The English court system was especially given to this kind of expense multiplication, for its basis was the adversarial system. Each side hired lawyers to pursue its arguments in court. The judge "kept the ring" and ruled on points of law, and at the conclusion of the trial the jury was asked to decide which lawyer had been the most believable. Such a method had even more opportunities than the French for long drawn-out wrangling, delaying, and consequent expense.

In New France, on the contrary, no lawyers were allowed. Most cases were heard before the intendant or before one of his subordinate officials, and no financial charges were made. In those cases that went to the courts, a fixed scale of fees, in all cases moderate, was in effect. In both instances, the judge was able at any time to decide what evidence he wished to take, and when he had heard enough. Cases were therefore disposed of with dispatch. The *habitants* became notorious for their resorting to the courts — but only if the authorities thought, on the basis of the preliminary examination, that there was a case to answer. In the English system a plaintiff could open proceedings on the flimsiest of excuses and compel an adversary to go to the trouble and expense of contesting what were clearly vexatious charges.

Then, too, the philosophy of the penal system in New France was a distinct improvement over the English. In England the system tended to be savage toward those found guilty. This is seen most clearly in the case of capital offences. In the English system there were many crimes for which the penalty was hanging — a list that continued to grow throughout the eighteenth century — and many in fact suffered that penalty. In New France, however, there were few such crimes, and hanging was rarely ordered: in all during the French régime, only 67 people were executed. Perhaps as revealing is that in the colony the authorities always had difficulty in finding a hangman, and that executions, far from being the popular spectacle they were in the English realms, or in France for that matter, were shunned and resisted. In short, in the matter of justice and its administration, New France represented an island of enlightenment where distributive rather than retributive justice seems to have been the rule.

Of course the whole system, like the absolutism of which it was a part, depended heavily upon the individuals who ran it. English detractors at the time and since referred to it as a system of rules, not laws, as an arbitrary tyranny, not a realm of liberty. Nevertheless, the evidence shows that the ordinary man in the *ancien régime* would have received a fairer verdict in New France than in almost any other European society. The liberty of England and her colonies was too often the liberty to take advantage of one's weaker neighbour, while New France's absolutism was frequently a system of countervailing tensions very far from arbitrary. It will be well to look more closely at the relation of ruler and ruled, and to examine the difference between absolutism and tyranny.

## — 3. A Distinctive Culture —

Enough has been said to indicate that the dichotomy of ruler and ruled that prevailed in *ancien régime* societies is not wholly satisfactory for New France. As one probes more deeply into the distinctive culture that arose on the banks of the St. Lawrence, it becomes apparent that the earlier queries were fully in order.

One trouble with the dichotomy is that the rulers tend to be seen as more monolithic than they ever were. In fact, tension rather than smooth coordination was the rule. *Seigneurs* would appeal to the authorities to be upheld against their tenants, and would be given support. *Censitaires* would also complain, however, and there would be times when they too would be vindicated. A nice instance of this seesaw came in 1711 when the king issued the two Edicts of Marly. One accused the *seigneurs* of failing to forward land settlement with sufficient vigour, and ordered that land should henceforth be conceded to settlers on demand, and in cases of failure the Quebec authorities were to make the grant and have the dues paid into the royal exchequer. The second took the *habitants* to task for being, in many cases, "content . . . with cutting down some trees" and failing to bring the *roture* into a fit state of cultivation. If after a grace period of one year better efforts were not put forth, the land was to revert to the *seigneur*. Similarly, the Church would complain of "two *habitants* . . . who were drunk during mass . . . and other parishoners . . . who leave the church during the sermon to smoke," and the authorities would step in to "prohibit . . . the sale of liquor . . . on Sundays. . . . Everyone is also prohibited from quarrelling . . . or talking in Churches; from leaving during the sermon and from smoking at the church door or about the church." However, when Laval thundered against those women who showed "a scandalous nudity of arms, shoulders, and throats, contenting themselves with covering them with a transparent fabric which only serves to give lustre to these shameful nudities," the authorities declined to act.

Even sharper was the tension that operated between governor and intendant. The ruling of 1675 sought to demarcate two distinct spheres, but of course it could not do so. The governor had prestige, the intendant had power. Both had claims, both had the ear of powerful men at Court. Colbert knew the limitations of the system, and rather wistfully wrote to Frontenac "it is impossible for the king's service to be effective unless there is complete accord between the two persons who have to act, exercise his authority, and work for the good of the people and the development of the colony." The population soon learned to play one authority off against the other, and the very possibility of such checking and balancing injected a libertinian element into the colony not at all intended by its designers.

The second reason for finding the dichotomy of ruler and ruled unsatisfactory is that it implies a subordinate element that has to be kept in its place, one that constantly threatens to erupt into anarchical violence and can be restrained only by ceaseless vigilance. It is clear that in New France, however, the many could not be put in their place. When the tithe was to be introduced at the French rate there was resistance, and State and Church backed down (How different from the mother country, where tax revolts provoked *dragonnades*, the most brutal use of soldiery to compel obedience.) When the *habitants* were ordered to live in villages the edict went unobeyed. When the *coureurs de bois* were told to stay in the colony and to obtain *congés* if they wished to trade, they scoffed at the prohibition. In this last there is a clue to the situation. The colony, perennially underpopulated, short especially of skilled labour (and even of unskilled: the regular troops were hired out as labourers), dependent on the fur trade, difficult to police on its borders, was simply unable to bring pressure to bear in the traditional way. As Radisson, himself a *coureur de bois*, boasted, "we weare Cesars, being nobody to contradict us." Early in the eighteenth century an official observed

firmness . . . is considered a crime in this country. The religious communities state that it is not the custom in New France to oblige them to contribute to the *corvées*; the nobility and officers of justice declare loudly that it violates their rights; the merchant says that it disrupts the order of his business; the farmer who is taken from his field and the craftsman from his shop obey only with difficulty. . . . There cannot be too much sternness in dealing with a people so unruly and so hostile to obedience.

Intendant Raudot offered a slightly softer explanation:

> The settlers of this country have never had any education because their fathers
> and mothers, like the Indians, have an inordinate affection for them during
> their childhood. Thus their faults remain unpunished and their temper is
> unformed. As there are no schoolteachers here, the children always remain
> with their parents, and growing up as they do without discipline, acquire a
> character that is hard and ferocious. They lack respect for their fathers and
> mothers as well as for their superiors and their priests. . . . I have done my
> best . . . to draw them from that barbarism and to cure them of the violence in
> which they are plunged by their ferocious manners. . . . But . . . they remain
> insubordinate for the most part.

The "rulers" soon learned, and on coming out from France took care to
bring servants with them; they knew they would not find them in the colony
itself. A similar point can be made with reference to urban industrial development: the independently-minded *habitant* who wished to work for another
in a business would go to great lengths to avoid appearing to be an employee,
and would even have an agreement drawn up in the form of a partnership so
as to hide the reality of the master/servant relationship.

The *habitants*, then, were scarcely ruled. This does not mean, however,
that they were fundamentally opposed to their superiors, or that they were
capable of articulating a counter-philosophy of their own. A mulish stub-
bornness they were quite capable of, but to suggest something in place of the
*status quo* was beyond them. Resistance was never concerted, and never possessed even that germ of a political philosophy that could be found in the
protests of the English colonies. It could hardly have been otherwise. Scattered widely over the colony and cut off from one another, they were still sufficiently caught up in the hardships of pioneering life to find considering alternatives an impossible luxury. Anyway, who would lead them?

There was no grouping among the nominal "rulers" that had cause to act
against the authorities. Church, *seigneurs* and businessmen all had occasion to
criticize, but in the last analysis they were happy with the *status quo*. English
detractors could point out that New France lacked newspapers, and so the
basis for public opinion; that there were no representative institutions to act
as a forum for debate; that religious pluralism was not countenanced. All this
was true, but beside the point. The ambitions of New France had quite different ends from those of New England. In both wealth was valued as a means
to an end. In the latter, wealth meant power, and political power at that. In
the former, however, it bought status. It was more important in New France

to have the outward marks of distinction than to possess the reality of power. Peter Kalm, the Swedish scientist who visited North America about 1750, never tired of comparing the two cultures. Since the expenses of his tour of New France were paid by the French authorities, his verdict has to be taken with a grain of salt. Even making these allowances, his judgment is worth pondering. He found that "in the English colonies . . . it was everybody's sole care and employment to scrape a fortune together . . . ," but they did not know how to spend it in a civilized manner. In New France, on the other hand, they went perhaps too far in the other direction. Kalm noted that even

> Frenchmen, who consider things in their true light, complain very much that a great number of the ladies . . . have gotten into the pernicious custom of taking too much care of their dress, and squandering all their fortune and more upon it, instead of sparing something for future times.

In this Kalm was echoing what the French Jesuit, Charlevoix, had earlier observed:

> There is a great fondness for keeping up one's position, and nearly no one amuses himself by thrift. Good cheer is supplied, if its provision leaves means enough to be well clothed; if not one cuts down on the table in order to be well dressed.

For Charlevoix, too, the contrast with the English was stark:

> The English colonist amasses means and makes no expense; the French enjoys what he has and often parades what he has not. The former works for his heirs; the latter leaves his in the need in which he himself is to get along as best he can.

A British observer in Montreal after it surrendered in 1760 wryly noted that "from the number of silk robes, laced coats, and powdered heads of both sexes . . . a stranger would be induced to believe Montreal is entirely inhabited by people of independent and plentiful fortunes."

The imperial connection was prized because it sustained and validated this world of status consciousness. The authorities upheld the social pretensions of the *seigneurs*. Not noble in themselves, they were yet well placed to obtain noble rank and certainly worthy of esteem. Thus the *seigneur* was allotted a special seat in the parish church, and was entitled to receive communion before other laymen. Commissions in the *Troupes de la Marine*, the regulars first sent to the colony in 1683, were reserved for the sons of *seigneurs*, enrolled as cadets at the age of 17. Paradoxically, a royal edict of 1685 also smoothed the way for successful businessmen to become nobles, in this way encouraging middle-class families to champion status consciousness and retarding the development of an alternative code. That edict ruled that in New France trade did not derogate from nobility, the aim being to encourage trade. The effect, however, was to free the upwardly mobile from having to spend a fortune on buying a venal *robe* office as the price of ennoblement, an obstacle of time and money. Now the assimilation was that much easier, and any questioning of noble standards that much weaker. For all these reasons the colonial elite had every reason to adhere to France, and to a status-conscious France at that.

Such an attitude affected the whole of society, and filtered down to the *habitants*. For them and their families public appearance mattered. Kalm claimed that many restricted themselves to a diet of bread and water, so that

> all other provisions such as butter, cheese, meat, poultry, eggs, etc. [may be sent] to town to get money for them . . . to buy clothes and brandy for themselves and finery for their women.

That conduct was geared to external show only, Kalm rubbed in when he wrote

> The women in Canada . . . seem rather remiss in regard to the cleaning of the utensils and apartments, for sometimes the floors . . . are hardly cleaned once in six months, which is a disagreeable sight to all who come from among the Dutch and English, where the constant scouring and scrubbing of the floors is reckoned as important as the exercise of religion itself.

Horses, because they were expensive and intimately associated with chivalry, were highly valued, to the extent that "it is a general complaint that the country people are beginning to keep too many horses, by which means the cows are kept short of food in winter." Status also helps to account for the lure of the *coureurs de bois*. Theirs was a life to be prized for its adventure and material rewards, but it was also attractive for its quasi-military *gloire* and because the *coureurs*, having been to the *pays d'en haut* where ordinary mortals did not venture, had status. Entirely congruent with such seeking and enjoying of status was the attachment of the *habitants* to their holy days, times when work was forbidden and occasions for the display of pomp and ceremony; until the very end of the French régime there were, in addition to the 52 Sundays, no fewer than 33 holy days of obligation, and when Bishop Pontbriand cut these down to 14 the resentment of the *habitants* was bitter.

The pattern of social relationships in New France, then, was one of acceptance. A preoccupation with status drained off energy that might otherwise have been critical, and the existing institutions were nicely calculated to provide support for status distinctions. If any one institution pushed too far, then acceptance might be tempered by a specific, limited refusal to go along. On the whole, nevertheless, the pattern was not challenged. This being so, the dichotomy of ruler and ruled ought to be replaced, perhaps by provider and provided. A useful way of looking upon New France is as a gigantic family. The head of the household is expected to protect, to guide, to initiate, to be firm when needed but to be forgiving when necessary — but not to act the tyrant. So it was with the Bourbons and their household of New France. Paternalism is a key element in absolutism.

The usefulness of provider and provided as an informing dichotomy to characterize New France lies in its ability to stress social welfare. If the term is not too fanciful, perhaps "monarchical socialism" might adequately sum up New France. From the earliest days, the various *hospitalières* had been prominent in the colony. This tradition of caring for the infirm, the destitute, the insane, the orphaned, even for the prostitutes, was one that only grew as the years passed; in 1730 the Blessed Marie Marguerite d'Youville founded the Grey Nuns to continue this commitment to care. The services that were provided were paid for in part by donations, but also in great part by grants from royal sources; the recipients were not turned away if they could not pay. For some a prepaid medicare system was available. For the regular troops special provision was made. It was, all in all, a humane and civilized treatment of social problems.

New France has had a bad press. After all, it lost to Britain in 1760, and its influential interpreter, who imposed his viewpoint for almost a century, was the American Victorian, Francis Parkman. To his many and colourful writings, Parkman brought an instinctive belief in rugged individualism and a contempt for paternalism. That Louis XIV "did for the colonists what they would far better have learned to do for themselves" was in Parkman's view nothing less than a crime, for it prepared the way for the inevitability of 1760.

> Root, stem, and branch [New France] was the nursling of authority. Deadly absolutism blighted her early and her later growth. Friars and Jesuits, a Ventadour and a Richelieu, shaped her destinies. All that conflicted against advancing liberty — the centralized power of the crown and tiara, the ultramontane in religion, the despotic in policy — found their fullest expression and most fatal exercise. Her records shine with glorious deeds, the self-devotion of heroes and of martyrs; and the result of all is disorder, imbecility, ruin.

Today the belief in classical liberalism that sustained Parkman's interpretation is not so easily maintained, and a different evaluation of New France becomes possible.

_____ **Suggested Reading**

The "standard" account of seigneurialism may be found in E.R. Adair, "The French-Canadian Seigneury," *Canadian Historical Review* (1954), and R.C. Harris, *The Seigneurial System in Early Canada* (1968). The querying of this interpretation may be seen in L. Dechèsne, *Habitants et Marchands de Montréal au XVIIè siècle* (1974), and A. Greer, *Peasant, Lord, and Merchant* (1985).

A more general coverage of the topics treated in this chapter is provided by Y. Zoltvany, *The Government of New France* (1971), and R. Donville and J. Casanova, *Daily Life in Early Canada* (1967). An overview of the structures is provided by A. Vachon, "The Administration of New France," *Dictionary of Canadian Biography, 1701-1740*.

Also useful are: J.-C. Falardeau, "The Seventeenth Century Parish in French Canada," in M. Rioux and Y. Martin (eds.), *French-Canadian Society* (1964) (a most interesting collection of material); W.J. Eccles, *Frontenac: The Courtier Governor* (1959). W.B. Monroe, "The Office of Intendant in New France," *American Historical Review* (1906). R. Cahall, *The Sovereign Council of New France* (1929). P. Deffontaines, "The *Rang*-Pattern of Rural Settlement in French Canada," in Rioux and Martin, *op. cit.*

On justice the most convenient is A. Lachance, *La justice criminelle du roi au Canada au XVIIIè siècle* (1978). There is also J. Dickinson, "La justice seigneuriale en Nouvelle-France," *Revue d'Histoire de l'Amérique Française* (1974).

Those who would like to contrast New France with New England (and what is history if it is *not* comparative?) should read C.S. Grant, *Democracy in the Connecticut Frontier Town of Kent* (1972).

M. Weber, *The Protestant Ethic and the Spirit of Capitalism* (1904) is a must. Those interested in applications of this approach to later Canadian topics·would do well to read A.R.M. Lower, "Two Ways of Life," *Canadian Historical Association Reports* (1943).

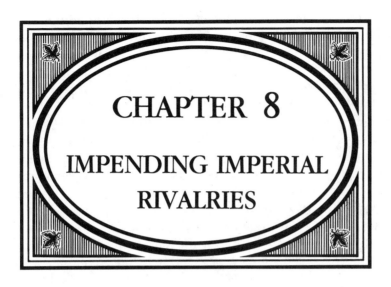

# CHAPTER 8

## IMPENDING IMPERIAL RIVALRIES

## — 1. Acadia —

The previous chapter was devoted to only one of the many societies that developed in northern America in the seventeenth and eighteenth centuries. Our concentration on New France was justifiable, for on the St. Lawrence the population rose to a significant level, some 65 000 at the time of the British conquest, and a way of life of some complexity and sophistication emerged. Nevertheless, there were other European presences in northern America at this period, and they too had their part to play in the unfolding of the Canadian experience.

Acadia, that vaguely defined approach to the St. Lawrence, had been settled before Champlain decided upon Quebec. Even after his removal, the French made various attempts to maintain themselves about Port Royal. In 1629 there was French activity on Cape Breton, and to support the all-important fishing industry a French outpost was maintained at Placentia in Newfoundland. From an early date, however, French claims were contested. In

1621 James I (in his capacity as James VI of Scotland) authorized William Alexander to "plant" New Scotland (the Latin affectation, Nova Scotia, was a later, Cromwellian touch). It was not until 1629, however, that settlers arrived, one party to the site of Port Royal, a second to Cape Breton, sailing in the wake of the Kirke brothers. In addition, there was the ever growing, but still stunted, establishment on Newfoundland, especially at St. John's.

Despite this activity, and signs that the Scots initiatives were promising, little came of these beginnings. The British, by the Treaty of St. Germain-en-Laye, handed back not merely Quebec but control of the Acadian region as well. Newfoundland was long seen as unsuited for colonization on account of the fisheries, so France was left to make good its claims. However, its efforts were halfhearted. The rescue that Louis XIV mounted in the 1660s did not apply to Acadia, and its fate may well stand as an example of what might have happened to Quebec had not the king stepped in with his full and unstinted backing. Not until the 1680s was something done for Acadia, when the fishing industry was reorganized through the Rochelle interests, and troops and naval supplies were dispatched to the area. Nevertheless, it was too little, too late. By this date France was preoccupied with war in Europe and, more to the point, New England had gone so far in its development that it overshadowed the fledgling French colony. New England fishermen and traders had established a stranglehold over the Acadian economy, and try as the French might to insist upon mercantalist self-sufficiency, the importance, even the necessity, of New England trade could never be denied.

Given such weak support and direction from home, the French effort in Acadia was a sorry one indeed. During much of the seventeenth century its development was hindered by vicious infighting between French interests, each claiming to enjoy royal rights to the area. A leading quarreller was Charles de la Tour who, in his attempt to hang on to his possessions, was not above paying homage for his lands to Alexander and through him to the Scots Crown. His backing both sides in this way was only realistic, however, for in the circumstances a British takeover of Acadia was not only possible but to be expected. Pressured by New England, Britain was to launch assault after assault on Acadia. As early as 1613 Samuel Argall had sailed from Virginia to attack Port Royal. In all, British forces conquered the whole or part of Acadia ten times in the seventeenth century. What fueled these attacks, especially on the part of the Americans, was a combination of avarice and religious fanaticism. The loot was not always to be found in the quantities rumoured, but the wish to deal a blow against Roman Catholicism was one that never failed to appeal. On the eve of the attack of 1690 the Massachusetts divine, Cotton Mather, claimed that

> The Question which we now have before us in short is this: Whether we will venture All, with an Hope to Perserve All, or Whether we will keep All, with an Assurance to [lose] All. . . . Who is on the Lord's side? Even so, who is for Jesus, against Satan, and who is for the true Christian, Protestant, Religion against Popery and Paganism?

Even over fifty years later, in the cooler eighteenth century, a Puritan warrior admitted

> how sweet and pleasant will it be . . . to be the person under God that shall reduce and pull down that Stronghold of Satan and sett up the kingdome of our exalted Saviour. O, that I could be . . . in that church to destroy ye images [there] sett up and [to have] ye true Gospel of our Lord and Saviour Jesus Christ [there] preached.

In such sentiments can the roots of Parkman's vision be seen.

Ignored by France and harried by its enemies, the colony's growth was understandably slow. As late as 1670 (a date when France recovered possession of Acadia after it had been in British hands for 16 years) the population was only 350. By 1686 it had risen to over 800, and by 1700 it was 2500. Such figures are tiny when compared with the total in the St. Lawrence, and even more insignificant when set alongside those of the English colonies. Many of the characteristics that marked the *habitants* could be found in Acadia, but not all. The colony lacked that flourishing and extensive fur trade that set the tone for so much of life along the St. Lawrence. Thus the élan that was so striking among the *habitants*, and that was fostered in the militia and the *Troupes de la Marine*, was noticeably absent in Acadia.

The two colonies had, nevertheless, much in common. The Acadians were farmers who were satisfied with what they had, saw no sense in change, and were not concerned with producing for the market. It was observed that they were "indifferent husbandmen in general, and do no more labour than what necessity urges them to." It must be admitted that they had even more reason than the *habitants* for such an attitude. Early Acadians had brought with them the technique of diking the marshy flats that bordered the many inlets that made up Acadia's coastline. The result was the reclamation of easily worked and tremendously fertile fields that gave them all the crops and all the forage they and their animals could desire. Nor was there any danger of exhausting this fertility: the dikes had only to be opened for the sea to sweep in fresh nutritious sediment, and the cycle could start all over again.

On this basis an egalitarian society of rude plenty grew up, knowing neither a rich elite nor an impoverished proletariat. The land gave so generously that they soon turned their backs upon the sea and allowed the New Englanders to monopolize the banks. The people, left for so long to their devices, organized themselves in extended families under patriarchs, and asked nothing better than to be left alone. As a society it was uneducated, becoming increasingly illiterate, and sinking into intellectual torpor; at the same time it was a singularly well-behaved, sober, and pious one. There truly was an arcadian existence. Already by the opening years of the eighteenth century it was being said of them that "they lived like true republicans, not acknowledging royal or judicial authority." The *habitants* themselves paid their cousins a backhanded compliment every time they used their saying to describe a stubborn fellow as "*entêté comme un Acadien.*"

Not even the final loss of French control to the British could shock the Acadians from their passive isolationism. In 1713 the Treaty of Utrecht ended the long drawn-out war that had pitted France against a European coalition headed by Britain. That war, the War of Spanish Succession, had broken out in 1702 when Louis XIV had accepted the throne of Spain on behalf of his grandson to whom it had been willed by the last, childless Spanish Hapsburg. The thought of the Bourbons adding a Spanish empire to the French was so frightening that all-out war for a decade was thought to be a worthwhile price to prevent the union. In the end the Bourbons did rule Spain, but France was so weakened and the two branches of the family were so far apart that the danger evaporated. By the terms of Utrecht, Acadia passed to Britain. The population was able to ignore the change in sovereignty, however. The early administrators, notably the Huguenot soldier Paul Mascarene, urged a policy of conciliation, arguing that it would be necessary to make the Acadians subjects first before making them good subjects. What he was referring to here was the initial attempt to have the Acadians swear unconditional loyalty to Britain so that they would be obliged to bear arms against its enemies, including the French, in any subsequent war. This the Acadians balked at, and Mascarene was prepared to accept a qualified oath that would have permitted neutrality towards France. There was sufficient ambiguity in the oath-taking for those on both sides to believe that such a modified loyalty had been agreed to. Certainly, after an early flurry of interest in this question, the Acadians were largely left alone and allowed to resume their inward-looking bucolic lives.

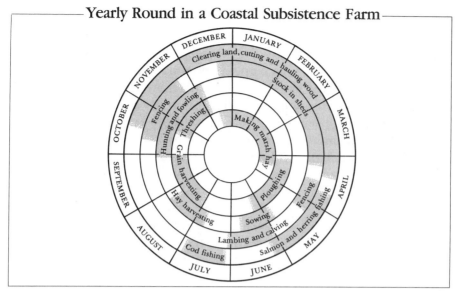

**Yearly Round in a Coastal Subsistence Farm**

SOURCE: R. Cole Harris, ed., *Historical Atlas of Canada*, Vol. I, *From the Beginning to 1800* (Toronto: University of Toronto Press, 1987), plate 32. Copyright © University of Toronto Press. Reprinted by permission of University of Toronto Press.

This policy was not to last, however. The French had had to give up Port Royal (renamed Annapolis Royal in honour of the British queen) and the surrounding settlements, and they had been required to withdraw from Newfoundland. They retained possession of the islands in the Gulf, notably Prince Edward Island (then known as Île St. Jean) and Cape Breton (Île Royale). On the latter the French determined to build a base to guard what remained of their colonial empire in northern America. At tremendous cost the fortress of Louisbourg was erected, to serve the needs of a fleet protecting the approaches to the St. Lawrence and to be a haven for privateers to prey on British and Yankee shipping in time of war. Attempts were made to have Acadians settle on the island, though few were prepared to exchange their familiar and fertile diked meadows, even when under alien authority, for the ruggedness of a fresh start on Cape Breton. The community at Placentia was moved, however, and in this way the new colony had the benefit of their fishing skills.

The growth of settlement was slow, and by the mid-1740s there were only some 4000 inhabitants (though it was able to support a dancing master). As such it posed little threat to Britain or to the English colonies, though its military potential and its success as a market (Louisbourg became the meeting place of French, British, New England, and Caribbean traders) once again attracted New England's attention. When war broke out in 1744 between France and Britain the traditional New England imperatives, booty and religion, went into action. A Puritan army, backed by ships of the Royal Navy, descended on Louisbourg in 1745 and captured it. Although the fortress was handed back by the Treaty of Aix-la-Chapelle in 1748, the question of the Acadians' loyalty had been brought up. There had been some Acadian support for France, in particular from the French priest, the abbé Loutre, who had great influence with the Indians. In 1745 a proposal to deport the Acadians was rejected as not feasible. Ten years later, however, when hostilities broke out in North America a year before the Seven Years' War was declared in Europe, the proposal was resurrected by the British lieutenant governor Charles Lawrence. Only after he had begun to round up and deport the Acadians was the matter considered by the imperial authorities. Faced with a *fait accompli*, they went along with their agent's action.

## Map 8.1: Greater Acadia, 1750

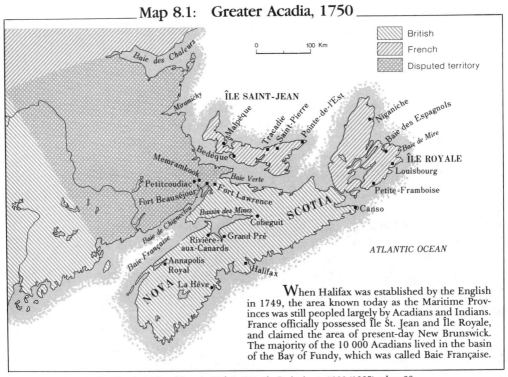

When Halifax was established by the English in 1749, the area known today as the Maritime Provinces was still peopled largely by Acadians and Indians. France officially possessed Île St. Jean and Île Royale, and claimed the area of present-day New Brunswick. The majority of the 10 000 Acadians lived in the basin of the Bay of Fundy, which was called Baie Française.

SOURCE: Harris, *Historical Atlas of Canada*, Vol. I, *From the Beginning to 1800* (1987), plate 30.

There were by this time some 15 000 Acadians. About 11 000 were shipped abroad, some to the English colonies in North America, some to the Caribbean. Others landed in England, still others in France itself. Louisiana received a share. Those not herded onto the boats escaped to live a haunted life in the woods, emerging years later to claim a place in their ancestral territory, to be joined by returning exiles from abroad. Ever since, debate has raged over the policy and its execution. Britain has been charged with the guilt of near-genocide. There is little doubt that such a drastic solution was not necessary, the vast majority of Acadians being neutral as they had claimed and the activities of the rest such that they could be contained.

At the same time it is well to remember that in the *ancien régime*, ideas about nationality and territoriality were very different from what they have since become. It was not unusual for an entire people to become new subjects of a conqueror overnight, and to be expected to be fully loyal to that conqueror, even to the extent of fighting his battles for him and against their former rulers. This had happened, for instance, to the people of Alsace; this predominantly German territory, part of the Holy Roman Empire for over 900 years, was forcibly "reunited" with France by Louis XIV in 1680. Henceforth its people were French, liable to the duties that fell on all subjects of the sun-king. Closer in time to the Acadian deportations, in 1746 Louis XV ordered that the conquered territories of the Low Countries be subject to the military draft. It may also be noted that in 1690 when Frontenac attacked New York, it was intended should the colony fall to New France to deport all the inhabitants to Pennsylvania or to England save for the Catholics. For that matter, the French themselves in 1751 threatened to deport the Acadians if they refused to swear allegiance to the king of France.

In the same way the charges of British cruelty in carrying out the policy have to be put in perspective. Undoubtedly there were some whose hatred of the Acadians spilled over into savage treatment, but equally clearly there were instances of helping as much as possible under the circumstances. Allowance must be made for the difficulty of the task (a large and unwilling population having to be seized in territory that favoured the would-be escaper) and for the peculiar framework of Acadian society. Réne Le Blanc complained that his family had been split up among different ships that eventually found their ways to different ports, although his wife and two children were with him. But then he had 18 other sons and daughters, and 150 grandchildren, all of whom he considered equally family.

Acadian developments by the mid-eighteenth century were merely small items in the clash of empires. Nevertheless, for the development of northern

America they had their importance. The stature of Louisbourg was such that in 1749 Britain decided to emulate the French example. The naval base of Halifax was constructed, and a surrounding settlement built up. So vigorously was this work carried on that within three years its population equalled that of Cape Breton. The base itself was to dominate the region, and remained a potent focus of imperial majesty for years to come.

The fate of the Acadians was a warning to their cousins on the St. Lawrence of what they might expect at the hands of a conquering Britain. When the Seven Years' War led to the invasion of New France, the fierce resistance of the people was largely inspired by fears of deportation. In the end Britain did not attempt to deport the 65 000 *habitants*; but then who would have imagined a deportation of 10 000? It was best to play safe and resist.

# — 2. The Mississippi Valley —

No sooner had settlement in the St. Lawrence Valley taken the place of mere trading than the question arose as to Canada's limits. As has been seen, the dynamic of the fur trade demanded an ever-expanding search for prime-quality beaver, but those in France who controlled the colony were not prepared to contemplate such a frittering away of resources. For Colbert in particular the first requirement was to build up a solid base of settlement in the region about Quebec. Later, when the population had expanded and a mature society had evolved, would be the time to spread further afield. Until then he insisted upon what historians have known as a "compact colony" policy.

The policy naturally appealed to the tidy absolutist mind, so much so that Colbert could even contemplate the loss of the entire fur trade: in that case "the settlers would be obliged to engage in fishing, prospecting, and manufacturing, which would yield them far greater benefits." As late as 1726 the minister of marine, Maurepas, was writing in that vein, lamenting the fact that whereas

> The genius of the people of New England is to labour to bring the soil into cultivation and expand slowly, the people of New France think otherwise, and wish always to press forward, with the result that the English colonies are more populous and more firmly established than ours.

However compelling the logic of the compact colony policy, it was powerless to withstand the imperative of the fur trade, and attempts to limit expansion were fated to remain Canute-like.

What vitiated the efforts of Colbert and those like him to control expansion was the fact that fur trading was not the only reason for pressing on beyond the pale. It might be possible to rail against the fevered search for beaver, but it was not so easy to refuse an opportunity to discover the route to the Far East. That was the prize that had dazzled Europeans from the first — indeed, it was the very *raison d'être* of their voyages to the New World. When colonists insisted to Colbert that they were really engaged in the vital task of exploring, and that any pelts picked up were incidental to the main task, there was little that could be said to counter them. This was doubly the case when the very governor of the colony found his own reasons for pursuing an expansionist policy. Frontenac, perpetually in debt like so many of his class and yet determined despite this embarrassment to live nobly, was keen to trade on his own account in the west and recoup something of his fortune. Thanks to his initiative Fort Frontenac was established in 1673 on Lake Ontario (the site of present-day Kingston). More significantly it was thanks to him that serious attention was given to discovering the river that the Indians called Mississippi and that led, they claimed, to fabled lands.

In 1673 Louis Joliet set out for that river. By 1674 he was back to report that he had journeyed on it far to the south. He had not reached the sea; however, he had gone sufficiently far to establish that its outlet was not the Pacific but the Gulf of Mexico. Even so, his report stressed the fertility of the prairies and the abundance of fur, and suggested that a start to settlement could be made in the Illinois country; he should himself be given the right to set up a post there. Colbert stood by his principles, however, and pointed out to Frontenac that

> You must on no account encourage [these new discoveries] unless there be a great need and some obvious advantage to be derived from them. You must hold to the maxim that it is far more worthwhile to occupy a smaller area and have it well populated than to spread out and have several feeble colonies which could easily be destroyed by all manner of accidents.

The lure of fur was too strong for such caution, and again with Frontenac's backing an expedition was sent into the Mississippi Valley. In 1678 La Salle departed from the St. Lawrence, ostensibly to confirm the course of the Mississippi but in reality to make his and his governor's fortunes. From now on the Mississippi Valley and the Great Lakes region were penetrated by French traders, and the beaver from these areas contributed to the glut that overwhelmed the colony in the closing years of the seventeenth century.

The collapse of the fur market was not the only problem, however. Colbert's premonition of "all manner of accidents" was being borne out. Increased trading in the west was stirring up Indian quarrels, both among the tribes themselves and against the French. The second Iroquois war had been dragging on since 1684, and now threatened to escalate still further in terror. The situation degenerated so far that large-scale military incursions, reminiscent of the Carrignan-Salières forays of 1666, had to be made into the Great Lakes region. This so angered the French authorities that they ordered the abandonment of the west. All the posts with a single exception were to be physically destroyed, but even a royal directive was impotent in the face of fur trading demands. Such was the outcry in the colony that the withdrawal was halted, and although trading was supposed to stop it continued as though the ban had never been decreed. In theory, however, the Colbertian compact colony policy had been reiterated.

Yet suddenly royal policy did an about-face. The most expansive imperialism displaced the existing caution. The *volte-face* was triggered by the impending death of Charles II of Spain and the imminent War of Spanish Succession. Louis XIV was now obliged to see the Mississippi, especially the delta, with new eyes. If his grandson was to be king of Spain it was imperative that France make good any claims it might have to the area. In the face of expected English opposition, a French presence on the Gulf would be well situated to challenge any English descent upon Mexico; at the same time it would be able to threaten English possessions both on the mainland and in the Caribbean. If on the other hand Spain did not go to a Bourbon but to an Austrian Hapsburg, France would be well placed to threaten Mexico. That the mouth of the Mississippi had become overnight a strategic centre in the coming European war was made plain when the French got wind of an English plan to plant a settlement there, peopled by Huguenot refugees. Thus in 1699 the *Canadien* Pierre Le Moyne, Sieur d'Iberville, was dispatched to take possession and to confirm the claims made earlier by La Salle.

From these beginnings the uncertain colony of Louisiana developed slowly. Great difficulty was experienced with the early site at Biloxi: the sea approaches were awkward, and the soil difficult to cultivate. Only with the removal of the capital to New Orleans in 1722 was the colony put on a firmer footing. Even then it was a weak growth, kept going for its military significance.

Shortly after this reversal of attitudes in the south, the north, about the Great Lakes, saw a similar development. Two very different factors were responsible. The first was the continuing need to prevent an Indian conflagration there. The second Iroquois war had been ended in 1701 and the colony was desperate to avoid a third. It was recognized that only the sending of French parties into the area would prevent hostilities. The second was the reordering of the Indian trade that threatened to take place in the wake of the Treaty of Utrecht. Clause XV of that treaty stipulated

> The subjects of France inhabiting Canada . . . shall hereafter give no Hindrance or Molestation to the Five Nations or Cantons of Indians, subject to the Dominion of Great Britain, nor to the other Natives of America, who are Friends to the same. In like manner the subjects of Great Britain, shall behave themselves Peaceably towards the Americans, who are Subjects or Friends to France; and on both sides they shall enjoy full Liberty of going and coming on account of Trade. As also the Natives of these Countries shall, with the same Liberty, resort, as they please, to the British and French Colonies, for Promoting Trade on one side, and the other, without Molestation or Hindrance, either on the part of the British Subjects, or of the French . . . .

This was a momentous development. In the first place it gave Britain a territorial claim that would be very embarrassing to the French. In the second, given that British trade goods were superior to and cheaper than French ones, western Indians were beginning to travel to Albany and desert their French allegiance. With time, the British traders would not wait for the Indians to come to them, but would go out to meet their suppliers on their own ground. The French, already accustomed to seeing the Great Lakes region as their monopoly, were horrified to see what the metropolitan peacemakers had allowed to happen. It was too horrible to contemplate and something would have to be done.

Thus, when the French heard of a projected British trading post at Niagara, they resolved to act. The British venture was perfectly legal under the terms of clause XV. However, the French preempted them. Obtaining the permission of a Seneca chieftain, in whose territory the post would lie, they erected one of their own in 1720. For the moment, decisiveness seemed to have preserved the French-Indian connection. However, all it had done in fact was to unleash a series of challenges and responses as the two sides vied for the control of the strategic centres. For example in 1727 the British established Oswego on the south shore of Lake Ontario. This development shocked the colonial governor, Vaudreuil, who wrote home that

> The news of this establishment on territory which has been considered, from all time, to belong to France appeared to him as much the more important as

he was sensible to the difficulty of preserving Niagara . . . and that the loss of Niagara would entail at the same time that of the entire Indian trade of the Upper country; for these nations go the more readily to the English, as they obtain goods much cheaper, and as much Rum as they please . . . .

He was so shocked, in fact, that he concluded that armed intervention would be necessary, and he ended his dispatch by asking "that extraordinary and considerable aid be sent . . . both in money and munitions of war, and a large number of guns and pistols. He also requires troops."

War did not break out, however. For their different reasons, Britain and France both desired peace in the years after Utrecht and, until the War of Austrian Succession in 1744, did everything they could to avoid an open break. Under cover of this extraordinary peace, the French rounded out their grasp of the Mississippi Valley-Great Lakes region, so that by mid-century their possessions ran in a great arc from Louisbourg, through the St. Lawrence, down the Mississippi to New Orleans. In between pullulated a dozen or so English colonies for whom westward expansion was merely a matter of time.

# — 3. Hudson Bay and the Far West —

The rivalry to the north went back to the closing years of the seventeenth century. In 1670 a powerful syndicate in England, including the backing of royalty, obtained a charter to realize a scheme put forward by two French men, Pierre-Esprit Radisson and the Sieur de Groseilliers. They had first-hand knowledge of North America and of the fur trade, having been *coureurs de bois* operating out of the St. Lawrence. Their plan was to approach the source of fur through Hudson Bay, and since the French authorities proved tardy in responding to their overtures they approached the English. The tradition of Frobisher, Davis, and Hudson had not been forgotten; indeed, it had been built upon in voyages such as those of Button (the first European in what is now Manitoba) in 1612 and Foxe in 1631, so the English were receptive to the suggestion. Very quickly the Hudson's Bay Company's posts in Rupert's Land (named after the first governor, Prince Rupert, cousin of King Charles II) posed a serious threat to the French.

It was a trade operated very differently from that of the St. Lawrence. The English did not go out to the Indians, but sat on the Bay and waited for them to come in to trade. It was not so much that they lacked the birch that would

## Map 8.2: France in America, 1663–1755

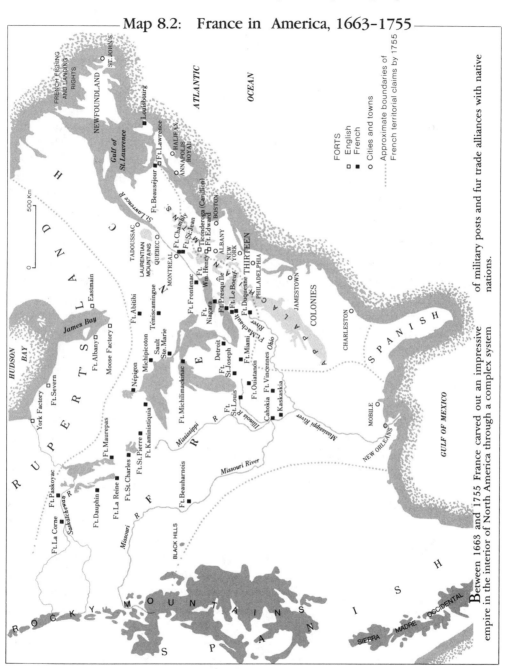

SOURCES: J. L. Finlay and D. N. Sprague, *The Structure of Canadian History*, 3rd ed. (Scarborough: Prentice-Hall, 1989), p. 68; Harris, *Historical Atlas of Canada*, Vol. I, *From the Beginning to 1800* (1987), plates 37–40.

have made canoe travel possible, nor that their traders came out for short stays and so did not identify with the land and its people. Rather it was that they could afford to wait. There were good reasons for the Indians to come in. The all-sea route meant that goods were cheaper, and also that much bulkier goods could be got to the Indians than was possible via canoe freighting. Moreover, English goods were frequently superior to those of the French. As early as 1673 it was being pointed out to the authorities on the St. Lawrence that "already we see that the establishment of the English on the great bay of the North . . . will cause a decided prejudice against [New France]. The English have already diverted a great many of the inland Indians . . . and attracted them to themselves by their great liberality. . . ." Much later, in the middle of the eighteenth century, the French authorities themselves were admitting that "the English have the better of us in the quality of merchandise in two important articles. The first is kettles — the second is cloth," They went on to explain that the Indians "have asked for kettles of yellow copper in bales one hundred pounds each . . . assorted by size each bale of twenty five to thirty kettles. Those which they have sent are almost all of the same size, poorly made and too heavy for the Indians." At the same time "the red cloth is brown . . .; the blue is equally of a very inferior quality to that of England and it is not surprising that when [the French] send envoys [to] the Indians they find no favour."

The Hudson's Bay Company represented a very real threat. More important than the quantity of furs they could intercept was the quality of them. The hat trade required a large proportion of coat beaver. The St. Lawrence trade always produced too great a proportion of parchment but the northern Indians who supplied the traders on the bay knew how to *engraisser* their skins. Moreover, narrow trading considerations apart, the potential threat that the English represented to the French-Indian alliances was a constant thorn in the French side. From their posts on James Bay such as Fort Charles and Moose Fort (the Bottom of the Bay) and from those like York Fort on Hudson Bay proper, the English could tap the furs from a vast hinterland.

The French attempted to counter with a Hudson Bay company of their own. In the 1680s there was the Compagnie de la Baie du Nord, in which the leading colonial merchant, Aubert de la Chesnaye, was prominent, but greater reliance was placed upon armed intervention. That the first attack took place during a time when the two metropolitans were at peace indicated how seriously the French saw the English threat. In 1686 the Chevalier de Troyes with a party of regulars and *coureurs de bois* made a striking overland journey in winter and took the English at the Bottom of the Bay by surprise. Three years later, with the rival traders jockeying for position in James Bay, European war broke out, and the scale of hostilities increased as both sides sent naval vessels into Hudson Bay. The fighting that resulted throughout the War of the League of Augsburg, 1689-97, was extremely confused, with forts changing hands constantly. Typical was the way in which Pierre le Moyne, Sieur d'Iberville, strove to possess York Fort: in 1690 he unsuccessfully attacked it; in 1694 he took it; in 1696 he lost it to the English; in 1697 he was back in possession. For the five years between the Treaty of Ryswick, that ended the war, and the outbreak of the War of Spanish Succession, the French were theoretically the owners of James Bay, and the English of the rest of Hudson Bay. After the French setbacks in the latter war, however, the Treaty of Utrecht gave the entire area to the British.

The impulse that led the French in the post-Utrecht reevaluation to move into the Mississippi Valley, also operated in the more northerly regions. The British might have unassailable title to Hudson Bay, but it would still be possible to outflank them by extending the French trading network further west from the Great Lakes. The new drive was signalled in 1717 when a new command was established, the *Postes du Nord*, centred on the north shore of Lake Superior about Kaministikwia. It became more significant in 1727 when Pierre Gaultier de Varennes, Sieur de la Vérendrye, was made commandant, and brought to the task of western exploration his very considerable talents together with those of his sons and nephew.

By 1731 a fort (St. Pierre) had been set up on Rainy River, and by the following year Fort Charles on Lake of the Woods. Fort Maurepas on the Red River followed in 1734 and Forts Rouge (at the confluence of the Red and the Assiniboine) and La Reine (present-day Portage la Prairie) in 1738. In 1742-43 two of his sons made a long journey from Fort La Reine that took them within sight of the Rockies. The area they explored, the present-day northern states, they found to be unsuited for their purposes, the trading of furs and the route to the western sea. Attention shifted northward. In 1750, a year after la Vérendrye's death, The Pas on the Saskatchewan was founded, and in 1753 Fort la Corne, named for the new commandant of the *Postes du Nord*, was established near the forks of the same river.

The Hudson's Bay Company could not stand by idly and see their trade cut off. The policy of sitting by the Bay would have to be modified. As early as the 1690s they had produced a *coureur* of their own, Henry Kelsey, who had ventured far into the western prairies, the first European to see the buffalo, but he was a man ahead of his company's time. This achievement was forgotten, even by the company that sent him, and nothing was done to follow it up. Only much later did the Hudson's Bay Company begin to move inland. In 1743 Henley House, upstream on the Albany River, which flows into James Bay, was built. It was a failed experiment, however, for it showed how unsuited the English traders were for life with and among the Indians. While they restricted themselves to their posts on Hudson Bay and dealt with the Indians at arm's length, quiet if not close relations existed. When they attempted to live at closer quarters, however, they antagonized the Indians, and in 1755 the Europeans at Henley House were massacred and the post given up. Yet the push inland had become necessary. In 1759 Henley House was rebuilt. Moreover, in 1754 Anthony Henday was sent to duplicate what Kelsey had done so long before. By the time he returned to York Fort a year later he had reached the foothills of the Rockies and obtained such a wealth of fur that the necessity of establishing inland trading could no longer be doubted.

En route Henday had encountered the French at la Corne and The Pas. At both he was well received: at the former "the Governor came with his hatt in his hand, and followed a great deal of Bowing and Scraping. . . . He treated me with 2 Glasses Brandy and half a Bisket." Such civility was possible in the northwest where contacts between the two powers were recent — and where the French were interested in trading away prime skins from Henday's Indians, which they did in part with the aid of "ten gallons of Brandy half adulterated with water." Even while this was happening on the fur frontier of the Saskatchewan, French and British were colliding on the settlement frontier of the Ohio. Any possible clash between French and British in the northwest was prevented even before it had begun.

## Suggested Reading

The Centenary Series volumes that cover this period are D. Miquelon, *New France, 1701-1744*, G.F.G. Stanley, *New France, 1744-60*, and W.S. MacNutt, *The Atlantic Provinces, 1712-1857*.

For Acadia, see N. Griffiths, *The Acadians* (1973), and *The Acadian Deportation* (1969). On the diking technique, see G. Wynn, "Late Eighteenth Century Agriculture on the Bay of Fundy Marshlands," *Acadiensis* (1979). For the French presence in the Mississippi Valley there are J.F. McDermott, *The French in the Mississippi Valley* (1965), and *Frenchmen and French Ways in the Mississippi Valley* (1969). W.J. Eccles, *The Canadian Frontier* (1969) is perhaps a more convenient *entrée* to this aspect of expansion. For Louisbourg, see J.S. McLennan, *Louisbourg* (1969). G. Rawlyk, *Yankees at Louisbourg* (1967), should be accompanied by S.E.D. Shortt, "Conflict and Identity in Massachusetts: The Louisbourg expedition of 1745," *Histoire sociale/Social History* (1972).

For northern and western developments, in addition to the Ray and Rich works referred to in Chapter 4, see G.L. Nute, *Ceasars of the Wilderness: Médard Chouart, Sieur de Groseilliers and Pierre-Esprit Radisson* (1943). W.R. Jacobs, *Diplomacy and Indian Gifts: Anglo-French Rivalry along the Ohio and Northwest Frontier*, (1950). N.M. Crouse, *La Vérendrye, Fur Trader and Explorer* (1956).

For a useful account that gives the feel of imperial rivalry on the ground there is W.A. Kenyon and J.R. Turnbull, *The Battle for James Bay* (1971).

# CHAPTER 9

## A MID-18th CENTURY BALANCE SHEET

## — 1. Canada vs. British North America —

Ever since Argall's descent from Virginia upon Port Royal, Britain and France had been contending for North America, but by the mid-eighteenth century the nature and scope of that struggle was changing. Both powers had used the long period of peace that followed the Treaty of Utrecht to expand their trade and commerce. In this France was making the greater strides, and its recovery from the defeats of 1713 was spectacular indeed. Not surprisingly there were those in Britain who felt that this resurgence made another war necessary, a preemptive strike to break France before it engrossed the trade of the entire world. A British commentator put it frankly in 1745 when he concluded that "our commerce, in general, will flourish more under a vigorous and well managed naval war, than under any peace." For him and his kind, and there were many of them, the war that was even then being fought (of Austrian Succession) was a great disappointment; its resolution was not the clear-cut recognition of supremacy that the hard-liners wanted, and they remained spoiling for a fight.

In the coming global confrontation, North America would have its part to play. Indeed, as the previous chapter explained, the situation there was extremely explosive and might have been expected to lead to war many years earlier. As it was, when the smash came, the first shots were fired in the New World two years before the first fired in the Old.

Those shots were fired in the Ohio Valley. Hostilities commenced there rather than in Acadia or Hudson Bay because the clash was triggered by the collision of fur trading and settlement frontiers. Hudson Bay was barely peopled; Nova Scotia, for all its impressive build-up about Halifax, was still tiny, and the earlier overspill of the population of Massachusetts into the area was a thing of the past. In the central and southern British colonies, however, the pressure of population was mounting. Since the beginning of the seventeenth century the move inland had been steadily underway, and the land between the seaboard and the Appalachian Mountains had been filling up. The English-speaking peoples were now poised to spill over into the trans-Appalachian west. That their numbers were reaching a critical point was signalled by two developments that deeply worried the French. In the 1730s the new colony of Georgia was launched. Its founding was evidence not only of a seemingly inexhaustible supply of fresh English-speaking colonists, but also of a forward policy that butted up against established Bourbon colonies, both French and Spanish; it was blatant provocation. Similarly provocative was the formation in 1748 of the Virginia Land Company. A group of Virginian speculators with impressive metropolitan backing obtained title to over 200 000 hectares in the Ohio Valley. Settlement could be expected to follow. The stark fact facing New France was the discrepancy in numbers: the French had perhaps 70 000 in North America, the British between one and two million.

Yet New France could be pardoned for remaining confident in the face of overwhelming odds. The British advantage was on paper; in practice their position was badly flawed. Numbers there might be, but unless they were united they would be of little use, and the colonies were notoriously jealous of one another. The fate of the Albany Conference in 1754 was evidence of their inability to act in concert. In that year the colonies were invited to meet with the Iroquois to decide upon a common policy in the light of mounting imperial tensions. These were real enough. Even while the Albany Conference was convening a Virginian force under George Washington had been sent into the Ohio Valley to protest the building of French forts there; a skirmish took place in which Jumonville, the commander of the French party, and nine of his men were killed. When Washington was challenged by French reinforcements he had to fall back upon Fort Necessity which, however, he was able to hold for only nine hours; soon he retreated ingloriously back across the mountains. Despite such tensions, interest at Albany was minimal. Only seven colonies took part, and Virginia itself, a key element in any proposed union, did not bother to attend. Moreover, within colonies there were frequently interests that preferred to avoid war with the French. A good example was the New York fur trading element, still largely of Dutch descent, that operated out of Albany. Their access to cheap and better quality trade goods meant an ability to drive a thriving illicit trade with Canadian *coureurs de bois*. Such traders could hardly be expected to favour an all-out war that would disrupt a flourishing commerce.

Set against British disunity was French unity of action. There might have been some uncertainty as to the authority of Quebec over Acadia, but it was understood that in time of war the governor of Canada was then in charge. Louisiana was a separate colony, it is true, but it was small compared to Canada and again, in the event of war, military operations were mounted from the St. Lawrence. The centralization of authority in Canada, and the absence of representative institutions, meant that private interests had less chance of sabotaging common decisions. When it came to mobilizing for war, the French effort was always more efficient.

On top of this was the fact that as fighters the French colonists were superior to the British. The years of frontier wars in which most of the people defended themselves against Indian attacks were long gone. Now the frontier was far inland, and generations had grown up that had not known Indian warfare. Colonial troops did enjoy their triumphs, notably against Louisbourg in 1745, but they were the exceptions. Usually their levies were poorly trained (even at Louisbourg the greatest number of casualties were the result of exploding cannons inexpertly served by raw recruits) and even worse disciplined. A British commentator was obliged to confess of his colonials, "our men are nothing but a set of farmers and planters, used only to the axe and hoe."

Not even their stiffening with British regulars could guarantee an improvement. European troops, trained in the almost balletic formalism of eighteenth-century warfare, were hopelessly disadvantaged in North American forests until they had had a chance to learn by their mistakes. Just what could happen to British regulars and colonial militia when up against superior guerillas was shown in 1755. To avenge Washington's failure of the previous year, an advance in force was undertaken into the disputed Ohio Valley. General Braddock was sent in command of two Irish regiments, and was joined by a regiment of Virginia militia. At the Monongahela River his force of almost 1500 men was caught by a Canadian-Indian detachment just over half its size, and in the chaos of bush warfare 977 men were killed or wounded; Braddock himself died of his wounds. His enemy's casualties were 39.

Such encounters point to a major reason for French confidence. In 1750 Canada was still a frontier society in a way that the English colonies had long since ceased to be. The defeat of the Iroquois had come in 1701, not even two generations before. Even after that date the long drawn-out settlement was at almost every point in contact with uncleared, unsettled wilderness where forest skills, if not always those of warfare, had to be practised. The fur trade still kept a disproportionate body of men (4000 had full-time jobs in the fur trade) intimately connected with the backwoods and their ways. The *Troupes de la Marine* might be French men who as often as not were employed in a civilian capacity to ease the drastic labour shortage of the colony. Their officers were colonials, however, and since it was a service where venality did not obtain, promotion was by merit and the professional standard was accordingly high. These officers were available to command the militia parties sent to carry on the *petite guerre*. It was a potent combination, and not surprisingly testimony to the effectiveness of the Canadian guerilla was plentiful. The British observer previously cited recognized that Canadians

> are not only well trained and disciplined, but they are used to arms from their infancy among the Indians; and are reckoned equal, if not superior in that part of the world to veteran troops [The Canadians] are troops that fight without pay — maintain themselves in the woods without charges — march without baggage — and support themselves without stores and magazines — we are at immense charges for those purposes.

Kalm noted "I have seldom seen any people shoot with such dexterity as these . . . , there was scarcely one of them who was not a clever marksman and who did not own a musket." Of their *coureur de bois* background he wrote

> It is inconceivable what hardships the people of Canada must undergo on their hunting journeys . . . . They often suffer hunger, thirst, heat, and cold, and are bitten by gnats, and exposed to the bites of snakes and other dangerous animals and insects. . . . By this means . . . they become such brave soldiers, and so inured to fatigue that none of them fears danger or hardships.

The Canadian militia, unlike its British colonial counterpart, was an effective as opposed to a paper establishment. As part of his paternal care of the colony, Louis XIV in 1669 had ordered the governor "to make the inhabitants expert in the use of arms and in military discipline." The order applied to all males between the ages of 16 and 60, though given the need to carry on the normal life of the colony, especially agricultural work, it was not possible to mobilize all these men at any one time; however, all were enrolled and in theory could be called upon. As might be imagined of the near-socialist régime that was Canada, the militia was to be provided with equipment, including muskets, at state expense.

Canada had good grounds for confidence, therefore. Even so, the position of the colony was precarious. The disparity in population was not to be ignored. Faced by the crushing British preponderance in numbers a Canadian invasion and conquest was out of the question. It might have been conceivable in Frontenac's day, if limited to the recently acquired and imperfectly assimilated New York; by 1750, it would have been impossible. The most Canada could hope to do was mount one of two holding operations until help could be provided by France. It could be an outright defensive posture behind the walls of Quebec and Montreal: this would be a poor choice, however, since it would mean abandoning the countryside to the enemy and the destruction of the source of food. The better way would be to mount a series of lightning raids against the British colonies, designed to keep them off balance and disinclined to risk heavier losses. This approach would not only preserve the colony from the ravages of war, but would exploit the particular genius of the Canadians for *la petite guerre*.

Nevertheless, either way could be nothing more than a holding action. The security of the colony would have to be guaranteed by France. This could be done by sending such vast quantities of men and munitions to Canada that a military solution would be possible. That a country would risk such a course of action in wartime must always be improbable and, given the nature of the Canadian defence problem, inconceivable in this case. As had been shown since the days of Champlain himself, the key to Quebec was the command of the Gulf of St. Lawrence. Any force in the citadel, no matter how strong, would have to do as Champlain did if confronted by a hostile navy cutting it off from France. In 1745 the French navy had not been able to defend Louisbourg against the British navy. What likelihood was there that the outcome on the St. Lawrence would be any different? No, the security of Canada would have to be gained elsewhere, by the use of French victories in Europe, say, that could be turned into bargaining counters: this happened in

1745-48 when Louisbourg was lost militarily but regained diplomatically.

Long-term security, then, was out of Canadian hands. All depended on the outcome of a game in which New France was merely a bit-player. What mattered was the relative standing of the two principal belligerents — and the valuation that France put on its North American colonies when it approached the bargaining table.

# — 2. Canada vs. France —

The truth was that France put very little value on Canada. Mercantilism still held sway, and a cardinal point of that doctrine was that colonies were valuable only insofar as they contributed to the well-being of the mother country. Colonial officials were reminded of this in no uncertain terms: "bear in mind that the colony of Canada is only as good as it can be useful to the kingdom"; "they must take as one of the chief objectives of colonies, that they were founded only for the benefit of the countries which formed them"; these were the sentiments that determined eighteenth-century reactions.

Canada provided goods that (apart from fur) could be produced in France itself. Accordingly the colony had little to recommend it. The West Indies, on the other hand, produced exotics that otherwise the French would have to buy from competing powers or do without. For this reason those islands were highly prized. Voltaire, the leading French writer of the day and the dominant intellectual of Europe, was all too typical in his evaluations. Canada he dismissed as "several acres of snow," and his other references were equally contemptuous: he wished "to see Canada at the bottom of the Arctic Ocean." Louisiana, however, he praised extravagantly, thinking its climate "the most beautiful . . . in the world" and capable of producing "tobacco, silk and indigo."

Such theoretical thinking was reinforced by more down-to-earth financial considerations. New France was poor. The greatest single export was fur, which as late as the 1740s amounted for 70 percent of the exports. Its yearly value was about 1.5 million livres. In contrast, the single Caribbean island of Santo Domingo produced, according to a highly placed official in the ministry of marine, "over 20 m. livres annually, an amount that can be doubled and some day may even exceed m." "Can we ever hope," he went on to ask, "that Canada will sell that much to France?" and concluded, "I even dare advance that the Island of Newfoundland and half of Santo Domingo are worth much more than all of Canada."

What was worse was that Canada was constantly running a deficit. Between 1729 and 1743 there were only three occasions when the balance of trade was in the colony's favour. Some deficits were extremely high: in 1735, it was over 600 000 livres in a year when total exports were only 1.7 million. Worse still was that Canada was so costly to operate. The money needed to administer, foster, and protect the colony was nearly always far greater than the income generated. In 1749, admittedly just after the War of Austrian Succession, it cost over two million livres to run Canada, but the yield from duties and so forth was only 233 000 livres. As time went on the situation only deteriorated. The massive graft of Bigot and his cronies, coupled with inflation and war expenditures, pushed the government's deficit to monstrous heights. The authorities warned that unless the colonial officials brought the mess under control, the king would have no option but to abandon the colony. The situation was so deplorable that even those who argued against Voltaire (and those who believed as he did) and urged the retention of Canada had to do so on military-political grounds. The Governor La Galissonière admitted that "Canada and Louisiana . . . are a burden to France" and owned that he would "not try to minimize their objection" to their retention. Nevertheless, he also stated that while

> We cannot deny that this colony has always been a burden to France and that it will probably continue to be so for a very long time to come . . . it is also the most powerful obstacle we can use to check English ambitions. . . . Since their strength grows daily, they will soon swallow up our island colonies as well as those we have on the mainland unless we find a way of limiting their progress.

Canada, thought La Galissonière, should be the perpetual thorn in Britain's side, and for this the outpouring of money was worthwhile.

The gross figures of trade and the cost of the government of Canada have long been known. So too has the correspondence of the officials. And so, in the manner sketched above, a view emerged early of a sickly economy, a parasite upon the main body politic, one lacking inherent strength and talent and so destined to remain one of hewers of wood and drawers of water. The view of Canada as a society of *habitants* ruled by the *seigneurs* and the priesthood was fully compatible with that of a backward economy. In the 1950s, however, a new interpretation of the economic viability of Canada began to be set forth. The originator of this revaluation was Maurice Séguin, and its leading scholarly proponent was Guy Frégault. Owing to their connection with the Université de Montréal the revaluation has become known as the Montreal thesis. It claims that *habitant-seigneur*-priest were but part, and not the most important part, of Canadian society, which possessed a full social development that centred upon a flourishing economy run by enterprising bourgeois.

Basic to the argument is a stress upon the indications of growth in the eighteenth century. There is no denying continuing population growth. The mere 2500 people of 1663 increased to over 55 000 by the mid-eighteenth century. The fur trade, which had languished in the last years of the seventeenth century and on into the eighteenth, had picked up and for the remainder of the French period was to enjoy success. Trade in wheat was growing, and Frégault provides the following statistics:

| Year | Cultivated land (arpents) | Wheat (minots) | Population | Wheat (minots/ capita) | Land (arpents/ capita) |
|------|---------------------------|----------------|------------|------------------------|------------------------|
| 1706 | 43 671 | 211 634 | 16 739 | 12.6 | 2.6 |
| 1712 | 54 297 | 251 453 | 18 712 | 13.4 | 2.9 |
| 1716 | 57 240 | 252 304 | 20 890 | 12.0 | 2.7 |
| 1721 | 62 145 | 282 700 | 25 576 | 11.0 | 2.4 |
| 1726 | 96 202 | 411 070 | 29 859 | 13.7 | 3.2 |
| 1732 | 133 263 | 468 219 | 35 478 | 16.9 | 4.1 |
| 1739 | 188 105 | 634 605 | 43 382 | 14.6 | 4.3 |

SOURCE: D. Miquelon (ed.), *Society and Conquest* (Copp Clark, 1977), p. 96.

He notes that "the table . . . clearly indicate[s] a turning point between 1721 and 1726." A major reason for this jump in wheat production was the requirement of Cape Breton: the new colony, particularly the workers and garrison of Louisbourg, demanded supplies that the island was not in a position to fulfill  but which Canada was. Other indicators show the same upward trend: sheep in Canada increased from 8500 to 26 000 between 1719 and 1739, pigs from 14 000 to 27 000, and cattle from 18 000 to 39 000.

Perhaps as important as these indicators is the evidence that the economy was diversifying and becoming more interrelated. The construction in the 1730s of a road between Quebec and Montreal was a sign of a new level of colonial integration. This period saw a spate of new enterprise: saw mills, tar, pitch, and resin works, were built; hemp, flax, and tobacco were cultivated; a cloth factory was begun; slate and tile businesses were founded. Pride of place, though, must go to the St. Maurice ironworks of 1733 and to the Quebec shipyards of 1739. The first produced an iron which modern analysis has shown to be comparable with that of Sweden, the leading eighteenth-century producer. The second was responsible for, among others, *Le Canada*, a 500-tonne merchantman, that was very well received in France (though it has to be admitted that *Algonquin*, a 72-gun ship for the navy, was not so highly esteemed; but then French naval yards had the highest standards in the world). At the same time trade was widening, and not only with Cape Breton. Trade with the West Indies was growing significantly, claims Frégault, and where some ten ships a year sailed from Quebec to the Caribbean by about 1740, by 1748 there were 28 such departures.

Using evidence of this kind, the Montreal school has insisted that the colony, far from being distinctive, was quite "normal." There may have been deficits, it is true, but Cameron Nish (not quite a Montrealer but very close to their position) is quick to point out that the same held true of many of the English colonies in America; it was a fact of life for certain units within a mercantilist empire. Much more striking than any overall deficit was the fact, for instance, that between 1745 and 1760 the colony counted 40 millionaires.

This was only the tip of the iceberg: a sizable sector of the population enjoyed a good income, whether from official salary, from the land, or from trade and commerce. There was money for investment, therefore, and buying and selling took on a new importance. This was signalled by the establishment in 1708 and 1717 respectively of exchanges in Quebec and Montreal, and even more by the permission granted in the latter year for both cities to have chambers of commerce with a sense of economic identity and syndics to speak on their behalf — when one remembers Colbert's dictum that "it is well that each speak for himself and none for all," the stature of the trading community is seen to be great indeed.

Like any normal colony, for instance, the British, Canada had at its head an interrelated group of families using positions of power to aid their control of the economy and access to government contracts — an establishment, in fact. Just as no one would deny the fundamental viability of the British colonial economies, so no one should seek to cast doubt on that of New France. Carl Bridenbaugh, the historian of British colonial society, chose to call his establishment an "aristocratic bourgeoisie"; Nish prefers the term "*bourgeois gentilshommes*." Both were almost contradictory phrases deliberately designed to draw attention to the interpenetration of trading and nontrading sources of power and profit.

The work of the Montreal school has been valuable, correcting as it does the earlier one-sided picture of Canadian society. However, it has to be said that as a thesis it has too many shortcomings. As may be imagined, there are a myriad points about which detailed dispute could take place. The claim by Nish, for instance, that Canadian deficits were no different from those of New England is questionable. It would seem that he has made no allowance for invisible earnings (notably freight charges); in the case of New England, which had a very well developed marine trade with the Caribbean and across the Atlantic, this would be a sizable sum; in the case of Canada it was, despite the spurt of shipbuilding, always minimal. However, it is not the technical side of the argument that is the most vulnerable: much more worrying is the fundamental criticism brought by Jean Hamelin.

This scholar, who stands at the head of the Laval school of interpretation, draws attention to the character of the wealth of Canada. He claims that much of it was spurious. Even before the boom period, as far back as 1685, the lack of coined money in the colony had been an embarrassment and a brake on economic activity. To remedy the situation the intendant, de Meulles, had issued playing-card money — cards signed by the authorities were promises to pay "real" money at a later date. There is, of course, nothing wrong with paper currency itself. Today it is used almost universally (where credit cards have not taken its place). The trouble comes if the use is not properly understood and more is issued than the state of the economy can justify. This happened to the first card money issued in Canada, and when it was finally redeemed in 1719 the king could afford to honour it at only 50 percent of its value. Stung by this fiasco, the authorities resolved never to repeat the experiment. However, the vast expansion of the economy that took place in the 1720s meant that the supply of coin was simply not sufficient, and in 1729 paper was once again permitted. As the boom continued the volume of paper became astronomical. In the end, with the loss of Canada, the Crown did not have to face the problem of redemption; but surely Hamelin is right in claiming that, had France hung on to Canada, "we are on . . . solid ground in asserting that the King would not have redeemed this paper at its face value" — for it stood at no less than 100 million livres. Moreover, these fortunes were built not only on inflation but also upon war profiteering. Hamelin uses the expression "sprouts of Mars" to describe many of the fortunes amassed in the period between 1745 and 1760 and to contrast them with more substantial profits gained through long-term, organic development.

The Laval school is equally keen to show that, while some *Canadiens* were undoubtedly among the establishment, the significant fact about this group is the dominant role occupied by those from France. A breakdown of ownership of bills of exchange in 1746 shows that 47 percent were held by French persons, with a further 14 percent held by those French who had come into the colony since 1730, leaving a mere 27 percent in the hands of *Canadiens* and long-settled French. Similarly, the import-export trade was 75 percent in the hands of non-*Canadiens*. Of the 70 merchants in Quebec in 1744 only 29 were *Canadien*, which causes Hamelin to ask, "Does this smooth French invasion of the internal market not presage the invasion of the English merchants in 1760?" Nor was there any indication that the French interlopers would eventually settle in the colony and identify with Canada. As far back as the time of Iberville the complaint that "the French . . . abandon the colonies and retire to France as soon as they have amassed a little wealth" had sounded forth. Hamelin wonders whether "the emigration of some of [the] businessmen in 1760, represented as a novel occurrence, was not in fact a repetition of a periodic phenomenon or the expression of a continuously occurring phenomenon that became more marked under the influence of exceptional circumstances in 1760?"

In view of this kind of evidence, it seems preferable to accept the testimony of Hocquart, intendant from 1731 to 1748, over the claims of the Montrealers. In 1732 Hocquart flatly stated, "it would be desirable to have rich merchants in this country, were they ever so few, for they would be in a position to trade and extend the posts, which now the modesty of their fixtures prevents their even attempting." He added despairingly, "you would find it difficult to credit . . . how small individual resources are in Canada." It has been countered that Hocquart was deliberately misrepresenting the situation. The French authorities were contemplating the imposition of a direct tax on the colony (something to cut down the deficit) and it is argued that Hocquart was "probably pressured by the economic elite" into trying any method to preserve their incomes. Nevertheless, it is hard to see why this French career bureaucrat should identify with a colonial establishment, and that so soon after coming out. The Montreal school notwithstanding, the existence of a substantial, solidly based bourgeoisie has yet to be established. Certainly the evidence collected by Intendant Raudot in 1708 on the Canadian businessmen presents them in a sorry light, for of 74 leading traders only 24 "have some possessions" and 15 "seem to have" — and as Hamelin points out a genuine bourgeois class does not spring up fully formed in a scant 40 years.

Equally disturbing to the Montreal interpretation is the fact that so much of the economic activity was initiated and fostered by the state. It had always been so. The early strides made in the 1660s had been under the intendancy of Talon, who disputes with Hocquart for the title of most effective administrator in French Canada's history. It is significant that both were ambitious traders who used every possible ounce of state backing to shape the economy. It was Talon who did so much for immigration, who established

131

tanneries and a brewery, who encouraged shipbuilding. Under Hocquart shipbuilding was once again taken up, the iron works were commenced, and so much else was done to further the economic development of Canada. Now there is nothing unusual in such a route to diversification. In most states handouts in one form or another have been at the base of private fortunes and economic investment. Frégault is to be commended for his realistic grasp of the fact that the war profiteering of the 1740s and after, and even the peculations of Bigot and his cronies, could have been ways to get resources into private hands for eventual industrial-commercial use. It is salutary to have Frégault lay to rest the Parkmanesque notion that investment has to be only private. This having been said, it still remains true that in Canada there was an unwillingness to use these handouts as a beginning; rather, they were seen merely as windfalls, sufficient in themselves.

At this point, one comes to the nub of the Montreal school's error: their failure to grasp the need of a bourgeois *mentality*, a sustained and rational approach to the mobilization of resources, for a society to transcend the traditional. Here one is driven back to the earlier point, that New France *was* a distinctive society (distinctive, that is, in comparison with the British colonies) that preferred present consumption to future growth. Money there might have been in the colony, but where was it spent? In 1754 money spent on importing liquor and wine was over 20 percent of the value of all imports. Money was spent on seigneuries, not so much for their cash value as for the tenants they supported and the status that they brought. In about 1700 the greatest trader was Aubert de la Chesnaye, but when he died he was in debt to the tune of 408 000 livres. The sum might have been unusually high, but his situation was all too typical; indeed, because of his dramatic rise and fall, one interpreter of his life has concluded that his example discouraged others from striking out on their own and that his failure was "not merely . . . that of an individual but, more basically, that of a type of entrepreneurship." As Hocquart complained, "there is no sight so common as a merchant who makes his fortune in Canada, but none so rare as one who is determined to build it up." Nish may have sought to challenge when he blended *bourgeois* with *gentilhomme*, but in fact he gave the game away. The compound is an unstable one, and in its disintegration Canadians chose the *gentilhomme* pole.

That there was no genuine bourgeois mentality in the colony is attested in many ways. The pointers range from the small and tangential to the large and structural. Revealing is the tendency of Canadians to go for the big splash, to prefer the dramatically huge to the more usefully appropriate. Thus, when they began shipbuilding they went in for monsters of a thousand tonnes rather than those of two hundred that the nascent trade needed; Hamelin does not hesitate to refer to this aspect of their dealings as "hugalomania." At the same time the lack of a bourgeois mentality both explains and is explained by the excessively military stamp that it bore. Military thinking, an aspect of the aristocratic code and profoundly antithetical to the true bourgeois outlook, permeated Canada. Commissions in the *Troupes de la Marine* drew off a disproportionate number of the elite of the colony, and meant that many fewer chose to go into trade and commerce. That commanders of the posts in the *pays d'en haut* expected to carry on fur trading and to make a tidy sum paradoxically confirms the point being made here: they were always few in number, the profit was always made on the side, and, most important, the possibility was looked upon as a lottery prize to be exploited in the short run, a stepping stone to something more worthwhile.

At the other end of the social spectrum, *habitant* life revealed how little the bourgeois transformation was at work in *Canadien* society. There was a growing demand for foodstuffs: they were needed not only for the Cape Breton trade but also for the colony itself, which required a reserve to carry it over the periods of shortage — in the last 20 years of French Canada the harvest failed eight times. Even without these spurs, it may be taken as a fact of *embourgeoisement* that attention will be given to rationalizing traditional agriculture, one of the most inefficient of all businesses and so susceptible of startling improvements. But what was the story of *Canadien* agriculture? It was and remained abysmally poor, an object of derision to American and European observers alike. Another glance at Frégault's figures will bear this out; wheat production per capita had gone up, but only because land cultivated per capita had increased even faster. It is clear that the extra yield was the dividend from fresh land just brought into cultivation, and equally clear that after a generation of overcropping that dividend would be exhausted: as far back as the 1680s there had been complaints of soil exhaustion. Nor is it possible to argue that given so much fresh land it made economic sense to cultivate extensively rather than intensively; the labour of clearing the forest was excessive, and great dividends would have followed the improvement of husbandry on the land already cleared.

Bourgeois attitudes were not filtering down in the countryside, but nor were they in the towns, by very definition the supposed home of such virtues. The *habitants* resisted any attempt to make them part of the normal work force of a society becoming bourgeois, and their mode of organization in disguised partnerships clung to older ways. It was significant that when the shipyards were started up, the labour had to be recruited overwhelmingly in

France. Those who immigrated from France in this period were little help, since they were not by and large artisanal material. Still, however few they were, and however low their standard, they were extremely welcome — only 11 percent of the artisan ranks were born in Canada. Legally and technically Quebec, Trois Rivières, and Montreal may have ranked as cities and towns, and so legally and technically some 20 percent of the population may have counted as urban, an extremely high figure for the day. Nevertheless, in no meaningful sense could their peoples be described as urbanized, as on the way to *embourgeoisement*.

At this point, a Montrealer might be heard to protest: all this takes time. The boom dated from the 1720s only. What was important was that the economy was expanding, investment was taking place, at least some *Canadiens* were taking part in the diversification and intensification and more could be expected to follow suit — in short, the process was underway and could be expected to develop *normally* unless somehow prevented. There is the key concept, as important to Séguin as to Frégault, that it is *normal* for an establishment to rationalize its pursuit of wealth, that it is *normal* for a society to develop from the traditional to the modern under the tutelage of the bourgeois. But how valid is such an assumption? That so many civilizations have come close to a bourgeois breakthrough (Hellenistic, Roman, Italian Renaissance, to mention some Western examples) only to slump back to an earlier · level would seem to indicate that the transition is not the norm. Indeed, it might argued that only one people has ever really made the transition — the Anglo-Americans. All other bourgeois societies were emulations, possible only after the pioneers had shown the way. From this perspective the development is not normal, but perverted. What has to be explained, therefore, is not why French Canada was prevented from following the same pattern as Anglo-America, but rather what impelled Anglo-America to pursue such an aberrant course.

To approach the problem in this way is to suggest that the Weber thesis still has much to offer. At the beginning of the twentieth century, the German scholar Max Weber examined the way in which Protestantism, especially in its Puritan and Methodist varieties, facilitated a shift away from group norms of present-centredness towards future-oriented individualism. The Protestant, armed with his or her own Bible, but deprived of a priestly mediator and the support of a sacramental system, was prey to psychological unease that could be assuaged through the gospel of work. The profits that accrued were not to be spent on conspicuous consumption, for that was pride, but were to be ploughed back into the rational expansion of the business. Thus emerged a gigantic cycle that revolved faster and faster at each investment, one that soon possessed a life of its own and destroyed the traditional balance between getting and spending. The Catholic scheme of things was quite otherwise. In Canada its injunctions flowed together with those of royal paternalism to produce a people secure in themselves, happy to indulge themselves when able, and permitted to drain off whatever unease might exist in vocations to priesthood, monastery, and nunnery, or else in pious offerings to the Church fabric. In Catholic New France the *bourgeois gentilhomme* was but a pseudo-bourgeois.

## Suggested Reading

Anyone interested in the American setting to the events of this chapter is directed to the relevant portion of L.H. Gipson's encyclopedic, *The British Empire Before the American Revolution* (1936-1970). The volume in the Centenary Series, G.F.G. Stanley, *New France: The Last Phase, 1744-1760* (1968) is more manageable. Other useful studies include: I.K. Steele, *Guerrillas and Grenadiers: The Struggle for Canada 1689-1760* (1969); G. Frégault, *Canada: The War of the Conquest* (1969); L. Kennett, *The French Armies in the Seven Years' War* (1967); A British equivalent is the misleadingly titled *Lord Loudon in North America* (1933), by S. Pargellis; see also P.E. Kopperman, *Braddock at the Monongahela* (1977).

The literature on the existence or otherwise of a bourgeoisie in New France is extensive. The beginner may embark on the topic through the very useful D. Miquelon (ed.), *Society and Conquest* (1977), where in addition to primary material and articles (translated where necessary into English) there is a convenient list of additional reading — altogether an excellent source.

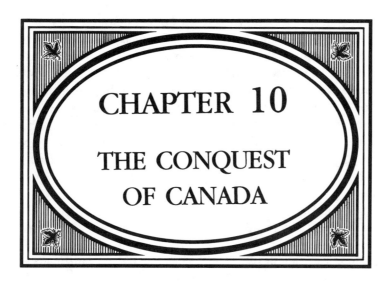

# CHAPTER 10

## THE CONQUEST OF CANADA

## — 1. Imperial Strategy —

What distinguished the Seven Years' War (which officially broke out in 1756, two years after hostilities had commenced in North America) from earlier wars between Britain and France was the determination shown by both sides to fight in North America with large bodies of metropolitan forces. The two powers had previously left the fighting there largely to colonials, perhaps helping out (as the British fleet did in 1745 at Louisbourg), but not committing large amounts of men or matériel to the struggle. Now this was to change.

In 1755 France dispatched no fewer than six regiments of regular troops to New France, four to Canada and two to Louisbourg. The following year a further two regiments were sent out, along with the leading general, Montcalm. There were plans to send even more soldiers to North America, — a corps of foreign troops in French service — but in the end these could not be spared. France was predominantly a European power with responsibilities on the Continent, and the demand for men was as pressing as it had been when it cut into Talon's plans for even greater immigration. Even so, the French managed to put no fewer than 6800 regular troops into New France, some 10 percent of the population.

Such numbers pale, however, when set against those that Britain was prepared to throw into the North American theatre. That aggressive war party alluded to earlier, which had called for a "vigorous and well managed naval war," hotly opposed to the French, was coming to power, and the hard-liners were prepared to use extreme methods to bring about the desired conclusions. Indicative of the mood of the day was an incident that originated in the very opening week of the war.

One of the prizes won by Britiain at Utrecht had been the island of Minorca in the Mediterranean. Its value was its ability to support Gibraltar, another prize of that war, and also to overawe the nearby French naval base of Toulon. With Britain's possession of Minorca, the Mediterranean was well on its way to becoming a British domain. The French were anxious to remove a presence so threatening to their security, and a fleet and landing force were sent under the command of La Galissonière (late governor of New France) to wrest the island from the British. The admiral in command of the British fleet sent to oppose this design was unable to prevent the island's loss. For this he was court-martialed, the charge being that he "did not do his utmost to take, seize and destroy the ships of the French King, which it was his duty to have engaged. . . . " Feeling ran high, and against the background of a mob-cry, "Hang Byng or look to your King," he was found guilty of misconduct and sentenced to death. As the log of HMS *Monarch* for 14 March 1757 laconically noted, "at 12 Mr. Byng was shot dead by 6 Marines and put into his coffin." The verdict of Voltaire, while formally equally laconic, was much more eloquent: "In [Britain] it is thought well to kill an admiral from time to time to encourage the others."

This harsh mood was epitomized by William Pitt the Elder, later Lord Chatham, who rose to supreme power during the war. He was a fitting representative of the new trading interest that was coming to dominate the politics of the period. The family fortune had been made by his grandfather, who had roared about India looting and exploiting. From this freebooter William Pitt had learned the importance of trade, and the need for hard-driving, perhaps unscrupulous methods. He had since developed a sense of the interrelatedness of trade, colonies, and naval power, and was particularly fascinated by the possibilities of North America. With his correspondent William Vaughan, a New Hampshire fish merchant, he had been discussing the strategic importance of Quebec since 1746. Not surprisingly, Pitt was the darling of the City interest, and in the days just before his entry into office he was the target of a "rain of golden boxes," testimonials in ceremonial caskets, as town after town vied to confer the freedom of the borough upon him. At a time when public opinion was just beginning to be a factor in politics, it was a dramatic witness to his ability to speak for the commercial class.

A leader like Pitt brought to the conduct of war a new singlemindedness. Small points serve to show how revolutionary his methods were. When it came to selecting commanders he was willing to break with the all-prevailing practice of choosing strictly on the basis of seniority. For example, James Wolfe, the commander of the attack upon Quebec, was picked over the heads of officers who would normally have received the command long before the relative junior. Similarly, the officer in charge of the invasion fleet that sailed up the St. Lawrence with Wolfe, Charles Saunders, was a junior. In the normal course of events he could not have hoped for the post. When it came to spending money and men, Pitt was prepared to be prodigal. The French recognized a novel approach, and soon it was being pointed out that "M. Vaudreuil [governor of New France] cannot have any knowledge of Mr. Pitt's project nor of the resolution to send thither such a large body of Regulars, a thing England has never done before." When the French got wind of a British proposal to send no fewer than 11 regiments to North America, in all some 10 000 men, it was observed that "Mr. Pitt has declared that if this considerable reinforcement be not sufficient, he will double and triple it." Pitt was as good as his quoted word; before the war was through, Britain had put 23 000 men into the American theatre. Then, of course, Britain was not engaged on the Continent except in a peripheral way, and so could spare such numbers.

Even more significant was the disparity in naval forces. At the opening of the war, Britain had 100 ships of the line against fewer than 70 for the French. This initial preponderance became only larger as the war progressed, for the British were able to make good their losses, and they had a superior merchant marine to draw upon as reserve personnel. In addition, Britain had over 100 frigates, fast sailers vital in mounting the blockades that bottled up the enemy fleet in port and that were such an important part of British naval strategy. Moreover, the British fleet had been taken in hand just before the outbreak of the war and licked into shape by George Anson. Everything from dockyard procedures to standardized equipment to officer promotion had been attended to, including the revision of the Articles of War that governed the fighting of battles and that made possible the execution of Byng. The

French, despite their lead in certain technical areas, did not experience such a housecleaning, and remained sunk in a defensive mentality that counted the preservation of its ships a victory. Against the all-or-nothing thrusts of Pitt it was a forlorn strategy.

# — 2. The Course of Conquest —

There was nothing original about Pitt's plan of attack — unless the weight of it be considered so. It was to follow the three traditional invasion routes, used so often in the past and to be used many times in the years to come, of the St. Lawrence, the Hudson River-Lake Champlain, and the Great Lakes. Since a ponderous advance that left little to chance was contemplated — memories of Braddock's defeat were all too fresh — 1757 passed with little accomplished. But in 1758 the triple assault was mounted.

It went ahead slowly. Pitt insisted that Louisbourg be taken before he would permit any force to ascend the St. Lawrence. Although the French had spent time, money, and effort on rebuilding the fortress after their return in 1748, there were still many flaws: the masonry was not of the best quality, food was in short supply, the troops were disaffected and close to mutiny, and morale was inevitably low. However, the presence of some naval forces strengthened the defence, and although Louisbourg eventually fell to the British, it withstood the siege long enough to prevent any attack on Quebec in that year. The story was similar in the far west, where a belated victory was finally won late in the campaigning season when the key to the French position, Fort Duquesne, was taken; it was suitably renamed Pittsburg. In the centre, however, the advance failed. The French under Montcalm defended Fort Carillon on Lake Champlain and the British commander attempted a frontal assault without the benefit of cannonade. He lost heavily and fell back in a near rout. Later he was replaced by Amherst, so opening the way for Wolfe, a subordinate at Louisbourg, to be given the St. Lawrence command. Thus the fighting broke off, to await the new campaigning season in the following year.

Time had been won by the French, but it could only work against them and for the British. In truth, the Canadian situation was a wretched one. Within the colony problem was piled upon problem. To begin with, there was a terrible shortage of food, the bad harvests being exacerbated by the need to mobilize so many of the militia. Food riots were close to occurring, especially when horsemeat became a staple of the diet. Montcalm tried to set a good example: "Horse meat is eaten at my home in every way, except soup. Small horse meat patties, Spanish style; horse meat stew; scalloped horse meat; horse meat steak on the spit with a good pepper and vinegar sauce; horses' feet baked in bread crumbs; hashed horse tongue with onions; horse meat ragout; smoked horse tongue, better than that of moose; horse meat pie, like hare pie. This animal," he concluded thankfully, "is much better than moose, caribou, and beaver." To make matters worse, the elite of the colony, the military officers and the Bigot circle in particular, were living an ostentatious life, consuming vast quantities of expensive food and liquor (in 1759 Abraham Gradis, a business associate of Bigot, chartered a ship, which he slipped through the British blockade; however, in place of desperately needed bread he filled it with wines and spirits, and for an outlay of 95 000 livres sold the cargo for 525 000 livres), gambling for huge sums, engaging in expensive and immoral entertainment, and generally flaunting their wealth. The mood was that of *après nous le déluge*.

Finally, it was clear that the sending of regular troops was not entirely advantageous. They were an added burden on the colony's resources. They contributed markedly to the disorganization of the colony, offending the underlying puritanism of the society with their dissolute ways. Above all, they sparked a quarrel between the *Canadiens* and the French, epitomized by the antagonism between Governor Vaudreuil and the commander-in-chief, Montcalm. Vaudreuil, the first *Canadien* ever to be appointed governor, was on very bad terms with Montcalm, a professional soldier used to European methods and style and openly contemptuous of things *Canadien*. Vaudreuil believed in a *Canadien* future; Montcalm was a convinced defeatist who felt that the most to be hoped for was to fight a rearguard action while a remnant got away to Louisiana. In February 1759, when Montcalm was placed in supreme military command, superseding Vaudreuil and even taking away his militia, relations between the *Canadiens* and the French, like those between the two individuals, reached their low point. Their enmity coloured everything; it pitted Vaudreuil and *petite guerre canadienne* against Montcalm and the regulars' defensive formalism; it set officer against officer, soldier against soldier; it poisoned the last days of the colony.

Externally the situation was equally bad. Time might have been of use to Canada had there been any possibility of reinforcements, but the authorities made it quite clear in 1759 that they were out of the question. It was due

# Map 10.1:   Showdown in North America

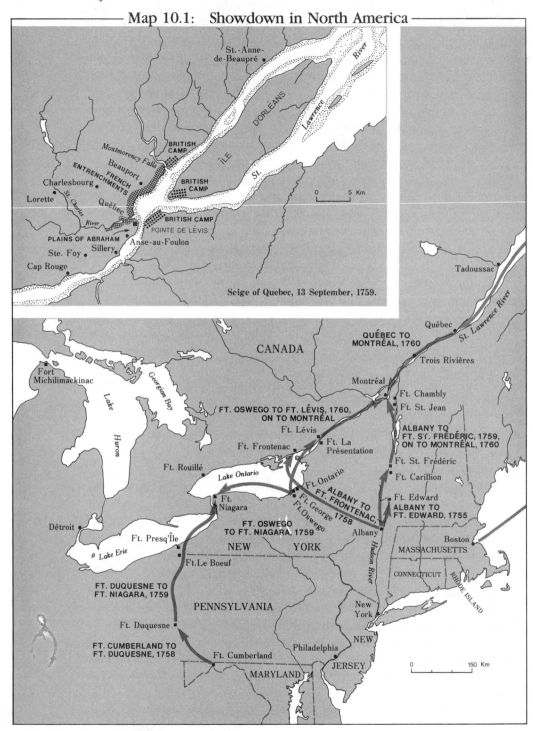

Seige of Quebec, 13 September, 1759.

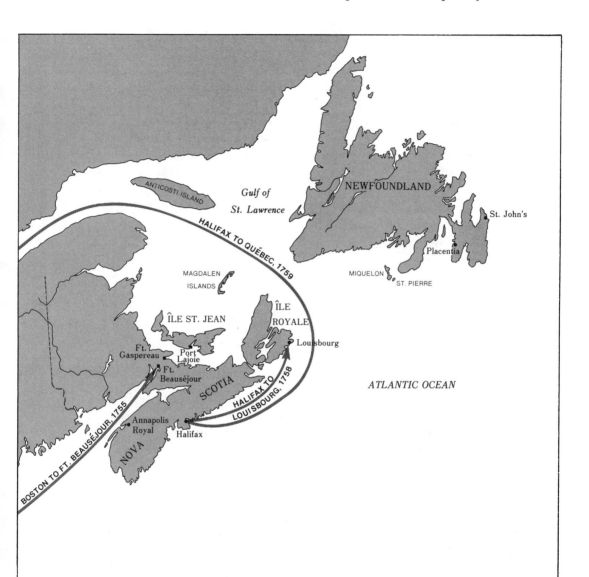

During the Seven Years' War, Britain either seized or forced the French to abandon their outposts of empire, and in a series of spectacular sieges, took Louisbourg, Quebec, and finally Montreal. By the Treaty of Paris of 1763 the French Empire in North America had been reduced to Saint-Pierre and Miquelon, two islands off the south cost of Newfoundland.

SOURCES: M. Trudel, *Introduction to New France* (Toronto: Holt, Rinehart and Winston, 1968), p. 88; Kerr, *Historical Atlas of Canada* (1975), pp. 26–8; Harris, *Historical Atlas of Canada*, Vol. I, *From the Beginning to 1800* (1987), plates 42–3.

partly to France's full commitment in Europe, partly to the anti-colonial mood (which has been touched on already) that could see no purpose in pouring resources into "a few acres of snow." Mainly, however, the British naval blockade was working so well that the very idea of risking men and supplies was unthinkable. It was frankly stated that nothing would be sent since "it would be much to be feared that they would be intercepted by the English on the passage." It was confessed further that against the Pitt machine nothing would be of use, for "as the King could never send you assistance proportionate to the forces the English are able to oppose against you, the efforts which would be made here would have no other effect than to excite the Ministry of London to much greater efforts to preserve the superiority it has acquired in [North America]."

This confession of naval inferiority is the key point. It accounts for the outcome of the war for Canada. In British history, 1759 is known as the *annus mirabilis*, the miracle year. In that single year victories were won around the world, from the Caribbean, where the sugar island of Guadeloupe was taken, to the European continent, where British troops were responsible for the victory at Minden, to India, where the French were ultimately defeated; the mob bawled out for the first time *Hearts of Oak*: "Come cheer up, my lads! 'tis to glory we steer/ To add something more to this wonderful year."

Prominent among the British victories listed for 1759 is the taking of Quebec. That it was a dramatic incident cannot be denied. Wolfe's decision to make the perilous ascent from L'Anse au Foulon to the Plains of Abraham, Montcalm's decision to sally forth and give battle, the manoeuvring for position, the volleys delivered from 40 metres that in less than three minutes shattered the French army and sent it running from the shelter of Quebec's walls, the added poignancy of the twin deaths of the commanders, the subsequent surrender of the city — all this has made the battle live in popular memory. How significant it all was, however, is open to doubt. Everyone remembers the battle on the Plains. How many know that the last battle between Britain and France in America was a year later at Ste. Foy, and that the French defeated the British and forced them in their turn to flee for the safety of Quebec's ramparts? In 1760 the French still controlled Canada, besieging Quebec. What defeated them was not the British army, but the British navy, for when in 1760 the first ship to sail up the St. Lawrence was seen to be HMS *Lowestoft* it was as clear as it had been in 1629 that capitulation was inevitable. The real peak of Britain's *annus mirabilis* was not the taking of Quebec, but the naval battles off Lagos in Portugal and in Quiberon Bay in Brittany, in both of which the French fleets were defeated decisively.

# — 3. Consequences for Canadian Society —

Quebec capitulated on 18 September 1759; Montreal was surrendered a year later on 8 September 1760, and with it Canada. Nevertheless, the war itself was not over, and even when the fighting was at an end there was the problem of peace. How much should be retained by the victors, and perhaps be the occasion for a war of revenge by the vanquished? How much should be handed back, and perhaps be the ground for a resurgent France? Although Pitt, by now out of office, wished to keep more rather than less, Britain eventually decided to retain Canada and hand back Guadeloupe. In North America France retained the fisheries only, being allowed to keep the tiny islands of St. Pierre and Miquelon off Newfoundland and having their right confirmed, included in the Treaty of Utrecht, of landing and drying fish on the Newfoundland shore between Bonavista and Point Riche. Many in Britain considered giving up a rich sugar island a poor bargain, for Voltaire had his supporters there too, and Pitt was not alone when he observed that "France is chiefly, if not solely, to be dreaded by us in the light of a maritime and commercial power — and therefore by restoring to her all the valuable West Indian Islands, and by our concessions in the Newfoundland fishery, we have given her the means of recovering her prodigious losses and becoming once more formidable to us at sea." The debates and peacemaking took time, and it was not until 1763 that the Treaty of Paris, that brought an end to the Seven Years' War, was signed.

To settle the form of the newly acquired colony took Britain even longer. In 1760 George II had died and been succeeded by his young grandson, George III. He was eager to reform the state of the nation, in particular its political life; to this end he pursued a more active role in forming and guiding ministries than his predecessor had done. This reassertion of the royal prerogative deeply disturbed the pattern that had grown up over the previous two generations, and a period of political instability ensued. Not until 1774, 15 years after the fall of Quebec, did the imperial parliament finally get around to legislating for the colony.

This act, the Quebec Act, was the culmination of a series of *ad hoc* initiatives, a drawn-out evolution. As such, it demands a separate chapter to itself (Chapter 11). However, one development that took place in the period 1759-63 was, in essence, a once-and-for-all decision: the response of the *Canadiens* to the question of whether to remain in Canada or to remove to France. It is true that exiles continued to arrive in France long after 1763, and indeed that there was also a reverse current of disappointed *émigrés* returning to Canada, the land of their birth. Nevertheless, the vast bulk of the outward migration took place immediately in the wake of the capitulations; it was a function of the shock of defeat.

The following questions are vital, for they have lain at the root of a controversy that has continued since the mid-nineteenth century. Did the exodus of *Canadiens*, in particular of the elite of the colony, take place on such a scale that it amounted to the "decapitation" of a society? Was the Conquest the reason why the *Canadiens* had been reduced to a proletarian status? The decapitation thesis, which sets out to prove these suggestions, has enjoyed a recent revival, and it needs to be examined.

The earliest advocates of the thesis stressed that many of the elite chose to leave for France, although they never spelled out just how many was "many," taking for granted that the exodus had been a large one. Only much later, towards the end of the nineteenth century, was an attempt to quantify the out-migration made. L.F.G. Baby traced the situation through the well documented family histories and extensive official papers of the period. After going through the various social categories, he concluded that there were remaining in the colony "a hundred and thirty seigneurs, 100 gentlemen and bourgeois, 125 prominent merchants, 25 jurists and men of the law of whom . . . several had even been in the Superior Council, 25 to 30 physicians and surgeons and an almost equal number of notaries." It was enough, he claimed, to "satisfy the political, intellectual, and other requirements of the population then living in the three towns of Quebec, Montreal and Trois Rivières." They made up "an adequate body of highly placed, enlightened, educated, and above all devoted men to counsel and guide their fellow countrymen in the wake of our catastrophe." This was not quantification that would satisfy modern standards — the percentage that 130 seigneurs constituted of the total pre-Conquest seigneurial class is not stated; "prominent merchants" is not defined; the inclusion of eighteenth-century physicians and surgeons among the elite is questionable since that age saw them more as barbers or artisans. Nevertheless, whatever the deficiencies of Baby's study, its main conclusions have been widely accepted. Something of the older view in muted form reappeared in the work of Robert de Roquebrune, where the total of *émigrés* was raised to 2000 (without any adequate explanation or documentation), but by and large Baby is taken to have painted an accurate picture.

When the decapitation thesis was taken up in the twentieth century, it was on a rather different basis. The roots of the reinterpretation lay in the University of Montreal, once again in the work of Séguin. There will clearly be a carry-over between those who believe that a *canadien* bourgeoisie had developed under the French régime and those who argue that only a social beheading prevented the flowering of that bourgeoisie and, under its tutelage, *canadien* society. Here again is the key to the Montreal approach: the interruption of a *normal* development is insisted upon. A clear statement of this line comes from Michel Brunet, the leading exponent of the decapitation thesis:

In 1760 . . . Canada included, as did all Western societies that evolved *under normal conditions*, a secular leading class comprised of administrators, soldiers, and businessmen. This elite . . . met the requirements of a modest colonial society of some 60 000 inhabitants. With the passing years, this naturally ambitious elite would have grown and would have played a more and more important role in the development of the country. The Conquest determined otherwise. [My italics.]

Despite a hankering after Roquebrune, Brunet accepts Baby's findings, and goes on to argue his case on other grounds. The picture he draws of the *Canadien* elite shows how they were reduced to a minority in the administration of the colony:

In 1779, the customs and postal service had 13 civil servants of whom one was *Canadien*. In 1781, a list of 22 senior government employees includes only one *Canadien* name . . . of a total of 38 justices of the peace, we find only 16 *Canadiens*. In the Council there were but six *Canadiens* in a membership of 22. From 1764 to 1791, 48 individuals served as councillors, 33 English-speaking and 15 French-speaking . . . the list of civil officers in the province for the year 1784 runs to some 136 names. *Canadiens* occupy 36 posts . . .

It is important to note that in making these points Brunet is not interested in the rightness or wrongness of these developments. Rather, he is emphasizing that a people who see their leaders discarded lose their pride, their belief in their own worth, and relapse into something of a childlike state of dependence. At the same time, one may ask just how many participants in administration is enough to convince a defeated people that they are being taken seriously and that it is worthwhile to work for further recognition.

As it was with administration, so too was it with the military. The seigneurs who were officers of the *Troupes de la Marine* were not used as the natural soldier-leaders that they were, and attempts to raise regiments that would take advantage of their services were stillborn. Only in 1796 was the Royal Canadian Regiment created for them, and by then an entire generation had gone by and the tradition had been broken.

Despite these other issues, Brunet concentrates on the question of the trading class. After recounting the problems facing the *Canadien* bourgeoisie he concludes "the *Canadien* businessmen had shown themselves incapable of holding their own against their English competitors. The Conquest had forced them to compete with unequal weapons." The difficulties were indeed daunting; the French Crown had repudiated most of the paper money, so many found themselves with their credit destroyed; the British government refused to allow delivery of goods from France already ordered and paid for; the need to transfer their European base from Paris to London put the *Canadiens* at a sudden disadvantage. It was inevitable, claims Brunet, that they should be squeezed out, and not only from overseas trade; soon the same was happening in other areas, such as the fur trade, where by 1767 the following pattern had developed: "Of 80 traders, 70 were *Canadien*; yet the list of businessmen who gave their guarantees of the good conduct of traders and hired men contained only 23 French names in a total of 40. . . ." (It should be noted that Neatby gives the figures as 29 out of 39. She challenges Brunet's picture of *Canadiens* without means, citing the example of the prosperous fur-trading family of Baby.)

Given that defeat can be traumatic, that *Canadiens* were pushed aside and faced tremendous difficulties, we must remember that other societies have gone through similar and even worse experiences. There is general agreement that British rule was humane; Brunet acknowledges that "the generosity of the conqueror, his benevolence, his solicitude for the general interest, and his spirit of justice gained him the hearts of the conquered." Other societies have used defeat, and even the feeling of being viewed with contempt, as a spur to their determination to rebuild what had been destroyed. Very much to the point in 1760 was the example of the Scots. The parallel is not complete, but instructive nonetheless. In 1707 the Act of Union swept an unwilling people into the United Kingdom, as very junior partner of England. Although Scots law was allowed to continue, the Scottish Parliament was abolished and token representation at Westminster took its place. Scots were despised in England as uncouth barbarians, and their way of life ridiculed unmercifully, and that in 1715 and 1745 parts of Scotland rose for the Stuarts against the Hanoverians did not help at all. Nevertheless, undaunted Scots very persistently struggled against the tide, thrusting themselves forward into prominent positions in politics, the civil service, the armed forces, and above all in the business world. It was not easy, but it showed what could be done. In contrast, Brunet conveys the impression that there was nothing that could be done by the *Canadiens*, that the odds against them were overwhelming.

One may find alternatives to Brunet's interpretations of the evidence. For instance, he notes the extensive fraternization from 1759 to 1763, which included instances of Canadian women marrying British soldiers. However, while he insists that it shows a people in disintegration, others might see evidence that there were good relations between two sophisticated peoples. Similarly, Brunet draws attention to the difficulty in finding *habitants* to volunteer for the paid militia recruited to deal with Pontiac's Indian rising of 1763, and interprets this as *habitant* antagonism to the British. One may consider, on the other hand, that the *habitants* were simply war-weary and more interested in putting their neglected farms back into commission than in campaigning in the wilds.

Brunet also notes that after the Conquest the Church became an extremely powerful leader in society. This had not been true of pre-Conquest Canada, where the secular authorities had been in control. The transition from religious to secular has been the norm in developing societies. To find the reverse taking place in Canada, a retrogression to a more primitive stage, Brunet argues, points to the catastrophic impact of the Conquest. Alternatively, however, it must be remembered that the Church had not been displaced by society so much as by the state, and there is a world of difference between them. The implicit argument here is that the forces of a secular bourgeois society are not free to develop unless the restrictions of organized religion are removed. However, in New France, the absolutist state itself had taken the restrictive place of the Church. After the Conquest, with the removal of that absolutist state, the church had come to fill the vacuum. Here was neither progression nor retrogression, but merely a substitution of one pre-modern mode for another.

Brunet seems to allow present-day outlooks to guide him, the perennial danger that the historian faces. He writes, for instance, that

> The haste of the conquered to submit to the authority of a century-old enemy, their docility, the servility of their ruling classes surprises a twentieth-century observer a little. The latter has been the witness of the courageous resistance of the countries occupied by the Germans during the course of the last war. The words 'collaboration' and 'collaborators' have a very bad press in our day.

Brunet does not account for the meaning and limits of nationality as understood in the mid-eighteenth century.

It can also be objected that there were more deep-seated reasons for *canadien* society's inability to overcome the obstacles. One is driven back to the fact that *Canadiens* gave up so quickly and so completely. It is well to remember that the bulk of the out-migration took place before it was known for sure that France would abandon Canada, a further reminder of Hamelin's contention that the colonial elite never particularly identified with Canada but with France, and that what happened in 1759 and 1763 was merely an intensification of long-standing tendencies. There did not arise from the ranks of the *habitants* replacements for those businessmen destroyed "in a competition with unequal weapons." Brunet actually destroys his case when he admits that "the financial losses [the *canadien* bourgeoisie] had suffered had . . . made them extremely timid. . . . The traders decided that it was wiser to sell their furs on the local market. The profits might have been more modest, but they seemed less risky."

Just as Frégault is replaced by Brunet in the Montreal school when it comes to the post-Conquest period, so too is Hamelin replaced by Fernand Ouellet in the Laval school. Central to Ouellet's criticism is that the *Canadiens* had not created a genuine bourgeois mentality, one that was on its way to pervading the entire society. Lacking such a mentality the *Canadiens* were in no position to adapt to the new challenges and new conditions operating after 1760. Especially since the beginning of the American Revolution, writes Ouellet, developments had been

> particularly disastrous for the French Canadian merchants . . . . Their weakness in the import sector, their exclusive liking for a world dominated by personal relations, their individualism, the attraction of the "noble" lifestyle, and the hold of family and religious values, explain . . . why they remained relatively stationary at a time when commercial capitalism was progressing. (*Economic and Social History of Quebec, 1760-1850*, 1980, p. 577).

Brunet refers to "timidity," Ouellet stresses traditional values. The two protagonists are here in agreement. French Canada from the first had been consumption oriented, it remained so during the critical years of the Conquest, on through the nineteenth century, and that outlook was still alive in the twentieth century. In the late 1950s the following attitudes, (to be found in M. Rioux and Y. Martin (ed.), *French Canadian Society*, pp. 271–95) were still being heard among French-Canadian entrepreneurs:

> I don't want to get too big. I'm happy so long as I get a comfortable living for myself and my family. . . . If I were rich I'd have more work and worry. It's no

use being a millionaire in the cemetery; I don't want to get too much bigger. What for? . . . You can't ask for more than three meals a day and a good bed; The money in this business came from my father, and my children and grandchildren have a right to it, too. So it would be wrong to risk it. Anyway, what's the use? Life is too short. Over the past ten years we could have expanded our business tremendously, but we haven't cared to do so. . . . Any surplus funds from the business go into real estate.

Frégault and Brunet would say that it was a mentality forced on the *Canadiens* by the Conquest; Hamelin and Ouellet would say that it was there from the beginning.

## Suggested Reading

In addition to the military studies listed in Chapter 9, the following are recommended: C.P. Stacey, *Quebec 1759: The Siege and the Battle* (1973); Y. Landry, "La Population militaire au Canada pendant la Guerre de Sept Ans," *Annales de démographie historique* (1978). Naval operations may be studied via J.S. Corbett, *England in the Seven Years War* (1918). Volume II of O.A. Sherrard's *Lord Chatham* (1952-58) deals with the war years.

Once again the reader is referred to Miquelon (see Chapter 9) for material on the decapitation thesis.

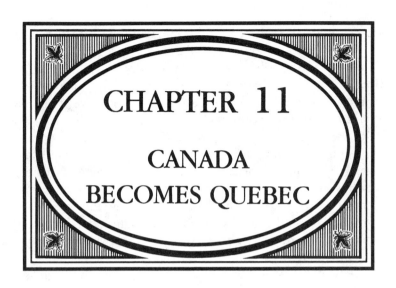

# CHAPTER 11

## CANADA BECOMES QUEBEC

## — 1. Imperial Aims —

The spoils of war were vast, and Canada was only one prize among many. Huge portions of the Indian subcontinent, counting inhabitants by the scores of millions, suddenly fell to British trading companies and gave rise to problems on such a scale that the British government was obliged to step in and regulate these possessions. In North America there was also a host of difficulties. Nova Scotia, which had barely been organized by the eve of the war, now had to manage the other portions of Acadia, the future New Brunswick, that had been ambiguously ceded in the Treaty of Utrecht and that now passed unambiguously to the British; at the same time the islands of St. John (later Prince Edward Island) and Cape Breton also became parts of Nova Scotia. To the south, both East and West Florida had been won from the Spanish. There were Caribbean acquisitions, too, notably, Grenada. It was not the sheer size of these new possessions that caused the difficulties so much as that for the first time Britain had to grapple with the problem of assimilating diverse cultures within the empire, something for which it had few precedents. For this reason, and because of the confused state of imperial politics at this period, the handling of Canada (renamed Quebec from the fall of 1763) was a mess. To understand what was intended, behind the welter of conflicting initiatives, it will be well to keep in mind the nature of the conquerors.

Britain had emerged over the past century as a first-class power, had made its claim, as a result of the Seven Years' War, to European if not to world preeminence, and was launched on a far-reaching transformation that would make it the first modern nation. The British elite had an arrogant confidence in their way of life, instinctively convinced of its superiority. At the same time, they were sure enough of themselves and their mission to be generous towards those they had conquered, and their conduct was generally humane. This attitude gave coherence to what otherwise was a very uncertain handling of Quebec.

The early moves to deal with Quebec were bound to be tentative. At the time of the capitulations it was not clear that the colony would remain British; moreover, a state of war still persisted. A military, *ad hoc* régime was inaugurated. This lasted, in fact, beyond the peace, and civil government did not return until late in 1764, at the end of the eighteen-month period granted to the defeated to wind up their affairs and leave if they so wished. Thus, for some five years in the case of Quebec and its surrounding region, four in the remainder of the colony, the conquered people experienced a rule that was not so much thought-out as instinctive. However, if that rule was instinctive and *ad hoc*, it was neither arbitrary nor without subsequent influence. Although the fact that the terms of capitulation were binding on a conqueror was not spelled out formally until 1774 when Lord Chief-Justice Mansfield declared that "articles of capitulation upon which the country is surrendered, and treaties of peace by which it is ceded, are sacred and inviolate, according to their true intent and meaning" (*Campbell v. Hall*, a case arising in Grenada but applicable to Canada), the British government had long acted on this assumption informally. When a study of Quebec was undertaken by the Board of Trade immediately after the signing of the Treaty of Paris, care was taken to circulate the capitulations of Quebec and Montreal, since it was "proper to examine, what Priviledges are reserved to His Majesty's New Subjects by the Terms of their Capitulations." The nature of the earliest British régime in Quebec requires, then, some examination.

The capitulation that mattered was that of 1760. Quebec City had been only one fortress, whereas Montreal was in effect the colony. In that surrender, the greatest number of articles dealt with the question of repatriation, whether of troops, civilians, goods or papers, and those that dealt with the society of Quebec were limited. In fact, only two social items appeared. One group of articles concerned the religion of the people. In Article XXVII Vaudreuil had asked that

> The free exercise of the Catholic, Apostolic, and Roman Religion, shall subsist, in such manner that all the states and the people of the Towns and countries, places and distant posts, shall continue to assemble in their churches, and to frequent the sacraments as heretofore, without being molested in any manner, directly or indirectly. These people shall be obliged, by the English government, to pay their Priests the tithes, and all the taxes they were used to pay under the Government of his most Christian Majesty [the French King].

To this Amherst replied, "Granted, as to the free exercise of their religion; the obligations of paying the tithes to the Priests will depend on the King's pleasure." Bishop Pontbriand having died just a short time before, Vaudreuil asked in Article XXX that

> If by the treaty of peace, Canada should remain in the power of his Britannic Majesty, his most Christian Majesty shall continue to name the Bishop of the colony, who shall always be of the Roman communion, and under whose authority the people shall exercise the Roman Religion.

Such interference by a foreign power was not acceptable and brought the curt response, "Refused." The other group had to do with the legal system. Article XXXVII granted that

> The Lords of the Manor, the Military and Civil officers, the Canadians as well in the Towns as in the country, the French settled, or trading, in the whole extent of the colony of Canada, and all other persons whatsoever, shall preserve the entire peaceable property and possession of the goods, noble and ignoble, moveable and immovable . . . .

It might be maintained that peaceable possession implied the continuance of the legal code that gave it meaning. However, the later attempt to spell this out in Article XLII, "The French and Canadians shall continue to be governed according to the custom of Paris, and the Laws and usages established for this country . . .," drew the riposte, "They become Subjects of the King." It can be seen from this that the British were prepared to be magnanimous up to a point (though they refused the French army the honours of war and insisted on the troops' laying down their arms) but were not prepared to make any significant concessions.

However, when James Murray took over from Amherst a rather more accommodating attitude became apparent. In 1762 Murray was required to make a report on the colony. His first observation was that "the Canadians are very ignorant and extremely tenacious of their Religion, nothing can contribute so much to make them staunch subjects of His Majesty as the new Government giving them every reason to imagine no alteration is to be attempted in that point." He appreciated the difficulty caused by Pontbriand's death, and went on:

> Care was taken under the former Government to keep up a great part of the Clergy French, especially the dignified part: To prevent the further importation of these, it would be necessary to encourage the natives to engage in the profession, which cannot be so well done, except the See is filled up, as without a Bishop there can be no ordination: some difficulty will attend this.

That Murray esteemed Catholicism for its social benefits rather than for its truths was further indicated by his comment that

> There are some few French Protestants in this Country who no doubt will be willing to remain, it would be a great comfort to these, if a Church was granted for their use, and some French Clergyman of sound sense and good Character, with a tolerable salary, was invited to settle among them, such an establishment may be attended with the further good consequences of enticing many of their Brethren in France, to come and enjoy that religious liberty after which they so ardently sigh, amidst a people sprung from the same origin, speaking the same language, and following the same Customs. It may likewise be conducive towards bringing about a Reformation, by slow degrees and must at least prove to the Canadians there is nothing in our Holy Religion repugnant to virtue or Morality.

If this was more accommodating than Amherst had been, it was only marginally so, and the same minimal concession to Catholicism was incorporated in the peace treaty. There it was agreed that

> His Britannick Majesty . . . agrees to grant the liberty of the Catholick religion to the inhabitants of Canada: he will, in consequence, give the most precise and effectual orders, that his new Roman Catholic subjects may profess the worship of their religion according to the rites of the Romish church, as far as the laws of Great Britain permit.

The sting was in the tail, for in Britain Roman Catholics had very little liberty and fewer rights — for instance they could not vote or sit in Parliament, hold commissions in the armed forces, be civil servants, take degrees at the universities, and so on. Nothing was said in the treaty about the legal system of the colony, or indeed about any other aspect of Quebec society, so the legal recognition of Canadian distinctiveness was minimal indeed. That this was intended was made very plain by the secretary of state in a dispatch to Murray in August 1763. The governor was to keep a close eye on the Catholic Church

> For tho' The King has . . . agreed to grant the liberty of the Catholick Religion to the Inhabitants of Canada . . . Yet the condition . . . must always be remembered, viz: As far as the Laws of Great Britain permit, which Laws prohibit absolutely all Popish Hierarchy in any of the Dominions belonging to the Crown of Great Britain, and can only admit of a Toleration of the Exercise of that Religion; This matter was clearly understood in the Negotiation of the Definitive Treaty; the French Ministers proposed to insert the Words, *comme ci-devant*, in order that the Romish Religion should continue to be exercised as in the same manner as under their Government; and they did not give up the Point, 'till they were plainly told that it would be deceiving them to admit those Words, for the King had not the Power to tolerate that Religion in any other Manner . . . .

With the realization that Quebec was to be kept came the realization that more formal arrangements would be necessary. A flurry of activity ensued. The Board of Trade was to examine "what New Governments should be established and what Form should be adopted for such new Governments?" In that examination they were to have as "a proper Object of Consideration, how far it is expedient to retain, or depart from the Forms of Government which His Most Christian Majesty had established in those colonies." When the response was forthcoming, certainly the Anglicizing and protestantizing assumptions were there, but there was also a realization that the making over of a colony in a new image was not something to be done overnight. The lords of trade observed

> It is obvious that the new Government of Canada . . . will . . . contain within it a very great number of French Inhabitants and Settlements, and that the Number of such Inhabitants must greatly exceed, for a very long period of time, that of Your Majesty's British and other Subjects who may attempt settlements. . . . From which Circumstances, it appears to Us that the Chief Objects of any new Form of Government . . . ought to be to secure the ancient In-

habitants in all the Titles, Rights and Privileges granted to them by Treaty, and to increase as much as possible the Number of British and other new Protestant Settlers . . . .

Between these last two imperatives was a tension only time would solve, and to handle it the lords of trade believed that the two "objects . . . will be best obtain'd by the Appointment of a Governor and Council under Your Majesty's immediate Commission and Instructions." In this way, they looked to an eventual British and Protestant colony, but recognized that until then Quebec would be distinctive and should lack that normal British element, an assembly.

The ministerial instability that was rife at this time was exacerbated by the shock, in the summer of 1763, of Pontiac's rising. The Indians of the Mississippi Valley, angered by the Anglo-American exploitation of Indian lands, formed an extensive confederacy and launched wide-ranging attacks against armed posts and settlers. Large stretches of the frontier were in chaos and casualties were high. The imperial government was advised by the lords of trade "that a Proclamation be immediately issued by Your Majesty . . . on account of the late Complaints of the Indians, and the actual Disturbances in Consequence." This advice was accepted, but if this was to be done "His Majesty is of opinion, that several other objects . . . might . . . be provided for at the same time: [including] To declare the Constitution of the New Governments, as established for the present, and intended in the future. . . ." The result was a hurried proclamation, drafted, revised, and concluded all in one week, that besides closing Indian land to settlement, so maintaining it as a fur preserve, sought to fill up the Floridas and Quebec and Nova Scotia — the two peripheries of British North America — with British settlers as soon as possible. The earlier recognition of local difficulties and of the necessity of time with which to overcome those difficulties was quite overlooked. Instead there was the blanket statement that "so soon as the state and circumstances of the said Colonies will admit . . . they shall . . . summon and call General Assemblies." For good measure, it was also stipulated that "We have given Power . . . to erect . . . Courts of Judicature . . . for hearing and determining all Causes, as well Criminal as Civil, according to Law and Equity, and as near as may be agreeable to the Laws of England. . . ."

In a sense, the royal proclamation was not so much a repudiation of the earlier approach as a speeding-up of the timetable; the instinctive preferences were now coming out rather more starkly than the ministers would on reflection perhaps have liked. Nevertheless, since the royal proclamation was in its very nature a public declaration, whereas the qualifications were restricted to a few politicians and civil servants, it was the former that attracted attention. Much the same point could be made about the instructions issued to Murray. There it was ordered that

> To the end that the Church of England may be established both in Principle and Practice, and that the said Inhabitants may by Degrees be induced to embrace the Protestant Religion . . . we . . . declare it to be Our Intention [that] . . . all possible Encouragement shall be given to erecting Protestant Schools . . .; and you are to consider and report to Us . . . by what other means the Protestant Religion may be promoted, established, and encouraged in Our Province . . . .

Once again it has to be recognized that such qualifications lacked the publicity the proclamation itself possessed, and the implication in the instructions of gradual transition was overlooked. The proclamation had said nothing of religion, but since it spoke of assimilating the constitutional arrangements of the new colonies to such "Manner and form as is used and directed in those Colonies and Provinces in America," which colonies and provinces were Protestant, it was pardonable to think Protestantism was imminent for Quebec.

Between the capitulations, the Treaty of Paris, the Board of Trade, and the proclamation, the situation was becoming more contradictory by the hour. Murray's actions did not help clarify matters. In 1764 he set up civil courts. An inferior court of common pleas was established in which French law was permitted where the facts seemed to warrant it (usually when both parties were *Canadien*). In addition, Roman Catholics were permitted to sit on juries, Murray justifying this breach of British law by pointing out that "as there are but two Hundred Protestant Subjects in the Province . . . it is thought unjust to exclude the new Roman Catholic Subjects. . . ." Similarly, Roman Catholic (that is, *Canadien*) advocates were permitted to appear in the courts, again a breach of British law. Murray's system was humane and meant well, but its *ad hoc* way was awkward and unclear and flew in the face of good legal principles.

The legal confusion was further evidence that the imperial government would have to come to grips with the question of Quebec. Nor did the evidence stop there. A ruling of the British attorney general and solicitor general baldly stated that "We . . . are humbly of Opinion, that His Majesty's Roman Catholick Subjects [in Quebec] are not subject, in these colonies, to the Incapacities, disabilities, and Penalties, to which Roman Catholicks in His

Kingdom are subject. . . ." In the same year, 1765, an awkward question was raised about the very basis of legality in the colony; since the proclamation had promised an assembly, could the legislation of a governor and council alone be valid? That it could not was the substance of Mansfield's judgment nine years later in *Campbell v. Hall.*

To overcome this confusion the North ministry brought in the Quebec Act in 1774. Since 1770 Lord North, with George III's backing, had been establishing himself, and the instability of the 1760s was over. It was possible to turn to colonial matters, and the Act of 1774 was the result. In examining this legislation it is essential to keep in mind that the solicitor general of the day called it "a bill of experiment," meaning that it was couched in general terms. As Guy Carleton, Murray's successor as governor and present in London during the preparatory drafting stages, put it, "the Act is no more than the Foundation of future Establishments." During debate, Lord North claimed "in a general plan of government, it is not possible to enter into detail what is proper or what is improper in Canada; it must be left to the legislature on the spot to consider all their wants and difficulties." This being so, in an age of mercantilist imperial centralization, a great deal would depend on the governor and the authorities at Westminster; thus, the instructions that accompanied the Act have to be read along with the more formal legislation in order to discover the intention of the Quebec Act.

The Act itself was solicitous of the welfare of the Canadians, and supported the institutions that were thought to be distinctively theirs. The free exercise of the Catholic religion was confirmed, and to this was added the right of the clergy to "hold, receive, and enjoy, their accustomed Dues and Rights." In other words, the tithe was reimposed, and only the qualification "with respect to such Persons only as shall profess the said Religion" prevented a full establishment of the Catholic faith. The entry of Catholics into office was made possible by substituting a new oath for those previously required. Civil law — contracts and land law in the main — was to be according to the laws of Canada; in other words, the French custom of Paris as modified by the ordinances of the French régime in the new world. (Criminal law was to be English.) Finally, the spectre of an assembly, in which the tiny Protestant minority would lord it over the mass of Catholics, who would be without votes or representatives, was again banished, it being "at present inexpedient to call an Assembly."

The instructions, which Carleton was to communicate to his council, had a rather different emphasis, however. The council was to consider whether the Laws of England may not be, if not altogether, at least in part the Rule for the decision of all Cases of personal Actions grounded upon Debts, Promises, Contracts, and Agreements, whether of a Mercantile or other Nature, and also of Wrongs proper to be compensated in damages.

This, if carried out, would remove a large part of the French civil law, and give frightening teeth to the provision in the Act itself that the laws and customs of Canada should prevail "until they shall be varied or altered by any Ordinances that shall . . . be passed in the said Province. . . ." Carleton was enjoined to remember that in matters of religion "it is a toleration of the free exercise of the religion of the Church of Rome only, to which they are entitled, but not to the powers and privileges of it, as an established Church, for that is a preference, which belongs only to the Protestant Church of England." Further in this connection, Carleton was to look for ways of undermining Catholicism: ordinands had to be licensed by the governor; only Canadians could be ordained; should the majority in a parish ask for a Protestant priest they should have their wish, and with it the tithes; Catholic priests proposing to marry should not be liable to any Roman penalty; above all, Carleton was "at all times and upon all occasions to give every Countenance and Protection in your Power to such Protestant Ministers, and School Masters, as are already established . . . or may hereafter be sent thither. . . ." The long range plan of Anglicization and protestantization had not been given up.

It was too much, however, to hope that a Quebec Act, especially one that was a "bill of experiment," would clear up a decade and a half of uncertainty and confusion. As the remainder of the chapter will explain, the colonial reception of the imperial enactments was rather different from that intended.

## — 2. Colonial Realities: The Church —

Initially, the intention of replacing Roman Catholicism with Anglicanism as the religion of the province seemed possible. In the immediate aftermath of the Conquest the situation of the Catholic Church was not hopeful. Support from France, which in financial terms had always been appreciable, ceased almost entirely, and only a small token, paid secretly, was sent by the assembly of the French clergy. Equally serious was the end of the supply of French priests. At the Conquest half the priests in the colony were from

France; even if the proportion of Canadians had been rising over the years, it was still not high enough for self-sufficiency. The interruption in the supply of priests was particularly worrying in the 1760s: as a result of deaths and returns to France the priesthood in Canada was down 25 percent within five years of the capitulation. Most daunting of all was the fact that the Church, now part of a state in which the monarch was, by virtue of the Elizabethan Act of Supremacy, head of the established religion, lacked a bishop, and accordingly no new priests could be ordained.

Yet the Church survived. A good deal of the credit must go to Murray. Although he was wedded to an eventual Anglicanization, he was equally wedded to a humane approach, and he was eager to act with courtesy towards the Church. At the same time, he was enough of a realist to know that Catholicism mattered deeply to the Canadians. "It is certain," he wrote, "that in the whole world there is no people more pious and more attached to its religion, than the *habitants* of Canada." If he could reassure them on that score, it would make his task of governing a defeated society that much easier. Accordingly, he gave orders that the Catholic religion was to be respected, and that troops encountering a religious procession in the streets should be suitably reverent. As early as 1762 he was paying a pension of 20 pounds to Jean Briand, the Vicar-General of Quebec, "for his good behaviour and as having little or no Income." Other priests besides received handouts from Murray for rebuilding purposes.

Undoubtedly the greatest service Murray performed for the Church was in backing the moves to have a bishop appointed. The obstacles to such an appointment seemed insurmountable. British opinion was hostile to Catholicism, and as late as 1780 London was given over to the mob for a week of looting and violence, the Gordon Riots, sparked by government "softness" towards Catholics. Thus, despite the finding in 1765 that the penalties attaching to Catholics in Britain did not operate in the colonies, the notion of a papal hierarchy having any standing in a British dominion was not countenanced. In evidence given in 1774 on the proposed Quebec Act, Advocate-General James Marriott argued that the Treaty of Paris had permitted "not the profession of the doctrines, but the profession of the exercise of external ceremonies . . . only," and he went on to claim that "the laws and constitution of this kingdom permit perfect freedom of the exercise of any religious worship in the colonies, but not . . . the maintenance of any foreign authority. . . ." Certainly, when Carleton was given his instructions in 1775, it was categorically stated that "all . . . correspondence with any foreign ecclesiastical jurisdiction, of what nature or kind so ever, be absolutely forbidden under very severe Penalties." It had also been pointed out in 1763, when the question of a bishop for Quebec had been first broached in London, that Maryland permitted the practice of Catholicism, but without a bishop.

Despite theory, and despite popular prejudice, the government was prepared to accept a compromise. A bishop would be elected by the Quebec chapter; in this way, a nomination by a foreign power, whether French or Roman, would be avoided, while at the same time the Protestant king of England would not have to impose his choice openly upon the Quebec Church. However, should the choice of the electors be unacceptable to the authorities, they could refuse to confirm it and have the process repeated. This, in fact, is what happened. The first choice was Montgolfier, superior of the Sulpicians, but Murray thought him unsuitable and refused to accept him. A second election chose Briand, who had been Murray's candidate for some time. Having been chosen, Briand was allowed to go to France — quietly — to be consecrated. On his return to Canada in 1766 he was officially to be known as the "Superintendent of the Romish Religion." Britain, in short, was turning a blind eye to the breach of its own laws and of the instructions that it would continue to issue.

The solution was as agreeable to Carleton as to Murray. In 1766, when the former replaced the latter, the pension to Briand was increased to 200 pounds a year, but Carleton had a more significant way of showing his approval of the bishop of his Church. When the Quebec Act gave rise to disquiet as Briand worried about the reference in it to the royal supremacy, and when rumour about the tenor of the instructions to Carleton began to circulate, the governor was able to reassure the bishop that all would be well. Carleton had already written to his superiors "that as the head of ecclesiastical arrangements, he may be left as much to himself as possible." He was as good as his word. He simply declined, in flat defiance of his orders, to communicate his instructions to the council. Only in 1781 did his successor make them openly known in the province. In this fashion, then, the more liberal thrust of the act was allowed to work untrammelled by the protestantizing intent of the instructions, and the Church was able to continue to reestablish itself.

There was, of course, a *quid pro quo* in all this. Briand had been chosen because he fitted in. From the first he issued *Mandements* that supported the new régime, and he ordered prayers during mass for the new king. He continued to be fulsome in his public utterances. Requests that priests aid the civil authority in controlling drinking dens and in apprehending deserters were passed on by the bishop. Moreover, when the governor chose to interfere in the running of the Church, he was not denied. Briand had long wanted to appoint a coadjutor to ensure the smoother working of the episcopacy, but Carleton kept holding the appointment up, and when he eventually permitted it he foisted upon Briand M. Desgly, an incompetent man who ought never to have been chosen.

There is warrant, then, for saying that in these years the Church was subserviant, but it had been under the French régime as well. Indeed, the early British rule was crucial in establishing the long-term health of the Canadian Church. It had been preserved. Furthermore, it had been Canadianized, the long tutelage to France having been forcibly broken. Finally, as it represented the whole body of Canadians, and was the only institution to preserve an unbroken continuity with the past, the Church came to speak for French Canada in a way that no other body could. In time its growing numbers and financial resources freed it from a narrow dependence upon the colonial government — though respect for constituted authority, so congenial to Catholicism anyway, and in particular for the English Crown, never disappeared — and it could strike out on a line of its own. That line was not the Gallicanism that had characterized it in the first half of the eighteenth century. The ties to absolutist France had been snapped: there was the Anglican Church, in its own way a "Gallican" institution, to be resisted. In reaction the Canadian Church developed an attachment to Rome that came to be a fierce ultramontanism. The religious pendulum, not for the last time, was swinging, this time back to the position of the early seventeenth century.

## — 3. Colonial Realities: The Bourgeoisie —

In the case of the Church the projects of the imperial legislators clashed with the realities of the colonial situation to produce something very different from the original intention. Even so, that clash occasioned little in the way of protest or rancour. It was otherwise with the British traders who entered the colony in the wake of the invading army and who continued to trickle in for some years. The quarrels they provoked sparked thunder and lightning.

The military authorities invited the entry of the traders, drawing attention to the immediate opportunities of provisioning the forces and also to the possibilities of the western fur trade, hitherto French. Some responded with alacrity: already by 1761 Alexander Henry was trading from the St. Lawrence by way of Michilimackinac. Pontiac's rising interrupted the westward flow, but by 1765 traders were once again being licensed for the *pays d'en haut*. Eventually, some 200 British Protestants moved into Quebec and Montreal, a tiny proportion of the total population but on account of their ambition, drive, and arrogance a significant interest group. They were cohesive, part of the conquering nation, articulate because of their knowledge of English ways and of the language, and determined to impress their viewpoint upon both colony and metropolis.

At first their relations with the French-Canadian bourgeoisie were good. In time they were destined to drive these competitors out of business, but that lay in the future. For the moment they had no quarrel with them on account of their race or culture. The Beaver Club was always open to French Canadians. Many of the traders took French-Canadian wives, as the leading examples of McTavish, Frobisher, and McGill testify. The plain fact was that the newcomers needed the skills of the old masters, and the profits to be made were enough for all. Their quarrels were with the British government, or more exactly with the authorities on the spot, in particular, Murray.

The clash was very largely one of personalities. The traders were "new" men who, succeeding by their own efforts, had embraced the trading ethic with fervour. They were single-minded, and contemptuous of anything and anyone who stood in the way of their potential fortune. Murray had to be their *bête noire*. He was descended from a landowning family and had been a professional soldier since his early manhood. Those years of military service had developed the chivalrous side of his nature and inclined him to be scornful of traders, to whom the notion of honour was so very different from his own. Very quickly his early commitment to the development of a trading empire on the St. Lawrence was tempered by his dislike of the agents of that development. He called them "the most cruel, ignorant, rapacious fanaticks who ever existed." In their turn, the traders, in a petition to the king, characterized their governor as given to "a Rage and Rudeness of Language and Demeanour" and guilty of the "most flagrant Partialities." The gap between the two parties was too wide to be bridged and in 1765 Westminster decided to recall Murray. In the following year he sailed for home and was replaced by Carleton.

Essentially the same collision took place. Carleton also was from a landowning/army background and his initial openness to the traders' viewpoint changed over the years until he, too, became hostile to their pretensions. More restrained than Murray, and also a better administrator, he did not suffer the same fate as his predecessor, but the same pattern of relationships prevailed nonetheless. That he suppressed information about projected changes in the civil law indicated just how far Carleton was prepared to go in keeping the trading interest within bounds. Temperament may have lain behind the quarrels, but the occasions were political. The first clash came in 1763 with the royal proclamation, which contained material that both delighted and enraged the British merchants. The promise of an assembly was received with joy. Given the thinking about the position of Catholics, it appeared that such a representative body would be composed exclusively of Protestants, elected exclusively by Protestants. This was to put the power of the colony largely into the hands of a few people. As the years went by, however, their joy turned to bitterness. The governors took advantage of the escape clause that decreed the establishment of an assembly "so soon as the state and circumstances of the said Colonies will admit" and put off its summoning indefinitely. In retaliation the merchants began to work over the governor's head, and in 1765 retained counsel in London at 200 pounds a year to lobby on their behalf. Their efforts were in vain. The Quebec Act did not grant them an assembly, and they continued to feel a deep sense of grievance.

It took time for disillusionment to sink in, but the proclamation contained one shock that made an immediate impact. The colony of Quebec was chopped in size, reduced to a mere parallelogram in the St. Lawrence Valley about Quebec and Montreal. The aim was twofold. In the first place it would make the colony a settled agricultural one, Colbert's compact colony in fact. Agriculture would become more important and the area would begin to appeal to that surplus population building up in the existing British colonies to the south. Secondly, it would deal with the problem that had caused the proclamation to be issued in such haste. The Ohio and Upper Mississippi Valleys were to be severed to form an Indian and fur preserve, so that the like of Pontiac's rising should never occur again. Within that reserve direct imperial control as opposed to colonial control would operate. This was a bad enough blow to the Montreal merchants and their belief in the natural right of the St. Lawrence to dominate the hinterland. Worse was the added stipulation that the fur trade should be tightly controlled and operated from fixed posts only. The previous French practice of going out to the Indians was to be given up, and the British inheritors of the trade predicted a speedy loss of furs to the French operating north out of New Orleans.

This decision did not stand the test of time. Settlers did not flood into Quebec for, as Carleton admitted, "the Europeans who migrate never will prefer the long unhospitable Winters of Canada to the more chearful Climates and more fruitful Soil of His Majesty's Southern Provinces." It proved impossible to arrange for a revenue to operate the imperial policing of the Indian territory. Far from its being an Indian reserve, empty of Europeans, there were European settlements already in the region, a prime example being the French-Canadian one at Detroit. Some jurisdiction more permanent and suitable than a military one had to be found for these settlers. Thus the Quebec Act undid the proclamation in this respect and restored Quebec to its former spaciousness. It was thought that this retrocession would be a sop to the merchants to set against their disappointment over the lack of an assembly.

It was something, but not enough to remove the sense of grievance that the British traders felt. In time the bad feeling engendered between merchants and bureaucrats widened to poison the atmosphere of the whole colony. The merchants, sensing themselves to be the representatives of a way of life profoundly at odds with an older more feudal conception, gradually extended their animosity to include any who seemed to uphold outdated ways. British increasingly confronted French, Protestant against Catholic. This development took place in part because the governors, by siding with the francophone Catholics against the anglophone Protestants, contributed to just such an identification.

## — 4. Colonial Realities: — *Seigneurs* and *Habitants*

From the moment of capitulation, a warm *rapprochement* developed between conquered and conquerors. The Canadians suddenly and to their surprise found that defeat was not the end of the world; indeed, it had positive advantages. While the war had continued, they had been filled with extreme anti-British propaganda. Their priests warned them of the religious perils to be expected at the hands of heretics. The example of the Acadians, some of whom had taken refuge in Canada, was constantly before them, and the invaders did not improve their image by their style of warfare. Military brutality, relearned against the Celts, this time in Scotland putting down the clansmen who had fought for Bonnie Prince Charles in the 1745 Rebellion, was widespread in the outlying areas and the Canadians feared the worst. Yet the horror stories did not come to pass. With the danger of guerilla attack removed, the British soldiery showed their other side, and quickly won the respect of the people. Murray helped greatly here, admitting to wrongs committed, obliging his troops to obey the law, even hanging those who looted. Deportation was not used. And religion, far from being extirpated, was protected. This reprieve, so complete in its reversal of the expected, had a profound psychological impact on the Canadians, easing for them the shock of defeat. When the British army showed itself willing to pay hard cash for produce, a sharp contrast with the bankrupt paper-monied French régime, many had cause to welcome the change of masters.

There was calculation in the British treatment of the Canadians. The governors realized that they would have to conciliate their new subjects. Any hopes of attracting large numbers of British settlers soon had to be given up, and in an early dispatch Carleton acknowledged that "barring a catastrophe shocking to think of this country must to the end of time be peopled by the Canadian race. . . ." The potential threat these numbers posed hung over the governors' heads. At the time of the capitulation, the war was still being fought, and who knew what relief expedition might be sent? After the peace the possibility of a French war of revenge and reconquest was ever present. Carleton in particular was preoccupied with this danger. For others the threat came not so much from France as from the British colonies to the south where already the first stirrings of the American War of Independence were being felt. Both Murray and Carleton were military men, so such considerations weighed heavily with them. They saw the *habitants* and *seigneurs* as ideal army material. "The Canadians are to a man soldiers" claimed Murray. Carleton was equally taken with their virtues, for they had "served with as much valour, with more zeal, and more military knowledge for America, than the regular troops . . . ." To this he added a significant statistic: the British troops numbered 1627, the British capable of serving as militia about 500, but the French Canadians could put 18 000 into the field.

Even without the threat of war, there was the question of ensuring smooth administration. To this end, the greatest possible continuity with the past was needed. Here, too, Murray and Carleton took care to see that the continuity was substantial. Murray showed no hesitation in commissioning French Canadians to handle administration under the military régime. He put one in charge of the north and one in charge of the south shore. In addition he appointed Sieur Jacques Allier civil and criminal judge in the parishes between Berthier and Kamouraska. The *capitaine de milice* was retained in office and given the task "to settle amicably as far as possible all differences which may arise amongst the inhabitants . . ., to hear all complaints, and if they are of such a nature that he can settle them, he shall do so with all due justice and equity. . . ." With the introduction of civil government the *capitaine* lost his judicial function, and in fact between 1765 and 1775 the office itself disappeared. However, the break in continuity was more apparent than real, for in their place were elected on the old principle bailiffs and sub-bailiffs. The reality of *habitant* self-government at the local level was kept up when the traditional marks of respect (such as the honoured place in church) were ordered to be observed. The two governors sought to introduce legal systems acceptable to the *habitants* and *seigneurs*. The main complaint of the British system was the delay and the cost in obtaining justice; as Carleton pointed out,

> The present great and universal Complaint arises from the Delay, and Heavy Expense of Justice; formerly the King's Courts sat once a week at Quebec, Montreal, and Three Rivers; from these lay an Appeal to the Council, which also sat once a Week, where Fees of all Sorts were very low, and the Decision immediate; at present the Courts sit three times a Year at Quebec and twice a year at Montreal, and have introduced all the Chicanery of Westminster Hall into this impoverished Province.

So, whereas Murray had sought to give satisfaction to the Canadians by setting up his hybrid court in 1764, Carleton preferred another tack. An ordinance of 1770 not only swept away the inferior jurisdiction of the justices of the peace, a blow against the traders who, as Protestants, filled these offices, but went on to establish courts modelled after those of the French régime — that is, expeditious and cheap, and sitting virtually year-round. The consummation of the policy of continuity, of course, was the Quebec Act itself, especially with the suppression of the accompanying instructions.

Calculation, however, was only part of the story. At bottom, that temperamental aversion to the traders was the same that drew *seigneurs*, *habitants*, and governors together, and as the force of one grew so too did the other reciprocally and in proportion. Murray, for instance, recognized the shortcomings of *habitants* and *seigneurs*: the former he described as "in general ignorant, for the former government would never suffer a printing press in the Country, few can read or write," though he did allow that they were "a strong healthy race, plain in their dress, virtuous in their morals and temperate in their living"; the latter he found "in general poor. . . . The Croix de St. Louis quite completed their happiness. They are extremely vain. . . . They were great tyrants to their Vassals. . . ." Yet in time he was prepared to say of them that they were "perhaps the bravest and best race upon the Globe." The *seigneurs* reciprocated: in petitions to the king they thanked him for "having given them as Governor, the honourable James Murray . . . this Worthy Governor whose clear sightedness, Equity, and wisdom continually afford him efficacious means for maintaining the people in tranquility and obedience," and testified that Murray, "by this affability, compelled us to love him." What Carleton liked was what he identified as a hierarchy of "Subordination, from the first to the lowest, which preserved the internal Harmony." The *seigneur-habitant* relationship, and the lack of representative democracy that went with it, instinctively appealed to him as the true basis for any society. For this reason Carleton, while in London, prevailed upon the imperial government to issue an ordinance in 1771 that empowered him "to grant . . . Lands . . . in Fief and Seigneurie." For the same reason he successfully campaigned against a provision in an earlier draft of the Quebec Act that would have allowed the holders of seigneurial land to convert it to freehold.

Murray, and to a much greater extent Carleton, had made their commitment to a traditional order, an order that in fact had never existed. Under the French régime the outward form was that of feudal overlord-dependent tenant. However, as has been shown, the *seigneur* was merely a land-settlement agent who enjoyed some status and whose sons were officers in the *Troupes de la Marine*, while the *habitants* were not in any meaningful sense his tenants so much as dependents of the king (if indeed of anyone). The British conjured up the ghost of a phantom, and if the Protestant traders came to believe in its reality and as a result harden their negative view of French-Canadian society, it did not fool the *habitants* or the *seigneurs*. Very soon events were to convince even Carleton that his reliance upon the traditional order, as he saw it, had failed.

--- **Suggested Reading**

The Centenary Series volume that deals with a Canada become Quebec is H. Neatby, *Quebec 1760-1791* (1966).

Two works by M. Trudel cover the transitional period: *Le régime militaire dans le Gouvernement de Trois Rivières* (1952), and *L'Eglise canadienne sous le régime militaire* (1956-57). See also M. Brunet, *Les Canadiens après la conquête* (1969).

The chief players in Quebec in this period are treated in R.H. Mahon, *Life of General the Hon. James Murray* (1921), and A.L. Burt, *Guy Carleton, Lord Dorchester* (1964). Opposing views of the latter's role in the genesis of the Quebec

Act are to be found in R. Coupland, *The Quebec Act* (1925), and C. Martin, *Empire and Commonwealth* (1929); H. Neatby, *The Quebec Act: Protest and Policy* (1972), provides primary material and differing interpretations.

The Indian Question is examined in H.H. Peckham, *Pontiac and the Indian Uprising* (1947), and W.R. Jacobs, *Dispossessing the American Indian* (1972).

Trading interests in Quebec are detailed in D. Macmillan, "The 'New Men' in Action: Scottish Mercantile and Shipping Operations in the North American Colonies, 1760-1825," in D. Macmillan (ed.), *Canadian Business History* (1972); W.S. Wallace, *Pedlars from Quebec* (1954); F. Ouellet, "Dualité économique et changement technologique dans la vallée du Saint-Laurent, 1760-1790," *Historie sociale/Social history* (1976).

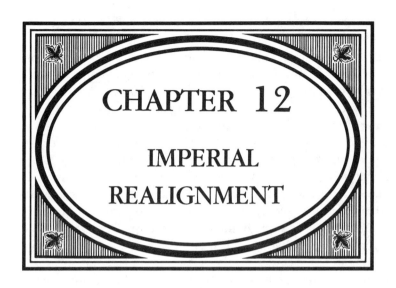

# CHAPTER 12

## IMPERIAL REALIGNMENT

## — 1. Reform and Reaction —

At the height of the Seven Years' War when matters were going badly for France, its chief minister, the Duc de Choiseul, ventured a prophecy. The loss of Canada, he predicted, would remove a salutary check to American colonial ambitions and within a generation they would have revolted against Britain and secured their independence. France would be revenged on her inveterate enemy. The events of the next two decades were to prove Choiseul· essentially right, though the dynamics of their development were infinitely more complex than he could have known.

Over the years a great variety of explanations have been brought forward to explain why the colonies rebelled. During the high-minded nineteenth century, the standard approach was to place the struggle on the lofty level of abstract constitutionalism. The British government, so the argument goes, in the years after the Peace of Paris, passed a series of laws that flew in the face of the accepted British maxim "No taxation without representation." In 1764 the Sugar Act raised the duty on that commodity. Duties had previously existed; indeed, that on sugar had been five shillings per hundredweight. The increase, to 27 shillings, represented something new, however, for the preamble to the Act made it plain that what was being attempted was not a duty to regulate trade in a mercantilist empire from which any income would be purely incidental, but rather a duty to raise a revenue. The former, colonists were prepared to concede, was proper, since for the empire as a whole the authority of Westminster was valid; the latter, on the other hand, was an illegal imposition, for no colonial assembly had given its approval.

A year after the Stamp Act, the constitutional case continues, the Stamp Act seemed to threaten British liberties in America even more seriously. That Act extended to the colonies the longstanding British requirement that official and legal papers pay tax in the form of stamps. This went a stage beyond the Sugar Act, which had still been an external tax, and in theory colonists not wishing to pay it could simply have refused to import sugar. The Stamp Act applied within the colony, to transactions that were not avoidable in the same sense; as such it was a matter that clearly ought to have come before a colonial legislature. Since it had not, the cry "No Taxation without representation" was properly raised. Indeed, the novelty was so pernicious that freedom-loving Americans rose up in justified anger and destroyed the stamps, drove out the tax officials, and went on to organize a boycott of British goods to show Westminster that they meant business. In this they were successful, and the Act was repealed.

Yet the British had not learned their lesson. The repeal was accompanied by a Declaratory Act that proclaimed the legality of the Stamp Act and reserved the right to impose similar legislation in the future. In 1767 Charles Townshend, the chancellor of the exchequer, brought in the duties named after him, taxes on paper, glass, paint, and tea. Once again a storm of protest arose. Once again the duties were removed — all except the tea tax. The agitation against this exception was kept up and finally, in 1773, British modifications to the tea trade provided the spark for the Boston Tea Party. A group of patriotic citizens "disguised" as Indians boarded an East India Company ship and dumped its cargo of tea into Massachusetts Bay. The oppressive British government responded with unnecessary severity. Four acts, known as the "Intolerable Acts," were passed to punish Massachusetts. The harbour was closed, destroying trade; the colonial council was abolished and replaced by one nominated by the Crown; the billeting of soldiers on citizens was arranged, so that the town might be bullied; and power was given to have trials removed to England if necessary.

Such in outline is the constitutional case, a litany of illegal or unjustifiable acts by the imperial authority that provoked the proper resistance of the colonies. A more cynical twentieth century has seen the struggle rather differently. Some, while not necessarily denying the power of such episodes to produce disaffection, have concentrated upon the economic factors. They have stressed that by the mid-eighteenth century the American colonies had reached a critical stage in their economic development. They had built up an extensive overseas trade, and intensive trading links among themselves into the bargain. They were outgrowing the mercantilist framework that kept them in subjection to Britain, and were ready to move beyond staple production to industrialization. At the same time, their population growth was continuing at a spectacular rate, and that too had reached a critical level. The pent-up population was ready to cascade over the Appalachian barrier and flood across the Midwest, but imperial policy, as announced in the royal proclamation of 1763, flatly opposed this development. However, the destiny of such a lusty child was not to be thwarted by parental prohibitions, and if Britain persisted in standing in the way of natural growth the inhibiting ties would have to be severed — with violence if necessary.

Yet others have explored the social dimensions. Rather than focus on the activities of the elite, whether politicians or merchants, they trace the hopes and aspirations of the ordinary man. They claim to have found a ferment of social revolution, a wish to throw off the old restraints on holding office, on political participation, on inheritance, on landholding, and so forth. This ferment was so powerful that it could not be contained within the existing imperial-centred framework, so heavily marked by the conservative, not to say reactionary outlook of old Europe. Therefore, an independent course of development became necessary.

These variants have been argued over, dismissed, resurrected with qualifications and ever-increasing sophistication, and combined for many years now. The understanding of the rebellion as it presently exists is complex indeed. But a history of Canada does not have to probe that understanding in any detail. Those seeking to understand Canadian history are interested in the War of Independence not so much for its own sake as because it impacted upon the emerging country in two ways. In the first place, the War of Independence produced a sizable body of pro-British diehards, the Loyalists, who preferred exile from America to acceptance of the new republic. Many of them chose British North America, and were a vital founding element in their adoptive home. Second, the very success of the American system, right on Canada's doorstep, continually posed fundamental questions to Canadians about their own identity; now that the British heritage had split into two strains, towards which should the Canadians gravitate?

These two questions direct examination not so much towards the ostensible causes of the breach as to the underlying mentalities that enabled the two sides to evaluate a given action, say the Stamp Act, in such very different lights. For this is the striking fact that has to be grasped. British opinion felt that the Stamp Act was perfectly valid, not onerous, and a statesman-like approach to paying off a crushing national debt largely incurred on behalf of the Americans and towards which they ought to contribute. The Americans equally sincerely felt that it was an intolerable imposition. The British were appalled and disgusted by the mob violence which greeted the tax. The Americans rejoiced in the valiant response of their citizens to attempts to enslave them. How was it that British attempts to give their empire the overhaul that it so obviously needed after the Seven Years' War led to such protests? How did reform produce such a reaction?

The starting point for the Americans was the very British one that, since humans were naturally avaricious after power, and that since there was a constant danger of despotism entrenched behind corruption, the proper system of political society was that of checks and balances. It was a theory that did not correspond to practice, but it was still deeply cherished because it marked Britain off from the absolutist French. It was a theory that received classic expression in 1765 in Blackstone's *Commentaries on the Laws of England*:

> And herein indeed consists the true excellence of the English government, that all parts of it form a mutual check upon each other. In the legislature the people were a check upon the nobility, and the nobility a check upon the people; by the mutual privileges of rejecting what the other has resolved: While the King is a check upon both, which preserves the executive power from encroachments. And this very executive power is again checked and kept within bounds by the two Houses, through the privilege they have of inquiring into, impeaching and punishing the conduct not indeed of the King, which would destroy his constitutional independence, but which is more beneficial to the public, of his evil and pernicious counsellors. Thus every branch of our civil polity supports and is supported, regulates and is regulated, by the rest: for the two Houses naturally drawing in two directions of opposite interest, and the prerogative in another still different from them both, they mutually keep each other from exceeding their proper limits. . . .

In Britain, as in America, there were those who feared that the balance was slipping, that the executive was becoming too powerful, a fear that surfaced dramatically in 1780 when John Dunning proposed and carried the motion at Westminster "that the influence of the Crown has increased, is increasing, and ought to be diminished." However, what is significant about the American treatment of this theme is the lengths to which they were prepared to go in opposing executive tyranny. What was in Dunning's case a nine-days' wonder was in the colonies a rooted maxim for the regular conduct of politics. In this respect the Americans would justify Murray's epithet "fanaticks."

The judgment that the times were corrupt pervaded the colonies. Not only was the mother country, in their view, sunk in decadence, so too were the Americans themselves. The feeling that liberty was in danger of being lost was intensified by the great religious revival that had worked its way through colonial society during the previous generation and more, a shattering experience that had riven the broad Calvinist tradition and given rise to "New Light" churches that channelled powerful impulses to find evil everywhere at work. This resurgent Puritanism was hostile to any suggestion of hierarchy. They looked upon Anglican efforts to have a North American bishop with horror as part of the imperial plan to subjugate free colonists: in 1765 it was claimed that "the stamping and episcopizing [of] our colonies were . . . only different branches of the same plan of power." That Quebec had been allowed a *Catholic* bishop filled them with fury. The old slogan "No Popery, no wooden shoes" rang again in this setting. Not surprisingly, that the Quebec Act appeared at the same time as the Boston Port Bill was taken as proof of a settled plan to subvert Protestant freedom, and that act was included among the Intolerable Acts.

The violence and the unreasonableness of this response draws attention to another characteristic of the American colonists, the tendency to political paranoia. The colonists believed that the actions of the British government were part of a vast conscious conspiracy to enslave them, but the reasons for the various taxing acts appeared acceptable to others. The British national debt was staggering and taxation was unbearably high; the Americans derived substantial benefits from membership in the world's then largest trading system, and ought to have paid something towards the operating costs; the existing system was run in so lax a fashion that while the average annual yield of the American customs was 2000 pounds the expense of collecting that sum was 8000 pounds; a second Pontiac's rising was to be avoided, so white settlers were to have been kept from crossing the Appalachians, and imperial troops were to police the region. To the Americans, however, none of this was acceptable: the taxes were, they believed, to establish a precedent that in time would crush the Americans. The troops were there to impose martial law. For far too many, everything Britain did was further evidence of a plot hatched against them. Thomas Jefferson summed up the prevailing opinion: "Single acts of tyranny may be ascribed to the accidental opinion of a day . . . [but] a series of oppressions begun at a distinguished period and pursued unalterably through every change of ministers too plainly prove a deliberate and systematic plan of reducing us to slavery." John Adams added the date of the "distinguished period": "the conspiracy was first regularly formed and begun to be executed in 1763 or 4."

Accompanying this paranoia was the belief that in such a desperate situation intolerance was a virtue and violence a necessity. At an early stage of protest, Patrick Henry ("Give me Liberty or give me death") proposed to the Virginia legislature that anyone who maintained that Westminster had the right to tax should be considered an enemy. That the suggestion was not adopted was irrelevant; Henry's sentiment was widely circulated and accepted. In 1772 the revenue cutter *Gaspee* ran aground; a Rhode Island mob attacked the vessel, cast the captain adrift in a small boat, looted and then burned the ship. The Boston Tea Party itself was not an isolated incident — there were other similar acts of violence.

Paradoxically, this almost totalitarian solidarity and herd-like suppression of dissent was accompanied by an individualism that could border on the anarchic. The colonies had a long tradition of allowing a person to do as he liked. Property was his to sell or to waste. His views were his to express with all the outspoken onesidedness that that might entail. This tradition led to the inclusion in the Declaration of Independence that man had a natural right to the "pursuit of happiness," a most extreme statement of individualism since no man could decide for another what constituted happiness. The tradition also led, after the war, to the invention of the constitutional convention. If society was to be properly constituted, it could only be after the people through their representatives, specifically chosen for this one purpose, had discussed the matter and drafted a constitution that was then approved by the free vote of all the citizens.

Such, then, was the American style. It was against such presumptions that Loyalism fought, and against which British North America reacted.

## — 2. Revolution Rejected —

When John Adams in the mid-1760s became aware that the real revolution, that of mentality, had taken place, he was sufficiently honest to admit that Quebec and Nova Scotia were unlikely to be part of that "Union," aroused by the Stamp Act, that "was never known before in America." "I pity my unhappy fellow subjects in Quebeck and Hallifax" he owned, noting that "Quebec consists chiefly of French men." In the case of Nova Scotia he ventured an explanation of their distinctiveness: "Halifax consists of a sett of Fugatives and Vagabonds . . . kept in fear by a Fleet and an Army." In this he was quite right. Halifax had been built as an answer to Louisbourg, and when that fortress passed to Britain, Halifax was free to overawe the surrounding area. At the same time the government contracts that inevitably went with such a presence naturally tied civilian fortunes to the imperial cause. Nevertheless, correct though he was, Adams did not see far enough. The evolution of Nova Scotia in this period was particularly complex; its distinctive roots went back to the effective foundation of the colony after the Treaty of Aix-la-Chapelle, 1748.

Nova Scotia rather than Quebec first furnished Americans with a foretaste of the new British attitude to imperial management. As a colony it differed significantly from Massachusetts, the dominant society of the region. Whereas Massachusetts had a long history of independent initiative, Nova Scotia had none. The former had been peopled by settlers who owed almost nothing to Britain other than their habits of mind; their work of clearing the land, subduing the Indians, and building their civilization in the wilderness had been overwhelmingly their own unaided effort. Their institutions fittingly mirrored their independence: local officials at the township level were elected by the citizens; the legislature of the colony was to a great extent free of imperial control; the council was elected. How different were arrangements in Nova Scotia! Its origin lay in a decision of Westminster to counter the French military threat; its early growth was at the hands of the Board of Trade; its officials were selected and closely overseen by imperial authorities. Although it had enjoyed an assembly since 1758, that body had none of the independence that marked that of Massachusetts, and the council was nominated.

With such beginnings it was difficult for Nova Scotia to experience that evolution in thinking that took place to the south between 1765 and 1775. Immigration from New England slowed, and by the mid-1760s the flow was if anything the other way, back to the future United States. British immigrants began to feature more and more in the makeup of the colony, so much so that by the outbreak of the war less than 50 percent of Nova Scotians were of New England origin. A colonial mentality permeated the province, which became plain when hostilities broke out. The inhabitants of Barrington admitted in a petition they wre sympathetic to the revolution, "having

Fathers, brothers, and children living [in Massachusetts]," yet when referring to the war they revealingly wrote of the fighting that "you" and not "we" were engaged in. The pro-American rebels of Maugerville acknowledged that it was "our Minds and Desire to submit ourselves to the government of Massachusetts' Bay," which has often been taken to show a revolutionary fervour; however, another interpretation is that even those opposed to Britain realized the impossibility of the colony's rebelling in its own right. The most that could be hoped for was a change of imperialisms.

War threw the raw, scattered, heterogenous population of Nova Scotia into confusion. Neither imperial loyalties nor rebel visions could provide that society with a sense of direction, a sense of self that would see it through the uncertainty. What did serve as a focus about which an identity could be formed was religion: on the very outbreak of war there arose in Nova Scotia a preacher of charismatic power that the times demanded. From 1775 until his death in 1784, Henry Alline dominated the colony and in so doing shaped it profoundly.

The religious milieu into which the newly converted Alline plunged was no less confused than the rest of society. The New Englanders who made up such a large portion of the colony had brought with them Congregationalism in the main, a church that was split into Old Light and New Light groupings as a result of the revival in America since the 1740s. In addition, New England settlers had brought Baptist, Quaker, and Presbyterian churches. From Britain came the Methodists and, as a sign of the greater imperial hold on this province, an Anglicanism that was always influential. It was a religious hodgepodge that prevented any one body imposing itself, and one in which an untutored preacher like Alline could move with effect. The test was vibrant preaching and dramatic conversion, a common factor to which the predominant Dissenting churches could all respond.

By all accounts Alline triumphed. He had his enemies, and there were regions, notably the garrison and administrative capital of Halifax, where he was not popular, but these were minor exceptions. He visited most of the colony, and was a success. People came by the boatload to the centres he was known to be visiting, and even after his departure interest would remain high. Thus at Liverpool, at the house of a disciple, "a large Concourse of People . . . near 150 attended, which till of Late is a very Strange thing in this Place, Such a Meeting having scarcely been Known in the Place Since the Settlement of it, till Since Mr. Alline was here." Even those who opposed him were obliged to take note of his message. Whether for him or against him Nova Scotian society was being drawn together and unified.

**180**

For the greater portion of that society, the lasting message of the Alline revival was a new sense of identity as "a People highly favoured of God." Revivalist religion is sectarian, an impulse that emphasizes the cohesiveness of the true believers who feel impelled to withdraw from a wicked society. In the future United States this impulse had, in the withdrawal from the British empire, gone on to swell into its own nationalism. In Nova Scotia on the other hand the sense of withdrawal was maintained in a purer form. If Britain was decadent, so too was New England. Evil and backsliding were to be found in both. Nova Scotia was a remnant, a migration from a migration, the quintessence of Puritanism. Alline described the movement that had brought himself as a boy from Rhode Island, together with so many of his listeners, as providential: "Your being called away from the approaching storm that was hanging over your native land, and sheltered here from the calamities of the sweeping deluge" was a true sign of election.

Secure in the knowledge that they were a chosen people, Nova Scotians could rise above the battle. This was the great gift of Alline to his people; he had offered to "lend you an annicient eye or discover to your view a map of the disordered world." They had accepted that offer, and the view of themselves as "a People highly favoured of God" proved very congenial to them.

John Adams had been right about Quebec, too. That province quite failed to protest the Stamp Act, the very touchstone of Americanism. The elliptical reason he gave for this distinctiveness was that in addition to being cowed by an army, the population was overwhelmingly that of "French Men." The implication was that such a people were not called to the defence of liberty, and events seemed to bear out this prediction. In 1774 the Americans issued a *pro forma* invitation to Quebec to join in the rebellion and send delegates to the continental congress. Massachusetts even dispatched an agent to coordinate agitation and hasten a declaration. However, a blunt statement was soon sent back by this agent that "there is no prospect of Canada sending delegates to the Continental Congress." Yet if Canada was not natural revolutionary material, it did not follow that the province could be ignored. If an invitation to join was not accepted, then conquest would be necessary: Canada, commanding the St. Lawrence route to the interior, was too valuable a strategic prize to be left to the British. In their hands it was destined to be the major jumping-off place from which to launch the invasion of the States. Thus, while Nova Scotia was largely ignored and invasion there amounted to little more than Jonathan Eddy and his ridiculous band of 28, no fewer than two armies, mustering at departure some 2000 men, determined on the conquest of Canada in 1775.

In part it was a traditional exercise. One force under Richard Montgomery, who as a member of Amherst's army had got to know the region 15 years before, invaded by the Lake Champlain route. A second, under Benedict Arnold, used the Kennebec and Chaudière rivers and suffered abominably. Montreal not being defendable, Carleton abandoned it and withdrew to prepare Quebec for a siege. Thus at the end of 1775 the remains of the two invasion armies began a forlorn attempt to take the citadel with insufficient supplies, cannon, and men (there were more within the walls than without). In desperation an assault under cover of darkness was mounted on the last day of the year, but there were many casualties, many more were taken prisoner, and Montgomery himself was killed. Despite these setbacks, the Americans hung on until the arrival in the spring of 10 000 British troops threatened to trap the invaders, whereupon they retreated precipitately.

This was the end of serious invasion scares on the St. Lawrence. A constant war of raiding was kept up, and the British recruited not only Loyalist companies from among the Americans but also used their traditional Indian allies. Prominent among these last was the Mohawk chieftain Joseph Brant. Nevertheless, a return to more formal manoeuvres on the pattern of 1775 was never attempted, although the Americans considered it, after 1777, when a British army from Quebec under Bourgoyne, invading through the Hudson Valley, had been forced to surrender at Saratoga, and especially after 1780, when the war seemed to be won. France, however, by then the all-important ally, vetoed the plan. The French implicitly accepted the dictum of Choiseul that a partitioned North America would prevent too great a show of independence; just as before 1763 American fears of French Canadians kept them dependent upon Britain, so now in the 1780s their fears of British North America would keep them dependent on France.

The war proved no danger for Canada in the long run. There had been anxious moments, but little more. What had been shocking, however, was the way in which the war years had overturned almost all expectations of the behaviour of Quebec society. In particular, Carleton's estimations were shown to be grossly mistaken.

In view of the governor's attitudes, and in view of the just-passed Quebec Act, it might have been supposed that the trading element would have been extremely hostile to the imperial connection and receptive to the Americans, but it was not so. A few merchants did declare for the rebels, of course. The vast majority, however, did not. They were terrified of what the colonial non-importation agreements would do to their fortunes, and they were too dependent on London to want to break that link. The fur traders especially recognized the way the St. Lawrence system did not fit into the one that would probably emerge from a victorious War of Independence. Carleton himself was forced to admit that his former estimate of their class was in need of revision.

By the same token, but with even more emphasis, he had to change his judgment of the *seigneurs* and the *habitants*. The former, rewarded with a power and recognition that dwarfed anything they had enjoyed under the French régime, responded with an arrogance and contempt towards the *habitants* that fell far short of Carleton's notion of *noblesse oblige*. For their part the *habitants* were deeply resentful of the way in which their traditional independence, grown all the greater in the years between the Conquest and the Quebec Act, was being curtailed. Therefore, when hostilities threatened, Carleton was forced to admit that care would need to be taken "to recall [them] to their ancient habits of obedience and discipline." As time went on, the situation grew worse. The militia frequently refused to muster. Too many were passive in the face of invasion, and some even gave aid to the Americans — Arnold's corps would not have survived had not *habitants* succoured them. The post-invasion inquests revealed a disturbing story. It was difficult to find militia officers who had done their duty to the fullest, and in 50 parishes not fewer than 37 officers had to be cashiered.

Two things saved the colony. The invaders behaved with arrogant stupidity: their prohibition on western trade alienated what little support they attracted from the merchant group; more seriously their Puritan contempt for the *habitants*, their Church, and their ways shocked the mass of the population. When Montgomery's successor wrote in a letter later captured and made public that the Canadians "were only one remove from the savages," and when it was reported that he had prohibited Christmas Eve mass, unflattering comparisons with British behaviour in 1760 began to be made. Second, as time ran on and hard cash ran out, the attempts to pay for goods in paper money completed the disillusionment.

The Church was true to form. Briand and his clergy cooperated with the civil authorities in ways that fully justified the reliance placed upon them by the Quebec Act. *Mandements* were issued enjoining loyalty to the British régime, and sermons were preached on the duty of obeying duly constituted authority. After the invasion, priests were used to establish the facts of what happened in the parishes, and ecclesiastical penalties (such as the withholding of the sacraments) were employed to ensure submission to the steps taken by the state; in one case an entire parish was laid under interdict. This is not to claim, of course, that Church commands always brought instant compliance, but in most cases they did, and without such backing the colony would have found it much harder to resist conquest by the Americans. Had the Church given even tacit support to the rebels the colony must surely have been lost.

Carleton and Quebec survived. He had done enough to justify public recognition and the award of honours. The British cabinet, however, remarked that "some parts of his conduct were doubtful"; his misrepresentation of the state of the colony, and his halfhearted measures against the rebels, particularly when they withdrew in the spring of 1776, were black marks against him. In 1777 his offer to resign was accepted in a manner tantamount to dismissal. A year later his place was taken by the Swiss mercenary, Frederick Haldimand.

In the diary entry of 1766 mentioned earlier, John Adams had gone on to discuss revolutionary sentiments in the Caribbean. No mention, however, was made of Prince Edward Island, Cape Breton, or of Newfoundland. Adams had every justification in ignoring them. Prince Edward Island was a tiny settlement of less than a thousand people; only in 1769 was it separated from Nova Scotia, and only in 1773 did it receive an assembly; it was being peopled by Highlanders, and was in no way attracted by the possibility of independence. Cape Breton was even more backward in its development and remained part of Nova Scotia. Newfoundland had over 10 000 inhabitants, but imperial theory still saw the island as a mere adjunct to the fishing industry; the people had little sense of community, lacked even the rudiments of civil government, and were oriented entirely towards Britain. All three islands were too dependent on Britain and the North Atlantic even to consider the possibility of joining the Americans.

## — 3. The Loyalists: Friends of Government —

The Loyalism of provinces was not the only kind. In every part of the Thirteen Colonies were individual Loyalists, men and women who for one reason or another could not go along with the majority. The depth of their Loyalism varied widely, from those who by keeping their views quiet were suffered to stay on in the eventual republic to those willing to speak out and risk tar-and-feathering, imprisonment, exile, and even lynching. Because of the wide range of commitment it is difficult to arrive at any precise estimate of their numbers, but the most thorough statistical account (by Wallace Brown) puts them at between 8 and 18 percent of the white population.

A further difficulty arises from the fact that the incidence of Loyalism was extremely spotty: few areas were homogenous. Even New York, Loyalism's area of greatest significance, exhibited a bewildering checkerboard of allegiances. Thus, making sense of the reasons for Loyalism has not been an easy task. Efforts to find a philosophic basis have not been successful, although it is possible to find individuals who espoused a political view at odds with the prevailing colonial mentality, men who were genuinely Tory in their opposition to the Whigs of the revolution. Charles Inglis, a leading Anglican from New York who later became Britain's first colonial bishop (in Nova Scotia) was prepared to reach back to the medieval tradition. Such men were, nevertheless, exceptions: when the Loyalists are examined as a whole, one finds as many Whigs as Tories.

The attempt to find a social denominator was no more successful. Again it must be admitted that there were high-status, rich individuals in the Loyalist ranks, but equally clearly there were plenty of the middling sort, and even of the poor. In 1778 Massachusetts passed an act banishing Loyalists, some 300 being listed by name. Their occupations were given, and these divide into three equal groups: a) merchants, professionals, and gentlemen; b) farmers; c) artisans, labourers, and small shopkeepers.

No more luck attended the attempt to make religion the basis of choice. Anglicans were well represented, it is true, but not disproportionately, and it must be remembered that the biggest bloc of signers of the Declaration of Independence were Anglicans. All denominations, in fact, were to be found among the Loyalists in too scattered a fashion for any pattern to be discovered.

However, one explanation has managed to fit this very diversity of response into a satisfying analysis. It has been pointed out that "all that the Tory regions, the mountain and the maritime frontiers, had in common was that both suffered or were threatened with economic or political subjugation by richer adjoining areas. The geographical concentration of the Tories was in peripheral areas, regions already in decline, or not yet risen to importance." It is stated further that "the Tories more commonly drew their recruits from the non-English than from the English parts of the community," and that "adherents of religious groups that were in a local minority were everywhere inclined towards Loyalism." Summing up, William Nelson, the author of this analysis, remarks that "taking all the groups and factions, sects, classes, and inhabitants of regions that seem to have been Tory, they have but one thing in common: they represented conscious minorities, people who felt weak and threatened."

Such an analysis points to what may be the best clue to the Loyalist phenomenon. Having rejected philosophical, social, and religious explanations of why some opted for Loyalism — that is, conscious motives — it would be well to consider the unconscious factors at work, to explore the temperament of those who rejected Whiggery. Members of minorities could not embrace the fanaticism that the Americans so enthusiastically practised; they sensed the threat to their distinctiveness. One Loyalist in exile in Britain observed, "the doctrine of toleration, if not better understood, is, thank God, better practised here than in America." Peter Van Schaack, a Whig who had his doubts and went Loyalist before rejoining the Republic, made his first switch in allegiance because he realized the totalitarian implications of New England Patriot behaviour.

> My difficulty arises from this, that taking the whole of the acts complained of together [the Sugar Act through the Intolerable Acts], they do not, I think, manifest a system of slavery, but may be fairly imputed to human frailty, and the difficulty of the subject. In short, I think those acts may have been passed without a preconcerted plan of enslaving us.

Here was an openness of mind shocking to the true Patriot; if he, thought Peter Oliver, had told his "deluded Followers that an Army of 30 000 Men were crossing the Atlantic in Egg shells, with a Design to roast the Inhabitants alive and eat them afterwards, the People would have first stared, and swallowed down the Tale whole."

Safely cocooned in their common sense, the Loyalists lacked that dynamic that drove their fanatical opponents on. It is significant that Loyalists were always weakly organized. The leaders were out of touch with each other, and often indeed did not know who they were; frequently it was only in exile that they became aware of their fellows. At bottom they believed that the froth of their enemies was an aberration, a temporary breakdown in the proper ordering of society, something that would soon blow over. It was the same attitude that made Carleton so dilatory in dealing with opposition in Quebec; decisive measures were not necessary, for the misguided would soon see the error of their ways.

This illusory optimism was rooted in an instinctive belief that change could only be for the worse. They may not have been philosophical Tories, but they were conservative in temperament. They feared change with a profound and unthinking fear, which was why cultural minorities were so receptive to Loyalism. Nelson's observation that Huguenots and Dutch Reformed who had become English-speaking were Patriots whereas those who retained their French or Dutch languages went Loyalist is extremely telling. In a slightly different context, but making essentially the same point, Nelson writes, "it was not oligarchs as such who became Loyalists, but only the weakest or least practical oligarchs."

Such was the Loyalist mentality. Of their number perhaps as many as 100 000 went into exile. Many, if they could afford to, made for Britain, others chose the Caribbean, but many elected to stay in North America. Over 25 000 made their way to Nova Scotia, and some 10 000 to Quebec. They took with them their temperamental presuppositions and in exile erected them into a more conscious philosophy. A major strand of this philosophy was a function of exile itself. The Loyalists were in danger of succumbing to an identity crisis. They had been persecuted, they had been uprooted — but for what? Those who went to Britain soon found themselves uncomfortable when confronted by a genuine Toryism, a genuine aristocratic society, and longed to return across the Atlantic. They realized that in repudiating the United States they could not have been repudiating America. Rather, they told themselves, they had been repudiating republicanism. What they favoured was British America, the British connection. By making a parade of their loyalty to the symbols of the British constitution, they could assure themselves that their sacrifice had not been in vain. Moreover, to cling was congenial to a people fearful of change. To be dependent was no badge of shame, but a guarantee of continuing purity. It is worthwhile underlining that future Tories had been as upset over the Stamp Act as had future rebel Whigs, but whereas the latter were prepared to go on and challenge Britain root and branch, the former drew back, believing in the ultimate good sense of the mother country.

The other main strand of the Loyalist philosophy was only partly a result of the exile experience; it was more the lesson of the rebellion itself. Their fear of change, their experience of the fickle nature of popular clamour, their treatment at the hands of the mob, heightened their belief that the many had to be kept in their place. As two leading Loyalists put it, "the larger bodies of men are, the more false importance they reflect on each other," and "mankind have seldom been assembled in great numbers for any useful purpose." The late catastrophe had been caused, they believed, by giving the mob, or even the democratic element, too great a leeway. Devices were needed to restore that balance that eighteenth-century man took for granted. A strong state-church — an established Anglicanism — would be useful. To stress the aristocratic element in society could only be beneficial, as would be the strengthening of the executive as against the legislature. In the reordering of British North America after 1783 there was ample opportunity for putting such thinking into operation.

## 4. Redrawn Boundaries, Remade Constitutions

To accomodate the irruption of so many newcomers Britain was prepared for a new beginning in British North America, but first it was necessary to decide just how much should belong to the republic. This task occupied the peace commissioners from 1782 until the Treaty of Versailles was concluded in 1783.

The British negotiations were carried on by governments in which Lord Shelburne's was the leading voice. His thinking was that of the advanced theorist, Adam Smith, whose *Wealth of Nations* had appeared in 1776 and who in attacking mercantilism had argued for *laissez-faire*. For this reason Shelburne was not particularly interested in hanging on to territory, for in the new age it would matter not a jot who controlled the land but who could produce and sell for less; to the most efficient would go the spoils. Shelburne was confident that Britain, already well launched on the Industrial Revolution, would be able to undersell the Americans for generations to come. Since a generous peace would draw the United States to Britain and away from France, which gave evidence of wanting to meddle in the North Atlantic fisheries again, he had every reason for being modest in his territorial demands. Thus, when a dividing line running through the Great Lakes was proposed, the British negotiators agreed.

There was considerable protest in Britain over Shelburne's approach. The mercantilists were still a force to be reckoned with; Britain was still in military control of the Old Northwest, had good claims to that part of America, and needed to yield nothing to the Americans in respect of it. Resistance to Shelburne was partly successful. His plan for virtual free trade between Britain and the United States was defeated, but on the boundary his concessions were allowed to stand, with the result that the American border ran much further to the north than the Americans had any right to expect. John Jay, the American negotiator, summed it up:

> It was impolitic for Britain to oppose America on the point of boundary because the profits of an extensive and lucrative commerce, and not the possession of vast tracts of wilderness were the true objects of a commercial nation.

. . . It was therefore not wise for Britain to think of extending Canada southward or retaining any part of a country which was not in her power to settle and govern.

The concession was galling to the Quebec fur traders, however. They petitioned Shelburne, pointing out that many posts would have to be given up, and that Grand Portage, the door to the far west, would now be in the hands of an alien power. Over 50 percent of the fur trade profits, it was alleged, came from the area now to be ceded. However, such protests counted for little when the reconstruction of an entire empire was at stake.

One consequence of the loss of the south shore of the Great Lakes was especially regrettable. That territory was the home of the Iroquois who had long been allies of the British. In 1775 the Americans had sought to make them neutral, saying that "this is a family quarrel between Us and old England. You Indians are not concerned in it." However, some Mohawk turned out for the British and helped delay Montgomery's advance. In time they were joined by other Iroquois, especially after their chieftain Joseph Brant returned from Britain in 1776. Neutrality was at an end, and most joined one or other of the combatants. When the terms of the treaty were announced, the Indians who had fought for Britain were shocked and furious. Not only had they lost territory, they had lost status. They had imagined that they were a sovereign people allied with the British. Now they had been disposed of like any subjects. They protested that

The English had basely betrayed them by pretending to give up their Country to the Americans without their Consent, or Consulting them[;] it was an act of Cruelty and injustice that Christians *only* were capable of doing, that the Indians were incapable of acting so, to friends and Allies.

To this, Shelburne could only reply that "the Indian nations were not abandoned to their enemies; they were remitted to the care of neighbours."

Brant did not wish to be "remitted to the care of neighbours." He made known his preference to settle in Canada. Haldimand furthered his request. Some of his people were settled near the Bay of Quinté, but the bulk moved to the Grand River to have "Six Miles deep from each side of the River beginning at Lake Erie, and extending in that proportion to the Head of the said River, which they and their Posterity are to enjoy for ever." Even then, despite imperial good intentions, problems arose. The authorities provided supplies and pensions to the Indians. They tried to prevent them alienating the land, or even leasing portions, to whites, so that advantage should not be taken of them. While the more traditionalist Indians were behind this policy, others argued that Indians should be allowed to manage their resources as they saw fit. There was more land, they claimed, than the Indians could possibly ever use. That dispute is still current, and litigation is underway about white "ownership" in the Haldimand Grant. Not for the first nor the last time, the limits of good intentions in Indian affairs were made evident.

Dwarfing this problem of relocation was that posed by white Loyalists. The large numbers of people descending on Nova Scotia caused more than material disruption. The Loyalists were contemptuous of the neutrals who had been, they thought, halfhearted in support of the British cause. Bad feeling was rife, and threatened to inject a jarring note into the legislature. The imperial government was happy, therefore, to hive off a new colony, New Brunswick, as a Loyalist haven. There were other advantages in dividing up Nova Scotia. Prominent Loyalists needed to be given "jobs," and the more colonies there were the greater the possibilities. Small colonies might be easier to control, and so avoid the late troubles. For these reasons, then, Cape Breton was also severed from Nova Scotia, and enjoyed an independent existence until 1820.

The reorganization of the Maritimes was a relatively straightforward matter. That of Quebec was not. It was not the handling of the bulk of the Loyalists that caused the problem. Haldimand, not wishing to complicate matters by having them link up with the existing English-speaking inhabitants, shunted them off to the shores of Lake Ontario where they were to hack a living out of the forest. There, to the west of existing settlement, it was easily possible to erect a province that would give them what they, as Americans, yet as Loyalists, wanted. In 1791 the Quebec Act was amended by the Constitutional Act and the colony was divided. The opportunity was grasped to make the new colony — Quebec west of Montreal, to be known as Upper Canada — into as close an approximation of Britain, constitutionally, as possible. The lessons of the American Revolution had been assimilated (and the looming excesses of the French Revolution were even then confirming them), and there was general agreement in the government at Westminster that the Second British Empire was to avoid the mistakes of the first by replicating on the Great Lakes that true balance of monarchy, aristocracy, and democracy that characterized the mother country. The executive was to be headed by a lieutenant governor, the representative of the king, armed with considerable powers. He could veto bills, and in addition might reserve bills for the approbation of the Crown itself; if this were not enough, the imperial authorities might disallow an Act within two years of its passing. Furthermore, there was provision in the Constitutional Act to render the executive free to a large extent of any financial control; no less than one seventh of the vacant land was to be set aside as a Crown reserve, the income from which, whether by sale or by lease, would give the executive the funds to develop the colony in the way it chose. Finally, the lieutenant governor was to be assisted by an executive council, whose members were to be appointed by him and were responsible to him.

Particular attention was given to the aristocratic element. It was the settled opinion of those who pondered the loss of the Thirteen Colonies that their great weakness had been the lack of a genuinely aristocratic chamber. Upper houses there were in the lost colonies, but they had no real independence and were not faithful transcripts of the House of Lords; frequently they were elected by the lower houses or had short lives. The Constitutional Act changed this radically. A legislative council was set up; its members were named by the lieutenant governor and held their seats for life. Indeed, there was an even more revealing provision written into the Act, namely the power to create an hereditary aristocracy with the right of summons to the legislative council — though in the event that part of the Act was never implemented.

A further novelty was introduced to buttress the emphasis upon the monarchical and aristocratic ethos. A natural concomitant of such a polity is an established church. To accompany the Crown reserve was an equivalent clergy reserve, again one seventh of the ungranted lands, intended to support the Church of England. In the time-honoured way, then, the natural alliance of Church and Crown would work to hold the democratic elements in due subordination.

If the framers of the Constitutional Act intended a close fit between British and Upper Canadian forms, they were fated to be disappointed. In part, this was due to ambiguities in the Act, ambiguities which in time would wreak havoc. The clauses dealing with the clergy reserve did not clearly and legally spell out that the Church of England should be an established church; references there were to Protestantism, but was this to be restricted to Anglicanism, extended to the Church of Scotland, or even applied to the sectarians who quickly came to represent the essence of the province's religiosity? In the years to come, wrangling over the clergy reserve would go far to ruin that balance and harmony that the authors of the Act intended.

The main cause, however, of the failure to assimilate Britain and the colony was the impossibility of making the democratic element conform to the imperial model. In Britain the House of Commons was an elitist body, filled with the sons of nobles, members of the establishment, and contained almost no one who could be said to represent the ordinary man; how could it be otherwise where deference was so marked and when the franchise was so restricted that in a population of some seven million perhaps some 100 000 at most had the vote? When Upper Canada was given an assembly, the vote was similarly given to any who met the English qualification. However, whereas in England the landholding pattern excluded most, in North America the wide availability of land meant that virtually every adult male was enfranchised. Broad democratic participation allied to shallow aristocratic roots (bear in mind, the planned hereditary component could never be realized) meant a lower house with a pronounced potential for making trouble.

"Defects" such as these, however, lay in the future. In 1791, under the tutelage of Governor Simcoe, the boast was the identity of parent country and child colony. This identity was made all the more striking when the law, both civil and criminal, was made English, and when seigneurial tenures were abolished to be replaced by freehold.

In Quebec east of Montreal, now to be known as Lower Canada, the identity was not to be so marked: the tension between conflicting outlooks was too strong. On the one hand were the merchants, both English- and French-speaking, who were in favour of ending Quebec's anomalous status and of moving the colony closer to the British norm, and who had been petitioning Westminster to this end since 1784. The recently arrived Loyalists naturally lent weight to their plea. On the other hand were the *seigneurs*, who asked for the *status quo* and rested their case on an interpretation of the Quebec Act as the inviolable "charter" of French-Canadian identity. Above all, there was the sheer mass of the population, still over 90 percent *Canadien*. The governor, Carleton, reappointed and elevated to the peerage as Lord Dorchester, was not able to side effectively with either party. Earlier he had given pledges to the French Canadians, and more recently he had done the same to the Loyalists, with the result that he felt hamstrung. "For my own part," he wrote to England, "I confess myself as yet at a loss for any plan likely to give satisfaction." Perhaps inevitably, the Constitutional Act in Lower Canada was a compromise between the two positions.

Constitutionally there was a parallel between the two Canadas. A powerful governor was provided with an executive council responsible to him; a legislative council on the nominated-for-life principle was established; an assembly was granted, again on the basis of a wide franchise; Crown and clergy reserves were set aside. Yet, to offset these Anglicizing elements, seigneurialism was retained (with the proviso that, in the case of new grants, freehold tenure might be used — The Eastern Townships were an anglophone enclave developed in the period after 1791), the *de facto* establishment of the Catholic Church was maintained, and French civil law persisted.

Formal concessions to the anglophones in Lower Canada might have been few, but even so a new atmosphere was evident after 1784 and 1791. The English element had been crucially enlarged, and merchant aggressiveness was given a boost by a Loyalist infusion that was distinctive and disruptive. After 1791 they had an assembly with the power to raise a revenue and so to foster their mercantile ends. Moreover, their familiarity with the parliamentary tradition, coupled with the francophone inexperience, meant an ability to dominate the democratic process in the formative years; they seized the opportunity to proclaim what they believed to be the superiority of their values. At the same time, the merchants were furious that the natural unity of the St. Lawrence had been broken, while the existence next door of an exclusively British Upper Canada tended to focus their resentment upon the French Canadians, for whose welfare the imperial authorities had sacrificed that of the English. The tone of English-French Canadian relationships was changing.

The view emerged that anything that had been left to the *Canadiens* had been so because it was insignificant or ephemeral; language, religion, and their own land system were increasingly becoming the marks not only of difference but of inferiority. Before 1791 Quebec had been a French-Canadian society with a tiny English element. Most inhabitants would have been conscious of the anglophones, if at all, as an élite, not really part of society. After 1791 Lower Canada became a dual society. For instance, after 1791, Protestantism became a meaningful alternative. Not only was a clergy reserve, as in Upper Canada, set aside for Protestants, but an Anglican bishop, Jacob Mountain, was appointed, and given a salary ten times that paid to the Roman Catholic bishop. This was to articulate a distinctively British set of values, and also to underline which was deemed the superior culture.

## Suggested Reading

The background to the rebellion of the Thirteen Colonies is traced in B. Bailyn, *The Origin of American Politics* (1965). The impact of the Navigation Acts and their administration is examined in T. Barrow, *Trade and Empire* (1960), and E.S. and H.M. Morgan, *The Stamp Act Crisis* (1953). See also B.W. Labaree, *The Boston Tea Party* (1964).

On those colonies that remained loyal, see G. Stewart and G. Rawlyk, *A People Highly Favoured of God* (1972), G. Rawlyk, *Revolution Rejected* (1968), and J.M. Bumsted, *Henry Alline* (1971). The older work of J.B. Brebner, *The Neutral Yankees of Nova Scotia* (1937), remains valuable. Quebec reaction to American initiatives is examined in A.S. Everest, *Moses Hazen & the Canadian Refugees in the American Revolution* (1976) and in G.F.G. Stanley, *Canada Invaded* (1973).

In general on the situation of the Atlantic colonies at this time readers may consult A.M. Clark, *Three Centuries and the Island: A Historical Geography of Settlement and Agriculture in Price Edward Island* (1959); F.W.P. Bolger (ed.), *Canada's Smallest Province* (1973); G.O. Rothney, *Newfoundland: A History* (1959); C.G. Head, *Eighteenth Century Newfoundland* (1976); A H. Clark, "New England's Role in the Underdevelopment of Cape Breton Island during the French Regime, 1713-1758," *Canadian Geographer* (1965).

The Loyalists have attracted a large and interesting examination. The following are recommended: J. Potter, *The Liberty We Seek: Loyalist Ideology in Colonial New York and Massachusetts* (1983); W.H. Nelson, *The American Tory* (1961); W. Brown, *The King's Friends* (1965); W. Brown and H. Senior, *Victorious in Defeat* (1984); a useful anthology is L.F.S. Lipton, *The United Empire Loyalists* (1967); D.V.J. Bell, "The Loyalist Tradition in Canada," *Journal of Canadian Studies* (1970); D. Stouck, "The Wardell Family and the Origins of Loyalism," *Canadian Historical Review* (1987). A particularly interesting study, since it forms part of a provocative and fruitful approach to Canadian History in general is K. McRae, "The Structure of Canadian History," in L. Hartz, *The Founding of New Societies* (1964).

The role of the Indians is studied in J.M. Sosin, "The Use of Indians in the War of the American Revolution," *Canadian Historical Review* (1965). See also C. M. Johnston, "Joseph Brant, the Grand River Lands, and the Northwest Crisis," *Ontario History* (1963), and *The Valley of the Six Nations* (1964).

The Constitutional Act may be examined through two volumes in the Centenary Series: G.M. Craig, *Upper Canada* (1963), and F. Ouellet, *Lower Canada* (1980). The genesis of the Act is described in the concluding chapter of the previous volume, H. Neatby, *Quebec: The Revolutionary Age* (1966). The operation of the clergy reserves is treated in G.A. Wilson, *The Clergy Reserves of Upper Canada* (1968).

# CHAPTER 13

## NEW BRITISH EMPIRE

## — 1. Business as Usual —

For Canada, the slogan of the last quarter of the eighteenth century was "business as usual." The political arrangements just arrived at were an expression of the belief that no change was needed, other than a return to the principles of true balance. It was to be the same in economic matters. Fur, which had been the mainstay of the northern colonies from the beginning, still held pride of place and the fur traders, rising to the challenges of the day, were going to continue to make even bigger fortunes.

The challenges the fur trade faced were very real. The opposition from the Hudson's Bay Company was telling. The new policy of going out to the Indians was beginning to bear fruit, and a series of leapfrogging exercises began, first with the Bay traders and then the Montrealers pushing ever farther across the continent. To the south, there was the problem caused by the United States. The Ohio-Mississippi triangle, the Southwest in fur-trading parlance, now belonged to the Americans. For some years after 1783 British traders and the military continued to hang on to the posts there, using as an excuse the fact that Loyalist claims for compensation (addressed in the Treaty of Versailles) had not been dealt with satisfactorily. This occupation could not last, however, and by Jay's Treaty in 1794 the evacuation of the area was agreed upon, to be completed within two years. Loss of the Southwest was bearable, however, for the superiority of the newly penetrated Athabaska region was patent. Concentration upon the Northwest followed.

Montreal responded to these challenges by experimenting with new structures to increase their operating efficiency. The first push in this direction came from the American invasion of 1775. At the advance of the invaders, all powder in Montreal was immediately thrown into the St. Lawrence. It was an understandable military precaution, but a disaster from the point of view of the fur traders, since it was an indispensable item in their outfits. At the same time, the authorities prohibited private vessels on the Great Lakes, since they could not risk supplies falling into rebel hands; here too, however, the disruption to the fur trade was catastrophic. To guard their interests, and to bring pressure to bear upon the military, the leading traders in 1779 formed themselves into a loose organization under the name of the North West Company. The arrangement was for one year only, but the usefulness of pooling resources was such that after further experiments a similar loose co-partnership, but this time to last for five years, was put together in the winter of 1783-84. This organization was to dominate Canadian economic life for the next generation and more.

Control of the North West Company was in the hands of the partners, leading Montreal houses that had shares in the venture. Thus, in the early days there were 16 shares, and firms such as those of the Frobisher brothers and of Simon McTavish held two each, while a trader like Peter Pond, a dynamic, illiterate, and unscrupulous fellow who had opened up the Athabaska region (and had probably murdered three men in the process), but who lacked the financial resources of the others, had to be content with one share. Over the years there were additions, deletions, and recombinations, but the names of Frobisher, McTavish, and McGillivray (the last were nephews of McTavish) remained prominent, indeed predominant. Nevertheless, if Montreal was the headquarters, care was taken to maintain good relations with the far extremities of the trading chain. Business affairs in London were in the hands of efficient firms, notably McTavish, Fraser & Co. and Inglis, Ellice & Co., that also had the ear of prominent politicians. Relations with the traders on the spot, in the far west, were excellent. The winterers were rewarded by having their fortunes depend upon the return of the trade, an incentive sufficiently powerful to be copied eventually by the Hudson's Bay Company. Moreover, the winterers were serving apprenticeships, the successful completion of which might secure entry into the ranks of the full partners. Above all, the importance of the winterers in the *pays d'en haut* was symbolized by the fact that membership in the Beaver Club was open only to those who had spent a year beyond the Grand Portage.

Such factors went far towards making Montreal able to compete by overcoming the disadvantages of a long supply line and the need for credit extending over several years. One more problem had to be overcome, however. The length of that supply line was such that the difficulties of merely staying alive threatened to leave no time for travelling and trading; days spent hunting deer or fishing were unaffordable luxuries when the race was on every season to escape before the freeze-up. This problem was solved, by Peter Pond it seems, when the Chipewyan secret of preparing pemmican was learned. As the old trader Alexander Henry put it in a letter of 1781, "it is not only the provisions for the winter season, but for the course of next summer, must be provided which is dry'd meat, pounded to a powder, and mixed up with Buffaloes' greese which preserves it in the warm seasons here." In turn the supply of pemmican became a sizable industry itself, one without which the conquest of its far-flung empire by Montreal would not have been possible.

The success of the Canadian fur trade and of that of the North West Company in particular was indicated by the analysis of 1795. It was reckoned that 11/14 of the fur trade in northern America was carried on by that company, with only 2/14 going to the Hudson's Bay Company and 1/14 to Canadian independents. So well entrenched was the company that the fur-trading imperative towards monopoly worked only in its favour. From time to time disagreements did arise in the close-knit world of the fur traders; from time to time political changes brought about commercial realignments. A good example of a challenge to the North West Company came in 1798, when Alexander Mackenzie led a protest rooted more in personalities than in anything else. At the same time, those outfits driven out of the Southwest, notably, Forsythe, Richardson and Company, were seeking to move into the Northwest. Their combination saw the foundation of the New North West Company (also known as the XY Company from the brand marks on their bales of goods). It had its successes, but by 1804 realism dictated its merging with the older "firm." The virtual monopoly had been reimposed.

On that basis there emerged in Montreal an elite with wealth and style. Fur traders bought *seigneuries*, built imposing mansions, and entertained lavishly. It was not a feudal society exactly, for the traders were too conscious of sound commercial practices — when McTavish died in 1804 leaving a fortune he took care to stipulate that no legacies over 100 guineas were to be paid out for seven years unless "sufficient money for that purpose shall have been realized . . . without loss or inconvenience to the concern or conerns in which I am now a partner." Yet there was something feudal about it, certainly something patriarchal: that same McTavish was known as "The Marquis" and bought up the ancestral clan home in Scotland. The wherewithal was available, and it must have seemed at the beginning of the new century that fur was to maintain its primacy, and within that primacy it was to be Montreal that should rule. Appearances were deceptive, however. The dominance of Montreal was to yield to York Factory, and fur was to give way to new staples.

## — 2. The Hudson's Bay Company Revitalized —

The North West Company had even greater grounds for optimism as they contemplated the fortunes of their one imposing rival. The Hudson's Bay Company was an all but lifeless hulk, drifting aimlessly, and looking to founder; its shares, which had recently traded at 250 pounds, were down to 50 pounds and the usual 8 percent dividend had to be halved and finally given up altogether in 1809. The North West Company seemed on the point of taking over its competitor; so aggressive had it become that it was negotiating for transit rights through the Bay, and it even sent its own ship into the area and set up depots on Charlton Island.

Any anticipated takeover was ruled out, however, when the direction of the Bay Company's affairs passed to new leadership. One of the new men was Andrew Wedderburn (he added the name Colvile about this time), the other, Thomas Douglas, Fifth Earl of Selkirk, who had married Colvile's sister in 1807. Colvile brought a new drive to the company, and a concern for efficiency. Under him waste was cut out, costs brought under control, and the system of using agents on commission in place of salaried managers, a system recently borrowed from the North West Company, was rapidly extended. Selkirk was deeply committed to overseas settlement as a means of relieving agricultural distress in the United Kingdom. The new methods which were remaking agriculture even as they were ushering in the Industrial Revolution were leaving large tracts of land depopulated. This was especially the case in Scotland, where overpopulation and inefficient farming were exacerbated by a massive shift to sheep runs. Selkirk, himself a Scot, saw British

## Map 13.1:  British North America in 1812

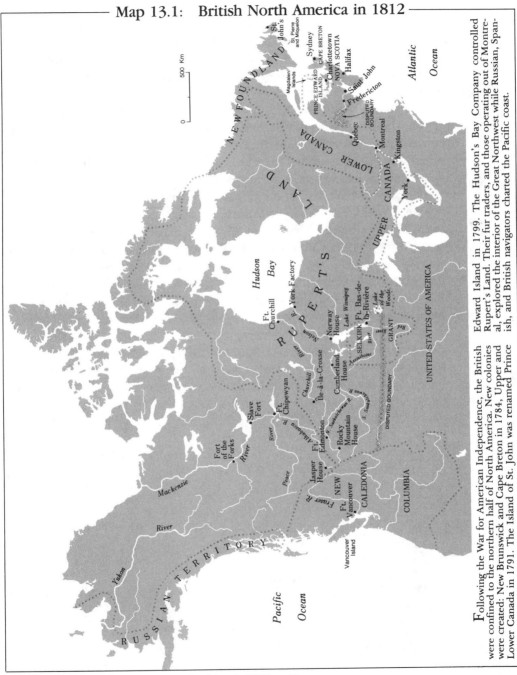

Following the War for American Independence, the British were confined to the northern half of North America. New colonies were created: New Brunswick and Cape Breton in 1784, Upper and Lower Canada in 1791. The Island of St. John was renamed Prince Edward Island in 1799. The Hudson's Bay Company controlled Rupert's Land. Their fur traders, and those operating out of Montreal, explored the interior of the Great Northwest while Russian, Spanish, and British navigators charted the Pacific coast.

SOURCE: Adapted from Kerr, *Historical Atlas of Canada* (1975), p. 40.

North America as a haven for the dispossessed farmers. He had previously experimented with colonies in Prince Edward Island and Upper Canada, but now, using his family connections with and shareholding in the Hudson's Bay Company, he thought to take up the colonizing provisions (so far unused) in that company's own charter. In 1811 the company granted him the colony of Assiniboia, 300 000 square kilometres surrounding the site of present-day Winnipeg.

The grant infuriated the Nor'Westers. The projected settlement lay athwart their supply line from the St. Lawrence to the Pacific slope. Agriculture and the fur trade had ever been antithetical, the former calling for a dense settlement that would disrupt wildlife, the latter requiring sparse settlement that would not disrupt the animal population, and for this reason alone the Montrealers were incensed. What made Selkirk's vision even more threatening was the strategic role that the Red River played in the Nor'Westers' system. There the Métis settlements, composed mainly of offspring of Indian women and French *voyageurs*, had specialized in preparing pemmican, the lifeblood of the extended trade. With the colony, an offshoot of the Hudson's Bay Company, astride this key portion of the lifeline, the two halves of the North West Company's operation would split apart and each would die.

The situation called for decisive action. At first it had seemed that the difficulties of the project would defeat it before it was launched; when Simon McGillivray, writing under a *nom de plume* in the *Inverness Journal*, pointed out the dangers involved he was able to dissuade many. It had seemed that the rigour of the climate, coupled with bad planning, would abort the expedition: of the advance party of 105 men that left in 1811 and was unable to get beyond the York Fort before the freeze-up, only 22 were in a fit state to accompany the governor, Miles Macdonell, to Red River the following summer. Finally, the difficulties of farming an unknown land had promised to complete the ruin of the plan, and in 1815, when the North West Company offered transport to Canada, the majority of the settlers gratefully accepted. Nevertheless, despite these setbacks Selkirk proved amazingly tenacious, and kept up the flow of immigrants (a cohesive party of Presbyterians from Kildonan seemed particularly promising). The Nor'Westers realized that sterner measures might have to be taken.

This realization became firmer after Macdonell had issued the Pemmican Proclamation. The failure of the first farming ventures encouraged the governor to safeguard the pemmican supplies. The North West Company representatives were told that in the yet uncultivated state of this country, the ordinary resources derived from the buffaloe and the wild animals hunted within the territory, are not deemed more than adequate for the requisite supply; wherefore it is hereby ordered that no person . . . shall take out any provisions, either flesh, grain, or vegetables, procured or raised within the said territory . . . for one twelvemonth from the date hereof . . . the provisions . . . shall be taken for the use of the colony. . . .

In pursuance of this edict, pemmican supplies were confiscated.

The rapidly degenerating situation was climaxed by resort to arms. In 1816 a party of Métis under their leader Cuthbert Grant was intercepted at Seven Oaks by the new governor of Red River, Robert Semple, and a detachment of his men; a challenge led to an altercation, and quickly to a scuffle. Someone fired, and a general shooting ensued. Semple was killed, along with 21 settlers; one Métis was slain.

Selkirk's response was to recruit Swiss mercenaries, members of the de Meurons Regiment just discharged from the British army. With their backing he confronted the Nor'Westers at their post at Fort William (now part of Thunder Bay), arresting some and seizing their papers for incriminating material. His warrant for taking the law into his hands was his commission as magistrate for the Indian Territories. However, his enemies were also prepared to use the law, and were able to get another magistrate to issue a warrant for Selkirk's arrest. Selkirk resisted this warrant, thereby putting himself in the wrong. Thus followed lawsuit upon lawsuit, both sides finding that the uncertainty about jurisdiction in the unformed territory beyond Upper Canada gave every scope for delay and prevarication. These suits settled nothing, but they did initiate a practice that continued for some time in the field. Accordingly both parties secured warrants, arrested competitors, and confiscated goods. In this novel form of guerilla warfare, the North West Company was the loser. The loose partnership gave under the strain, with some wishing to avoid any repetition of lawlessness. The Hudson's Bay Company was stiffened at the crucial moment by the appearance on the scene of George Simpson, who from his arrival in 1820 was to dominate the fur trade for the next generation. The Nor'Westers' partnership agreement was due to be renegotiated in 1821. Bowing to the inevitable, they coalesced with their rivals. The logic of a monopoly in the trade had once again triumphed, and since the geographical advantage of Hudson Bay over the St. Lawrence was undeniable, it was the Bay Company that came out on top.

## Map 13.2: Exploring the Great Northwest

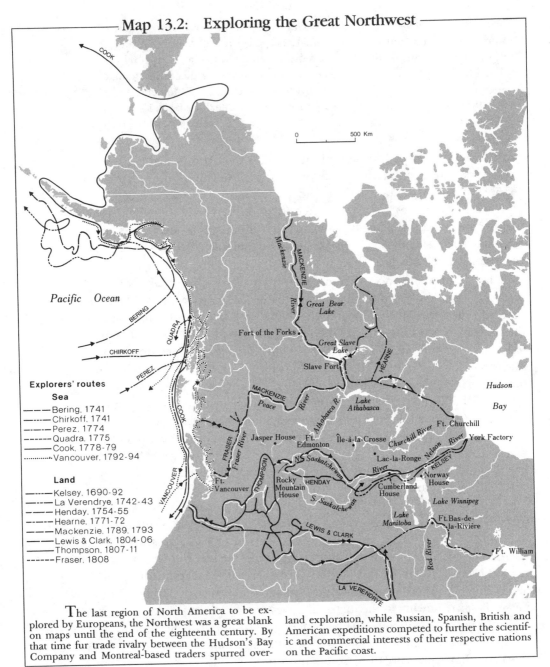

**Explorers' routes**

**Sea**

— — — Bering, 1741
— - - — Chirkoff, 1741
— · · — Perez, 1774
———— Quadra, 1775
———— Cook, 1778-79
············ Vancouver, 1792-94

**Land**

— - - — Kelsey, 1690-92
— - — La Verendrye, 1742-43
———— Henday, 1754-55
— · · — Hearne, 1771-72
———— Mackenzie, 1789, 1793
———— Lewis & Clark, 1804-06
———— Thompson, 1807-11
— — — Fraser, 1808

The last region of North America to be explored by Europeans, the Northwest was a great blank on maps until the end of the eighteenth century. By that time fur trade rivalry between the Hudson's Bay Company and Montreal-based traders spurred overland exploration, while Russian, Spanish, British and American expeditions competed to further the scientific and commercial interests of their respective nations on the Pacific coast.

SOURCES: Kerr, *Historical Atlas of Canada* (1975), p. 20; Harris, *Historical Atlas of Canada*, Vol. I, *From the Beginning to 1800* (1987), plates 58, 67.

The imperial authorities were eager to endorse the new arrangement. The legal problems sparked by Selkirk's venture were worrisome. More threatening were the signs of foreign interest — Russian and American —in the Northwest. The Act of 1821, "For regulating the Fur Trade and establishing a Criminal and Civil Jurisdiction within certain parts of North America," gave its blessing, then, to the coalition, and confirmed the Hudson's Bay Company in its monopoly in Rupert's land. The rest of the Northwest was to be a monopoly for the coalition for 21 years. Thus did the roaring days of the fur trade draw to their conclusion. That fur was now challenged by new staples only hastened that transformation.

## — 3. New Staples: Wheat —

In the two Canadas, and especially in the upper province, grain became a leading article of commerce. Already by 1802 around 30 000 tonnes were being exported down the St. Lawrence, of which a surprising amount was from a colony not even a generation old. This impressive start was due largely to the nature of the colony's birth. Upper Canada had been peopled by Loyalists, farmers familiar with North American agricultural techniques and expert in clearing the heavily forested land. Indeed, so proficient were many at this backbreaking task, they did not wait to become farmers but sold up and moved on, preferring to be "professional pioneers" who carved a clearing out of the waste every six or seven years. Moreover, the imperial authorities were generous: the land was given to the Loyalists free; food was furnished gratis for two years; implements were provided free or at reduced cost; grist mills operated toll-free until 1791. In short, the pioneers were not obliged to waste their all-important capital in getting started, but had enough to take care of emergencies and to take advantage of opportunities as they arose. In addition, the settlers had convenient markets in the early days. Whereas other pioneers often had only fellow pioneers to sell to (not the most affluent of buyers), the Loyalists of Upper Canada could sell to the fur trade (this outlet dried up only after 1821 when provisioning was done exclusively via Hudson Bay and Red River, and by then Upper Canada was over its growing pains), to the British garrisons such as the one at Kingston, and even to the American military posts that had been set up in the wake of Jay's Treaty. All told, the early settlers of Upper Canada had great advantages over those in otherwise similar circumstances, and the experience stands as a solid testimonial to state paternalism.

That there were great attractions for agriculturalists in the province was borne out by the growth of population and by the appearance of a booming land market. By 1812 there were over 75 000 inhabitants. This seems a tiny figure when set against the later totals, but a comparison with that of New France puts it in its proper light: in 30 years, Upper Canada had exceeded the population that it took New France a century and a half to build up. It was an impressive beginning to what was to be continued growth.

The speculation in land was equally impressive. It is at first difficult to see how land speculation could even exist in the province. The government's policy (if indeed it invited the term) was to make free grants to those wishing to become farmers; it went further, limiting the size of grants so that, in theory, only genuine settlers could obtain land. Practice was, however, quite divorced from theory. The land was virtually the governor's to dispose of, and it was often given away in huge blocks as a means of rewarding officials. In 1800 some 50 000 hectares were awarded to the members of a Lower Canadian Assembly Committee studying abuses in the granting of land; the grant was approved by the Duke of Portland in London, who earlier had called for land grants to be made in "a prudent, temperate and judicious manner." Retired military men were frequently singled out for large grants, as it was hoped that they would lend a suitable tone to society and also be an added protection in time of war. Loyalist grants were sometimes not wanted by the recipients. This was especially true of those made to the children of Loyalists, many of whom preferred to work the father's farm in the expectation of inheriting it and who were glad to obtain some capital in exchange for distant waste land. Above all, there was the system of leaders and associates, a well-tried system in all parts of America. Wealthy speculators such as John Richardson would come forward claiming to represent a syndicate of *bona fide* would-be farmers. They would petition for a large amount of land, undertaking to pay the survey and the legal fees. Once in possession of the land the fake associates would be bought off, perhaps for the price of a drink, and fade away, allowing sales to genuine farmers. In these various ways, then, speculators were able to amass vast parcels of land. In Simcoe county, an extreme case, as late as 1854 over 50 percent of the land was in the hands of speculators.

It was in the speculators' interests to cater to the farmers by establishing stores in the new settlements. There they sold the farmers the implements they needed and the clothes and provisions they could not or would not provide for themselves. In return, they took the products of the land and disposed of them, usually downriver in Lower Canada. Potash was often the first "crop" a farmer had; it was the fruit of the ashes obtained from burning the immense piles of trees felled in the very first years, and Europe was voracious in its demand for potash for fertilizer, soap-making, and for the textile industry. Beef and pork were also in demand, going to the United States and to the other British North American colonies, though very soon the advantages of the American Midwest phased out these specialties. The main interest was grain, especially wheat, and it was reckoned that this crop accounted for one third of all cleared land. Here Britain was the great buyer, needing the hard North American wheats to blend with its own softer varieties. The British Corn Laws of 1815, especially in their revised form after 1822, gave mercantilist protection to colonial wheat as against foreign. Even before this, Upper Canada was discovering the attractions of the new staple. As early as 1794 the governor of Upper Canada, John Simcoe, noted with surprise that in Kingston "the fur trade . . . seemed no longer the principal object of attention," and in that year the town was shipping grain down the St. Lawrence. By 1801 Durham boats with their greater capacity had to be introduced to handle the increased traffic. The stream continued to swell, interrupted only by war, and by 1820 around 15 000 tonnes were being exported from Upper Canada alone. Most of this was American wheat and flour, but by 1845 over half the exports were Canadian.

Volume such as this proclaimed what had been recognized for some time: the St. Lawrence, despite its marvellous advantages, would need to be improved by the building of canals. The commercial elite, that blend of old fur magnates and newer grain traders rooted in both the Canadas, wholeheartedly espoused the doctrine of improved waterways. This was the case moreso after the success of steam had been demonstrated: the first steamer, the *Accommodation*, had worked the St. Lawrence in 1809. Resolute and sustained action had to follow. In time it did. The Lachine Canal was begun in 1821 and finished in 1824. The Carillon, Chute à Blondeau, and Long Sault on the Ottawa River were completed in 1834 and gave improved access as far as the mouth of the Rideau River. The St. Lawrence was further improved by the Beauharnois (1842-45) and the Cornwall (1834-43) which together permitted steamboats to navigate as far as Kingston and Lake Ontario. Already that lake had been joined to Lake Erie by the Welland Canal, the first boats passing through in 1829 and an improved route completed by 1833. In addition, the Rideau Canal linked Bytown (present-day Ottawa) with Kingston, but this was primarily a military venture built at imperial expense so as to avoid the St. Lawrence route and its dangerous exposure to American domination.

These improvements were a striking achievement, but politically they were extremely disruptive. As Chapter 15 will show, they exacerbated tensions between the two Canadas and sharpened racial animosities.

## — 4. New Staples: Timber —

Britain had long looked to North America as a source of timber. A country that depended on its "wooden walls" (as Britain termed its navy/ships) to the extent that Britain did had to keep an eye open for sources of supply. As far back as 1705 an imperial statute had sought to safeguard the Crown's right to suitable timber and to foster that trade in North America. However, the fact that the Baltic supply was of better quality and cheaper to transport, and that there were longstanding links with that source, meant that no significant Atlantic timber trade developed until everything suddenly changed. In 1807 Napoleon blocked British access to the Baltic, and in desperation a new source had to be developed immediately. The sudden imposition of crushing duties on Baltic timber (Memel fir rose from 73 shillings a load in 1806 to 340 shillings in 1808) coupled with the absence of duties on colonial timber, gave the new trade a preference that immediately called it into vigorous life. The artificiality of this trade, born by belligerency out of mercantilism, was seen in the fact that by 1827 it was reckoned that to keep the Canadian trade alive required a British "tax" of 900 000 pounds per year. A desperate war had required desperate methods, and the trade having reoriented itself so nobly it was only right that it should continue to enjoy protection.

Sheltered in this way, the Canadian timber exports rose spectacularly. That of staves went up fourfold between 1805 and 1811, of deals (that is, sawn lumber at least eight centimetres thick) twelvefold, and square timber (that is, logs some six metres by three fifths) no less than twenty-four-fold. By 1819 one in every seven British ships was engaged in the timber trade of British North America. The commitment of the British colonies in America to timber was even greater: by mid-century wood products were 44 percent of all exports from the two Canadas; in the case of New Brunswick it was an amazing 78 percent.

The income generated by this trade was huge, but little went to Canadians. The big houses were overwhelmingly owned or dominated by Britons. A good example was the giant Gilmour, Rankin & Co., an offshoot set up by the Glasgow house of Pollock, Gilmour & Co., which sent representatives when the Baltic duties were imposed. From time to time native concerns emerged: Cunard's, a branch of the shipping firm, was one, but in its titanic struggle with Gilmour, Rankin & Co., it overreached itself and went bankrupt in 1848. Others tended to be taken over by the British and became branch plants. For too many Canadians timber was a "gambling" trade, and they declined to enter it, preferring the smaller but safer profits to be made in land speculation, grain forwarding, and the like. They reasoned that timber was liable to sudden and alarming fluctuations, that there were too many opportunities for total loss either in bringing logs to Quebec or on the high seas — this last was all too possible since timber ships were old and notoriously overloaded. Even so, there was remarkably little turnover in the trade, the established houses being able to ride out the ups and downs of the market. The reluctance of Canadians to take part in directing the trade seems in fact to have been a psychological failure of nerve. Accordingly profits tended to slip away from Canada.

Already the mixed nature of the blessings of the timber rush becomes apparent, which further examination only confirms. Benefits proved illusory not only at the controlling end. The lower end, the shanty men who went out to the forest in the winter and cut timber, and the *draveurs* who in the spring guided the logs downstream to Quebec or St. John, also enjoyed dubious benefits. The work was long, arduous, and dangerous: in 1845 on the Ottawa alone no fewer than 80 lives were lost in the drive and to logjams. The monotony of the camps and the dangers of the drive were exorcised in the roistering that took place when the men were paid off. A year's wages would disappear in an orgy of overindulgence. Penniless, the shanty man would be obliged to sign on for another year merely to get by. There were some who resisted temptation and used their cash to get themselves started on a farm or in a business, but these were the exceptions. For the majority the attempt to combine farming and lumbering was usually disastrous; as early as the 1820s a commentator noted that the timber trade "may rather be termed as necessary evil than a benefit to a young country. The settler . . . from Europe . . . if he . . . devote himself steadily to agriculture . . . will . . . become eventually independent; but he is more frequently tempted by his first little gains to engage in 'lumbering.' " The proper balance between the two occupations was almost impossible to find, the result being that as New Brunswick's timber exports rose, so too did the imports of food stuffs.

The deleterious effects were not confined to the purely economic. Especially in the early days the trade tended to inspire contempt for law and order. Philemon Wright, an American (but no Loyalist) who opened up the Ottawa in the winter of 1805 and went on to become a pillar of respectability, was openly contemptuous of legality, sending his crews in to cut timber on reserve land if he thought he could get away with it. He could console himself with the thought that if he did not steal it, one of his rivals undoubtedly would. Among the crews themselves a similar lawlessness prevailed. Pitched battles between rival gangs were frequent, notably those between the Irish Shiners and the French Canadians for control of the Ottawa in the mid-1830s. The world of lumber encouraged a piratical, catch-as-catch-can attitude, an acceptance of a carefree outlook on life.

The method of "making timber" was just as primitive. Square timber was demanded, and as time went on the proportion of this product rose at the expense of deals. Europe always looked with suspicion on North American deals since they were not sawn with the care that the Baltic traders managed, and were liable to more warping on the long Atlantic haul. Wright discovered this to his cost, because his experiments in sawn lumber found no takers and he quickly went back to trading in square timber.

To obtain the desired article whole forests were razed. First the smaller trees and shrubs had to be chopped down to give access and to provide a bed for the pine. Many trees, once felled, had to be discarded, as inspection might reveal rot in the heart of the wood; in that case the entire tree would simply be abandoned. If the tree passed inspection, then the gang would set to work with their broadaxes. The first, the liner, removed the bark and marked the dimensions of the finished log; the second, the scorer, would rough-trim the trunk to the lines; finally the hewer would smooth-finish the job, working so expertly that the two finished sides would appear to have been planed. The trunk would then be rotated and the process completed for the remaining two sides.

By the time an area had been "lumbered out," a mess of tangled scrub, discarded pines, and wood chips littered the ground. As it dried it provided ideal material for forest fires. Not many were as destructive as the one on the Miramichi in 1824, which killed 160, destroyed 600 buildings, and consumed timber stands valued at half a million pounds, but the havoc they wreaked in sum was awful.

Getting the logs to tide water was also primitive. Drams or cribs, rectangles some ten metres by thirty, were built. Sticks were laid within and over the frame, the whole kept together by pegs and withes; these last were thin saplings twisted together to form a kind of cable. Some ten drams were then joined and the result was a raft, the product of a season's work in the bush. They could be of monstrous dimension; one seen in the 1840s was reckoned to be over a hectare in extent, which is appreciably more than the size of a football field. These ungainly monsters were vulnerable to the rapids, and in

1829 Ruggles Wright, Philemon's son, introduced timber slides after seeing their operation in the Baltic. However, with that exception, rafting remained a primitive art, awe-inspiring and even majestic, but undeniably primitive.

It has sometimes been alleged in defense of the timber trade that it at least opened the country up for agriculture by doing some of the preparatory work of clearing, but the tangle left by the woodsmen was hardly an improvement. Anyway, pineries were on sandy soil unsuitable for agriculture; the pioneers learned to choose land by the kind of trees it bore and it was well said in an 1820s handbook that "Pine, hemlock and cedar land is hardly worth accepting as a present." If anything, the timber trade probably had a detrimental effect upon settlement patterns, a price still being paid today.

The two leading historians of the timber trade, A.R.M. Lower and M.S. Cross, have recognized its romantic aspects. At the same time, however, they have recognized its darker side, its failure to contribute as it should have to the development of the colonies. In their different ways they echo the warnings of Peter Fisher, a New Brunswicker writing in 1825. He observed:

> The persons principally engaged in shipping the timber have been strangers who have taken no interest in the welfare of the country; but have merely occupied a spot to make what they could in the shortest possible time. Some have done well, and others have had to quit the trade; but whether they won or lost, the capital of the country has been wasted, and no improvement of any consequence made to compensate for it, or to secure a source of trade when the lumber shall fail. Instead of seeing towns built, farms improved and the country cleared and stocked with the reasonable returns of so great a trade; the forests are stripped and nothing left in prospect, but the gloomy apprehension when the timber is gone, of sinking into insignificance and poverty.

## Suggested Reading

As a background to company histories of the fur trade, readers may want to consult E.W. Morse, *Fur Trade Canoe Routes of Canada* (1979). On the Hudson's Bay Company: G. Williams, "Highlights in the History of the First Two Hundred Years of the Hudson's Bay Company," *The Beaver* (1970), and D. MacKay, *The Honourable Company* (1966). For the North West Company, see M.W. Campbell, *The North West Company* (1957), and E.E. Rich, *Montreal and the Fur Trade* (1966). For the imperial and American setting, there is the older but still useful A.L. Burt, *The United States, Great Britain, and North America* (1940).

The collision of the two companies in Assiniboia is well treated in W.L. Morton, *Manitoba: A History* (1957). The major project of publishing Selkirk's writings, edited by J.M. Bumsted, will be invaluable; see J.M. Bumsted (ed.), *The Collected Writings of Lord Selkirk* (1984) (volumes in progress). Important recent work on the Métis includes J. Brown, *Strangers in Blood: Fur Trade Company Families in Indian Country* (1980), and S. Van Kirk, *"Many Tender Ties": Women in Fur Trade Society* (1980).

The land question of Upper Canada is treated in *Land Policies of Upper Canada* (1968), by L.F. Gates. There is also a host of articles coming out of the work headed by D. Gagan; see, for example, "Property and Interest: Some Preliminary Evidence of Land Speculation by the 'Family Compact' in Upper Canada, 1820-1840," in *Ontario History* (1978). Also important is C.G. Karr, *The Canada Land Company* (1974). The agricultural history of the province is set out in R.L. Jones, *History of Agriculture in Ontario* (1977). Important also is D. McCall, "The Wheat Staple and Upper Canadian Development," *Canadian Historical Association Reports* (1978). The Lower Canadian wheat economy is examined in T.J.A. LeGoff, "The Agricultural Crisis in Lower Canada, 1802-12," *Canadian Historical Review* (1974).

A classic (with all that is implied by that term) is D.G. Creighton's, *Commercial Empire of the St. Lawrence* (1937). A treatment of transportation in the region is G.P. Glazebrook, *A History of Transportation in Canada* (1964). A more specialized study is H.J. Aitken, *The Welland Canal Company* (1954).

The timber trade is covered by A.R.M. Lower, *Great Britain's Woodyard* (1973). The New Brunswick experience is dealt with by G. Wynn, *Timber Colony* (1981). There is also D. McCalla, "Forest Products and Upper Canadian Development, 1815-46," *Canadian Historical Review* (1987). The more social aspects of the trade are to be found in M. Cross, "Lumber Community of Upper Canada, 1815-67," *Ontario History* (1960), and "The Shiners' War: Social Violence in the Ottawa Valley in the 1830s," *Canadian Historical Review* (1973).

Economic treatments that provide a useful framework are D.L. Marr and D.G. Paterson, "Renewable Natural Resource Exploitation," in *Canada: An Economic History* (1980), and M. Watkins, "A Staple Theory of Economic Growth," *Canadian Journal of Economics and Political Science* (1963).

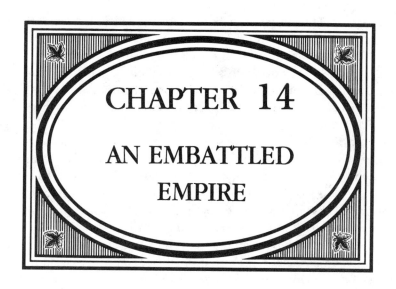

# CHAPTER 14

## AN EMBATTLED EMPIRE

## — 1. War Threatened and War Renewed —

Between 1793 and 1815, with only a short break from 1801 to 1803, Britain was once again locked in war with her inveterate enemy, France. So far these Revolutionary and Napoleonic Wars have been alluded to only with respect to their impact on the timber trade. Of course war on such a scale had to have a wider impact, and this chapter will sketch something of the effects the worldwide struggle had upon British North America.

Any war with France had to revive the spectre of a resurrected French Empire in the New World. Fears of French intervention in Canada and what had been Acadia were not without basis. In 1793 and 1794 there were rumours of impending French invasions, given substance in the latter year by the presence in New York of a French naval squadron. In 1796 these fears were borne out when a naval force landed to attack St. John's, Newfoundland; however, the strength of the defense dissuaded the French and they withdrew without causing significant damage. Lower Canada was visited by

French agents. The bordering state of Vermont, which had been an independent republic from 1777 to 1791 and which still hankered after its autonomy, was dickering with the French, and its leading citizen, Ira Allen, was in Paris from 1790 to 1800 exploring possible annexation. There, too, rumours of invasion circulated, this one planned for 1797. Somewhat later even distant Upper Canada was fearful lest the French reestablish their former hold over the Indians and turn them against the British.

In time, fears like these were seen to be insubstantial. Another fear, however, overshadowed that of military invasion, and had a major bearing on developments in Lower Canada. What distinguished this war from previous French wars was that France had succumbed to godless revolution. Within a few years of 1789 the revolution had gone so far as to repudiate religion, to institute the cult of the Supreme Being, and to persecute the Catholic Church. The king had been guillotined, and absolutism toppled. In the view of many a *Canadien*, evil was loose in the land. Napoleon could not remedy the situation; the emperor had the sense to return to hierarchy and centralization, but his concordat with the Pope made a servant of the Church and degraded its head. For true Catholics, Napoleon was the "Anti-Christ." This characterization of France and its leader came early to Lower Canada's bishop, Plessis. He raged against "those monstrous principles preached by Diderot, Voltaire, . . . Rousseau, . . . D'Alembert and other deists of the century." A victory for France would mean that

> In the midst of your cities the deadly tree of liberty will be planted and the rights of man will be proclaimed. . . . Your laws will be made a mockery and a plaything for the arrogant foes of the human race; you will share in all the pitiable woes of the fate befallen France; you will be free, but with a freedom of oppression, which will make the dregs of the citizenry your masters and cast into the dust the estimable leaders who now possess your affection and confidence.

He warned against

> The seductive expressions of liberty, philanthropy, fraternity, equality and tolerance [which] have been eagerly seized and repeated by every mouth. The sovereign authority of the Prince has been called tyranny; religion, fanaticism; its consecrated practices, superstition; its ministers, imposters; God Himself, an illusion! When once these barriers are down, what will become of Man, my brothers? Left alone with his depraved reason, is there any misdoing of which he is incapable?

It was truly a world turned upside down that the bishop identified, and the vast mass of the population accepted his every word. The arrival in Lower Canada of 45 emigré French-speaking priests could only reinforce such attitudes.

The French Revolution effectively severed what remained of French-Canadian links with the former metropolis. When it came to deciding between "home" and religion, the latter won out convincingly. For this reason the French Canadians were all the readier to embrace anti-Americanism. Since the War of Independence, French-American contacts had always been close: the revolutionary agents, such as Henri Mazières, who slipped into the colony did so via the United States; both countries were republics. By the early years of the nineteenth century French-Canadian newspapers were insulting the Americans by comparing "Yankis" (itself a term of abuse in French-Canadian mouths) with "Austrogoths, Vandals, [and] Cannibals." As anti-Americanism increased, so too did protestations of loyalty to Britain and the British constitution, inspiring for instance, the following doggerel:

> Yes, proud English, never doubt,
> Side by side we will win out,
> For you will find our arms are stout.

Such loyal outpourings had been sparked by a clash between Britain and the United States in 1807 that was a commentary on the influence of the Napoleonic Wars and a foretaste of an even greater clash to come. In that year the British vessel *Leopard* had stopped the American *Chesapeake* on the high seas: deserters from the Royal Navy were known to be aboard. Shots had been fired, some of the crew of the *Chesapeake* had been killed, and four men were taken off by the boarding party. This was an insult to American sovereignty, but the British felt that a desperate situation justified desperate remedies. Their losses through desertion were reaching crisis proportions. The British navy was at sea in all weathers, blockading hostile coasts for as long as the ships remained seaworthy; the crews were wretchedly provisioned, and were forever risking death-dealing engagements. However, skilled seamen could be sure of employment in American ships under peacetime conditions, with excellent rates of pay, and no questions asked. It was to stop this fatal haemorrhaging that the *Leopard's* captain acted as he did.

Impressment was not the only ground for American anger. Their sense of outrage was intensified when the two principal belligerents resorted to economic warfare and in so doing squeezed the United States between them. Late in 1806 Napoleon, by the Berlin Decrees, ordered the closing of the continent of Europe to British trade. In retaliation the British issued Orders-in-Council proclaiming Europe blockaded and requiring all neutral shipping

213

to put into British ports to obtain clearance before proceeding to the continent. Napoleon's counter was the Milan Decrees of 1807 that ordered the taking of any ship that complied with the British order or that even permitted British inspection on the high seas. For neutrals it was an impossible position, and for the Americans, whose carrying trade had grown by leaps and bounds during the 1790s, especially galling. Coming on top of the *Chesapeake* incident it infuriated many Americans, often as much against the French as against the British.

The incidents of 1807 did not lead to war. President Jefferson was convinced that hostilities could be avoided by the use of economic sanctions. At first a Non-Importation Act was attempted since the United States was a desirable market for both Britain and France. When this did not work, an Embargo Act was tried by which American shipping was forbidden to trade with either country. The only results were the ruin of the American marine and the growth of the smuggling trade. The Embargo Act had to be replaced by a Non-Intercourse Act, but this was only slightly less harmful to the Americans' own carrying trade.

Five years of economic sanctions did not work. In 1812 James Madison, Jefferson's successor, declared war. There were many reasons, but the deciding one seems to have been the feeling that something had to be done. America was the only republic left in the world, and her supine acceptance of insults from others appeared to confirm the worst fears of many, that a republic could not command the virtues necessary for survival. A gesture was needed, and it did not really matter against which power war was declared. Since Britain was still seen as the great enemy, since it was felt that a second War of Independence was required to complete what was only half done in the first, and since Britain's actions had been accompanied by an arrogance that Napoleon had been careful to avoid, Britain was the chosen target. That the War of 1812 was declared five days after Britain lifted the Orders-in-Council was as fitting as the fact that it ended with the Battle of New Orleans, fought two weeks after peace had been concluded. Gestures obey a logic of their own, and it was in keeping with the mood of the "war hawks" that Henry Clay boasted that "the militia of Kentucky are alone competent to place Montreal and Upper Canada at your feet."

Clay's mood was not shared by all, however. America went to war in 1812 a badly split nation. The New England states in particular were hostile to the president and the "war hawks." It was their carrying trade that above all had been hit by the Embargo Act, and they preferred the risks of smuggling to the uncertainties of outright war. So strongly did they feel about the matter that in 1814 their delegates assembled at Hartford in a convention that threatened to do for New England what the Philadelphia Convention had done for the United States. At the same time the governor of Massachusetts sent an agent to Halifax to discuss the possibility of a separate New England peace and alliance with Britain. Only the prompt and favourable Treaty of Ghent in 1814 prevented such developments.

In the event, the two years of war made little difference to the United States. On the colonies of British North America, however, the impact was rather more profound. The next three sections will trace this impact on the other regions.

## — 2. A Phoney War —

In the Atlantic region, the War of 1812 climaxed a war situation that had prevailed for some 20 years. The Revolutionary and Napoleonic Wars that had raged since 1793 with only a brief respite between 1801 and 1803 could not but affect such a strategic portion of the ocean. War on such a scale provided a tremendous fillip to economic development. From 1793 the presence of the fleet, the prizes of the privateers, and the expansion of the garrisons meant an injection of much needed purchasing power. Naturally enough, Halifax secured most of the bounty. Indeed, so great was its pull that New Brunswick actually lost ground in the 1790s. However, when the war resumed in 1803 the economic growth was so dramatic that all parts of the region stood to benefit.

The imperial authorities recognized that the coming struggle would be a titanic one, and there was a tightening up of mercantilism to enable the empire to mobilize its every resource. For some time before this, the United States had been granted privileges within Britain's trading area, notably in the West Indies. This privilege was withdrawn, and the Atlantic region was the main beneficiary. When Jefferson collaborated by embargoing American trade, the gains to the Atlantic colonies mounted higher and higher. For both Nova Scotia and New Brunswick the value of the West Indies trade more than doubled in the five years before 1812. The authorities further capitalized upon this novel state of affairs when they passed the Free Ports Act in 1807, a development that drew hundreds of American ships to designated colonial ports in defiance of United States' laws. Moreover, after 1805, Britain knew she was supreme at sea; the crushing victory at Trafalgar over the combined French and Spanish navies had seen to that. Safe from danger, the Royal Navy could be used piecemeal in convoy work, and Maritime shipping began to sail the Atlantic, building up a carrying trade with Europe as well. For these reasons, then, the economy began to boom, and, of course, there was always the timber trade.

Even the outbreak of the War of 1812 could do little to upset this development. Given the New Englanders' refusal to embrace the war, military activity in the Atlantic region was bound to be subdued. Even had the Americans of the Northeast shown more belligerency, they would have had to recognize that Halifax was too powerful a citadel for them to attack. As it was, far from wishing to assault the city, New Englanders wished to trade there. On the British side there was no eagerness to mount an attack upon the neighbouring states. Hostilities could only weaken the "neutrality" of the New Englanders and perhaps drive them into the arms of the "war hawks." To guard against such a development, the commander of the British forces explicitly declared that he aimed "to avoid committing any act which may, even by a strained construction, tend to incite the eastern and southern states." So quiet, in fact, was the Atlantic theatre that it was felt that the 104th Regiment, raised in New Brunswick, could be spared for duty in a more threatened area. In the depths of winter the regiment was marched over 1100 kilometres, largely on snowshoes, to Kingston in Upper Canada, a tremendous undertaking accomplished in only 52 days.

This exploit led to the only aggressive land engagement in the Atlantic region. Noble though the march of the 104th had been, it nevertheless revealed how precarious and unnecessarily long the route between Halifax and the St. Lawrence was. Accordingly, the imperial strategist decreed that the New Brunswick boundary should be moved to the west at the expense of Maine. In the late summer of 1814 a British force landed in United States' territory and occupied some 160 kilometres of coast and its hinterland. Although the inhabitants showed no distress over their change of nationality, and although to dislodge the British might have been more than the Americans were prepared to undertake, the Treaty of Ghent largely nullified this expansion. However, the boundary remained uncertain until 1842 when it was essentially settled by the Webster-Ashburton Treaty.

So buoyant was the region that even Newfoundland experienced the surge. The fishing was in an excellent state: the French had lost their privileges and had been cleared out of St. Pierre and Miquelon (developments once again reversed at the peace table); the Mediterranean was open to British traders and export opportunities there were magnificent. The old view of

## Map 14.1: War of 1812

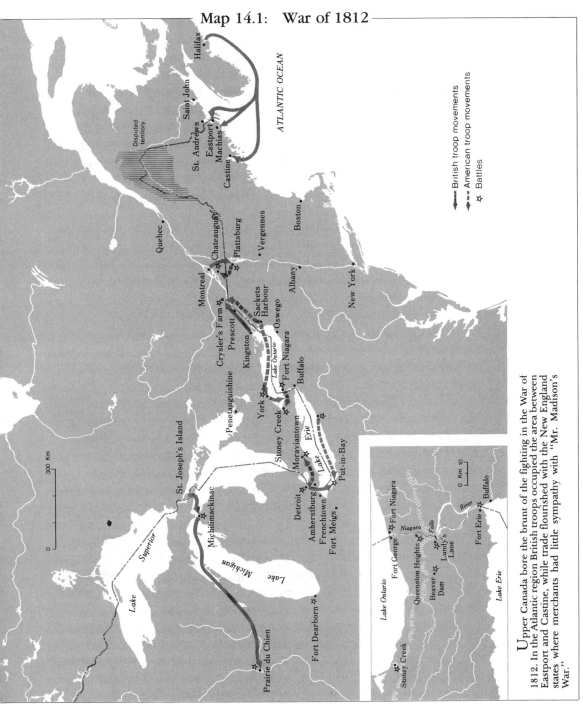

Upper Canada bore the brunt of the fighting in the War of 1812. In the Atlantic region British troops occupied the area between Eastport and Castine, while trade flourished with the New England states where merchants had little sympathy with "Mr. Madison's War."

SOURCES: Kerr, *Historical Atlas of Canada* (1975), pp. 38–9; R. Douglas Francis et al., *Origins: Canadian History to Confederation* (Toronto: Holt, Rinehart and Winston, 1988), p. 209.

the island as a platform on which to dry fish and do little else — certainly not to cultivate the soil, which was technically illegal — was already breaking down, especially as the sedentary fishing took over from deep-sea fishing carried out from the ships themselves. This new-found prosperity speeded the transformation, and it was no accident that the opening years of the nineteenth century were crucial in shifting the colony towards a more normal development. Among the key indicators, the following originated in the first decade: a postal service, the first newspaper, the first hospital, and the first political pamphlet. In 1813 the new stage was signalled when the ban on cultivation was lifted.

The war did not have a spectacular impact upon the region. Nevertheless, in the quickening of the pace of economic development, and the laying of the foundation of a vast carrying trade, the beginnings of Atlantic pride and confidence that was to mark the people throughout the nineteenth century are to be traced. If there were few heroic set-piece battles to be incorporated into the emerging mythology, there was enough in the privateering and the exploits of the 104th to reinforce their Loyalist heritage.

# — 3. Birth of a Nation —

Lower Canada had much more to fear than the Atlantic colonies. It contained two centres that, unlike Halifax, could be taken and would provide rich prizes: Montreal was, as in 1775, not easily defensible, and Quebec, as always, was vulnerable in winter when naval support could not be provided. An elementary strategy would have seen that a successful attack on Lower Canada would have left the other British colonies without adequate support. In fact, the Americans declined to attack the lower province, preferring instead an assault upon the upper.

When war was declared, the American decision was, of course, not known, and fears for Lower Canada were compounded by its economic and political state. There was no great optimism over its ability to withstand an American invasion. When Sir James Craig arrived as governor soon after the *Chesapeake* incident and talk of war was current, he expressed decided unwillingness to arm the militia lest it go over to the enemy. If it is thought that his was a wrong reading of the situation — and Craig had served in North America in the War of Independence and had seen for himself the woeful performance of the Canadian militia at that time — his successor, the francophile Sir George Prevost, was only slightly more confident, describing the militia in 1812 as "ill-armed and without discipline."

What had unsettled the province was a massive economic and social readjustment over the previous twenty-odd years. In the 1790s economic growth had been impressive. With wheat prices in England rising 41 percent in that decade, the possibilities for the Lower Canadian farmer were excellent. The massive exports of wheat and flour noted in Chapter 13 are tribute to the grasping of opportunities. During the same period fur prices also were rising. If that trade was no longer dominant, it was still significant. Money was plentiful, therefore. The *seigneurs*, however, were not prospering. They had shown little ability to profit from the new arrangements and theirs was a class fast declining. The following verdict, passed by a rising star (Louis-Joseph Papineau) on a leading representative of the old order (Duchesnay) is revealing:

> He lived on seven or eight hundred louis a year, saving nothing, and half of this revenue came from positions that died with him. Thus we see yet another of these old families fated to pass into obscurity, for it is left with negligible fortune and no influence or education.

The vacuum that threatened to form was filled by a new group. The farmers who were the main beneficiaries of the boom conditions, due to their *Canadien* heritage did not use their growing purchasing power to consolidate their newly won positions and to move on to higher levels of economic organization. Rather, they consumed their surplus in buying status, sending their sons to school and college and having them enter the professions. Notaries, advocates, doctors, pharmacists, surveyors — all increased their ranks in the opening years of the nineteenth century. The swing was mirrored in the composition of the assembly; whereas the professions were but 18 percent in 1792, they were 29 percent by 1800 and 35 percent by 1810. On the other hand, the merchant element had declined from 59 percent through 37 percent to 31 percent.

The boom did not maintain itself: the *habitant* remained bound to traditional cultivation methods, which were ineffective. Every spring the thawing ice carried away a winter's accumulation of farm-yard manure that the farmer dumped there rather than carried to his fields. Rising yields were due only to the fresh lands that were brought under the plough, and when they were no longer available, soil exhaustion quickly reduced the crop. By the 1830s Lower Canada was unable to feed itself and had to import its breadstuffs.

The *habitants'* difficulties were such that they were reduced to growing the despised potato.

The bursting of the bubble of prosperity meant reduced opportunities. An oversupply of professionals lacked the positions for which they had trained. Unemployed and underemployed, they were a talented, literate, and vocal proletariat that easily inclined towards critical attitudes. Dissatisfied with the existing state of affairs, they were leaders in search of a cause and of a public.

Against this background the province began to split along ethnic lines. That dualism of conqueror-conquered foreshadowed in the Constitutional Act now became overt. The new economic pattern could only foster it. The fur trade had kept alive an Anglo-*Canadien entente*, but that trade was now in decline. The new staples, wheat and timber, were mushroom growths where the controlling firms were British and where French-Canadian participation was restricted to the lowest level of *habitant*, lumberjack, and *draveur*. In these new businesses there was no equivalent of the Beaver Club with its easy social intercourse of anglophones and francophones. When the Chamber of Commerce was set up in Quebec City in 1809, not a single director bore a French-Canadian name. About this time the mouthpiece of the English party, the Quebec *Mercury* (founded 1804), began openly to rail against French Canadians as an inferior people, delighting for instance in reprinting passages likening them to Australian aborigines or New Zealand Maoris. Prevost recognized the polarization and in dispatches home wrote of "the divisions in the House of Assembly [that] have become national in character. . . . the baser part of the English population . . . treat their French fellow subjects in a manner which is highly insulting. . . ."

This deplorable development had become institutionalized in 1805, when the Gaols Bill was debated. There was agreement that new jails were needed, but on the question of financing them there was complete lack of agreement. One party, largely identified with the English merchant group, wished the money to be raised by a land tax. The other, largely identified with the *habitants* and their spokesmen the professionals, preferred a tax on goods entering the country. More than the debate itself, the aftermath of the decision (which was for a customs duty) showed the way in which passions were being inflamed. The English merchants refused to give up the fight. They worked to have the bill disallowed by the imperial authorities. The Montreal merchants gave a magnificent dinner at which the following toasts were drunk:

6th - The honourable members of the legislative council who were friendly to constitutional taxation, as proposed by our worthy member in the House of Assembly.

7th - Our Representatives in the provincial parliament, who proposed a constitutional and proper mode of taxation, for building gaols; and who opposed a tax on commerce for that purpose, as contrary to the sound practice of the present state.

\*    \*    \*

12th - May the commercial interest of this province have its due influence on the administration of its government.

For publishing an account of these proceedings the editor of the Montreal *Gazette* was haled before the assembly, and for taking his part the editor of the *Mercury* was in turn arrested. This latter had certainly let himself go. He had assimilated Napoleon and the French Canadians and had written

It is certain that nothing could be more gratifying to our arch-enemy and the French nation, than a prohibition on our presses. The usurper well knows the wholesome truths they teach, how strongly they initiate a hatred of tyranny; how ardently they cherish that noble, that inspiring passion, a love of country, when every Briton so sensibly feels that the cause of his country is his own. . . . We know ourselves to be beyond the reach of his arms; but where will not Italian art and French cunning insinuate themselves. . . . Wherever French councils prevail, there follows immediately a spirit of persecution and cruelty.

A much more fruitful response to the *Gazette* and the *Mercury* was the founding in 1806 of *Le Canadien*. There its leading light Pierre Bédard set out to educate French Canadians in the ways of British constitutional and parliamentary practice. Copious extracts from Locke and Blackstone were printed along with commentaries on their applicability to Lower Canada. Meanwhile, a lively political battle was carried on in the press. Some wondered if the still infant assembly could withstand the pressures, and how the colony would react to invasion.

When hostilities did break out, the fears proved short-lived. In part this was due to Craig's work. He soon formed the opinion that *Le Canadien* was a dangerous publication and dismissed all connected with it from their militia positions. In 1810 he ordered the arrest of the printer and editors of the paper, including Bédard, who was eager to make a martyr of himself. In the long run, this brutal, frontal assault helped weld the French-Canadian party together, and give it a sense of mission. In the short run, however, the absence of Bédard and the others deprived the group of leadership, something that was not really provided until the 1820s with the emergence of Louis-Joseph Papineau as the dominant figure.

Too much should not be made of this factor, though, in accounting for the absence of disaffection in 1812. Much more significant was that there were few who looked upon the possibility of annexation by the United States with favour. The English party was in favour of maintaining the imperial connection; the timber merchants needed the imperial preference; the fur trader still had hopes of wiping out what he saw as the mistakes of 1783 and 1794. Even the *habitants* were keen to serve in this war: the downturn in the economy led many a son to leave the farm or workshop for the militia. Once again, however, the Church was the firmest in its protestations of loyalty. So powerfully did the Church back the civil authorities that even officials in distant London were impressed. When it was recommended that Plessis be given a seat in the legislative council and that his title as Roman Catholic bishop of Quebec be openly recognized, there was no refusal.

Finally, it must be insisted that for all the critical tone of Bédard and *Le Canadien*, it was restricted to a limited target. They hit out against Craig, and against arrogant merchants. Otherwise, there was much that was conservative in their critique. Leaders such as François Blanchet, who had been trained as an apothecary at Columbia University in New York, were the exception, and most were products of the seminaries and *collèges* of the colony. These were Church-run institutions, where habits of deference and a sense of hierarchy were inculcated. These men were not frontier democrats. Moreover, their distrust of things American was thorough-going, and linked up with deep-rooted ways of thinking. Fully in the *ancien régime* tradition they inveighed against the greedy qualities of the Americans, their sordid scramble for profit, their ignoble buying and selling. They scorned "a mercantile aristocracy, the most abominable, the most pernicious of all orders." To resist such contagion they championed the agrarian myth. *Le Canadien* referred to the French Canadians as "les enfants du sol." They saw a prosperous peasantry as the necessary basis of any well-established society. The prosperity it provided was genuine, unlike the meretricious wealth that a commercial-industrial civilization produced. *Le Canadien* summed up the case against "les Yankis" as follows:

> Canada can never achieve a great measure of prosperity through commerce . . .; its natural leaning is to agriculture, which, of all conditions, is the least precarious. . . . It can readily be concluded that commerce in no way profits Canada as certain would have it believed, that only a small number of individ-

uals make fortunes from it, and that most of the inhabitants, particularly in the cities, have only an illusory appearance of wealth.

This stress upon the precariousness of commerce reveals the continuities between New France and Lower Canada.

The devotion at once to the British connection and to the agrarian myth was curious but not impossible. That it was elaborated by lower middle-class professionals and Churchmen was only slightly less surprising. Nevertheless, anti-Americanism was able to bring these two champions together effectively. Before the threat of invasion, abbé Lartigue, later bishop of Montreal, announced a novel identification: in calling upon French Canadians not to "disregard the most sacred duties of religion" and not "to fail in loyalty and courage at this critical time," he went on to speak of "our national honour," and to ask "what nation was ever more valiant . . ., more devoted to its Prince than the Canadian nation?" The fusing of nationalism and Catholicism was to run as an informing thread throughout Canadian history.

The war even provided the heroic incident that could serve to symbolize the birth of the new nationalism. The Americans never grasped the need to mount a serious attack upon the lower St. Lawrence. When they did move against Lower Canada their efforts were vitiated by their militia's refusal to cross state lines. Nevertheless, there was just enough activity to provide an engagement in 1813 at Chateauguay. It does not matter that it was more of a skirmish than a battle, the Americans losing some 50 men and the French-Canadian militia some 25. It does not matter that the French-Canadian commander, Charles de Salabery, was a regular officer in the British army (who had spent time seeing to the suppression of Ireland). It was a French-Canadian victory and the myth transmitted was that of Thomas Chapais, the nineteenth-century nationalist historian:

> It rightly marks a glorious day for our race. It was primarily a French-Canadian victory. It is ours and no one can take it from us. . . . Chateauguay was our reply to Craig's . . . imputations. Chateauguay was our revenge. Chateauguay was the assertion of our undeniable loyalty and ardent patriotism. Chateauguay was an heroic illustration of our national spirit. . . .

# — 4. A Loyal Province in the Balance —

Upper Canada was to bear the brunt of invasion. Since Jay's Treaty the expanding United States had been consolidating its hold on the old Northwest, and was coming to grips with its Indian "problem." In 1794 Mad Anthony Wayne defeated the tribes of the area at the battle of the Fallen Timbers. In 1811 this was followed up by the battle of Tippecanoe in which the promising Indian coalition put together by Tecumseh was defeated. Now, it was felt, two birds could be killed with one stone: war in the far west would gain British territory, but it would also lead to Indian "pacification."

The capture of Upper Canada from the British appeared to be an easy matter since so few of the inhabitants were British. From the beginning of the colony's life settlers had been pouring in from the United States as part of that westward expansion that paid so little attention to political boundaries. Indeed, the Upper Canadian authorities eagerly welcomed such settlers, for these late Loyalists, like their earlier cousins, possessed the skills needed to tame the virgin land. The invading commander, General Hull, recognizing the part that family ties might play, issued a proclamation that said in part:

> Raise not your hands against your brethren. Many of your forefathers fought for the freedom and *Independence* we now enjoy; being children therefore of the same family with us and heirs to the same heritage the arrival of an army of friends must be hailed by you with a cordial welcome. You will be emancipated from tyranny and oppression and restored to the dignified position of freemen.

As hostilities commenced, the best hope of the Americans seemed likely to be fulfilled. The mood of the colony was largely one of defeatism. Lieutenant-Governor Isaac Brock reported that

> Legislators, magistrates, militia officers, all have imbibed the idea [that the province must fall], and are so sluggish and indifferent in their respective offices that the artful and active scoundrel is allowed to parade the country without interruption and commit all manner of mischief. They are so alarmed of offending that they rather encourage than repress disorders and other improper acts.

Brock attempted to control the situation by having the assembly pass laws to strengthen the militia, to suspend *habeas corpus*, to proclaim martial law, and to turn over surplus funds. All four requests were denied. Brock summed up the position as "most critical, not from anything the enemy can do, but from the disposition of the people — The population, believe me, is essentially bad." If matters improved from this low point as time went on, there was still much to be desired. Two members of the assembly and one ex-member went over to the Americans; so many of the rank and file did so that a unit of the American army, the Canadian Volunteers, was formed from their number, and in 1814 at Ancaster Assizes, 15 of them were convicted of treason and eight were hanged.

Yet the colony did not fall. The ability to attract the Indians to the British side was an important factor here. In the first days of the war the commander in the far west quickly put together a force of regulars, North West Company *voyageurs*, and Indians, and captured the American post at Michilimackinac. This had a dramatic effect on Indian morale — and also on poor Hull, who complained that the surrender had "opened the northern hive of Indians and they were swarming down in every direction." Brock got on well with Tecumseh, of whom he said "a more sagacious or a more gallant Warrior does not, I believe, exist," and an effective alliance resulted.

The initial success was swiftly followed up. It might have been expected that Brock, with only one regiment of regulars and a disaffected population, would have settled for a fighting withdrawal. Instead, he decided on the offensive. He moved against Hull's superior numbers at Detroit, cut his lines of communication, and let it be understood that the Indians were about to be loosed. Hull surrendered. When soon afterwards, a second American invasion threatened, this time by way of Niagara, Brock was present to impel his forces against them. The battle of Queenston Heights was another triumph for his aggressive tactics. That Brock was killed in the fighting only heightened the sense of the heroic.

The Americans never recovered from these early reverses. During 1813 they were able to win the naval supremacy of the Great Lakes, which made possible the capture and destruction of York (later Toronto). By 1814, however, the tide was once again in Britain's favour. The battle of Lundy's Lane was a standoff, but since it was followed by an American withdrawal the colony had reason to congratulate itself. Control of the Lakes began to pass to the British, and the sacking of York was revenged by the Royal Navy when it burnt the American capital, including the White House.

Honour was even, and both sides were prepared to talk peace. The British were in a strong position, and at Ghent might have insisted upon concessions. In particular, they might have stuck by their initial demand for an Indian territory south and west of Lake Erie. Such a buffer zone would have wiped out something of the stain left by their treatment of their allies in 1783 and in 1795 (after Fallen Timbers), and would, incidentally, have been popular with the fur traders. However, the American negotiators proved surprisingly adamant. It has been suggested that only their long absence from the United States, which blinded them to the poor state of their badly divided country, enabled them to be so uncompromising. The British were in no mood to haggle. Political conditions in Europe were unsettled, and everyone was sick of war. On the basis essentially of the *status quo ante*, the Treaty of Ghent was signed at the end of 1814.

For all its seeming uselessness, however, the War of 1812 had had a dramatic impact on Upper Canada. Sir James Yeo, the Royal Naval commander on the Lakes, might point out that

> The experience of two years active service has served to convince me that tho' much has been done by the mutual exertions of both services, we also owe much, if not more, to the perverse stupidity of the Enemy; the impolicy of their plans; the dissensions of the Commanders, and lastly between them and their Ministers of War.

Historians since might agree that only the presence of British regulars saved the colony, and the others, from the Americans, but that was not how the colonists themselves saw it. As early as 1812 Rev. John Strachan (later Anglican bishop of Toronto) preached a sermon in which he claimed

> It will be told by the future historian, that the Province of Upper Canada, without the assistance of men or arms, except a handful of regular troops, expelled its invaders, slew or took them all prisoners, and captured from its enemies the greater part of the arms by which it was defended. . . . And never, surely, was greater activity shewn in any country than our militia have exhibited, never greater valour, cooler resolution, and more approved conduct; they have emulated the choicest veterans, and they have twice saved the country.

The "militia myth" launched here did not lack for elaborators. An intensified sense of the "Loyalist Province" developed, British in its manly repudiation of republicanism. The former openness to American settlers was disowned: henceforth they would be kept out, and British migrants would be prized for "the speedy settlement in such a manner as shall best secure its attachment to British Laws and Government." The Rush-Bagot agreement that disarmed the Great Lakes is taken as a first step towards the "Undefended Border," but it is well to remember that it originated not as part of a good neighbour policy but as a measure of quarantine.

## Suggested Reading

The coming of war in 1812 may be traced in B. Perkins, *Prologue to War: England and the United States, 1805-1812* (1963); R. Horsman, *The Causes of the War of 1812* (1968); J.W. Pratt, *Expansionists of 1812* (1965); and R. Brown, *The Republic in Peril* (1964). The war itself is covered by G.F.G. Stanley, *The War of 1812* (1983); M. Zaslow (ed.), *The Defended Border* (1964); and by J.M. Hitsman, *The Incredible War of 1812* (1965). The aftermath is the subject of C.P. Stacey, *The Undefended Border: The Myth and the Reality* (1962). In a different way is S.F. Wise and R.C. Brown, *Canada Views the United States: Nineteenth Century Political Attitudes* (1967).

For the wider setting of British North America two works by G.S. Graham may be cited: *Empire of the North Atlantic* (1974), and *Sea Power and British North America, 1783-1820* (1941). Also to be included here are H.C. Allen, *Great Britain and the United States: A History of Anglo-American Relations, 1783-1852* (1954), and J.L. Wright, *Britain and the American Frontier, 1783-1815* (1975).

For Lower Canada, the LeGoff article referred to in the last chapter may be supplemented by R.L. Jones, "Agriculture in Lower Canada, 1702-1815," *Canadian Historical Review* (1946); G. Paquet and J.P. Wallot, "The Agricultural Crisis in Lower Canada, 1801-1812: A Response to T.J.A. LeGoff," *Canadian Historical Review* (1975); and J. McCallum, *Unequal Beginnings: Agriculture and Economic Development in Quebec & Ontario until 1870* (1980). The Gaols Bill controversy may be followed in J.P. Wallot, "La Querelle des Prisons," *Revue d'Histoire de l'Amérique Française* (1960-61), while the *Canadiens'* impact is conveniently handled by L.A.H. Smith, "*Le Canadien* and the British Constitution, 1806-1810," *Canadian Historical Review* (1957).

The role of the Indians in the Upper Canadian war effort is described in S. Wise, "The Indian Diplomacy of John Graves Simcoe," *Canadian Historical Association Reports* (1953); R. Horsman, *Expansion and American Indian Policy, 1783-1812* (1967), and "British Indian Policy in the Northwest, 1807-1812," *Mississippi Valley Historical Review* (1962).

The tone of Upper Canadian society in this period may be judged from J.L.H. Henderson (ed.), *John Strachan: Documents and Opinions* (1959); S.F. Wise, "Sermon Literature and Canadian Intellectual History," in J.M. Bumsted (ed.), *Canadian History before Confederation* (1972); "God's Peculiar Peoples," in W.L. Morton (ed.), *The Shield of Achilles* (1968); and "Upper Canada and the Conservative Tradition," in E. Firth (ed.), *Peoples of a Province* (1967).

# CHAPTER 15

## AN AGE OF REFORM

## — 1. The North Atlantic Setting —

By war's end the British possessions in North America revealed a rapidly maturing character. There were, of course, exceptions. Newfoundland still lagged in its development; significant progress had recently been made, and the population had shot up to some 60 000, but its anomalous past continued to weigh heavily. Only in 1820 was the practice of having justice administered by the senior naval officer in the vicinity abandoned and common law practices introduced; only in 1825 was the governor given a council; and only in 1832 was an assembly granted. Even then the inclination to make these forms work was lacking, the people having for too long been without self-government: politics had degenerated to such a level that the clock had to be put back. Half the representatives could be elected but the rest had to be appointed. Another exception was in Red River, where the population was tiny and remained so for many years. In addition, the vast region subject to the Hudson's Bay Company, including the Pacific coast, was sparsely populated, and a non-aboriginal society would be some time yet in establishing itself in those areas. On the other hand, the Maritimes and the St. Lawrence had long been settled, were growing in numbers, and were well on their way towards developing sophisticated cultures.

A sign of the times was the reunion of Cape Breton and Nova Scotia. The crudity of this tiny unit — it had only 6000 people at the time of Ghent — had not seemed out of place in an earlier age, but as other settlements developed the island seemed increasingly out of place. The occasion for the reunion was the realization that, given the royal proclamation of 1763, which had promised an assembly, the levying of taxes by council alone (there being no assembly in Cape Breton) was illegal. In 1820 its separate existence was ended. The enlarged Nova Scotia had close to 90 000 inhabitants at this date. New Brunswick, by its first census of 1824, had some 75 000. Even Prince Edward Island had over 25 000. The two Canadas, of course, were by far the largest; Lower Canada numbered 360 000 and the upper province about 100 000, impressive figures indeed. Not all the inhabitants had gone beyond the raw, frontier stage, but many had, and for them there was an ever-growing leeway for reflection, for the wider view, and more immediately for politics.

The changing nature of society is revealed by two crucial indicators. The first is the spread of the newspaper. Mention has already been made of the Quebec *Mercury* and *Le Canadien*. These were by no means the first, but a spate of significant foundings took place from the war's end, and the standard account of journalism in Canada dates the second period, that of "thickening growth," from 1807. The six newspapers in the Canadas in 1813 had become nineteen by 1824 and fifty in 1836. The growth in the Atlantic region was not as spectacular, but there were some notable foundations in the period and there, as on the St. Lawrence, an impassioned debate was possible.

The second indicator is interest in universities. A charter for Kings' College, York (what later became the University of Toronto) was obtained in 1827, though its predominant Anglicanism caused protest and held up the project for some years. The Methodists of Upper Canada established what became known as Victoria College, Cobourg, in 1836; it later affiliated with the University of Toronto. In Lower Canada the seminary had existed since 1663, but in 1821 McGill was chartered. Denominational diversity in the Maritimes led to many foundations. The Anglican King's College at Windsor, Nova Scotia, dated from 1788 but was remodelled in 1827; the Presbyterian Pictou Academy began in 1816; Horton Academy at Wolfsville, a Baptist college, was founded in 1828; in addition there was the nonsectarian Dalhousie, chartered in 1818 but functioning only from 1838. New Brunswick had its

King's College at Fredericton from 1828. What later was named Prince of Wales College in Charlottetown dated from 1834. Such fragmentation may not have been efficient, but nevertheless it was a tribute to colonial vitality.

It is necessary to stress the fact of colonialism. The greater part of the colonial elite was imported, along with the bulk of the ideas, the habits of mind, and the framework of discussion. It was a world in ferment that poured its opinions into British North America: the two major sources of inspiration, Britain and the United States, were both caught up in fierce debate over the direction society ought to be taking. At this period, the North Atlantic community was at its liveliest, and British North America was able to share in it to the full.

For Britain the post-Waterloo years meant the release of pressures long bottled up by the war. Even before 1793 the Industrial Revolution had been at work, disrupting traditional patterns of economic and social organization and introducing alien forms in their place. The need to fight a generation-long world war had speeded up the transformation and intensified the growing pains. Now, with the need to concentrate solely on survival removed, an explosion followed. All manner of viewpoints were articulated. The teachings of Adam Smith were elaborated and the triumph of *laissez-faire* brought nearer. Yet the liberalism that championed this way of thinking was challenged. A reawakened Tory philanthropy, sickened by industrial and urban problems, called for a recognition of *noblesse oblige*. On the other wing the Philosophic Radicals, followers of Jeremy Bentham's scientific calculus of "the greatest good of the greatest number," advocated practical measures to deal with sanitation, prison reform, poor relief, and the like. Meanwhile the working class was producing its own leaders and articulating its own critique of society, pressing for the legalization of trade unions (secured in 1824-25), and building such self-help organizations as the Cooperative Movement. In addition, it mounted the Chartist agitation from 1838 to 1848, a massive and sustained attempt at far-reaching reform of politics and a potent means of educating the working class. Over all this vast ferment of ideas hovered the religious revival, felt by most, but experienced most intensely by the Methodists and dissenting Protestant sects which together gave rise to that most characteristic nineteenth-century phenomenon, the nonconformist conscience.

Of the many political clashes spawned amid this intellectual and political effervescence, two may be singled out as of major importance. The first was the struggle for Catholic emancipation. Since the sixteenth century, and more particularly since the Glorious Revolution of 1688, Catholicism had been proscribed. This had posed the problems that assailed New France in

1763. There, because the colony was so far away and posed so little danger, its problems could be ignored, but in England itself and most notably in Ireland, there was no blinking them away. Indeed, since Catholicism in conquered Ireland had become a badge of national resistance to England, the persecution of the faith had become worse as the eighteenth century went on, not better. When the Revolutionary and Napoleonic Wars once again threatened to make Ireland the back door into England, and when the Irish rebelled against their conquerors, the quasi-independence of Ireland was snuffed out: in 1801 the Irish Parliament was abolished and its representatives were swallowed up at Westminster.

In the 1820s a reviving nationalist movement was launched by Daniel O'Connell, at once Catholic and nationalist. Using the parish priests in a painstaking organizational effort, and raising funds on the new principle of mass contributions of a trifling sum each week, O'Connell put together an impressive political machine. Its power was demonstrated in 1828 when O'Connell stood in the Clare by-election and was elected. By the law as it then stood, he was not permitted to take his place at Westminster. The government of the Duke of Wellington was faced with the choice of upholding the law and provoking civil war in Ireland, or granting Catholic emancipation. Such was the strength of O'Connell's movement that they changed the law.

The change was momentous. The prevailing orthodoxy had been that there had to be a state church (Anglicanism), and that the church-state identity had to be insisted upon at all costs. Only Anglicans could be fully loyal. However, now the idea had been permitted that loyalty could flourish in diversity. Pluralism could make for strength, not weakness.

Hard on the heels of Catholic emancipation, the second major problem, the question of Parliamentary reform, came up. The voting qualification dated from the fifteenth century, and not surprisingly no longer corresponded with social realities. By 1830, out of a population of some 16.5 million in England and Wales, considerably fewer than half a million had the vote. Worse still was that the constituencies had been frozen since the seventeenth century, and similarly failed to correspond with reality; huge cities like Manchester and Birmingham went unrepresented, while rotten boroughs like Old Sarum which lacked permanent residents returned two members.

After almost two years of fierce political fighting, the Great Reform Bill was passed in 1832. By its provisions the vote was extended to more people, and on a new principle. No longer was the possession of freehold land (a rarity in England) the essential basis for the franchise; rather the value of property an individual possessed became the test. At the same time, a beginning was made toward the notion that representation should be based on population: rotten boroughs were suppressed and the seats transferred to the Manchesters and Birminghams of the industrial regions. Like Catholic emancipation, the Reform Bill had shown that nothing, including the English Constitution, was immune to change, and that the many, if properly organized, could wrest concessions from the holders of power.

Yet what is striking about the British evolution is its halfheartedness, its unwillingness to abandon deferential patterns, and the lingering remains of the former state. Thus, completion of the political reforms took four further acts like that of 1832, and not until 1929 did all adults receive the vote (all adult males were enfranchised only in 1918). In fact, the chief architect of the Great Reform Bill, Lord John Russell, was so convinced that it was the last word in reform that he was known as "Finality Jack." The actual addition to the number of voters was derisory: fewer than a quarter million were added to the electoral rolls. Nor did religious tests disappear completely overnight. They continue to exist vestigially, and there are still offices in Britain closed to Catholics, including that of the monarchy itself.

Against this tardiness, American development was swift indeed. Already before 1820 many states had recast their constitutions to give adult (white) male suffrage. In many states, religious pluralism was an accomplished fact — although anti-Catholicism was nevertheless widespread and virulent. The noteworthy development in the United States in the 1820s was the extension of such beginnings, a program bound up with the name of the president from 1829 to 1837, Andrew Jackson.

Jacksonianism could be summed up in the slogan liberally used at the time, "Equal rights for all, special privilege for none." In line with that sentiment, the following innovations took place. The nominating convention dates from the 1820s, a device ostensibly to give the ordinary citizen a say in the choice of candidates and to take the nomination out of the hands of the professional caucus. The usefulness of having a "man of the people" as a presidential candidate dates from this period; Jackson himself, a jack-of-all-trades who had been soldier, land speculator, lawyer, and farmer, was in this mould, but a better example of this style was the successful naming of William Harrison for president in 1840. An unknown, Harrison was elected after being boomed as the victor at Tippecanoe, for having had the sense to be born in a log cabin, and for not having developed any refinement. Devotion to simplicity was applied to office-holding. Bureaucrats did not have to be experts; indeed, it might be better if they were not, for experts tended to lose contact with real people and genuine concerns. Any loyal citizen could turn his hand to almost any job. The test was less technical competence than commitment to democratic principles, and this could be judged by the people at large: the election of officials from poundkeeper to judge to members of the electoral college became the rule.

If one American political issue is selected to set alongside Catholic emancipation and the Reform Bill in Britain, it would have to be the Bank issue. With their belief in equal opportunity, dislike of special interest groups, and distrust of experts, Jacksonians hated the Federal Bank of the United States. It was so arcane as to seem magical. To Jackson himself the Bank came to stand as a symbol of everything rotten in the republic, as a monster poised to destroy simple virtue. He determined to kill it, and after a bitter struggle succeeded. His veto on the rechartering was given in 1832.

Clearly, the American reform style was very different from the British. In a sense, however, they were similar. Both were attacks on oligarchy, assaults on the inner groups that ruled simply because they always had ruled. When it came to oligarchies, British North America also had its share. In every colony there was a close-knit body that seemed to enjoy disproportionate power and have undue access to favours. The Canadas were the worst offenders here, in part because the Constitutional Act of 1791 had so openly favoured an oligarchic structure as a means of curbing democratic excesses. In Lower Canada reformers identified the "Château Clique"; in Upper Canada their target was the "Family Compact."

From the end of the War of 1812, criticism mounted. To the south was the example of Jacksonianism, a standing reproach to imperial style. From Britain came not only reform ideas, but also the very people who by sheer weight of numbers would disrupt the established pattern: following the war, American immigration was reduced as that from the British Isles was immensely increased. This flood is so important that it warrants a separate section to itself.

# — 2. Immigration —

Until the end of the Napoleonic Wars the prevailing view in Britain was that emigration ought to be discouraged. This was due in part to the unexamined belief that the population was dangerously low, perhaps even declining. It was due in part also to mercantilist thinking that held that population was too valuable a commodity to allow it to slip away into another's possession. The loss of artisans was to be guarded against above all, and statute legislated against their emigrating and taking with them special skills and trade secrets. However, the most immediate reason for discouraging emigration was the need for personnel with which to fight the war. For all these reasons, the Passenger Vessels Act was passed in 1803 to lay down minimal standards for ships taking emigrants across the Atlantic. The reason was not a humanitarian concern but a wish to raise costs and dissuade intending passengers.

Ideas were changing by the time of Waterloo. The first British census was taken in 1801 and continued at ten-year intervals. It was no longer possible to deny that the population was large and increasing very rapidly. Then, too, mercantilist dogma was yielding to *laissez-faire*, and the repeal of the legislation against artisanal emigration in 1824 was another victory for the emerging orthodoxy. Of course, the coming of peace destroyed at a stroke the artificial war economy, threw hundreds of thousands out of work, and spread poverty on a huge scale. Poor relief, which had been increasing in cost for many years, surged still further and placed unbearable pressure on those who otherwise might have weathered the storm. All the while the accelerating impact of the Industrial Revolution kept the economy in a precarious state. Emigration began to seem attractive, not simply to the disadvantaged who wanted out, but to the comfortable who feared revolution unless something were done. The case of Ireland loomed disproportionately large. The population there was increasing at a frightening rate, well on its way to its all-time peak of eight million in the 1840s, a figure far above that of today's population. This overpopulation was impossibly balanced on one crop, the potato, and when that failed from 1845 to 1848, the ensuing famine killed well over a million. With such developments in the background, the older views gave ground. The Passenger Vessels Act of 1803 was repealed in 1827 and although subsequent legislation was put in its place, the requirements were very low, for now the aim was to speed emigration.

These "push" factors were aided by others akin to colonial "pulls." The timber ships that sailed in such numbers were often without a return cargo since few would entrust valuable goods to such unseaworthy vessels, but at trifling cost they could be converted to carry desperate people. Passages could be bought cheaply, and many who intended from the first to immigrate to the United States entered the New World via British North America in a timber ship. Especially after the repeal of 1827, transatlantic fares were low; before 1827, a ratio of one passenger to every five registered tons was permitted, after 1827 the ratio was often one to one, or even worse; on 5 July 1831 the *Ulster* from Londonderry docked at Quebec with 505 passengers although the ship was only 334 tons. The overcrowding was incredible, and an observer at Liverpool described the cramming of 86 emigrants into a hold measuring seven and a half metres by seven metres. Under conditions like these pestilence was inevitable, and it was said that "the harbor master's boatman had no difficulty, at the distance of a gun-shot, either when the wind was favorable or in a dead calm, in distinguishing by the odour alone a crowded emigrant ship." Emigrant ships were worse than slavers, for while every slave lost at sea meant reduced profits, every passenger so lost represented gain in supplies and room.

A second "pull" was the organization of land companies. In 1826 John Galt took the lead in organizing the Canada Company, which took over reserve land in Upper Canada. Eight years later he repeated the scheme with the British American Land Company in Lower Canada. In the Maritimes the New Brunswick and Nova Scotia Land Company was set up in 1832. These companies used aggressive methods, publicizing the virtues of their lands and of a fresh start in the New World, and maintaining agents in Britain to assist those interested.

Between the "push" and "pull," the number of "voluntary" emigrants rose steadily. Between 1815 and 1850 three million left the British Isles. Two million of these went, directly or indirectly, to the United States, but one million remained in British North America. In 1832, an early peak year, 66 000 poured into the country. With an exodus on this scale it was no wonder that the government soon abandoned assisted settlement schemes. There were military settlements in the years immediately after 1815: in Nova Scotia a new road between Halifax and Annapolis was dotted with such villages, though only a few survived; in New Brunswick the 104th was paid off with land on the upper St. John River; and Upper Canada, for obvious strategic reasons, received its share of such settlements. In 1819, for the first time, the government spent public money to send emigrants to the colonies, and two Irish ventures resulted. However, this government involvement was considered to be too expensive when so many "volunteers" crowded forward. The figures tell the tale: between 1815 and 1825, assisted emigrants totalled just over 7000, while "volunteers," unassisted, exceeded 66 000.

The immigrants were a mixed blessing. They tended to avoid Nova Scotia, except as a place of entry, but New Brunswick received some 5000 per year throughout the 1830s, Lower Canada perhaps 3000, with the bulk going to Upper Canada — between 15 000 and 30 000. Even Prince Edward Island, groaning under an unsatisfactory landholding system, grew by immigration in this period. So too did Newfoundland. Immigrants brought with them much-needed capital, for not all were destitute. They contributed necessary skills such as up-to-date farming knowledge, crafts for both town and countryside, and in many cases the sheer muscle power that was so very much in demand. They staffed the various levels of officialdom, taught in the schools and universities, and wrote for the expanding press. However, set against these gains was the resentment they often provoked. Too often, as in the plague years 1832 and 1834, they brought cholera. When they were not accused of bringing disease, they were considered guilty of wage-cutting. Frequently they were disruptive, which was especially true of the Irish. Even when they were not physically awkward, their separateness could be viewed negatively: the colonies of Highlanders that maintained the Gaelic language were cases in point, and where they were Catholic as well, the resentment was apt to be intensified. When times were good, tension tended to be muted, but at any downturn in the economy the immigrant could serve as a point about which to crystallize hostility. In the long view the sums of money that the colonies had to find to relieve immigrant distress were an investment in the future that paid good dividends, but in the immediate view they were often the cause of bad blood and savage politicking.

## __ 3. The Revival of Nationalism __ in Lower Canada

The polarization in Lower Canada, which had begun early in the century but had been arrested by the War of 1812, was noted in Chapter 14. It now continued and deepened. The population was still increasing at its accustomed high rate, so much so that overpopulation became the problem. There was land enough, but not in an available form. Too much was locked up in the reserves. Too much was freehold land in the townships, and although *habitants* were beginning to move on to this land, they preferred to settle in the seigneuries that were more familiar (both geographically and legally). The seigneurs were not making concessions, however. Their refusal was quite illegal, since the whole aim and purpose of seigneurialism was to settle willing farmers on the land upon request. However, the pressure on the land meant that farms that ought to have been granted *gratis* could now be sold, and further that withholding land for even more profitable sales in the future became an attractive speculation. Under-the-table deals became common, and fewer and fewer *habitants'* sons could become *censitaires*. An agricultural proletariat was developing, with in some areas 40 percent of heads of families being landless. At the same time the subdivision of existing holdings accelerated:

## Map 15.1: British North America's Mercantile Economy

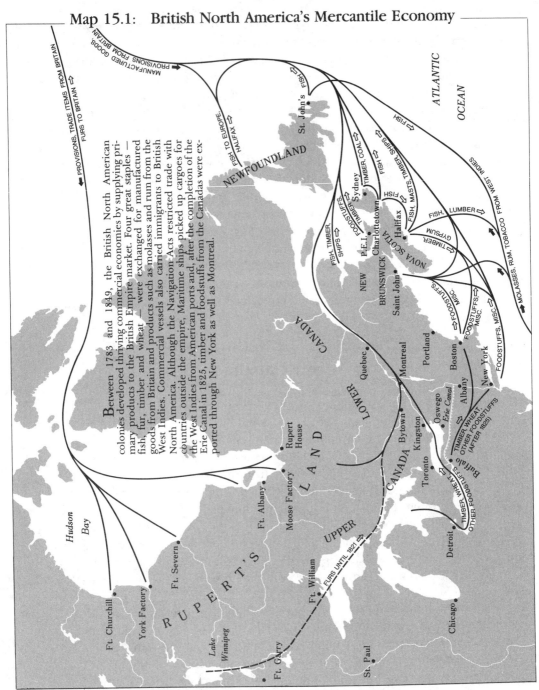

Between 1783 and 1849, the British North American colonies developed thriving commercial economies by supplying primary products to the British Empire market. Four great staples — fish, fur, timber and wheat — were exchanged for manufactured goods from Britain and products such as molasses and rum from the West Indies. Commercial vessels also carried immigrants to British North America. Although the Navigation Acts restricted trade with countries outside the empire, Maritime ships picked up cargoes for the West Indies from American ports and, after the completion of the Erie Canal in 1825, timber and foodstuffs from the Canadas were exported through New York as well as Montreal.

SOURCES: Kerr, *Historical Atlas of Canada* (1975), pp. 46–7; Harris, *Historical Atlas of Canada*,
Vol. I, *From the Beginning to 1800* (1987), plate 68.

by 1831 about one third of farms were less than fifty *arpents*, too small to be really viable. The contrast with a recent and well-remembered age of plenty was galling.

A souring mood was made even more bitter when the traditional wheat economy collapsed. The general ineffectiveness of Lower Canadian agriculture has been mentioned — little improvement took place and soil exhaustion continued. Then, in the mid-1830s, disease appeared in the colony and decimated the wheat yield. A massive shift to the coarse grains had to follow, meaning fewer cash exports and poorer eating. On top of the crop failure of 1836 came the commercial smash of 1837 (a universal North Atlantic phenomenon). When the dust had settled, the figures showed the magnitude of the revolution. Whereas wheat had accounted for some 70 percent of total agricultural production, it now (according to the 1844 census) amounted to no more than 4.4 percent.

While rural Lower Canada was slipping deeper and deeper into economic crisis, the economic dominance of anglophones was seen to be growing in step. Their control of the timber trade has been noted. It was the same with the banking system. In the mini-boom that followed the Peace of Ghent, a rash of banks had been founded — the Bank of Montreal in 1817, the Quebec Bank and the Bank of Canada in 1818, and the City Bank of Montreal in 1831. In these crucial ventures French Canadians were unrepresented: in 1831 they held only 19 percent of the Quebec Bank stock, and only 2.9 percent in the Bank of Montreal. So it was in that other boom-sector, transportation: in the nine largest concerns, French-Canadian investment was only 2 percent. Even in the small-scale rural business world the disproportion was glaring. Thus, in 100 rural parishes studied for 1831 the British were only 7 percent of the population but accounted for 20 percent of the businessmen; in Rimouski in 1842, only 5 percent of the population was anglophone, but 50 percent of the businessmen were anglophone (F. Ouellet, *Lower Canada, 1791-1840* (1980), p. 161).

Racial division was reaching paranoid levels. In 1832 the cholera epidemic broke out, brought by the hapless migrants crowding into Quebec. It proved frighteningly easy to whip up hatred against foreigners, and to make them scapegoats for *habitant* misery. Xenophobia grew to such proportions that the retention rate of migrants in Lower Canada dropped dramatically: in the early 1820s about one third had remained in the colony, and even in the late 1820s almost a quarter had done so, but by 1835 the figure had dropped to 8 percent and by 1836 to 4 percent. Of course, the agrarian crisis noted above played its part, but the fear of *habitant* aggression was clearly a factor, too.

Amid such tensions the growth of a *patriote*, nationalist party went ahead. Just as Governor Craig had fostered that growth in the earlier period, so now did a successor, Dalhousie, who was in office between 1820 and 1828. For all his good qualities — indeed perhaps because of them, since his devotion to duty was rooted in a Scots-Presbyterian dourness — Dalhousie was unable to work with the representatives of the French-Canadian party that controlled the assembly. In particular, he quarrelled with the emerging leader, Louis-Joseph Papineau.

At first Dalhousie had shown favour towards him. The criticism that Papineau kept up, however, notably over the governor's favoured scheme for the union of the Canadas, changed all that. In 1822 a bill was brought in at Westminster to reunite what had been sundered in 1791. The major reason for the initiative was the merchants' need for improved waterways to carry the staples to the Atlantic and British manufactured goods inland. This need was considered vital after 1817: in that year New York began work on the Erie Canal designed to bring traffic from the Great Lakes down to New York City. However, Upper Canadian and Lower Canadian merchant willingness to spend public monies was constantly vetoed by Lower Canadian *patriote* refusal to enrich a "foreign" element at the expense of the *nation canadienne*. For the same reason, they were appalled by the union scheme: it would be costly and moreover would lead to the submergence of *canadien* ways in religion, civil law, and landholding. When Papineau worked against union, he lost Dalhousie's good will. Had the governor been in the colony in 1824 when a new assembly was elected, he would not have accepted Papineau as speaker. When he forced an election in 1827, he repudiated the assembly's renewed choice of Papineau as speaker.

The attempt to maintain an earlier view of royal supremacy was to attempt to put the clock back impossibly far. Opponents within the colony and at Westminster mounted an impressive attack. The authorities made no attempt to save him, and in 1828 Dalhousie was kicked upstairs to become commander-in-chief of the forces in India. Moreover, a British Commons' committee on Canada reported in favour of the assembly in its stands against executive power. By the close of the 1820s, then, it looked as if reform in Lower Canada could proceed smoothly.

It was not to be, however. The assembly did not take the findings of the Canada Committee as a basis from which slowly to elaborate a new concept of imperial-colonial relationships. There was no willingness to experiment along British lines by moving executive and assembly closer together, a step along the way to responsible government. One way to do this would have been to have prominent members of the assembly take seats in the executive council. The offer had been made by Dalhousie early in his governorship to Papineau, but it was refused. Dalhousie's successor, Kempt, made an offer to John Neilson, the leading moderate *patriote* (not to be confused with the Nelson brothers, Robert and Wilfred, who were radicals), but that too was declined. Rather, the *patriote* party showed a sudden eagerness to follow Papineau in novel directions that owed nothing to British practice.

The evolving radicalism owed something to the French revolutionary tradition. Enlightenment notions had made a belated appearance in the colony, and when Papineau was enjoying the peak of his popularity in 1835, he was greeted in Trois Rivières by a banner proclaiming *"Vive le peuple souverain, la liberté, l'égalité"*; later still, the *Marseillaise* would be heard during demonstrations. However, it was always more rhetoric than substance, for such traditions held little appeal in a province that had given shelter to royalist and Catholic *émigrés*. The Irish example was also drawn upon, and in time Papineau would be called the Daniel O'Connell of his people. An observer admitted "it is astonishing how much the name of Daniel O'Connell is known and used among the Canadians. I have seen in the most distant situations little framed engravings of 'O'Connell the man of the People' suspended on the walls in juxtaposition with the Virgin and the Crucifix in the Bedchamber of the French Canadians." Nevertheless, the major attraction — for the leaders certainly — was the American vision of reform, Jacksonian democracy.

Signs of this orientation could be discerned as early as 1829, when Papineau chose the legislative council as "the origin of all the abuses which impose strain on the provinces." The council was that oligarchic body deliberately set up in 1791 with the aim of keeping a democratic assembly within due bounds. It could veto any assembly bill, and frequently did so. Papineau was now to demand the American solution of a popularly-controlled council, one elected by the people and not nominated by the executive and imperial authority. He announced that it was "not in the mother country, nor in the rest of Europe, . . . that we should seek examples; it is rather in America. . . ." He went on to say that "it is certain that before very long, all America should be republican. . . . Only in a general elective system is each on a perfectly equal footing with another. . . ." Soon he added the need for popular conventions to arrange the framework of the new order.

This reform strain was summed up in the *Ninety-two Resolutions*, passed by the assembly in 1834. Some 30 dealt with the evils of the legislative council, and number 42 rhetorically asked if "there was not in the two Canadas a

241

growing inclination to see the institutions become more and more popular, and in that respect more and more like those of the United States," and wondered whether "it would be wise that the object of every change made in the institutions of the province should be to comply more and more with the wishes of the people, and to render the said institutions extremely popular . . . ." The same resolution roundly answered, "Yes, it would be wise; it would be excellent." On a more mundane level, number 75 observed

> That the number of the inhabitants of the country being about 600 000, those of French origin are about 525 000 and those of British or other origin are about 75 000; and that the establishment of the civil government of Lower Canada for the year 1832 . . . contained the names of 157 officers and others receiving salaries who are apparently of British or foreign origin, and the names of 47 who are apparently natives of the country, of French origin, . . . the latter class being of the most part appointed to the inferior and less lucrative offices . . . .

In all, with only one significant exception, it was a full statement of a republican position. The exception was the omission of any condemnation of seigneurialism. An "Americanizing" document might have been expected to declare for freehold land, but Papineau himself believed passionately in seigneurialism and the patriarchal mode that accompanied it, and the resolutions touching on the land issue (numbers 56–62) were supportive of "feudalism."

In the election of 1834, the *patriote* party showed itself well organized and able to appeal to the voters. They were able to make much of the "Montreal Massacre" of two years before when the troops, fearing that the crowd at a by-election was getting out of hand, fired at and killed three *Canadiens*, "not," as Papineau later claimed, "because the people were guilty of poor conduct, but because they were *Canadien*." They were able to discipline those members who had had the temerity to vote against the *Ninety-two Resolutions* in the assembly; 17 of the 24 who voted against did not run for reelection. When all the votes were finally tallied, the *patriote* sweep was seen to be all but complete. They captured every seat in Quebec and Montreal. In the seigneurial areas 41 *patriotes* were returned by acclamation. Of votes cast, the *patriotes* took no less than 77 percent. The English party was reduced to nine members. Deadlock loomed, and Britain sent out Lord Gosford as governor and high commissioner with orders to report fully on the situation.

While this was happening divergent views were crystallizing. The British party was shocked into action. Their organizing of a British Rifle Corps was suppressed by Gosford as too provocative, but they reorganized themselves as the Doric Club and took to brawling in the streets. More principled was the attempt to found a *via media* between the *patriotes* and the reactionaries. The lead here was taken by John Neilson, a former *patriote* who could not accept the extremism of the *Ninety-two Resolutions*. The Constitutional Association of Quebec was set up to champion reform within the framework of "the just subordination of the colony to the parent state." The declaration of the association drew attention to the totalitarian dangers implicit in the *patriote* organization and message, and warned of "a dangerous ascendancy over this class of the population [the inhabitants of the French origin]" acquired by them. It was a sign of the times when *Le Canadien* spoke out on the side of moderation and became in effect a supporter of the government.

Such declarations of support were welcome, but none was equal to that provided by the Church. As on previous occasions, the hierarchy came out publicly for law and order. Lartigue was the leader here. He had his nationalist *bona fides*, and no one could deny his commitment to *la nation canadienne*. However, as his pronouncement of 1812, quoted in Chapter 14, made plain, it was a Catholic nationalism that he championed. As Papineau became more and more anti-clerical, and as the *patriotes* became more and more secular in their thinking, Lartigue began to draw back. He was not pleased when the assembly passed a Schools Act in 1829 that bypassed the Parish Schools Act of five years before. The new Act gave control to trustees who had no necessary connection with a parish, and there was no reference to religious teaching. Financing was in the hands of the assembly. Lartigue was so hostile that he said of the *habitant* children that "it would be better for them to have no literary education at all than to risk a bad moral education." In 1831 an assembly bill, the "Loi des Fabriques" that was vetoed by the council, aroused his wrath by introducing democratic controls in the running of parish affairs. Thus, by the time Gosford had his report ready, Church opinion, especially at the higher level, was hardening against Papineau.

After Gosford had reported, the British government made its response to the *Ninety-two Resolutions*. They were fewer in number and more brutally outspoken. The Ten Resolutions of Lord John Russell, issued in 1837, stated "that in the existing state of Lower Canada, it is unadvisable to make the Legislative Council of that province an elective body." They went on to provide the governors with funds should the assembly persist in withholding supply until alleged grievances were remedied. This blank refusal infuriated the *patriotes*. The extremist *Vindicator*, edited by Papineau's Irish lieutenant E.B. O'Callaghan, warned

> The die is cast; the British ministry have resolved to set the seal of degradation and slavery on this province, and to render it actually, what it was only in repute – the 'Ireland' of North America . . . . One duty alone now remains for the people of Lower Canada. Let them study the history of the American revolution.

*Patriotes* followed this advice. A boycott of British goods was planned. The *Fils de la Liberté* were set up on the model of the American Sons of Liberty. Extralegal associations such as the Assembly of Six Counties were founded. Papineau reminded his listeners that "the Americans began with passive resistance before taking to arms. . . . Our cause is much more just than that of the old colonies." By the late fall of 1837 the situation was explosive. Lartigue chose his moment and issued a *Mandement*, enjoining support for the authorities on all good Catholics. Gosford chose his moment too, and called out the troops. In doing so he surprised the *patriotes*, who had set 4 December as the date of the revolutionary convention. Caught unprepared, the rebel forces were brushed aside at St. Denis and St. Eustache. Papineau and others fled to the United States. From there, sorties were made in the following year, especially by the real extremists such as Robert Nelson, but neither they nor the *Frères Chasseurs* (Hunters' Lodges) they founded could do anything against the military's savage reprisals. The Lower Canadian Rebellion of 1837-38 was a resounding failure.

# 4. Republicans Rejected: The Case of Upper Canada

In Lower Canada, the appeal of American republicanism had been restricted to a portion of the elite. The majority of the inhabitants were insulated from that appeal by language, by religion, and by an already old tradition of looking upon their neighbours as damned "Yankis." In the case of Upper Canada, however, this insulation was lacking, and thus American republicanism was much more pervasive.

To begin with, there was the population itself. True, legislation in 1816 discouraged the immigration of Americans, but they did not disappear immediately, and since they were more than 50 percent of the population their leaven continued to work powerfully. Official attempts to limit their role in the colony only served to highlight their identity. During the 1820s the "alien-question" was a major one. It began in 1821 with the election of Barnabas Bidwell to the assembly; he was an American and had in fact served in the United States congress. The assembly expelled him, but on moral rather than legal grounds, and the question was reopened when his son, Marshal Spring Bidwell, came forward at the ensuing by-election. The assembly allowed him to take his seat, although he was an alien. The vote showed a split between the more loyalist eastern portion of the colony and the western, late loyalist areas. Attempts to legislate the position of aliens continued to split the province: an assembly bill would have confirmed American settlers in their property and political rights, but the council would confirm only the former. Not until 1828 was an act passed that quietened the problem, though it did not wholly solve it. Through it all, Americans remained numerous and prominent, and in 1836, when the governor, Sir Francis Bond Head, reported home on the assembly he had inherited, he identified 13 out of a house of 60 as Americans.

It was not only American individuals who appealed against British ways. The very example of republican success just across the border was extremely telling. On many issues American practice compared favourably with the colonial, to say the least. A leading example was the land grant system. In the United States the policy was one of cheap cash sales accomplished in a simple and efficient manner. The would-be farmer in Michigan, say, became "lord of the soil in fifteen minutes." In Upper Canada, however, he would be "tormented with office fees, petitions, affidavits, council days, locations . . . and is wearied out of his life before he gets his business done," and would end up paying a high credit price on which he would pay interest. The existence of Crown reserves was an impediment to settlement, for they held land off the market and kept it in an unimproved state that lowered the value of neighbouring farms. The whole land issue was given great publicity when in 1817 a Scots immigrant, Robert Gourlay, began a survey — complete with questionnaire — about the condition of the province. Ostensibly it was to aid emigrants from Britain by providing information, but it turned out to be an embarrassing critique of the executive as set up under the Act of 1791. Question 31 was devastating, for it was the open-ended: "What, in your opinion, retards the improvement of your township in particular, or the province in general; and what would most contribute to the same?" The response stressed the disadvantages caused by the land reserves, which prevented contiguous settlement, and emphasized the shortcomings of an immigration policy that retarded population growth. Gourlay was led to demand a legislative enquiry. When this failed, township meetings leading to a convention, a strategy reeking of republicanism, were called for. In 1819 Gourlay was arrested and convicted under an 1804 wartime Act regulating the conduct of immigrants, and was expelled from Upper Canada. He became a martyr to many, and the superiority of the American system became all the clearer to them.

One aspect of the land question eclipsed even this, however. The Crown reserve was not the only one complained of; there was also the clergy reserve, and it raised issues over and above that of land granting. It will be remembered that these lands, one seventh of the ungranted land of the colony, had been set aside in 1791 for the support of the "Protestant Clergy." The intention, presumably, had been to establish the Anglican Church, the established Church in the mother country. Certainly the Anglicans in the province assumed this to have been the case, and their leader, John Strachan, later the first bishop of Toronto, an ex-Presbyterian with all the proverbial ultraism of the convert, was insistent on this interpretation. Since he was a member of the Family Compact, had been a member of the executive council since 1815 and of the legislative council since 1820, and moreover since he had been the educator of many of the high officials, he was able to go far in having his interpretation accepted.

However, his interpretation was not completely accepted. The characteristic of Upper Canada in its social-religious style was its repudiation of both Anglicanism and Catholicism in favour of sectarianism. The raw, thinly settled backwoods were not suited to the parish organization and educated priesthood of the Churches, but the itinerant pastors of the Baptists, Congregationalists, and Methodists (and to a lesser extent of the Presbyterians) were right for the frontier. Their non-intellectual traditions appealed to a population unable to provide for lengthy intellectual preparation. Above all, the enthusiasm, the playing on emotions long starved of outlet in the isolation of the forest, were just what was needed. Upper Canadians turned to sectarianism with a vengeance.

The sectarian lobby was outraged by the pretensions of the Anglicans. They campaigned to have the reserves applied to all Protestant groupings — and here they had the letter of the Constitutional Act on their side. Their first success came in 1820 when the colonial office stated that the Presbyterian Church of Scotland might share in the reserves. By 1826 the assembly was on record as favouring equal access by all Protestant groupings. Two years later, the imperial Canada Committee (the same that had come out against the Lower Canadian oligarchy) stated its belief in equal sharing. Yet the problem could not be settled. It dragged on and on, and in 1840 the Governor Lord Sydenham described it as "the one great overwhelming grievance — the root of all the trouble of the Province — the cause of the Rebellion — the never failing watchword at the hustings — the perpetual source of discord, strife, and hatred." Only in 1854 were the reserves secularized and the dispute stilled. All the time that the wrangling continued, the example before everyone's eyes was an America where church establishment had been swept away, and support for religion was on the voluntary basis.

Upper Canadians naturally differed in the extent to which they accepted American values, and in the lengths they were prepared to go in weaving all their criticisms into an assault upon the Family Compact. Nevertheless, some were prepared to go all the way, and considered the province utterly corrupted by the British oligarchy. The spokesman for these extremists was William Lyon Mackenzie, a Scot who began his *Colonial Advocate* in 1824 and steadily became more strident in his criticisms until he led the Upper Canada Rebellion in 1837. A convenient summary of his creed (much more succinct than the famous *Seventh Report on Grievances* of 1835, the counterpart of the *Ninety-two Resolutions*, by which the Upper Canadian assembly formally went on record as favouring republicanism) may be found in the proclamation and constitution he issued after the rising had taken place. It opened with a ringing repudiation of European ways:

> For nearly fifty years has our country languished under the blighting influence of military despots, strangers from Europe, ruling us, not according to laws of our choice, but by the capricious dictates of their arbitrary power. They have taxed us at their pleasure, robbed our exchequer, and carried off the proceeds to other lands . . .; they have . . . ruled us, as Ireland has been ruled, to the advantage of persons in other lands . . . .

After more in this vein, Mackenzie listed his objectives; they included

> Perpetual Peace, founded on a government of equal rights to all, secured by a written constitution, sanctioned by yourselves in a convention . . . .

> A Legislature, composed of a Senate and Assembly chosen by the people.

> An Executive, to be composed of a Governor and other officers elected by the public voice.

> The people to elect their Court of Request Commissioners and Justices of the Peace — and also their Militia officers, in all cases whatsoever.

> A frugal and economical Government . . . .

The Jacksonian inspiration is patent.

As events were to show, such views, whatever their diffusion, were not enough to spark a successful rebellion: in Upper Canada, even more clearly than in Lower Canada, the Rebellion of 1837 was a resounding failure. Only a tiny handful marched down Yonge Street in Toronto; when fired on, it dispersed. One man had been killed, two died of wounds, and there was hardly any further loss of life. Mackenzie fled to the United States and from there made his way to Navy Island, whence he issued the proclamation and constitution mentioned above. However, in the case of the upper province there was no equivalent to the 1838 activity that took place in the lower.

For all its failure, a rising had taken place. For all its lack of support, inclinations to republican patterns had been strong. In explaining Mackenzie's failure it may well be that timing is the all-important factor.

In many ways, republican hostility to British methods had been more intense in the 1820s than in the 1830s, yet it was not intense enough to produce rebellion. Since then there had occurred a challenge to American presuppositions. A major factor in shifting the balance of opinion was the change in the population. The American element had been frozen since 1816; the British was growing rapidly. Recent immigrants in themselves tend to be a stabilizing force, preoccupied as they are with getting established and looking to authority to show the way. Moreover, certain strains among the immigrants intensified the loyalist cast of mind. There were many half-pay officers among them, instinctively obedient to British law and order and dependent on the imperial connection for their pensions. There were many Protestant Irish, members of the Orange Lodge. This organization, founded in Ireland in the late eighteenth century, was devoted to upholding the British Protestant monarchy as a means of keeping Catholics in their place. There was also a dramatic defection from the sectarian ranks that had backed reform against the Family Compact. Until 1828 the Methodists had been dependent on the American organization. In that year, however, they abandoned that link and joined up with the British Wesleyan Methodists. The Wesleyans were notoriously Tory and had a horror of democracy. Mackenzie always looked upon Egerton Ryerson, the leader of Methodism in Upper Canada, who broke with the radicals in 1833, as a traitor.

Since the War of 1812 the colony's mood had vacillated. An initial pro-Americanism had weakened, and the loyalist myth had intensified. By the 1830s a realignment of the colony's basic stance was potential. It became actual due to a governor prepared to come forward and act as a focus about which the emerging consensus could rally. That governor was Sir Francis Bond Head.

Like so many other governors in the post-Waterloo years, Head had been a military man, but he was not merely a martinet. His was a lively mind, and he was naturally attracted to the progressive forces at work about him. After working for a mining concern in South America, he became an assistant-commissioner for the New Poor Law in East Kent. In 1834 the traditional scheme of poor relief had been taken in hand by Parliament in the rush of progressive activity that followed the Reform Bill. The thinking behind the New Poor Law was Benthamite. The commissioners showed themselves aggressive modernizers, determined to improve the lot of the working people, if necessary by imposing unpleasant courses of conduct for their own good. The openhanded provision of outdoor relief was to be given up, and in future was to go only to those inside the workhouse. There the régime was deliberately to be made unpleasant, one degree less "eligible" than that of the poorest working labourer outside. In this way the poor would be terrified into finding work and living frugally — in fact, they called the workhouses "bastilles." Head was in complete agreement with such thinking. Further examples of his Benthamite outlook were his favourable contrasting of German educational interest with English lack of concern, his preference for modern subjects over the classics, and his anticipation of Lord Durham in offering Lower Canada the choice between being "disloyal and anti-commercial" or "commercial and loyal." Given his scale of values he might have concluded that go-ahead America proved the superiority of republican ways. However, that country was in the grip of the many, who, he believed, could never be trusted to identify true progress. He was delighted by the American panic of 1837, for it confirmed his suspicion that their success was meretricious and could not last. He saw true balance between progress and stability in Britain. When all allowance has been made for Head's elitism, he was a progressive, and the banner that greeted him in Toronto, "A Tried Reformer," was not impossibly wide of the mark.

Soon after his arrival, Head plunged the colony into an election. He took the leading part, scandalizing the more staid by his impetuosity and by even appearing on the hustings. His pitch was earthy realism, which contrasted strongly with Mackenzie's devotion to abstract principle. "Can you do as much for yourselves," he asked, "as I can do for you? If you choose to dispute with me, and live on bad terms with the mother country, you will, to use a homely phrase, only quarrel with your own bread and butter." This was fully in keeping with his diagnosis earlier that the province needed "capital and population," roads and railways (the latter were still extreme novelties, even in Britain), which hit home with significant sections of the population. In 1834 the Canadian Alliance of Toronto had called for close links with any body "in Lower Canada or the other colonies, having for its object 'the greatest happiness of the greatest number'." Others demanded "the improvement of the land we live in, rather than . . . the consideration of abstract questions of Government."

The election was a triumph for Head. The reformers were routed, and the leading radicals, including Mackenzie, failed to keep their seats. They claimed, not surprisingly, that their loss was due solely to the governor's use of bribes and bullies, and was not an adequate reflection of public opinion. A little later the Toronto civic elections took place; Head crowed that the voters "unequivocally expressed their verdict in my favour, by exterminating the twenty republican candidates from every single ward of the city, and by electing in their stead staunch Constitutionalists, who in every instance excepting one, had majorities of more than two to one over their opponents."

The colony had indeed expressed a preference for unspectacular gains over spectacular moral crusades, confirming a choice that the loyalists had made in the previous century. Not that reform was unthinkable — far from it — but reform was to be pragmatic and low-key, and to take place within a firm framework of a known imperial connection.

## __ 5. The British Mode Vindicated: __ Reform in the Maritimes

As the two Canadas saw the republican mode of reform pushed to the point of rebellion, any form of change became, for the moment, impossible. Alternatives, even those more in tune with British constitutional evolution, had to wait for a more auspicious juncture.

That British way was to disregard its own eighteenth-century theory, which had held that there should be a separation of powers and a balance among them. In fact, there never had been in Britain the separation demanded by the theory, and the interpenetration of the executive and the legislature had long been a part of constitutional life. Now a similar arrangement of executive and assembly was being urged in the colonies. The two Baldwins (W.W., the father, and Robert, the son) had been pressing for such a system in Upper Canada since the 1820s. It was what would be called "Responsible Government," the idea that the government of the day (the executive, that is, the executive council or the cabinet) should be responsible, that is, answerable, to the public opinion of the day as revealed in the composition of the assembly and located within the majority party there. Thus, so long as the government can command a majority of the votes in the lower house it may continue in office; however, should it lose a vote on a significant issue it must resign and make way for one that can win a majority.

As these Canadian beginnings were pushed aside by republican pressures, the pace of British modes was being set in the Maritimes. Here was something of a surprise. Two obstacles stood in the way of any fusion of executive and legislative personnel. One was the prevailing colonial practice that councillors were appointed for life, to be removed only for completely unacceptable behaviour. Thus, in Nova Scotia in 1830, of the 12-member council one had held office since 1811, one since 1808, one since 1802 and one since 1788! Such an entrenched group could not be responsive, let alone responsible, to changing public opinion. This obstacle was shared by all British North American colonies, but the second was peculiar to those of the Maritimes. In those three colonies the executive council was not distinguished from the legislative council, a separation that had been made by the Constitutional Act for the Canadas but which did not apply in the Maritimes. Given this fusion of functions it was impossible to conceive of an executive changing from time to time in response to changing public opinion without forfeiting in the legislative council that remoteness from democratic pressures that was held necessary in any truly stable society. To have the legislative function of an upper house "responsible" would be akin to having the House of Lords dependent on the many, and tantamount to letting in elective upper chambers through the back door.

Yet despite these obstacles, changes in direction of Responsible Government did come. The start was made in New Brunswick. Owing to the timber boom, the executive was in a very strong position. The Crown had huge reserves of land much in demand by timber barons who were willing to pay high prices for access to the pineries. The Crown was making so much merely from these sales that it was amassing a fund, the interest from which alone threatened to make the executive free for all time from dependence upon assembly votes for funds. However, the executive agent in charge of timber concessions, Thomas Baillie, made enemies, and against him and his councillor clique the timber merchants began to work. It was a struggle that gained momentum in 1833 when the imperial government split the council into two, on the lines of the two Canadas: Baillie was in the smaller executive council, but his opponents were relegated to the larger legislative council.

When Baillie's rivals began to organize they realized that the assembly was the obvious base from which to fight. That body could be made to appear as the bastion of popular resistance to an oligarchy entrenched in the executive council. The issue on which they would give battle would be the traditional constitutional one of an assembly's right to control financial matters. The dispute was taken to Britain where a parsimonious imperial government was eager to find ways of getting colonies to pay their own expenses. There a deal was struck: if the assembly would vote a permanent civil list that would pay the salaries of the chief executive officers, the Crown would hand over to the assembly the control of its lands and hence control of access to timber. Thus Baillie's rivals triumphed. The seal was set upon the assembly's victory when in 1837 Baillie's leading opponent, Charles Simonds, was given a seat on the executive council; the seat was given not in recognition of Simonds' personal qualities but because he was a leading member of the assembly and so could be said to represent public opinion.

The situation in New Brunswick by the end of the 1830s was not Responsible Government. The executive council as a whole did not mirror public opinion. Moreover, it was the governor who decided which of the individuals enjoying public confidence should be invited into that council, not public opinion as revealed by the standings in the lower house. Even so, the merging of executive council and assembly had been taken one step further, and to that degree Responsible Government was closer to realization.

Much the same development occurred a little later in Nova Scotia. There the leading reformer was Joseph Howe. He had leaped to prominence in 1835 when he was put on trial for publishing in his paper, *The Nova Scotian*, an attack upon the magistrates that, since they were appointed by the council, was also an attack upon that body. Against all the odds, and against the law as it then stood, the jury acquitted him. Suddenly a popular champion, Howe stood for the assembly and was elected. Immediately in 1836 he moved into action, securing the adoption of the Twelve Resolutions. The sting was in the twelfth:

> Resolved, that as a remedy for these grievances, His Majesty be implored to take such steps, either by granting an Elective Legislative Council, or by such other reconstruction of the local Government as will ensure responsibility to the Commons, and confer upon the People of this Province, what they value above all other possessions, the blessings of the British Constitution.

The attempt to pass off an elective upper house as part of the British constitution was an impossible one, and it may be supposed that Howe was using it as a bargaining ploy. Certainly, he gave up his resolutions and himself moved an alternative which ran

As a remedy for these grievances, we implore Your Majesty to grant us an Elective Legislative Council; or, to separate the Executive from the Legislative Council; providing for a just Representation of all the great interests of the Province in both; and by the introduction into the former of some Members of the popular Branch, and otherwise securing responsibility to the Commons, confer upon the People of this Province what they value above all other Possessions, the blessings of the British Constitution.

This moderate, conciliatory formulation met a ready response from Lord Glenelg, the British minister for the colonies. At a time when extremism in the Canadas was mounting, the attitude of Nova Scotia seemed reasonable, In 1837 the council was split as New Brunswick's had been four years earlier, and four members of the assembly were included in the executive council.

Two years later, in 1839, the following circular was sent by the colonial secretary, Russell, to all colonies with representative institutions:

[The governor] will understand and will cause it to be made generally known, that hereafter the tenure of colonial offices held during Her Majesty's pleasure, will not be regarded as equivalent to a tenure during good behaviour; but that not only will such officers be called upon to retire from the public service as often as any sufficient motives of public policy may suggest the expediency of that measure, but that a change in the person of the governor will be considered as a sufficient reason for any alterations which his successor may deem it expedient to make in the list of public functionaries, subject of course to the future confirmation of the sovereign.

Again it is to be noted how far from Responsible Government this is; but at the same time it does facilitate that doctrine.

In Prince Edward Island the evolution was rather different. In that colony there was a serious split between the absentee proprietors who controlled the land and who had allies among the Island's oligarchy and officialdom, and the tenants who wanted the government to repossess the land and regrant it. This popular movement found its champion in William Cooper and enjoyed its triumph in 1838 when his "Escheat Party" won 18 of 24 seats in the assembly. Cooper's solution was not along British lines but rather the republican one of an elected legislative council. However, his embassy to London in 1839 to press his ideas on Lord John Russell was a failure. He was refused any interview, and while the council was split into executive and legislative branches, and while two assemblymen were taken into the executive council, this was done more in emulation of other Maritime developments than in deference to Prince Edward Island itself or to Cooper. Rather, the extremism of the land question encouraged the imperial authorities to stand firm, and the Escheat Party collapsed totally by 1842.

The contrast between New Brunswick and Nova Scotia on the one hand and the two Canadas on the other (and not so clearly between them and Prince Edward Island) provides a clue to the explanation for the success there of Responsible Government and for the repudiation of republicanism. Both New Brunswick and Nova Scotia were homogeneous provinces, and that in a double sense.

In the first place, they were essentially loyalist (and not late loyalist, either) in their composition and outlook. What this meant was that loyalty to the British connection could be taken for granted, and a critic did not risk labelling himself disloyal merely because he pressed for change. Howe himself was a good example. He was the son of a loyalist who had been a magistrate in Nova Scotia. Thus, when the son printed criticisms of magistrates it was not the same as when Mackenzie, a newly-arrived Scot who visited Washington and became a Jacksonian, mounted his attacks. Who could doubt the *bona fides* of one who exclaimed "I am a dear lover of old England, and to save her would blow Nova Scotia into the air or scuttle her like an old ship"?

Second, the politically active belonged to one stratum of society. In the case of New Brunswick there was nothing genuinely popular about the dispute: Simonds was every bit as much a member of the Family Compact as was Baillie, the only difference being that Simonds was an "out" while Baillie was already "in." It is true that in Nova Scotia the council was heavily Anglican whereas five sixths of the people were not, and that most of its members came from Halifax, so that the colony as a whole was poorly represented on the council. Nevertheless, the opposition never took the populist tone it had in the Canadas or in Prince Edward Island. Howe was a Halifax man who never articulated a backwoods protest. He was concerned very little with religion and did not champion a sectarian crusade. In both colonies, for all the disputes, political discourse was singularly free from rancour organized into movements. It was no aberration when Howe in 1840 entered a "Tory" executive council.

Nova Scotia and New Brunswick, in fact, were duplicating the evolution of the mother country in that the key developments were taking place "within doors" and only later were being reported to the people at large. On the contrary, in the two Canadas and in Prince Edward Island, the leading edge was to be found in forces organized outside the charmed circle, forces that brought pressure to bear upon the political elite. There was about New

Brunswick and Nova Scotia an instinctive acceptance of the rules of the game as played in the Britain of the second quarter of the nineteenth century, and an absence of that popularism that vitiated smooth development elsewhere. However, as the experience of the next few years was to indicate, the rules of the game were suddenly to change. An earnest of that revolution was the dispatch to British North America of Lord Durham as governor and investigator of the confused situation after 1837.

## Suggested Reading

For the development of Canadian newspapers, see W.H. Kesterton, *A History of Journalism in Canada* (1967). The histories of many if not most Canadian universities are available; they are too numerous to be listed here. On education in general, see J.D. Wilson, R.M. Stamp, and L.P. Audet (eds.), *Canadian Education: A History* (1970), and R. Harris, *A History of Higher Education in Canada* (1976).

Immigration is covered in H.I. Cowan, *British Emigration to British North America, 1783-1837* (1962); V. Macdonald, *Canada 1763-1841: Immigration and Settlement* (1939); and M.A. Jones, "The Background to Emigration from Great Britain in the Nineteenth Century," *Perspectives in American History* (1973). A specialized study is O. MacDonagh, *A Pattern of Government Growth: The Passenger Acts and their Enforcement* (1961). On cholera there is G. Birtson, *A Darkened House* (1980).

Lower Canadian nationalism is the subject of H.T. Manning's, *The Revolt of French Canada, 1800-1835* (1962). Also important are F. Ouellet, *Social and Economic History of Quebec, 1760-1850* (1980); "Le Nationalisme canadien-français," *Canadian Historical Review* (1964); and W.H. Parker, "A New Look at Unrest in Lower Canada in the 1830s," *Canadian Historical Review* (1959). For Papineau consult F. Ouellet, *L. J. Papineau* (1961), and *Papineau: Textes choisis* (1958).

On the Union project, see W. Ormsby, "The Problem of Canadian Union, 1822-28," *Canadian Histocial Review* (1958), while for British attitudes in the period immediately following, see P. Burroughs, *The Canadian Crisis and British Colonial Policy* (1972), and *British Attitudes Towards Canada* (1971).

Lartigue's response to rebellion is examined in F. Ouellet, "Le Mandement de Mgr. Lartigue de 1837 et la réaction libérale," *Bulletin des Recherches Historiques* (1952).

G. Filteau's three-volume *Histoire des patriotes* (1938-39), covers the Lower Canadian rising. That of Upper Canada is dealt with in chapters in F. Landon, *Western Ontario and the American Frontiers* (1967). Also to be consulted are A.B. Corey, *The Crisis of 1830-1842 in Canadian-American Relations* (1941), and O.A. Kinchen, *The Rise and Fall of the Patriot Hunters* (1956).

For the background to Upper Canada's rebellion, see G.M. Craig, "The American Impact on the Upper Canadian Reform Movement before 1837," *Canadian Historical Review* (1948). S.R. Mealing edited and introduces a reprint of R. Gourlay, *Statistical Account of Upper Canada* (1974). D.W.L. Earl (ed.), *The Family Compact* (1967) is also useful. A. Durham, *Political Unrest in Upper Canada, 1815-36* (1927), still retains its place. For the religious dimensions, see J.S. Moir, *Church & State in Canada West* (1959), and G.S. French, "The Evangelical Creed in Canada," in W.L. Morton (ed.), *The Shield of Achilles* (1968), and *Parsons and Politics: The Role of the Wesleyan Methodists in Upper Canada and the Maritimes, 1780-1855* (1962). A good approach to Mackenzie is via A.B. McKillop's edition of W. LeSueur, *William Lyon Mackenzie* (1979). Bond Head may most conveniently be approached through S.F. Wise's edition of F.B. Head, *A Narrative* (1969), though it must be said that Wise is less than fair to his subject.

The literature on Responsible Government in the Maritimes is full. To be singled out are W.S. MacNutt, "The Coming of Responsible Government to New Brunswick," *Canadian Historical Review* (1952) and W.R. Livingston, *Responsible Government in Nova Scotia* (1930), and *Responsible Government in Prince Edward Island* (1931). Newfoundland's special case is treated in G.E. Gunn in *The Political History of Newfoundland 1832-1864* (1966). They all may be set against P. Burrough's, "The Determinants of Colonial Self-Government," *Journal of Imperial and Commonwealth History* (1978).

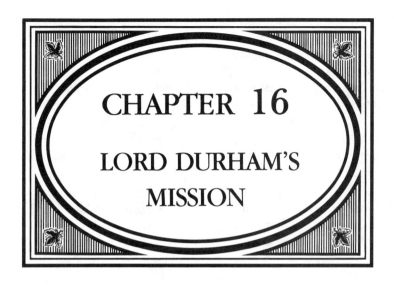

# CHAPTER 16

## LORD DURHAM'S MISSION

## — 1. Radical Jack in British North America —

The news that Lower Canada had burst into rebellion plunged the British government into deep gloom. Lord Melbourne's ministry was in a precarious position. The recent election of 1837 had returned a House where the Whigs were kept in power only by an alliance with the Radicals, and even then their majority over the Tories was a scant 12 votes. Since Radicals like Hume and Roebuck had been siding with Canadian radicals and reformers for many years, even calling for the abandonment of the colonies, it looked as though the government might lose its majority and have to resign. Melbourne was desperate for a remedy that would at least buy time.

The solution he hit upon was to ask John George Lambton, first Earl of Durham, to go out as governor general and high commissioner. The Earl was known as an advanced Whig, almost a Radical in fact. The son of one of the few Whigs to have voted against repressive measures at the time of the Revolutionary Wars, he had developed into a fierce defender of the reform cause.

He had spoken in favour of liberal concessions to Catholics and Dissenters. He had supported mechanics' institutes and the newly founded University of London, established to contest the privileged position of Oxford and Cambridge. He was eager to take up progressive ideas, and rejoiced in being one of the first to light his residence with the newfangled gas lights. Above all, he had taken a lead in resurrecting the issue of parliamentary reform, speaking out for it as early as 1819. So prominent was he that when in 1830 Prime Minister Earl Grey (his father-in-law) felt that the time was ripe to make it a government issue he appointed Lambton to the committee of four that drafted the Reform Bill — and since Lord John Russell was one of the four it was a case of balancing "Finality Jack" with "Radical Jack." By 1837, such a figure could be counted on to impress the Radicals at Westminster, and there was an even chance that he might impress the Canadians, too.

Durham's reputation as an advanced thinker must not disguise the fact that he was also very much an aristocrat. Stemming from an old established family (his grandfather had refused a peerage) that had made a fortune from the collieries of the northeast of England, the "King of the Coal Country" was determined to parade that high station he thought was rightfully his. He was avid for recognition, and openly pursued titles and decorations. When he agreed to go to Canada, he insisted upon a fittingly impressive retinue, and took along no fewer than eight *aides-de-camp* (it was pointed out that Wellington in the Peninsula actually fighting Bonaparte never had more than six). Merely to unload the plate, furniture, racehorses, and his other equipment at Quebec took two full days. That he entered that city on a white charger was only in keeping. Accompanying this vanity was what many opponents took to be an aristocratic temper and impulsiveness. He was always liable to break out in awesome displays of rage, and his tendency to make rash decisions, to issue ultimatums if at all checked, was notorious. In his defence it should be said that he was a lifelong sufferer from migraine, which could prostrate him for days at a time, and that his family life was tragic: his first wife (whom he married clandestinely when he was 19) died after only three years, and later, within the space of a little over three years, so had his mother, son, and three daughters. However, these facts were not always known or remembered, and the general impression was of a headstrong, willful man. The fact remained that too often what he did was intolerable. Melbourne said of him, "What he did was often right, but always so done as to be totally indefensible."

His stay in Canada was typical. Appointed early in 1838 he delayed his journey out for no good reason, except, as critics said, to be able to proceed with due solemnity. He put the delay to some good use, however, by reading up on the background and digesting opinions. On arrival he made a virtual clean sweep of the existing government, installing men from his entourage in the vacancies: Edward Gibbon Wakefield and Charles Buller were the most important, the former being put to work on a report on Crown lands and emigration, the latter on municipal institutions. This fresh start gave him an initial popularity with the French Canadians. However, not all the consequences of his new-broom approach were satisfactory. One of his appointments was that of Thomas Turton, his legal representative, whom he appointed to the executive council; this appointment proved disastrous. Not only were Turton's personal qualities dubious, but his knowledge of the law was not up to the mark, either. A problem that had confronted Durham from the moment he landed was what to do with eight leading rebels then being held in jail. To pardon them would be to show weakness. To put them on trial before a jury would doubtless lead to acquittal in the face of the evidence. To pack a jury would be distasteful. Durham thought he had effected a neat compromise when be banished them to Bermuda. However, Turton ought to have spotted that to do so was to exceed Durham's commission, which applied to British *North* America only. The action was illegal, and the eight could have brought actions for wrongful arrest. The Melbourne government, which knew that any attempt to indemnify the Canadian officials involved would lead to a defeat in the House of Commons, declined to uphold Durham. Impulsive as ever, Durham resigned. Just as typically, he chose to issue a proclamation to the Canadians in which he accused the home government of sacrificing the colonies' true interests. It was a woeful breach of good manners, and helped erode what support he still retained.

The result was that when Durham wrote his *Report*, he did so as a private citizen. The government was not particularly anxious to have it, and the *Report* saw the light of day only because it was leaked (probably by Wakefield, who was a journalist) to the *Times*. Put out under such unpropitious circumstances, the *Report* had virtually no impact, and as far as Britain was concerned might almost never have been.

Yet it did have its significance. In the colonies the ideas that Durham espoused might have been in the air for a long time. The novelty of 1839, when the *Times* printed the *Report*, was that now an ex-governor-general and high commissioner, a belted earl no less, one who had sat in the British cabinet, had been ambassador to Russia, and had even been rumoured as prime minister, had enshrined such ideas in a formidable document. Étienne Parent translated it and it appeared in his *Le Canadien*, while in Upper Canada "Durham meetings" sprang up across the province. The Maritimes, too, were caught up in the discussion, and Prince Edward Island's thinking in particular was jolted into new channels. Not everything championed by the Durham *Report* appealed to everyone, of course, but as the following sections will demonstrate, the debate it unleashed, the questions it identified, and most importantly the legitimation it conferred, were vital stages in the evolution of British North America.

## — 2. Durham's *Report* —

There was something for just about everybody in the *Report* — and by the same token just about everybody had grounds for being disappointed. The two sides of the Earl, the radical and the traditional, were responsible for stirring up profound disagreement in British North America. Only one point in the *Report* did not further split colonial opinion. Even before leaving Britain, Durham had concluded that the union of all the British colonies in North America would be desirable. Such an arrangement would foster a deeper sense of nationalism with which to oppose American encroachment. (Durham the modernizer, in company with many of his contemporaries, was fascinated by the United States and suspected it to be the wave of the future.) At the same time a union would create an entity of sufficient size to swallow up the petty tensions that so often consumed colonial energies. Once in British North America, however, Durham had to recognize that feeling against his plan was widespread and passionate. Most disturbingly this feeling was most powerful in the Maritimes, colonies quite free of the taint of rebellion, and Durham had the sense to realize that it was pointless to push for a British federation. The most that could be hoped for was some outline that would encourage eventual participation in some form of union, and the *Report* included the hope that "any or all of the . . . North American colonies may . . . be . . . admitted into the union."

Durham's point of departure was the belief that the colonial-British link ought to be maintained. The reason was that the colonies were too valuable a dumping ground for the "suffering classes of the mother country" to be allowed to slip away. The colonies were, he claimed, "the rightful patrimony of the English people, the ample appanage which God and Nature have set aside in the New World for those whose lot has assigned them but insufficient portions in the Old." This backhanded compliment was overlooked by those who valued the imperial connection and wanted it preserved. Radicals in Britain and extremists in the colonies who looked to annexation to the United States were disappointed.

Loyalist joy was not unalloyed, however. Despite the fact that Durham had spent only five days in Upper Canada, a good deal of the *Report* dealt with that colony; indeed it could hardly have been otherwise, when the colony had adopted the *Seventh Report in Grievances* and had engaged in rebellion. The commission learned enough to castigate the Family Compact. The backwardness of the province when compared with the neighbouring states was stressed: the *Report* stated that "there must have been something wrong to have caused so striking a difference in progress and wealth between Upper Canada and the neighbouring states of the Union." The wretched policy and administration of the land granting agencies was pilloried; the clergy reserves were singled out for especial blame as a formentor of discord. Durham did not mince words;

> Everywhere needless delays have harassed and exasperated applicants; and everywhere, more or less, I am sorry but compelled to add, gross favouritism has prevailed in the disposal of public lands. The evils produced by the system of reserving land for the clergy have become notorious . . . .

Reformers, whose ranks had been thinning since their rout by Bond Head in 1836, felt vindicated and experienced a surge of confidence.

Reform happiness was crowned when they read of Durham's acceptance of the principle of Responsible Government. During his lightning trip to the upper province, Durham had met the two Baldwins. They had explained to him the ideas they had been mulling over for some years, and followed up this initiative in written communications. They proposed that in matters of domestic concern, the Crown should be governed by the advice of the executive council alone. That executive council, moreover, should be entirely composed of those who belonged to the majority group in the assembly. Durham put it as follows in the *Report*:

> It is not by weakening but strengthening the influence of the people on its Government, by confining within much narrower bounds than those hitherto allotted to it, and not by extending the interference of the imperial authorities in the details of colonial affairs, that I believe that harmony is to be restored . . . . It needs no change in the principles of government, no invention of a new constitutional theory, to supply the remedy which would in my opinion, completely remove the existing political disorders. It needs but to follow out consistently the principles of the British constitution, and introduce into the Government of these great Colonies those wise provisions, by which alone the working

of the representative system can in any country be rendered harmonious and efficient.

A beauty of the proposed reform was that it did not depend on legislation; "This change," noted Durham, "might be effected by a single dispatch containing such instructions." It was necessaary only to stipulate which issues remained of imperial concern, and hence beyond this proposed reform. Durham gave them as "the constitution of the form of government, the regulation of foreign relations and trade . . . and the disposal of public lands." These were wide exemptions, and it was not clear that domestic and imperial issues could always be distinguished as easily as Durham implied, but the magnitude of the novelty remained.

The Family Compact, the Chateau Clique, and many loyalists, too, were deeply disturbed by Durham's acceptance of reform thinking. Nevertheless, on one other aspect of the *Report* they found themselves in agreement with its author. When it came to the French Canadians, Durham was, they felt, sound. His attitude to this numerically dominant element gained emphasis from the fact it was presented with the dramatic effect of a conversion. When he set sail from Britain, confessed Durham, he had viewed the

> quarrel which I was sent for the purpose of healing [as one] between the executive government and the popular branch of the legislature. The latter body had, apparently, been contending for popular rights and free government. . . . I looked on it as a dispute analogous to those with which history and experience have made us so familiar in Europe — a dispute between a people demanding an extension of popular privileges, on the one hand, and an executive, on the other, defending the powers which it conceived necessary for the maintenance of order.

As he experienced the situation on the spot, however, Durham was forced to recant his original views; now, he realized, he had missed the point. "I expected to find a contest between a government and a people; I found two nations warring in the bosom of a single state: I found a struggle, not of principles, but of races."

Durham did not stop there. He went on to describe the French-Canadian race, by which he meant "culture" or "identity," not a genetically determined entity, in terms that pleased the Loyalists. In Whig fashion he rooted their mentality in the fact that in the seventeenth century they never knew the blessings of a "Glorious Revolution." "The institutions of France," he declared, during the period of colonization of Canada, were, perhaps more than those of any other European nation, calculated to repress the intelligence and freedom of the great mass of the people. These institutions followed the Canadian colonist across the Atlantic. The same central, ill-organized, unimproving and repressive despotism extended over him. . . . Under the same institutions they remained the same uninstructed, inactive, unprogressive people. . . . They clung to ancient prejudices, ancient customs, and ancient laws, not from any strong sense of their beneficial effects, but with the unreasoning tenacity of an uneducated and unprogressive people.

Durham did allow that they were "mild and kindly, frugal, industrious and honest, very sociable, cheerful and hospitable, and distinguished for a courtesy and real politeness, which pervades every class of society." When all allowance had been made, however, "they remain[ed] an old and stationary society, in a new and progressive world." This was music to the ears of the thrusters of the St. Lawrence society. That French-Canadian passivity, considered so detrimental to canal improvements, had been recognized; now, perhaps, something would be done in the interests of development.

The Earl's reading of the situation allowed of only one solution. The French Canadians must be submerged beneath an Anglicizing tide. Two methods would bring this about. Renewed immigration from Britain would eventually swamp superior French-Canadian numbers. This would take time, however, and the perceived seriousness of the situation demanded immediate action. Therefore, despite the resistance to any plan of union, that of the two Canadas at least would have to be insisted upon. It was to be expected that the French Canadians would be as hostile as they had been to the union proposal of 1822. Many of the Family Compact and of the loyalists, those who set an inordinate store by the purity of the British connection, were not keen, preferring the old alternative of annexing Montreal to Upper Canada and in effect abandoning the French Canadians. Even so, many more, such as the entrepreneur William Merritt of Welland Canal fame, were in favour of union.

Union also made it possible to champion Responsible Government and at the same time deny it to the French Canadians. That race, it was believed, could not be trusted to use Responsible Government in a proper, that is, a progressive manner, but in a Union in which the English-speaking modernizers would have the direction of affairs, correct political principles would coincide with desired economic and social goals. In the long run, this would be for the good of the French Canadians themselves and, as Durham took care to point out, "the alteration of the character of the province ought to be immediately entered on, and firmly, though cautiously followed up." He nevertheless warned that "in any plan . . . with this end in view, the ascendency should never again be placed in any hands but those of the English population."

Such were the main recommendations of the *Report*: union of the Canadas, Anglification, and Responsible Government. How these proposals would fare would depend upon the imperial government (which had virtually disowned the *Report*) and the balance of forces in British North America.

# — 3. Implementing Union —

To replace Durham the British government chose Charles Edward Poulett Thomson. The choice indicated how seriously, if belatedly, the government was now taking Canadian affairs. Thomson was an up-and-coming politician. A Benthamite (he had been personally aided by Bentham in 1826 when he first ran for Parliament), he was wedded to the latest ideas of reform founded upon efficiency and carried out by a technocratic elite. He was himself from a trading background, having served the family firm in Russia and in the London headquarters. He had risen quickly at Westminster, and already had been president of the Board of Trade before ill health caused him to withdraw from Parliament. In 1839 he was available, and Melbourne's government was delighted to send him out to Canada. He landed at Quebec in October 1839, and almost immediately began to arrange the union of the two colonies.

In the case of Lower Canada, there was no great difficulty. During the rebellion the constitution of the province had been suspended, the governor administering the colony with the aid of a nominated special council. With these arrangements still in place, Thomson was able to ram through the proposed Union Bill in two days, and never more than three of eighteen councillors voted against any item. It was well for Thomson to use this method of proceeding. Like Durham, and in keeping with the Benthamite tradition, he ignored French Canadianism. They represented, he believed, an outmoded mentality, and their distinctive ways were to be erased as soon as possible. "Racial" pride was not something that the technocratic calculus took into account, and to threaten its disappearance caused no qualms to "right thinking" people. Thomson judged that

> If it were possible, the best thing for Lower Canada would be a despotism for ten years more; for, in truth, the people are not yet fit for the higher class of

self-government, scarcely indeed, at present, for any description of it. Here there is no such thing as a political opinion. No man looks to a practical measure of improvement. Talk to anyone upon education, or public works, or better laws, let him be English or French, you might as well talk Greek to him. Not a man cares for a single practical measure — the only end, one would suppose, of a better form of government. They have only one feeling — a hatred of race.

Such a quotation is a useful epitome of Benthamite sentiment, with its stress upon "improvement" and "practicality" — and also a useful reminder that the "racial" slurs could be applied to English- and French-speaking elements.

Upper Canada presented more of a challenge. There the constitution remained in force, and there was an assembly to be dealt with. As has been mentioned, there was also resistance to union with French Canadians. Thomson had to mobilize his great skills in order to overcome it, but eventually he secured support for his draft bill.

Certain leading provisions made it possible for Upper Canada to accept the loss of identity. It was agreed that there should be equal representation from the two sections (to be renamed Canada East and Canada West); although the former had 650 000 inhabitants to the latter's 450 000, each was to have 42 members. This went beyond what Durham had recommended; in his thinking it would be enough to have the unified colony as a whole represented, the English-speaking element in Canada East (some 150 000) joined to those in Canada West being enough for an anglophone majority. The new proposal in theory meant an even greater certainty of being able to keep the French Canadians in their place. A second proposal that appealed to many doubters was the decision to make the debt common to the unified province: since Upper Canada had in pursuit of river improvement run up a debt of 1.2 million pounds, whereas Lower Canada's was a paltry 95 000 pounds, the former gained a tremendous windfall at the expense of the latter. To sweeten the deal further was Thomson's negotiating with Westminster for an imperial guarantee of 1.5 million pounds. The formal announcement was not made until later, but the likelihood of some largess played a role from the beginning. Finally, there were two other provisions included in the draft bill that appealed to Upper Canada: the capital was to be in Canada West (to Toronto's surprise and chagrin the choice was Kingston), and English was to be the sole language of record (though French might be used in debate).

Such, in broad outline, was the scheme that Thomson laid before the Upper Canadian assembly. It was accepted, and the imperial Parliament went ahead with the Union Bill. In recognition of Thomson's skill in obtaining it without a fresh outbreak of revolution, the grateful ministry raised him to the peerage as Baron Sydenham of Sydenham and Toronto.

There remained one final step before Sydenham could feel that union was wholly consummated. An election had to take place for the united province's first Parliament. The return of an anti-union majority would make a mockery of what had been achieved, and even a sizable bloc of repealers would cast a pall over the proceedings.

Nothing, then, was to be left to chance. In the tradition of Bond Head, Sydenham threw himself into the fray, acting less as governor than as party manager and prime minister. A brazen gerrymander of French-Canadian constituencies was carried out, whereby the English-speaking and mercantile elements were better represented. Polling stations were carefully sited to put Sydenham's critics at a disadvantage. Troops were available to keep order at the public and open voting that obtained in pre-ballot-box days — at the request of ministry candidates only. Land patents were rushed through to qualify additional voters — if they were likely to be sound voters. The effort worked; when the weeks-long polling was finally over, Sydenham had reason to congratulate himself. An estimate of the group breakdown in the 84-member assembly gave 24 government men, 20 French Canadians, and 20 moderate reformers. From these the governor expected to be able to consolidate a centre party that would avoid the factionalism of earlier days.

It is impossible to say just how Sydenham's design might have developed. Overworked, never strong, Sydenham died in September 1841 following a fall from his horse. Had he lived, and had he continued in office (which was not certain, for he felt he had done the job he was sent to do and wished to return home), he would have found that he needed to rethink a basic assumption. Earlier, in comparing the two halves of the province, he had written, "It is [in Lower Canada] a bad prospect, . . . and presents a lamentable contrast to Upper Canada. There great excitement existed, the people were quarrelling for realities, for political opinions, and with a view to ulterior measures." At the time he made the comparison, he meant to praise Upper Canada, and dismiss Lower Canada for its want of political awareness: implicit was the view that the French Canadians would be amenable and could be led by the livelier English-speakers. As events were to show, this was a woeful misreading of the situation. Stung by the contempt of Craig, of Durham, of how many others, and now by Sydenham, the French Canadians reacted by asserting their nationality and parading a sense of pride in their race. Far from being amenable, they showed themselves implacable and determined to form a solid bloc in defence of their rights. With the political ferment in Canada West leading to party fragmentation, the very reverse of what Sydenham implied came to pass. The French Canadians could exercise a veto power, and without their concurrence no public business could be carried on. As Sir Charles Bagot, Sydenham's successor, wrote to the colonial secretary, "It is impossible to disguise from oneself that the French members of the Assembly possess the power of the Country, and whoever directs that power . . . is in a situation to govern the Province most effectually." It will be worthwhile to examine this resurgent *nationalisme*, for it helped dictate the evolution of Canada, and of *Canadien*-British relations in particular.

## — 4. *Canadien* Reaction —

"They are a people without history or literature." These words about the *Canadiens* attributed to Durham were a final straw for François Xavier Garneau. They brought back to him the unhappy days of articling in a Scots lawyer's office where his fellow students, anglophones, had jeered at him "What are you, then, you French Canadians, you haven't even a history!" He resolved to supply that deficiency, and in 1845 appeared the first part of his *Histoire du Canada*. In the dedication to the governor-general he wrote that

> I have undertaken this work with the aim of restoring the truth, so often disfig-
> ured, and of turning back the attacks and insults to which my compatriots have
> been and daily are subjected by those who at one and the same time wish to
> oppress and exploit them. I think that the best way of doing this is to set forth
> quite simply their history.

Thus was conceived the best known riposte to French Canada's detractors, and a landmark in the emerging Quebec consciousness.

Best known, but by no means alone, Garneau's *cri-de-coeur* was echoed by others in the 1840s, a decade that witnessed a renaissance in Canada East that was to be observed in every aspect of society.

It was a vibrant period of French-Canadian letters. Both Quebec City and Montreal had two biweekly newspapers devoted to political reporting, analysis, and education, the *Journal de Québec* and *Le Canadien* in the former, *L'Aurore* and *La Minerve* in the latter. In addition, there was a host of lively, including satirical, papers. The 1840s saw the appearance of works that were to be classics of French-Canadian literature. The first significant novel, P.J.O. Chauveau's *Charles Guérin*, came out in 1846, and in the same year was published *Le Jeune Latour* of Antoine Gérin-Lajoie, who was later to be the author of the quintessential *habitant* novel, *Jean Rivard*.

The extent of the ferment at work in Canada East was well shown by the founding in Quebec and Montreal of the *Institut Canadien*, societies for advanced discussion and where, as time went on, the European liberal tradition was eventually imported. In these *Instituts* radical ideas including anticlericalism were developed, ideas that were soon to coalesce into the *Rouge* party. It was from this background that the typically entitled *L'Avenir* emerged together with its leading advocates, the Dorions. This tradition was never a major one in French Canada, but that it existed at all is a tribute to the intellectual excitement of the time. It can never be forgotten how powerful a role the Church had played in Quebec, nor that in this very decade it was rising to a peak of influence. Indeed, the outstanding example of French-Canadian vitality was provided by the Catholic community.

The Church had always championed *la survivance*, claiming to represent the *Canadiens* in a way that no other institution possibly could. Now, with Durham and Sydenham launching assaults upon their distinctiveness, the ecclesiastics did not disappoint their flock. Their task was made easier by the fact that the entire body of the faithful experienced a revival that put it in a fit state to resist the lure of assimilation. Two figures stand out in the crusade to make Catholicism a living reality to the ordinary *habitant*, preachers who in their very difference from each other illustrate the wide span of the revival's appeal. The first was the native priest, Father Chiniquy, who led a movement for moral reform, for temperance especially. Eventually he fell foul of his superiors, was excommunicated, and gravitated to the Presbyterians. Nevertheless, before this happened he had tremendous successes. The second was Bishop Forbin-Janson, a French aristocrat, a charismatic preacher able to draw crowds of up to 10 000 at a time. Thanks to workers like these, the Church was reinvigorated in the 1840s.

Thus conditioned, the Church was directed by able leaders. The dominant French-Canadian prelate in the coming generation was Bishop Ignace Bourget of Montreal. He had been assistant to Lartigue (indeed, it had been at Bourget's consecration in 1837 that Lartigue had opened the campaign against Papineau), and on that Bishop's death in 1840 he took over in his own right. Bourget was a man of ability and, above all, of firm views firmly stated. He was keen to reestablish links with Europe: thanks to him representatives of French orders were brought to Canada and in 1842 the Jesuits were once again on the St. Lawrence. It was also thanks to him that in 1841 the Church acquired its own newspaper, *Les Mélanges Religieux*, soon ably edited by a rising politician, Hector Langevin. Bourget quickly made his mark, and made everyone aware that he was a thoroughgoing ultramontane — that is, he championed the view that the Church was more the mistress than the handmaid of the state.

It was not long before issues arose that gave Bourget and the Church an opportunity to stress their commitment to *la survivance*. Inevitably, education was one. The Benthamite Durham *Report* had included an appendix dealing with the school system, and predictably had recommended one based upon the United States and Prussian models: in the interests of technocratic efficiency there should be a unified, secular, state-run system. In one of his last acts, Lartigue had denounced such an approach: the schools, he said, would be "*écoles neutres*" and it would *décatholiser* the province. Early numbers of the *Mélanges Religieux* continued to attack the Durham proposals; one very tellingly pointed out that

> Elementary schools open to all beliefs will cause the destruction of all belief and as a result of all morality individual and public . . . . Wherever the Catholic clergy instruct and direct, there is loyalty, morality, progress, peace, and happiness. Catholic influence creates neither fanaticism, nor religious quarrels, nor any disunity whatsoever.

These echoes of the Church's loyalty to the British connection and of its work for due subordination availed little, and the Act of 1841 went through essentially as the *Report* had wanted. Nevertheless, four years later Church pressure began to pay off. In 1845 the law was modified so that the parish once again became the basis of the school system, and commissioners were elected on a denominational basis with the *curé* given *ex officio* powers as "visitor." A year later the modification was even more to the Church's liking. Now the *curé* was given veto power over hirings and the choice of text. These were impressive gains for French-Canadian distinctiveness, and proof to many that the Church did guarantee *la survivance*.

The second issue was the Jesuits estates question. During the French régime the Jesuits had amassed considerable landholdings, some 350 000 hectares. Soon after the Conquest, however, the Order had been suppressed by the papacy, and the holdings had been taken over by the Crown with the stipulation that they should be used for educational purposes. The question now arose of what should happen to them. There were those who argued that the assembly had rightfully inherited them from the Crown in 1832. On the other hand, many maintained, especially the ultramontanes, that the Crown had had no right to them and that they should go back to the Church. The dispute spilled over into a wider political framework. Proponents of the first solution were in effect taking a Benthamite individualist position, and would have been happy to see the proceeds spent on any Canadian child, whether in Canada East or Canada West, Catholic or Protestant. Supporters of the second, on the contrary, were upholding a corporate view of society whereby Catholic charity should be directed to Catholic ends via Catholic agencies. In the end, the issue was settled by an act passed as late as 1888, but its discussion in the 1840s kept the claims of the Church and of French Canada in the public eye.

The turnabout in *canadien* fortunes was startlingly fast. In 1837 they had been reviled as rebels and degenerates, but already by the early 1840s they were reasserting their rights. Their self-confidence was back and with it a pride in their "race." In this, Sydenham's successors played their role, in part because they were the men they were, and in part because they calculated that by giving due recognition to the *Canadiens* they could best avoid another rebellion. The days of Peninsular veterans sent to hold down distant colonies was passing. The three who followed Sydenham, Sir Charles Bagot, Sir Charles Metcalfe, and Lord Elgin (the stopgap Earl Cathcart may be ignored), were all from a different world. Cultured and sophisticated, essentially aristocratic, they wanted to get along with the French Canadians, saw the usefulness of conciliating them, and had the ability to charm them. Bagot, for instance, took pains to write to the archbishop of Quebec in his own hand and in French. He took care to appoint *Canadiens* to offices wherever possible. When it came to deeds (or lack of them) he could be equally Francophile; thus he postponed (indefinitely as it turned out) the ordered assimilation of the court procedures of Canada East to the English model, and he paved the way for the School Acts of 1845-46 when he made the office of superintendent an empty one with two assistants beneath it — one for Canada East (and Catholic) and one for Canada West (and Protestant). Elgin was personally equally forthcoming and equally successful, and when he read the Speech from the Throne in French as well as in English he forever endeared himself to the *Canadiens*. That the provision of the Union Act, that English alone be the language of record, was repealed in 1848 was a fitting tribute to him. Even Metcalfe, who as will be seen quarrelled with an important section of French-Canadian politicians, could appreciate their culture and identify with them, and be respected and even loved in return. He was especially remembered for arranging the pardon of the exiles of 1837-38, an issue that, more than any other, had agitated the colony and fostered bad blood.

Of Durham's three proposals, the first, union, had carried. The second, anglification, had failed: there was to be no assimilation to British ways. But what of the third, Responsible Government? This is the most difficult to pass judgment upon, for when it was conceded it was under circumstances very different from those Durham had in mind.

## — 5. Implementing Responsible Government —

The evolution of Responsible Government had been a long one. In 1828 Dr. W.W. Baldwin had written to the colonial office suggesting

> A provincial Ministry, If I may be allowed to use the term, responsible to the Provincial Parliament, and removable from office . . . when they lose the confidence of the people as expressed by the voice of their representatives in the Assembly . . . .

By 1839, when an ex-governor-general and high commissioner called for the doctrine to be implemented, a clear statement of imperial policy was required. In the same year Russell, the colonial secretary, made the position clear. Writing to Thomson, he enjoined him "to refuse any explanation which may be construed to imply an acquiescence in the petitions and addresses on this subject." He went on to lecture Thomson on the reasons for this negative:

> If we seek to apply such a practice to a colony, we shall at once find ourselves at fault. The power for which a minister is responsible in England, is not his own power, but the power of the Crown, of which he is for the time the organ. It is obvious that the executive councillor of a colony is in a situation totally different. The Governor, under whom he serves, received his orders from the Crown of England. But can the colonial council be the advisers of the Crown of England? Evidently not, for the Crown has other advisors, for the same functions, and with superior authority. It may sometimes happen, therefore, that the Governor receives at one and the same time instructions from the Queen, and advice from his executive council totally at variance with each other.

The answer was, in Russell's view, self-evident, and a little later that newcomer to the scene, Prince Albert, the Queen's consort, reiterated the fact;

> I don't think the Crown of England could allow the establishment of a responsible government in Canada as that would be tantamount to a declaration of separation from the mother country. If the Governor-General is constitutionally bound to act according to the advice of his responsible government, how is

he to obey the instructions which the Queen's government may think it proper to send to him?

At the same time, however, Russell recognized that to deny the principle was one thing, to accept at least part of the Durham proposal another. In that same dispatch to Thomson he observed

> The Queen's Government have no desire to thwart the representative assemblies of British North America . . . . Her Majesty has no desire to maintain any system of policy among her North American subjects which opinion condemns . . . . While I have thus cautioned you against any declaration from which dangerous consequences might hereafter flow, . . . it may be said that I have not drawn any specific line beyond which the power of the Governor on the one hand, and the privileges of the Assembly on the other, ought not to extend. But this must be the case in any mixed government. Every political constitution in which different bodies share the supreme power, is only enabled to exist by the forebearance of those among whom this power is distributed.

Moreover, it will be recalled, this was written at the very time that Russell changed the terms of the tenure of executive office, which indicated that he was prepared to act on his beliefs.

Thomson went some way in keeping with this advice. His executive council was staffed by those who, since they had seats in the assembly, could be presumed to enjoy the confidence of the voters; however, his anti-*Canadien* prejudice was such that not a single French Canadian was included in the' government. Thomson's was certainly not Responsible Government, since the choice of members was in the governor's hands and since patronage remained his. Nevertheless, it was "an administration . . . responsive but not responsible to the representatives of the Canadian people." It was a system in which the key figure was the governor. Russell's dispatch revealed that harmony was nicely balanced between competing forces, a precarious balance that had to be constantly maintained by the governor's intervention, and a balance fatally easy to destroy.

This was soon made clear. When Sydenham died late in 1841, and Bagot took his place, the province had a governor whose view of the possibilities differed considerably from his predecessor's and from his masters' at Westminster. As early as the summer of 1842 he was called upon to show his colours. The executive council informed him that they were losing the backing of the assembly and risked defeat, because the French Canadians' bloc voting was coming back to haunt Sydenham's successor. The *Canadiens* formed the nucleus of an opposition large enough to deny the executive council and bring public business to a halt. What could Bagot do? Any attempt to add individual French-Canadian members to the council would fail, for the mass of their bloc would accuse them of having sold out, of becoming *vendus*, and *canadien* hostility would only have been intensified. The alternative was to take in a French Canadian as the acknowledged leader of the French-Canadian bloc. But was there such a leader, given that in 1840 French Canada as a whole, from archbishop to simple *habitant*, had been against the union? Fortunately for Bagot, there was such a man: Louis-Hippolyte LaFontaine.

Close to Papineau until the outbreak of the rebellion, LaFontaine managed to avoid full complicity in the rising. During the preparations for the first elections of 1841, he considered the possibilities for one passionately devoted to *survivance*. Unlike so many others, he decided that *survivance* could be best achieved by accepting union, but then going on to demand Responsible Government. Achieving that, *Canadiens* could be *maîtres chez eux*, masters of their own destiny. When he addressed the electors of his constituency in Terrebonne in 1840 he expressed this belief, and it became in effect a manifesto for a party. It was not representative of all French Canada by any means, but as time went on LaFontaine was able to emerge as the dominant *canadien* politician. Meanwhile, his commitment to Responsible Government led him into an alliance with Robert Baldwin and Francis Hincks, leaders of the Canada West reformers who were pressing for the same system of government. It was an arrangement whose strength and usefulness was shown when the reform forces in Canada West could get LaFontaine returned for Fourth York in 1841, after he had been defeated in Terrebonne by Sydenham's machinations. A year later, the reformers of Canada East were able to reciprocate, making it possible for Baldwin to be returned for Rimouski.

When Bagot made his offer to LaFontaine the French-Canadian leader accepted. That the arrangement met with approval was seen by the vote in the assembly: 55 in favour, and only five opposed. It should be noted, however, that the reconstituted government was not a Responsible Government. The initiative still came from the governor, and the council still contained members from other than LaFontaine's grouping, members, indeed, who were antipathetic. Bagot was sufficiently Benthamite to believe that "the future lay with *judicious selection*, no party being barred except where their conduct should have made recognition of them impossible to a self-respecting governor." Yet the new arrangement was a major step in the direction of Responsible Government, and Bagot observed to the colonial secretary that "whether the doctrine . . . is openly acknowledged, or is only tacitly acquiesced in, virtually it exists."

This was too much for his superiors. The colonial secretary, Lord Stanley, felt that Bagot had gone too far, and he reiterated the principle enunciated by Russell: "Your position is different from that of the Crown in England." Then he went on in a Sydenhamite fashion.

> The Crown acts avowedly and exclusively on the advice of its ministers, and has no political opinions of its own. You act in concert with your Executive Council, but the ultimate decision rests with yourself, and you are recognized, not only as having an opinion, but as supreme and irresponsible, except to the Home government . . . .

The man chosen to hold the line, and if possible to recover lost ground, was Metcalfe; he had done brilliantly in India and Jamaica, and perhaps could do equally well in Canada.

In Jamaica, Metcalfe's above-party direction of affairs had led to the extinction of "factionalism." He proposed the same approach in Canada, writing to Stanley that

> The course which I intend to pursue with regard to all parties, is to treat all alike, and to make no distinctions. . . . [I want to] bring into the public service the men of greatest merit and efficiency without party distinction. . . . The idea of governing according to the interested views of a party, is odious.

Given such an outlook, it could not be long before a crisis was provoked. In November 1843 it occurred. His own summary runs as follows:

> On Friday Mr. LaFontaine and Mr. Baldwin came to the Government House, and . . . demanded of the Governor-general that he should agree to make no appointment . . . without previously taking the advice of the Council; that the lists of candidates should in every instance be laid before the Council; that they should recommend any others at discretion; and that the Governor-general in deciding, after taking their advice, shall not make any appointment prejudicial to their influence.

These demands if granted would have cut the ground from beneath the governor. He refused to comply, and accepted the resignation of the entire council with one exception.

Metcalfe fought back. Adopting the style of Bond Head and Sydenham (that is, he would fight his own a battles, including elections) he prepared his counter stroke. He reverted to eighteenth-century practice and determined to build an assembly majority for his ministry. This, of course, was in flat contradiction to Responsible Government and modern practice: today an assembly majority is decided and then it produces a ministry from its ranks. Carrying on the government was at first difficult for Metcalfe. The assembly had approved a motion regretting the passing of the ministry by 46 to 23. Metcalfe merely prorogued Parliament. He had a problem finding members willing to serve on the council, and for a long time it consisted of only three. Nevertheless, patient work brought the numbers slowly up, and to Denis-Benjamin Viger, a leading French-Canadian politician from a pre-LaFontaine period, he was even able to add Denis-Benjamin Papineau, brother of the great Louis-Joseph and a bearer of the *mystique* of the *patriote* tradition. The governor and Viger hung on grimly until, in the fall of 1844, they judged the time ripe for a trial of strength. An election was called.

The result was a vindication of Metcalfe's courage. It was seen that the executive council woud be able to survive a vote of confidence, but it was a tight-run thing. In Canada East LaFontaine had carried all before him, winning 28 seats. Viger himself had gone down to defeat (twice, in fact; in those days voting was spread out over weeks, and once defeated a candidate could move on to another constituency and try again), and only two French-Canadian supporters of the ministry had been elected. However, in Canada West, it had gone 30-12 for the ministry, and with 8 supporters from the Townships of Canada East, it was enough for victory. When all returns were in, the governor felt confident that he had some 46 voters to his opponents' 38. Yet if the result lacked clarity, it certainly disproved the contention that Responsible Government was necessarily the wave of the future. When in the following year Viger and a supporter were returned in by-elections in Canada East, it was increasingly evident that Metcalfe's system had an appeal.

Then suddenly everything changed. Metcalfe was dying of cancer, and left the colony at the end of 1845, brave to the end despite excruciating pain. Overshadowing the personal tragedy was an imperial one that brought a revolution in its train. In that same year the Irish potato crop failed. By 1846 it was clear that here was no isolated setback, but the beginning of a famine of unprecedented proportions. Before it had run its course, over a million had died, and a further million had been forced into exile. To meet such a catastrophe, the British government suspended the Corn Laws so that the desperately needed supplies might be got into Ireland. The gradual replacement of mercantilist protection by *laissez-faire* free trade was telescoped into a few short years, and by 1849 the last pillar of the old system, the Navigation

Laws, had been repealed; henceforth, all goods might be shipped in any bottom. The impact of these developments on the colonies was shattering.

Here it is sufficient to note the impact on constitutional arrangements. The old prohibition on Responsible Government had derived its validity from the fact that the empire really was one. In a free trade setting, on the other hand, there was less need to coordinate policy, less occasion for dispute between centre and periphery. Those four areas enumerated by Durham as ones where the imperial authority should retain supremacy were now much diminished in scope and the grey areas of ambiguity much reduced. Indeed, in the new framework, Britain was eager to press Responsible Government on the colonies, and that is why the *concession* of Responsible Government is a better formulation than the *winning* of it.

It was in the governorship of Lord Elgin that Metcalfe's stand was given up. Early in 1848, following an election, it became clear that the ministry no longer enjoyed the confidence of the assembly; the reformers defeated it by a vote of 54-20. Elgin called upon the leaders of the Reform party, Baldwin and LaFontaine, to form a government, and it was that government that set policy and controlled patronage. That it was the genuine article was proved the following year. An act was passed, the Rebellion Losses Bill, to compensate those who had suffered during the tumult of 1837-38. Diehard loyalists were opposed since in the review it was proposed to compensate those guilty of treason — Wolfred Nelson had a claim in for 1200 pounds. When the bill passed, they fully expected Elgin to exercise the Crown's veto, for how could the Queen's representative accept disloyalty and reward it? Elgin shared this view of the bill, but signed nonetheless. A loyalist mob rioted and the Parliament building (moved from Kingston to Montreal) was burnt to the ground. Nevertheless, mob fury could not reverse what Elgin had done.

It might be said that the Rebellion Losses Bill was no true test of Responsible Government. Even if Elgin was opposed to the measure, it did not run counter to imperial interest. Within ten years that situation had arisen, however. In 1859 Canada passed an act that levied a 20 percent duty on imports in order to finance public works. Manufacturers in Britain rightly interpreted this as incidentally giving Canadian producers protection, and in a petition to the British government called for the disallowance of the colonial legislation on the grounds that it ran counter to imperial policy. The colonial office made representations to Canada in this sense, but was met with the firm statement that

> Self-government would be utterly annihilated if the views of the Imperial Government were to be preferred to those of the people of Canada. It is therefore

the duty of the present government distinctly to affirm the rights of the Canadian legislature to adjust taxation of the people in the way they deem best.

The colonial office backed down.

It was the Maritimes, however, that provided the best illustration of the power of imperial initiative in bringing about Responsible Government. Nova Scotia was the colony where the doctrine was first applied, even before Canada. In 1847 the governor, Sir John Harvey, was acting just as Metcalfe had: he believed in the superiority of all-party ministries, and was attempting to reconstitute the Conservative council by bringing in leading Liberals. He thought that Responsible Government was "peculiarly inapplicable to the conditions of a single colony . . . by its direct tendency to array one class of Her Majesty's subjects against another . . . and thus to produce and to perpetuate agitation and render repose impossible." However, this was no longer 1843-44. The new colonial secretary, Earl Grey, and the Whig Government were not prepared, like Stanley and the Tories, to support a governor who took such a line. Dispatches from Grey to Harvey (and the same instructions went to the other colonies) made it plain that full Responsible Government on the British pattern, *i.e.*, party government, should be allowed. Thus, when in the election of 1847 the Conservatives under J.W. Johnston failed to elect a majority in the assembly and early in 1848 lost a vote of confidence, there was no repeat of the Metcalfe-Viger tactic. Harvey immediately called upon the Liberals to form the government, which they did, under Howe and James B. Uniacke.

Colonial reluctance to embrace Responsible Government had been evident in Nova Scotia. If Howe and Uniacke had won, it had not been overwhelmingly, and roughly half the population that voted was happy to support Conservatives wedded to Harvey's view of politics. In New Brunswick colonial foot-dragging was even more marked. In that province it would have been difficult to find political parties, an indispensable prerequisite to Responsible Government. New Brunswickers prided themselves on being "independent," and this showed in the habit that continued there of allowing private members to introduce money bills; in that way, colleagues could support logrolling projects for each other and keep their constituents happy. However, it also meant that the government could not control the disposition of public funds, and so lacked an essential means of maintaining party cohesion. This practice had been prevented in Canada when in 1840 Westminster modified the Union Bill by writing in the requirement that only the executive council should initiate a money bill. Lacking this reform New

Brunswick could stick by an outmoded system, so that Responsible Government was more an empty theory in that province than a reality. To make matters worse, the executive council itself valued its members' independence more than cabinet solidarity: in 1851 the governor asked its advice on whom to appoint chief justice, but it disagreed among itself and would offer no advice, with the result that the governor made his own appointment and demonstrated that Responsible Government was in abeyance. Not until 1854 was the lost ground recovered; in that year, for the first time in New Brunswick's history, a government fell and was replaced following the loss of a vote of confidence in the assembly.

Prince Edward Island laboured under the disadvantage of its small size. When in 1847 Grey asked the governor for his views on the possible introduction of Responsible Government, Sir Donald Campbell eventually replied that

> Before a community is fit to receive that system, it is essential that it should have . . . diffused throughout its whole extent, individuals possessed of property, education, and intelligence in such numbers as to insure that whatever political party may from time to time gain ascendency in the Assembly, its ranks will always be able to furnish men desirous of devising useful measures, capable of conducting the government, and to whom from their respectability the administration of the affairs of the colony may be safely entrusted.

But, he went on

> This Island . . . has (with the exception of Charlottetown) no towns of any consideration where enterprize and intelligence are congregated . . . I do not believe that from the East to the West point, twenty men could be found possessed of the general knowledge and those enlarged views necessary for the originating and perfecting any important measure.

Nevertheless, Grey was once again more prepared to foster Responsible Government than to impede it. In this case he was encouraged when the assembly refused supply in 1850, and a dispatch to Campbell's successor, Sir Alexander Bannerman, ordered that the system be implemented. Again, like New Brunswick, however, it was some time before the system was more than a mere formality.

The cases of New Brunswick and Prince Edward Island were minor imperfections, however. The larger colonies, Canada and Nova Scotia, had Responsible Government, and in time their example would pull the rest into line. For the moment the striking fact was the acceptance of the doctrine.

The doctrine, of course, had its two sides. Accepting the benefits also meant accepting its costs, and as the 1840s indicated the latter might have outweighed the former.

------------------------------------------------- **Suggested Reading**

While W.S. MacNutt's volume on the Atlantic provinces continues to 1857, the Centenary Series volume on the Canadas becomes J.M.S. Careless, *The Union of the Canadas, 1841-57.*

Durham's biographer remains C. New, whose *Lord Durham* appeared in 1929. His *Report* may be studied in G.M. Craig (ed.), *Lord Durham's Report: An Abridgement with Introduction* (1963). Also to be read is the revisionist G. Martin, *The Durham Report and British Policy* (1972).

The working out of the new constitutional-political arrangements may be followed in P.G. Cornell, *The Alignment of Political Groups in Canada 1841-67* (1962); W. Ormsby, "Sir Charles Metcalfe and the Canadian Union," *Canadian Historical Association Reports* (1961), and *The Emergence of Federal Concept in Canada 1839-1845* (1969), which downplays Responsible Government; G. Metcalf, "Draper Conservatism and Responsible Government in the Canadas, 1836-1847," *Canadian Historical Review* (1961).

On various aspects of French-Canadian resurgence see, in addition to the Ormsby book just cited (which describes among other things the abandonment of anglicization), J. Monet, *The Last Cannon Shot* (1969); J.P. Bernard, *Les Rouges* (1971); M. Trudel, *Chiniquy* (1955); L. Pouliot, *Mgr. Bourget et son temps* (1955-1972); M. Lajeunesse, "L'évêque Bourget et l'instruction publique au Bas-Canada, 1840-1846," *Revue d'Histoire de L'Amérique française* (1970); N.F. Eid, *Le Clergé et le pouvoir politique au Québec* (1978).

For an overview of the entire political-constitutional development in this period, see P.A. Buckner, *Transition to Responsible Government* (1985).

# CHAPTER 17
## A MODEST PROSPERITY

## — 1. Annexation and Reciprocity —

When mercantilism collapsed, so too did many a fortune in British North America. Writing in 1849 Lord Elgin judged that "prosperity in most Canadian towns, and more especially in the Capital [Montreal], has fallen 50 percent in value within the past three years." The Chatham, New Brunswick, *Gleaner* would have agreed; its issue of 4 December 1849 reported that "on Wednesday last a property in Lower Cove was put up to auction at the Coffee House Corner. A few years since it cost £900; and £500 it was said had been often refused for one of the two lots. On Wednesday both were purchased . . . for £575. . . . This shows a depression of some 90 percent, within a few short years."

It is not at all certain that the economic collapse was caused by the ending of mercantilism. Far more may have been due to worldwide factors than to the ending of protection and the opening up of the shipping lanes. That is irrelevant, however; what mattered was the interpretation of events made at the time by those whose fortunes were affected, and many were convinced that the blame lay with Britain.

In 1843 imperial legislation seemed to promise continuing colonial preference. The Canada Corn Act of that year fixed the tariff on wheat and flour entering Britain (in that country "corn" does not mean maize but grain) at the nominal rate of one shilling a quarter; all other wheat and flour was to bear discriminatory duties. Moreover, American wheat and flour exported via Canada was to be considered Canadian when entering Britain, and hence liable to the one shilling a quarter charge only. The effect was impressive. In 1843 exports from the St. Lawrence were 33 000 tonnes. Now, at last, the vast expenditures for canal improvement seemed about to pay off. Merchants and speculators invested heavily, increasing the milling capacity of the province and expanding the freighting and storage capacity. A year later, exports rose to 66 000 tonnes.

Then came the shock of repeal. As one investor remembered, "in 1843 we triumphed, so I commenced my Welland Mills and finished them about mid-summer . . . ; my mill has done nothing since it was finished." Between 1847 and 1848 wheat and flour exports dropped from 106 000 tonnes to 60 000 tonnes, while New Brunswick timber fell from 290 000 tonnes in 1846 to 150 000 in 1847. A prominent Canadian businessman, Isaac Buchanan, wrote to the London *Times* of 6 February 1846 complaining that "England has dishonourably broken the promise of protection to Canadian wheat and lumber made by every Ministry from the timber panic of 1806 downward." He followed up this charge by warning

> that as there remains no longer any but the slightest bond of interest between Canada and the Mother Country, no reason can be given why Canadians should risk their lives and property in defending nothing, or should allow Canada to be any longer used as the battlefield of European and American squabbles.

(This was the time of British-United States tension over the Oregon territory.) To rub salt into the wound, in 1846 the United States passed the Drawback Act that permitted Canadian grain for export to pass through the United States in bond without paying duty. In this way, much traffic that might otherwise have used the St. Lawrence was drawn into the Erie system.

For the tottering merchant community, reeling from disaster to disaster, the passing of the Rebellion Losses Bill in 1849 was the last straw. The orgy of smashing and burning that paralyzed Montreal (and led to that city's losing its capital status) was the expression of a group that had seen its economic position shattered and its loyalty spurned. In a bitter about-turn it called for what previously it had execrated — the end of the British connection and annexation to the United States.

Annexation had its proponents throughout British North America. In the Maritimes, apart from New Brunswick, it was admittedly weak. However, timber having been so heavily hit, New Brunswick was prepared to consider new solutions: at that colony's initiative an unofficial intercolonial conference took place in Halifax in 1849. LaFontaine was in the chair, and Howe was secretary. New Brunswick's delegates spoke of annexation in vague and nebulous terms. Canada West had its pockets of annexationist sentiment, notably around Kingston and Toronto. In a by-election in 1849, Peter Perry, a "republican" from the old days and a member of the assembly of Upper Canada from 1824 to 1836 who now was widely perceived as having annexationist leanings, was returned by acclamation. (To offset this, however, William Lyon Mackenzie wrote from his American exile to say that had he been in Canada he would have worked "not only to keep Canada separated from this country, but also to preserve the British connection, and to make that connection worth perserving.") Nevertheless, it was Montreal where the movement had its greatest strength.

From that city an Annexation Manifesto was put out in October 1849. It opened with a conspectus of the lamentable state of the colony:

> Our Provincial Government and civic corporations embarrassed, our banking and other securities greatly depreciated, our mercantile and agricultural interests alike improsperous, real estate scarcely saleable upon any terms, our unrivalled rivers, lakes and canals almost unused; whilst commerce abandons our shores, the circulating capital amassed under a more favourable system is dissipated, with none from any quarter to replace it.

It went on to compare the province unfavourably with the neighbouring states — "'Whilst the adjoining states are covered with a net-work of thriving railways, Canada possesses but three lines which, together, scarcely exceed fifty miles in length" — and quickly came to the alternatives before the people. "The Revival of protection in the markets of the United Kingdom" was rejected since "the millions of the mother country demand cheap food, and a second change from protection to free trade would complete the ruin which the first has done much to achieve." The second was "the protection of home manufactures," but this would fail without access to the United States market since Canada was so small. "A federal union of the British American Provinces" was no remedy, since this would be too small to absorb all the goods produced. "The independence of the British North American colonies as a Federal Republic" was not possible since "the acquirement of a name and character, among the nations, would, we fear, prove an over-match for the strength of the new republic." The fifth possibility, "reciprocal free trade with the United States, as respects the products of the farm, the forest, and the mine," was imperfect because it would do nothing for the manufactures and would leave untouched the political evils facing Canada. Thus it was concluded "there remains but one to be considered . . . . THIS REMEDY CONSISTS OF A FRIENDLY AND PEACEFUL SEPARATION FROM BRITISH CONNECTION, AND A UNION UPON EQUITABLE TERMS WITH THE GREAT NORTH AMERICAN CONFEDERACY OF SOVEREIGN STATES." From start to finish the document was devoid of any appeal to higher principles; only the economic benefits were dwelt upon.

Within a week or so over one thousand had signed the manifesto. Many prominent businessmen were among that number, and many who later ecame prominent in government, too: John Redpath, the sugar baron, as president of the Montreal Annexation Association, and signers included William Molson, John Rose, later head of the Grand Trunk Railway and a cabinet minister, A.T. Galt, a father of Confederation, D.L. Macpherson, lieutenant governor of Ontario, and John Abbott, prime minister of Canada, 1891-92.

There was one other source of support for annexation. In 1845 a pardoned Papineau had returned from exile. He had never come to terms with the union, and now he threw himself and his backing into the annexation campaign. *L'Avenir* took up the issue and there developed the idea that the fate of Louisiana showed that *la survivance* could be better ensured if *Canadiens* became part of the United States than if they followed LaFontaine's siren song and remained in a union with *les anglais*. The paper had made a bow in the direction of the economic argument, and hard on the heels of the manifesto had proclaimed

> Since the 92 resolutions, we have not seen a better statement of the principles and a more faithful picture of the needs of the country. It appeals to all classes and parties to forget their former reasons for dissension, to unite, in order to obtain what the country needs most urgently, prosperity with annexation.

The real interest, nevertheless, was one that had begun to be discussed even before annexation became a burning topic.

They say that the British government is just and strong. Beyond the 45th parallel there is a government which, . . . fearlessly grants its subjects what is just and reasonable. Our brothers in Louisiana, French like us, have learnt that. That government would grant us what we ask for, and require of us only that we submit to the general laws of the United States as sovereign. Far from extinguishing the sacred flame of nationality that burns in our hearts, it would rekindle it and foster it; for that government well understands that in confiding the defence of the St. Lawrence to the French of Canada it would be as well defended as was New Orleans by the French of Louisiana.

So wrote *L'Avenir* as early as February 1849, and it kept up this message. After the manifesto had appeared it took its own petition to Quebec City and obtained some 600 signatures.

The annexation movement proved, however, to be short-lived. Both the agitation of the Montreal businessmen and of the *Rouges* for annexation faded quickly. The alliance of English-speaking Tories wanting economic deliverance and *Canadiens* stressing a statehood which, like Louisiana's, "is still French and Catholic because it is democratic" was even more bizarre than was normally possible in Canada's case and was fated to break up. Moreover, in the case of the major element it was a passing petulance, an excess that would be forgotten as soon as a more acceptable alternative emerged. This, in fact, was ready and waiting, for even before turning to annexation British North Americans had been discussing reciprocity.

The attraction of reciprocity gained immensely when annexation burst on the scene. Now, in addition to its own virtues, was the argument that only reciprocity could head off annexation. In almost all parts of British North America a considerable body of support grew in favour of reciprocity between 1848 and 1850.

In Canada, especially Canada West, the reformers were keenly in favour. Their staple had been badly hit and they were convinced that they had everything to gain and nothing to lose by allowing the free trade of natural products between the colony and the United States. Hincks argued strongly for the measure, as did Merritt of Welland Canal fame. Together they pressed the case upon Elgin, who was quickly to be a leading advocate of the idea.

In Atlantic Canada it was much the same. Prince Edward Island, in fact, was so eager that in 1849 it translated feeling into fact by passing an Act for Reciprocity, to go into effect whenever the United States should pass an equivalent; in this, the island colony was ahead of Canada which, behind Merritt's lead, passed a similar act a little later in the same year. In both cases, lack of American action meant failure. New Brunswick had called the 1849 meeting in Halifax, and its governor, Sir Edmund Head (cousin to Bond Head), was, like Elgin, constantly working to bring about reciprocity. Even Nova Scotia, dependent on the fisheries and hence leery of any agreement allowing Americans greater access to its waters, initially lent its support to the rest of British North America, although it eventually moved against reciprocity. Only Newfoundland was, at this stage, strongly opposed: when invited to the Halifax gathering in 1849 the colony refused, stating baldly that "the Council . . . express their entire conviction that no advantage to be derived from a reciprocal free trade with the United States of America, would compensate for the concession to the citizens of that Republic of a participation in the Fisheries of this Colony."

Despite this fine show of interest in reciprocity, little was accomplished. The imperial government sent a representative to Washington in 1849 but continued efforts yielded no results. Meanwhile, as trade began to pick up worldwide, the impetus for reciprocity in British North America began to fade. Yet within a short while, the two major partners, Britain and the United States, began to find renewed interest in the proposal, and once again negotiations were undertaken. On Britain's part, the motivation was the realization that if the colonies were to begin paying for their own defence and for the costs of the immigration service, about which awkward questions were being asked at Westminster, the prosperity and morale of the colonies would have to be improved. Moreover, here was a chance to settle the fisheries question and to remove a potential source of dispute with the United States. On the United States' part, there was the sectional rivalry that led to the Civil War, and both North and South wished for their own reasons to see British North America strengthened by reciprocity. The former argued that it would lead to annexation and be an accession to Northern strength, the latter that it would stave off annexation and so prevent Northern gains! The British having pressured the Americans by enforcing the existing limitations on their fishing in British colonial waters, and the Americans having prepared the way by bribing colonials and Americans to the tune of $118 000, Elgin was dispatched to Washington in 1854, ostensibly for the social round. Thanks to his charming ways, reciprocity was achieved. As a Washington paper implied, who could resist?

> More was accomplished last evening [at a ball at the British legation] than has been accomplished from the days of Ashburton [in 1842; Ashburton for Britain settled the Maine-New Brunswick boundary dispute with Daniel Webster in that year] to the advent of Elgin . . . . The large and brilliant company broke up at a late hour and departed for their respective homes — pleased with their

courtly and courteous host; pleased with the monarchical form of government in England; pleased with the republican form of government in the United States; pleased with each other, themselves, and the rest of mankind.

Reciprocity was to run for ten years. It provided that the fisheries on the Atlantic coast north of the 36th parallel were to be open to fishermen of both countries. A list of natural products was drawn up which should be admitted duty-free into the British North American colonies or the United States. Americans were to be free to navigate the St. Lawrence, paying only those tolls that the colonists paid; in return, British subjects were to be free to sail on Lake Michigan.

News of the treaty was warmly greeted in British North America. Merritt, as might have been expected, believed "its beneficent effect on both sides of the boundary, has exceeded the expectations of its most sanguine promoters." Doubters like Newfoundland and Nova Scotia were won over. It was hard to be critical when the figures were so impressive: Canada's exports to the United States doubled in the first year of reciprocity; in Atlantic Canada the impact was not as dramatic, but exports did rise from $2.2 million in 1854 to $3 million in 1855 and to $3.8 million in 1856. This growth may have taken place even in the absence of the treaty, but to people at the time the value of reciprocity loomed large. As much as the economic benefits there were the psychological ones. The feeling abroad was that the colonies now had a guarantee of support. Having successfully buried the memory of 1849, the 1850s were to be seen in retrospect as a golden age.

# — 2. Staple Revolutions and Staple Traps —

In fact, the 1850s were for many societies a golden age. A worldwide economic upturn was experienced. In 1848 gold was discovered in California, three years later in Australia. In both cases the effect was extremely beneficial. The increased amount of gold in circulation had a mildly inflationary effect that acted as a tonic. The new economic activity it called into being was salutary, especially the shipping of people and cargo halfway round the world. Nor can the psychological impact of the discoveries be ignored. Recovery in Britain was marked, and it was appropriate that 1851 saw the first of the World's Fairs, the Great Exhibition at the Crystal Palace, at which faith in an ever expanding economy was celebrated. Even the wars of the period acted to fuel growth: The Crimean War of 1854-56, when Britain and France fought Russia, boosted the economy, and British North America did well out of the hostilities when wheat supplies from Russia were cut off and extra shipping was demanded.

Nevertheless, the outstanding reason for the British North American boom was the impact of the United States. Initiatives in that country were having spinoff effects on its northern neighbours in ways never before experienced. Immigration was running at tremendous levels: Europe had seen widespread revolutions in 1848 and exiles were streaming to the New World; Ireland had just gone through a famine. British North America was not favoured by these newcomers; indeed, so many were leaving the British colonies for the United States that many areas were suffering actual population loss. America was nevertheless the land of growth, and as its population boomed, so too did the demand for foods of all kinds. One odd, but as it turned out crucial development, was the surge in beer drinking. From the 1850s the German community in the United States grew significantly. At the same time there was a new federal tax on whiskey. The consumption of beer rose enormously, and barley was in great demand. Since it was held that Canadian barley produced a superior brew, a new export trade to the United States developed.

More significantly, this massive population growth was helping to force the industrialization of the country. Although development was puny compared to what would happen from the 1870s on, it still marked a breakthrough to a new level of economic activity. A good index of industrialization was railway construction. By 1850 the United States had 15 000 kilometres of track, with more being laid every year. Here the impact on British North America was two-fold. First, there was the direct demand for materials used in the construction, such as wood for ties and wagons and foodstuffs for the gangs. Dwarfing this effect was the fact that American railways tapped the latent supply of British North America and made possible trades that previously had been hopelessly uneconomic. For instance, dairy products, livestock (especially sheep and pigs, which could not be driven like cattle), eggs, and fruit became sought after from great distances. Thus the Ogdensburg Railway of 1850 drew off the produce of Canada West and transported it as far as Boston.

The Civil War of 1861-65 hugely intensified American demand. Oats and barley were needed as never before; livestock was taken in great quantities; and while the demand previously mentioned had tended to favour Canada above all, now the Maritimes enjoyed an especial advantage. The war disrupted the American merchant marine, and the colonials could now take up the slack. The American fisheries were in disarray, and again Maritimers could benefit. When it came to running the Union blockade, taking war goods to the South or cotton to England, the Maritimers were well placed to run the risks and make the exceptional profits.

So it was that a measure of diversification was fostered in the Maritimes. The old staples continued to provide the basis of the economy. Fish continued to be caught and sold in vast amounts, a trade in which Nova Scotia was predominant. The British West Indies, the United States, and the Mediterranean continued to take the harvest of the banks. In New Brunswick, timber was still far and away the biggest industry. Forest products were declining in relative importance, it is true, but the figures were still impressive: in 1853 they accounted for 82 percent of all exports, in 1861 for 76 percent, and in 1865 for 66 percent. In sum, the economy was buoyant, and shipping began to rise with its crest.

In shipbuilding New Brunswick took the lead. Already by 1854 over 40 ships of 1000 tonnes or more were launched in that province. The totals continued to grow, and other colonies took part in the industry; by 1874 it peaked with 185 000 tonnes constructed in British North America. During those twenty or so years, the Maritimes earned an outstanding reputation for design, workmanship, and hard sailing. Typical of the breed was the *Marco Polo*, built in Saint John in 1851 as a timber drogher. A year later, somewhat modified, it was put on the Australia run. Before leaving Liverpool its master, the legendary driver James "Bully" Forbes, announced his intention of sailing there and back within six months, a feat never before achieved. By making the outward passage in 76 days and the return in the same number, he had enough time in hand for a leisurely turnabout in Melbourne. There was justification for the banner hoisted from fore- to main-mast in Liverpool, "THE FASTEST SHIP IN THE WORLD," and every reason for thousands to flock to see her.

Owing to the *Marco Polo* and many another like it, "Bluenoses" were recognized worldwide for their excellence (the term was then applied to all vessels built in British North America, to full-rigged ships as well as to coasting schooners). Equally well known was the Maritime carrying trade. Here Nova Scotia was the leader, building a huge fleet that travelled the newly free-trade world in search of cargo. By the 1870s Nova Scotia had no less than 490 000 tonnes in the trade, while New Brunswick had 300 000 (Canada East, by then Quebec, had 221 000). Altogether, British North America had the world's fourth largest merchant marine.

This, however, was as far as diversification went. Nor was it maintained for long. There was, perhaps, a foretaste of what was to happen when the *Marco Polo* was sold to the Black Ball line of Liverpool, or when the master of all clipper designers, Donald McKay of Nova Scotia, decided to work for Boston interests. The Maritimers would not transcend their golden age of the 1850s. Even then, steam was changing transportation out of all recognition; in 1840 steamships did 14 percent of the world's carrying, by 1860 it was 32 percent, by 1870 it had risen to 49 percent and by 1880 it was 62 percent. Nevertheless, Maritimers clung to the wooden ship. The many small ports of the region gave a bias towards medium-sized vessels, but the bigger steamer was not to be stopped. The bigger steamer required not only a bigger port but also a tributary hinterland tied to it by that other steam innovation, the railway engine. This was a transition the Maritimes never successfully made. The long tradition of localism was never surmounted. The political habit of having members of the assembly vote small-scale public works projects for each other's ridings prevented the emergence of a unified outlook, able to take a broader view of a colony's interests. In this connection, the failure of local government in the Maritimes, and of a municipal taxing structure that would have taken care of small-scale improvements and left the assembly freer for the major undertakings, was an especially fatal flaw. The result was that even those places initially at an advantage failed to take full advantage of their position. In 1845 when Samuel Cunard, the founder of a maritime dynasty, moved his terminus from Halifax to Boston, the writing was perhaps already on the wall.

It was a different story in the Canadas — though only in part. There the 1850s saw a pattern of diversification much as the Maritimes initially had. It was well that such a movement was possible. In Canada East the old staple, wheat, had already collapsed; in Canada West the same fate threatened — not that the farmers recognized the danger, for the figures seemed to bear out an optimistic assessment of wheat's future. The millers and forwarders might have been ruined by abolition in 1846, but for the farmers the future looked rosy. In the early 1850s they exported 80 percent of their wheat surplus, and received 75 percent of their cash income from that one crop. Wheat and flour made up over 50 percent of all the exports of Canada West. Between 1850 and 1856 (the year the Crimean War ended) wheat exports almost doubled and the value tripled; in the latter year wheat exports peaked at 255 000 tonnes.

However, the situation was precarious. In district after district, wheat midge decimated the crop. The continued reliance on one crop was

## Map 17.1: Shipbuilding in the Maritime Colonies

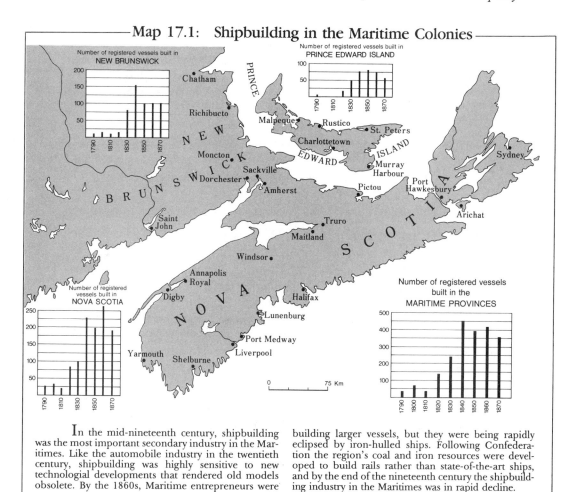

In the mid-nineteenth century, shipbuilding was the most important secondary industry in the Maritimes. Like the automobile industry in the twentieth century, shipbuilding was highly sensitive to new technological developments that rendered old models obsolete. By the 1860s, Maritime entrepreneurs were building larger vessels, but they were being rapidly eclipsed by iron-hulled ships. Following Confederation the region's coal and iron resources were developed to build rails rather than state-of-the-art ships, and by the end of the nineteenth century the shipbuilding industry in the Maritimes was in rapid decline.

SOURCE: Adapted from Finlay and Sprague, *The Structure of Canadian History* (1989), p. 155.

inevitably causing soil exhaustion. The president of the Agricultural Association of Upper Canada had said as early as 1847

> It is mortifying to hear remarked by those lately arrived from Great Britain, where the land is cultivated in a very superior manner, that some parts of Canada look as if the people had farmed themselves out. Yet mortifying as it is,

these are the remarks we are compelled to listen to, and cannot contradict. Facts are stubborn things; for in many parts of Canada such an exhausting course of culture has been pursued, without adding what was necessary to sustain the productive powers of the soil, that it has become so reduced, and the yield consequently so small, as to scarcely adequately remunerate the cultivator for the expense of harvesting. . . .

Furthermore, with virgin land coming into cultivation in the American middle west, the outlook for the Canadian farmer was deteriorating. The full danger of the situation was revealed by 1870 when the average yield per farm fell from the 3.6 tonnes of 1860 to a mere 1.6 tonnes.

Increasing American demand for products other than wheat therefore came at an opportune time. By 1852 an observer in Canada East was able to write,

There is no doubt that our market for horses, cattle, sheep, pork, and butter, is likely to improve, rather than get worse. . . . When we came to Canada [about 1830] there was a large importation of horses, beef, pork, mutton, cheese, poultry, and other things to this country from the United States. The case is now exactly reversed . . . and there is every probability that this new market is likely to increase every day.

The same was even truer of Canada West, where the continuing wheat boom meant there was more capital with which to make the transition. However, there was more to it than this. In Canada West there was a receptivity to change, an eagerness to try new ways, that seemed to be lacking in the East. Recently, attempts have been made to exonerate the *habitant* from the charge of inefficiency, stressing the fact that he lacked the elbow room to improve his farm and methods. These attempts have not disproved the original view that failing French-Canadian farms taken over by English or Scots immigrants could be turned around. It may be countered that immigrants would have greater capital resources behind them; nevertheless, a *habitant* community could have raised capital cooperatively (like the early building societies) had the initiative to do so been there initially. By 1860 Canada East had 73 agricultural societies; Canada West had 315. An early attempt to found an agricultural college in Lower Canada in 1833 failed two years later because of inadequate backing. Later attempts to do so in the 1860s lagged because of poorly chosen and unmotivated students. Another example of poor management was the French-Canadian breed of horse, a major export. So eager were its breeders to cash in on its popularity, they exported every stallion in the colony and the breed became extinct. Finally, the contrast with Canada West was nowhere more evident than in the awarding of prizes at agricultural exhibitions: in Canada East prize money was distributed among many categories and doled out in tiny amounts, with $8 going to the winner, $7 to the runner-up, and so on down to $1 and even to 50 cents; in Canada West the gap between winners and runners-up would have been significant.

In the case of Canada East diversification meant little more than the replacement of one form of subsistence by another. In Canada West, on the other hand, diversification was part of a continuous process of specialization that raised cash incomes to new levels. The point may be made in many ways. One convenient way is to contrast the number of mechanical mowers and reapers in use in the two halves of the province: by 1871 Canada East's total was 5149, Canada West's (with only a modest lead in population) 37 874. Another is to point out that between 1850 and 1870 the cash income of the farmer of Canada West never fell below four times that of his counterpart in Canada East — and on many occasions it was as much as ten times higher.

This wide diffusion of purchasing power, coupled with an entrepreneurial mentality, permitted the growth of specialized trades catering to a mass market. A rash of towns was the result. In the Maritimes, self-confident urban centres were rare: there was Halifax and Saint John, but Charlottetown could not be included, and Yarmouth and Moncton soon applied to have their municipal charters taken away; Fredericton became a city only because in 1848 it was given a bishopric — a feudal rather than mercantile conception. In Canada East there were Quebec City and Montreal, and then Sherbrooke and Trois Rivières, lagging far behind. In Canada West, however, there was a host of towns eager to grow, five of which aspired to regional prominence — Toronto, Hamilton, Kingston, Ottawa, and London. By today's standards they were small, and the hinterlands they served tiny — London was 7000 in 1851, Kingston less than 12 000 — but the urbanization of that part of the province was well underway. By 1870 there were 81 towns in Ontario (that is, places with populations of over 1000); the corresponding figure for Quebec was 27. Even allowing for the difference in population the difference in pattern is obvious.

The response of British North America to urbanization and industrialization has to be examined. First, it is necessary to look at a development already touched upon tangentially — the impact of the railway on British North America.

# — 3. The Transportation Revolution —

Old Winter is once more upon us, and our inland seas are 'dreary and inhospitable wastes' to the merchant and to the traveller; — our rivers are sealed fountains — and an embargo which no human power can remove is laid on all our ports. Around our deserted wharves and warehouses are huddled the naked spars — the blasted forest of trade — from which the sails have fallen like the leaves of autumn. The splashing wheels are silenced — the roar of steam is hushed, — the day saloon, so lately thronged with busy life, is now but an abandoned hull, — and the cold snow revels in solitary possession of the untrodden deck. The animation of business is suspended, the life blood of commerce is curdled and stagnant in the St. Lawrence — the great aorta of the North. On land, the heavy stage labours through mingled frost and mud in the West — or struggles through drifted snow, and slides with uncertain track over the icy hills of Eastern Canada. Far away to the South is heard the daily scream of the steam-whistle — but from Canada there is no escape: blockaded and imprisoned by Ice and Apathy, we have at least ample time for reflection — and if there be comfort in Philosophy may we not profitably consider the PHILOSOPHY OF RAILROADS.

This arresting passage is the opening to T.C. Keefer's *Philosophy of Railroads*, which first appeared in 1849. By 1853 it had gone through four editions, and evidently it caught the mood of the day. The comparison with the United States was timely. It was not merely that, at a date when America had 15 000 kilometres of track, Canada had less than 100. It was, rather, that the very *raison d'être* of Montreal and of the St. Lawrence transportation system seemed to have been called in question. Despite the large sums expended to improve the river and to catch up with the Erie Canal, the Americans had once again jumped into the lead by moving beyond mere barges and into railroads. For Keefer and his many admirers, it was necessary either to follow suit or go under.

In a concise pamphlet, buttressed by statistical appendices, Keefer elaborated upon this central message. Separate sections were devoted to the benefits of speed, economy, regularity, safety, and convenience that the railroad would confer. Special attention was given to economy. He pointed out that "friction on a level Railway [is] only from one-tenth to one-seventh of that upon the roads." He went on to observe

If this be the effect of the rail alone, it is needless to enlarge upon its power when travelled by an iron horse, with which hunger and thirst are but metaphorical terms, which knows no disease nor fatigue, and to which a thousand miles is but the beginning of a journey, and a thousand tons but an ordinary burthen.

Turning to his overwhelmingly agricultural readership he pointed out what neighbouring American lines were already bearing out, that "the essence of a Railway system is *to increase its own traffic*, adding twenty-five percent to the value of every farm within fifty miles of the track [and] doubling that of those near it." Regularity was also stressed, for "Railways in the winter season have no competitors."

The use made of such arguments, backed up with statistics, was impressive, but no less impressive was the framework in which the whole case was presented. Keefer accurately caught the mid-Victorian mood, the faith in progress and the ability of modern methods to transform every facet of society. In a passage redolent of Adam Smith's "Hidden Hand" Keefer rhapsodized,

> Nothing would be a more powerful antidote to [the existing] state of primitive, but not innocuous simplicity, than the transit of Railways through our agricultural districts. The civilizing tendency of the locomotive is one of the modern anomalies, which however inexplicable it may appear to some, is yet so fortunately patent to all, that it is admitted as readily as the action of steam, though the substance be invisible and its secret ways unknown to man. Poverty, indifference, the bigotry or jealousy of religious denominations, local dissensions or political demagogueism may stifle or neutralize the influence of the best intended efforts of an educational system; but that invisible power which has waged successful war with the material elements, will assuredly overcome the prejudices of mental weakness or the designs of mental tyrants. It calls for no cooperation, it waits for no convenient season, but with a restless, rushing, roaring assiduity, it keeps up a constant and unavoidable spirit of enquiry and compassion; and while ministering to the material wants, and appealing to the covetousness of the multitude, it unconsciously, irresistibly, impels them to a more intimate union with their fellow men.

This was the very epitome of free-trade expansionism, and Keefer was popular.

The realization of his dreams fell woefully short, however. In the Maritimes there had been planning on a large scale. An early attempt to link New Brunswick with Quebec had fallen through when territory through which the route was to pass was awarded to the United States by the Webster-Ashburton Treaty; not until the spur of the Corn Law Abolition was a modified version of this line taken up again, and even then progress lagged. However, in 1850 an ambitious scheme brought together delegates from New Brunswick and Nova Scotia, from Canada, and from New England. Newfoundland also was represented. The projected line was aptly known as the Intercolonial. Howe journeyed to London to obtain the imperial backing necessary for such a line, since the Maritime colonies clearly could not afford to pay their share of such an undertaking. Initial reports suggested that Howe had succeeded, but since the line ran too close to the American border, the British government finally refused. The Intercolonial had to wait until Confederation.

Meanwhile, New Brunswick made slow progress with a line to Woodstock, and did better with one from Saint John to Shediac that joined the St. Lawrence and the Bay of Fundy. Nova Scotia constructed lines from Halifax to give access to those bodies of water, too. That, however, exhausted the colonial abilities for the moment; yet some idea of the revolution they wrought may be gained from the following development. These lines were publicly built and run through railway commissioners. The difficulty in raising sufficient funds was enough to modify the uneconomical custom of allowing private members to introduce money bills, and in New Brunswick in 1857 and in Nova Scotia in 1860, the British and Canadian practice of restricting their introduction to members of the executive was decided upon.

The Canadian experience, however, did not suggest that parliamentary practice had much to do with probity when it came to railways. As the tortuous story of railways chartered, amalgamated, bought out, and leased indicated, there was ample scope for the most extensive corruption.

The first significant Canadian venture came in response to an American initiative that coincided with Montreal's fears for its future. John A. Poor, of Portland, Maine, was determined that his city should supplant Boston as the Atlantic terminus. To this end he proposed a line to link Portland with the traffic of the St. Lawrence at Montreal. In 1845, Canada chartered its section, the St. Lawrence and Atlantic. Prominent in the company was A.T. Galt, director of the British America Land Company, which had extensive holdings in the Eastern Townships, an area to be traversed by the line. However, early construction was hampered by a shortage of funds, and Galt was delighted to come to an understanding with Francis Hincks, at that time finance minister in the Canadian government. In 1849, Hincks put through the Guarantee Act, whereby the government undertook to guarantee the interest up to six percent on half the bonds of any reputable railway; the test of a reputable railway was one of at least 120 kilometres. A little later, a Municipalities Act permitted local authorities to invest in railways. This method of increasing capital was used to excess: the tiny but ambitious settlement of Port Hope invested to the tune of $740 000, although its population was only 4000. The St. Lawrence and Atlantic was able to take advantage of the Guarantee Act, and was kept alive. More importantly, perhaps, Hincks had had his eyes opened to the possibilities of railway promotion and manipulation.

Better fortune attended the second major Canadian system. What became the Great Western began life in 1834 as the London and Gore Railway. The economic collapse of 1836-37 and the rebellion had prevented any further development, but in 1845 it was resurrected, the leading figure being Sir Allan MacNab, the Tory knighted for helping put down Mackenzie and his following. This politician, who would be premier of the province, was fully in the mainstream of Canadian life when he announced "Railways are my politics." His line linked Hamilton with Niagara on the one hand and Windsor on the other, and soon a connection with Toronto was completed. It was well placed to take advantage of a dense population and an area not served by canals. Moreover, it was able to act as a "short cut" for existing American lines. The Great Western had its moments of doubt, but eventually established itself as a paying proposition.

As these two systems took shape, it became clear that the central section cried out for completion. At the time when the Intercolonial was being born, a line down the St. Lawrence Valley and on to the far west of Canada was considered strategically necessary. More to the point, if the St. Lawrence and Atlantic was to have any traffic, and Montreal a future, it was necessary to tap into the Great Western and divert its flow away from Niagara and the New York route. Hincks began to air proposals for a Grand Trunk Railway, to run from Windsor to Toronto to Montreal and beyond; east of Montreal would be a link with the St. Lawrence and Atlantic, but also a line from Point Lévis to Trois Pistoles on the lower St. Lawrence for an eventual linkup with the Intercolonial. The prospectus of 1853 painted a glowing picture of the possibilities; it was, it was claimed,

the most comprehensive system of railway in the world. Protected from the possibility of injurious competition for nearly its entire length by natural causes as well as by legislative enactment, it improves the traffic of a region extending for nearly 800 miles in one direct line. . . . Commencing at the debouchment of the three largest lakes in the world the Grand Trunk Railway of Canada pours the accumulating traffic throughout the entire length of Canada. . . . The whole future traffic between the western regions and the east, including Lower Canada, parts of the state of Vermont and New Hampshire, the whole of the state of Maine, and the provinces of New Brunswick, Nova Scotia, Prince Edward Island, and Newfoundland, must therefore pass over the Grand Trunk Railway.

As reassuring, no doubt, was the fact that the president of the Railways was Sir John Rose, the solicitor general for Canada West, and the directors included Hincks and four other cabinet members.

As it emerged from the original shell of the Intercolonial, the idea had been for a publicly built, publicly owned line, but as it took shape under Hincks's hands, it became a private venture. The company's handling of its responsibilities was in no way superior to that of the Maritime provinces. The corruption was such that critics took to referring to the line as the "Grand Trunk Pig," so much was the company-to-government relationship like that of hog to trough. An Englishman, sent out to represent the shareholders who were overwhelmingly from Britain, remarked, "Upon my word, I do not think there was much to be said in favour of the Canadians over the Turks when contracts, places, free tickets on railways, or even cash was in question." Capital was in short supply. Already by 1855 the company was broke and had to be bailed out by the province. The same thing happened a year later. By 1861 its deficit was $13 million. By 1867 the provincial debt on account of the Grand Trunk was $26 million.

Nevertheless, the line had been built. It leased the St. Lawrence and Atlantic. It built the main line from Montreal to Toronto, and eventually built its own western extension to Sarnia by way of Guelph. By 1860 the total length of track in British North America was 3200 kilometres. These lines may have been politically objectionable, since they spawned so much corruption. They may have been economically unsound, since apart from the Great Western they were built ahead of settlement and in losing competition with American lines and Canadian waterways, and they were so often poorly constructed and hideously expensive to maintain. However, psychologically they worked. They gave the settlers that feeling, so forcibly championed by Keefer, of being part of something up-to-date and exciting. It was a formula whose magic was to work for many years to come. At the very end of the century the duplication of Grand Trunk and Great Western was to be paralleled on a much vaster scale as two additional transcontinentals were added to the

## Map 17.2: Canals and Railways in British North America

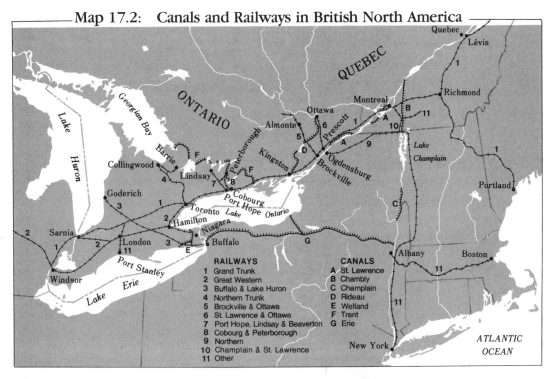

**RAILWAYS**
1 Grand Trunk
2 Great Western
3 Buffalo & Lake Huron
4 Northern Trunk
5 Brockville & Ottawa
6 St. Lawrence & Ottawa
7 Port Hope, Lindsay & Beaverton
8 Cobourg & Peterborough
9 Northern
10 Champlain & St. Lawrence
11 Other

**CANALS**
A St. Lawrence
B Chambly
C Champlain
D Rideau
E Welland
F Trent
G Erie

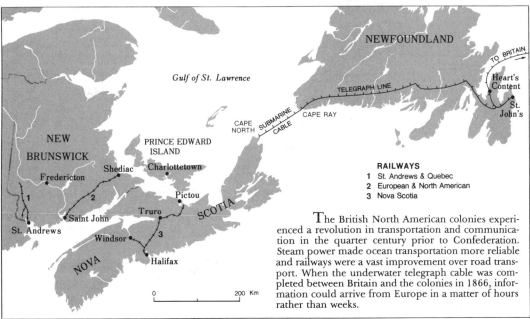

**RAILWAYS**
1 St. Andrews & Quebec
2 European & North American
3 Nova Scotia

The British North American colonies experienced a revolution in transportation and communication in the quarter century prior to Confederation. Steam power made ocean transportation more reliable and railways were a vast improvement over road transport. When the underwater telegraph cable was completed between Britain and the colonies in 1866, information could arrive from Europe in a matter of hours rather than weeks.

Canadian Pacific. By the 1920s Canadians could boast that they enjoyed (if that is the word) the greatest per capita length of track in the world.

This is to look far to the future, however. In the 1850s the spread of railways was within bounds. Yet already it was reshaping relationships — and not only the economic. In an anticipation of McLuhan, Keefer had written that "Steam has exerted an influence over matter which can only be compared to that which the discovery of Printing has exercised upon mind." The final section of this chapter must deal with the vast transformation that mid-Victorian development brought to British North America.

## — 4. Industries, Tariffs, Cities —

Not before Confederation, and indeed not for many years thereafter, could it be maintained that British North America was an industrial society. The characteristic institutions of such an order were almost wholly lacking. In Canada only three cotton-spinning mills were established between 1844 and 1860. Even the disruption caused by the American Civil War, both to Britain and to the United States, made little difference, for only three more were added, as well as one in Saint John, New Brunswick. Woollen mills were more common, but their very number (91 in Canada West and 31 in Canada East) indicates that they were small-scale local affairs, manufacturing a crude product for a limited local market. In wool and cotton alike the traditional suppliers, Britain and the United States, maintained their dominance for many years. Iron-working was developing in the 1860s as a railway network spread, but once again it was a scattered small-scale business: in the Maritimes, where the raw materials were to be found, several attempts to launch the trade failed, and only the Saint John iron-rolling mill was successful. Nova Scotia began to develop its coal reserves, but when set against the fisheries and shipping that trade was on a small scale. It is true that by the 1860s Canadians were manufacturing farm machinery from pilfered American designs, but this was a time when the implement business was tiny and localized. Timber-related manufacturers were just beginning, including furniture-making. There was, of course, always beer-brewing. All told, however, the manufacturing component of the economy was small, and it was trade and commerce that made up the vast bulk of the non-farm sector.

Given the undeveloped states of manufacturers, any attempt to win protection failed. There had always been those who had refused to accept the imperial sellout of 1846 as final. Within a year, R.B. Sullivan, a Canadian cabinet minister and soon-to-be judge, was speaking out in Hamilton (the leading hotbed of protectionism, and home of the prominent protectionist *Spectator*); there he was reported as saying,

> What I find fault with . . . is a state of things that leaves this country without moneyed capital of its own. This is produced by our not having manufacturing enterprise and capital here. Our manufacturing towns are in Great Britain and the United States, whither the profits of our industry flow, without our having the benefit of capital in the country, creating, reproducing more capital, as it should be under a better system.

By 1852, hope of a return to protectionism seemed to be reviving. A convention was held that brought together protection-minded Boards of Trade; it was chaired by Hugh Allan, founder of the steamship line and later of the C.P.R. Hincks, the Canadian finance minister, repudiated his earlier free-trade views. An assembly debate considered, though it did not approve, a motion "to foster and encourage those branches of native industry for which this country possesses natural advantages" by tariff reform. The mover noted that

> With every natural facility, and the bounties of nature strewed about us in the utmost profusion, with elements of wealth on every hand, we are still but an agricultural people, — without manufacturers, without railroads, and without ourselves possessing the means wherewith to build them. No wonder we are obliged to have recourse to English capitalists and English contractors for our contemplated Grand Trunk line; and obliged, if built at all, to construct it at double the expense it would otherwise cost. Those who are dependent upon England for their clothing and knives and forks and spoons, must also necessarily be dependent upon her for their railroads.

The real push came in 1858 with the founding in Toronto of the Association for the Promotion of Canadian Industry. The lead was taken by Isaac Buchanan; it was he who had written in such bitter terms to the *Times* in 1846 to protest the repeal of the Corn Laws, and he was now the editor of the Hamilton *Spectator*. He went out of his way to state that

> We can afford to speak more plainly than men who for a moment would doubt their own loyalty, we being of that class who would stick to the old flag, right or wrong; and we cannot find words sufficiently eloquent to denounce those ignoramuses who would try on old country theories . . . in a new country like Canada. Though this country is not, and we trust never will be, republican, its

material interests are the same as those of our republican neighbours. Canada, therefore, wants no untried theory of trade and industry, seeing that we have the actual and dearly-bought experience of the United States.

An appeal to the imperial connection did no harm at a time when British immigration was peaking and the Crimean War was recently over.

The protectionist wave spent itself; it was before its time. It is true that in these years the tariff went higher and higher. Revision began in 1847 when, as a consequence of the imperial conversion to free trade, the colonies were permitted to set their own. Initially, the average tariff on American goods was reduced from 12 percent to 7.5 percent, while that on British goods was raised from 5 percent to 7.5 percent. In 1856 the average rate went to 15 percent. In 1858, the year of the Association for the Promotion of Canadian Industry and a visit by its delegation to the finance minister, William Cayley, the rate was pushed up to 20 percent. A year later, A.T. Galt, Cayley's successor, added a further 5 percent. It was this last tariff that had wrung protests from English manufacturers and from the colonial office, and had elicited a firm rejoinder from Canada so that Westminster backed down — a development referred to in Chapter 16 in the section on Responsible Government. However, the explanation for these tariffs is to be sought not in the prompting of a manufacturing lobby, nor in the government's wish to nurse infant industries to adulthood, as in the need to raise a revenue to pay for the ever-mounting railway deficits. It is significant that the highest duties were on luxury items such as tobacco, coffee, spice, and liquor. When the ministers described the tariffs as "incidentally" protectionist they were speaking the truth. With the Maritimes maintaining lower average duties than Canada, British North America for the present resisted joining the protectionist camp.

Industry, then, was not the dominant factor in the 1850s and 1860s, yet these were decisive decades for industrialization. In the discussion of the staple developments the inability of the Maritimes and of Canada East to break free was noted. In the survey of railway construction the lag of the Maritimes and of Canada East was noted. The widening gap between Canada West and the rest of British North America becomes evident in this period. In this connection the movements of population are revealing. In 1861 the populations of the colonies were as follows: Newfoundland, 130 000; Prince Edward Island, 81 000; Nova Scotia, 300 000; New Brunswick, 250 000; Canada, 2 508 000 (Canada East, 1 112 000; Canada West, 1 396 000). Two facts stand out. The absolute predominance of Canada is marked, roughly two and a half million to three quarters of a million, and the disparity is even more marked if Newfoundland is kept separate — it had always lagged in its development ("by far the greater parts of Newfoundland . . . were as primitive as when Cabot had first sighted her rocky coast"), and Responsible Government came only in 1855. Second, the rate of growth also favoured Canada. In the Maritime provinces the population in 1848 was some 560 000, so that the increase by 1861 was in the order of 12.6 percent. For Canada, the 1851 figure was 1 842 000, which meant an increase of 34.5 percent. For Canada West the increase was 45.6 percent. These figures indicate that not only was Canada West perceived as the best place for making good economically, but that the very growth of population was making possible that economic advance.

The essence of what was happening in British North America may be seen in the metropolitan evolution of the time. The term "metropolis" is reserved for those cities large enough to dominate a hinterland so that even fair-sized urban concentrations can be made dependent on them, especially for financial services and cultural leadership. The classic examples in earlier Canadian history would be Versailles/La Rochelle acting as the metropolis for New France, or London as metropolis for the whole of British North America. It was in London that backing was found for commercial ventures such as the fur trade and the wheat and timber staples, and it was from London that fashion (whether in bonnets or in philosophy) radiated. As J.M.S. Careless has pointed out, a nice analogy is with the feudal system, and just as there could be great lords dependent on the king but who in their turn had lesser nobles dependent on them, so too a great metropolis like London could have subordinate centres, each of which in its own sphere acted as a metropolis. Thus, in the earliest days of New France, Quebec City might be looked upon as a metropolis. In time, however, Montreal's control of the fur trade enabled it to break free and then to take Quebec City in tow. Certainly with the growth of grain-forwarding and banking in Montreal, that city left its French-Canadian rival far behind.

What is striking about British North America at mid-nineteenth century is the way in which population growth, changing transportation links, and increasing industrialization favoured the emergence of two metropolises and two only. From what has been said, the Maritimes and Newfoundland would not be able to find a candidate. In W.L. Morton's standard account of Canada from 1857 to 1873, Saint John, New Brunswick, is not even mentioned in the index. Halifax does appear, but only because in scattered, underpopulated Nova Scotia the naval base had an imperial significance quite disproportionate to its economic standing. Equally clear, the rival to Montreal ought to come from booming Canada West. It was, in fact, Toronto.

What enabled Toronto to escape Montreal's orbit was that New York was a metropolis, too, and engaged in a fierce rivalry with Montreal for the control of the upper midwest. The building of the Erie Canal had underlined that rivalry, and the two cities had vied for the riches of the frontier ever since. Toronto could play the one against the other, finding between them the room to grow itself. Its position enabled it to overtake centres in Canada West that had once been bigger and seemingly more important (such as Kingston, an older loyalist centre and onetime provincial capital), and to beat back the challenge of upstart newcomers (such as Hamilton, which boomed in the 1840s and 1850s but later fell back). In Toronto's favour was not the port — that advantage was shared by a host of competing towns along the lakefront, including Kingston. Rather, what was crucial was its ability to act as a centre for the emerging rail network. The Grand Trunk (though it was a Montreal line) gave access to the east and the west; the Great Western (though that line too was not based in Toronto) gave access to the Niagara peninsula; above all, the Northern Railway was the key. This line, a truly Toronto line, was opened to Collingwood on Georgian Bay in 1855. It was the real secret of Toronto's growth — east-west through traffic proved illusory, but north-south feeders opened up new sources of supply and new areas of demand. This was something that Kingston, for example, was never able to manage, in part because its "back country" was not as rich as Toronto's and so did not cry out for rail development; consequently, that city stagnated.

On the basis of these advantages, and behind the lead of ambitious entrepreneurs, Toronto went from strength to strength. It developed banks with which to challenge the hegemony of Montreal. In 1850, only two of the five banks in Toronto were not Montreal-based, but in 1866, the Bank of Commerce began an effective challenge to Montreal's dominance. Insurance companies and building societies were growing, the Canada Permanent dating from 1855. In the same year the Stock Exchange was built. By the 1850s the expanding possibilities were beguiling the city's leaders, and they were looking for new territory to enfief. Canada West having exhausted the best farmland, and business eager for new markets, they turned their gaze to the lands of the Hudson's Bay Company. Toronto's interest in the northwest dates from 1856.

Montreal realized it was facing a formidable rival. In fighting back it had powerful weapons. It was a larger city than Toronto, and through it came many of the migrants to British North America. In addition, because the agriculture of Canada East was still in an unhealthy state, and because new lands there were not opening up fast enough for the still growing population, *habitants* were flooding into Montreal to provide a pool of cheap labour. The city's financial power was great — it was always believed in Canada West that Bank of Montreal hostility killed the Bank of Upper Canada, which went under in 1866. Financial power applied in Montreal meant capital-rich businesses operating up-to-date machinery in well-built and efficient premises. Montreal's position was strategic, and as the metal trades grew in importance the city was especially well placed to take advantage: at this date the pig iron for British North America was imported from Britain, and there was a significant freight saving in selling in Montreal rather than Toronto. In addition, Montreal had boot and shoe factories, woodworking businesses, tobacco, sugar and many other manufactures. By 1870, the industrial value added in Montreal exceeded that in Toronto, Kingston, Hamilton, London, and Ottawa (the five largest cities in Canada West) put together. There was, however, one oddity about Montreal's early lead: the city did not sell significantly to its immediate hinterland, for Canada East's *habitants* were poor and aimed for self-sufficiency. Rather, Montreal sold to British North America as a whole, and so depended on access to, and preferably control of, a transcontinental transportation system.

As the two metropolises reached out, they did so culturally as well as economically. At various times both were the provincial capital; and as politics became more compelling and full-time a political culture grew up in the two cities. Previously, politicians had been local bosses who took time off to go to the assembly; now they were becoming big-city men who occasionally had to run down to their constituencies. Similarly, opinions became centralized in the metropolis and then diffused over the rail network; the older provincial newspapers were giving way before the likes of *La Minerve*, edited in Montreal by George-Etienne Cartier, and George Brown's *Globe*. Both cities were the seats of leading universities, and from them future leaders of society returned home with metropolitan notions. In this connection, attention may be drawn to the Normal School in Toronto, where the majority of the province's English-speaking school teachers were trained. Then, too, both cities were in the nature of religious "capitals."

If the 1850s and 1860s are decisive for industrialization, they are no less so for urbanization. Especially in Canada, the older scale of things, the older pattern of living, was giving way to a newer and more sophisticated ordering. Pioneering was now for most people in British North America a faint memory.

--------------------------------------------------- **Suggested Reading**

The Centenary Series volume which deals with British North America between 1857 and 1873 is W.L. Morton, *The Critical Years (1964).*

The revolution in British imperial thinking and its impact on British North America may be approached through P.J. Cain, *Economic Foundations of British Overseas Expansion 1815-1914* (1980) (which draws attention to the different interpretations current in the field); G.N. Tucker, *The Canadian Commercial Revolution* (1936); D.F. Warner, *The Idea of Continental Union: Agitation for Annexation to the United States* (1960); D.C. Masters, *The Reciprocity Treaty of 1854* (1961); L.H. Officer and L.B. Smith, "The Canadian American Reciprocity Treaty of 1855-66," *Journal of Economic History* (1968); R.H. MacDonald, "Nova Scotia and the Reciprocity Negotiations, 1846-1854," *Nova Scotia Historical Quarterly* (1977).

Economic developments in the period may be traced in H.C. Pentland, *Labour & Capital in Canada* (1981); D.S. Macmillan (ed.), *Canadian Business History* (1972) (various chapters); D. Sutherland, "Halifax Merchants and the Pursuit of Development, 1783-1850," *Canadian Historical Review* (1978); E.W. Sager and L.R. Fischer, "Atlantic Canada and the Age of Sail Revisited," *Canadian Historical Review* (1982), and *The Enterprising Canadians: Entrepreneurs and Economic Development in Eastern Canada 1820-1914* (1979); for a more colourful account of Maritime sail, see S. Spicer, *Master of Sail* (1968); an outgrowth of a large-scale collaborative study is K. Matthews and G. Panting (eds.), *Ships and Ship Building in the North Atlantic Region* (1978); G. Tulchinsky, *The River Barons: Montreal Businessmen and the Growth of Industry and Transportation, 1837-1853* (1977).

Railways are examined in H.V. Nelles (ed.), *Philosophy of Railroads, and Other Essays by T.C. Keefer* (1972); A.W. Currie, *The Grand Trunk Railway of Canada* (1957); C. Wallace, "Saint John Boosters and the Railroads in the Mid-nineteenth Century," *Acadiensis* (1976).

Urbanization is explored in D.C. Masters, *The Rise of Toronto 1850-1890* (1947); M.B. Katz, *The People of Hamilton* (1976); J. Spelt, *Urban Development in South-Central Ontario* (1972); G. Tulchinsky (ed.), *To Preserve and Defend: Essays on Kingston in the Nineteenth Century* (1976); J. Petryshyn (ed.), *Victorian Cobourg* (1976). Metropolitanism in Canada is always connected with J.M.S. Careless: see his "Frontierism, Metropolitanism, and Canadian History," *Canadian Historical Review* (1954).

# CHAPTER 18

## Federal Union

## — 1. Political Deadlock —

Whatever the economic well-being of British North America at mid-century, politically the situation was discouraging. To a great extent British North America was merely sharing in the malaise that marked the parliamentary systems of the day and that did not spare the one at Westminster. The old eighteenth-century politics was well and truly dead. In that system, the executive was formed, which proceeded to build itself a majority in the Commons by the distribution of places and patronage; it was a stable system and by and large ministries endured. By the later nineteenth century the modern system was well established. In this system, parties organized outside Parliament compete in elections, and the winning group proceeds to form the government; this system, too, is stable, and today the fall of a government due to the erosion of its voting strength in the Commons is altogether exceptional. However, from the 1840s to 1860s was a transitional period. The old mechanism had broken down but the new had not yet fully emerged. Without adequate means of disciplining the private member, ministries were impotent; the independents enjoyed their heyday, free to vote as they pleased and to change their allegiance at the drop of a hat. In British North American parlance, it was the age of the "loose fish."

The Atlantic provinces experienced this problem as much as anywhere. The deep-rooted localism referred to earlier only exacerbated the difficulty of managing the House, and made sustained commitment to larger projects difficult. To the colonists, such an approach was by no means unpopular, but the governors, men for whom the wider concerns had to matter and who were familiar with the rather more disciplined ways of British politics, were unhappy with the situation. From them came much of the impetus for some kind of British North American Union, for they felt it would curb petty parochialism and elevate the tone of politics.

Yet the Atlantic could afford to jog on; the blemishes were not fatal flaws. In Canada, however, the evils of the system were blatant. It was not merely a question of a little instability, a lack of discipline. Deadlock, shady maneuvering, and impotence disgraced the parliamentary scene.

It has been pointed out how the Durham-Sydenham plan of assimilation was abandoned before the 1840s were through. A double system of law within one colony meant having two attorneys-general and two solicitors-general. A recognition of Catholic claims to a separate religious educational system meant the splitting of the superintendency of schools. The grant of equal standing to the French language was another retreat from assimilation. Very quickly it was appreciated that the colony was two sections, and that the logical political conclusion of abandoning monoculture was the doctrine known as the "double majority." First put forward in 1845, that doctrine held that a law could be passed only if it could command a majority from the section affected by it. The doctrine was never accepted as an official part of the Canadian constitution, and even those who favoured that approach on occasion could disregard it on others. Nevertheless, such a doctrine was required in fact, and a governor admitted that "you may judge how the difficulty of my position has been complicated by this quasi federal question, which I am bound to treat as theoretically absurd, though I know full well that in practice it must be looked to." Whether openly acknowledged or not, the principle of duality was so well understood that after the coming of Responsible Government (and in some cases even before) ministries were double-headed; the LaFontaine-Baldwin government was only the first of many.

The coincidence of sectional discord and an age of "loose fish" meant that Canadian politics had to be turbulent and sterile. It was easy to use questionable methods to win even righteous ends, and easy to feel that some group somewhere was taking unfair advantage. The debates over education provide a very good example of this kind of politics. In 1850 the system in Canada West was overhauled. A clause permitted Catholic parents (if sufficient in number) to demand a separate school for their children; previously they could only request such a school. The majority of Canada West's staunch Protestants considered this to be unwarranted interference with *their* schools. Their resentment was much greater three years later when a new School Act went so far as to establish separate school boards in Canada West and to give them the right of taxation to maintain their schools; moreover, those who contributed tax money to Catholic schools were excused taxes to the common schools. When it became known that the Act of 1853 carried only with the help of the votes from Canada East the bitterness was great.

In the face of what they saw as "papal aggression," the Protestants of Canada West rallied behind the voice of "voluntaryism," George Brown. It was the belief of this Scots Presbyterian, widely propagated through his *Globe*, that Church and State should be quite separate, and he began a crusade to undo the work of 1850-53. "The state shall have nothing whatever to do with religious teachings in any shape," he thundered. "Let our school system be destroyed, and what remains to us of hope for the country?" Distrusting all things French Canadian, he broadened his campaign to include alteration of the terms of union. The equal representation of East and West permitted the former to impose its will on the latter; that, he insisted, must be changed to "representation by population," for by mid-century the West had surpassed the East in number of people. It was a bitter agitation, and combined with the structural difficulties threatened to paralyze politics.

Turbulence and sterility were also evident in the unscrupulous politicking by which ministries were sustained or defeated. The troubles of the age of "loose fish" were aggravated partly by the singular lack of political issues. The reformers had little else to agitate for since Responsible Government had been conceded. The Tories, having seen the imperial connection cease to be an issue, had lost their extremist tinge. Thus, these two groupings drew together to give rise to that quintessential Canadian phenomenon, the broad centre party. The union was consummated when Augustin-Norbert Morin, an author of the *Ninety-two Resolutions*, formed a government with Sir Allan MacNab, the rebel-chasing baronet of 1837. This fusion left the advanced position very poorly represented. In Canada West there were the Clear Grits, agrarians faintly tinged with American notions and given to democratic and egalitarian ideas. They were rescued from political limbo by Brown, who gave them leadership, the sophistication of his metropolitan background, and a reasonableness previously lacking. In Canada East there were the even more unrepresentative *Rouges*, led by A.A. Dorion, eighteenth-century anticlericals in a sea of ultramontane *Bleus*. These two opposition parties had little in common, and between them Brown and Dorion were to help demonstrate the impoverishment of Canadian politics in the 1850s.

The election of 1857 returned a shaky Macdonald-Cartier centrist government. In July 1858 it fell on a vote to accept the Queen's choice of Ottawa as the colony's capital. The governor asked Brown to form a government. For French-Canadian backing, Brown asked Dorion, who agreed, and the Brown-Dorion ministry was sworn in. Within 24 hours the government had been defeated. The ousted centrists had moved a vote of non-confidence, arguing that the known incompatibility of Clear Grits and *Rouges* made any such coalition absurd. The manoeuvre might have been legal, but it was irresponsible: the ministry should not have been condemned in advance but allowed to carry on the colony's business and judged on its record.

This did not exhaust the chicanery. The governor did not feel he could grant Brown a dissolution since an election had only recently taken place; indeed, he had told Brown this when inviting him to form the government. A.T. Galt was asked to make the attempt. He declined. The governor then turned to Cartier, who agreed, bringing in Macdonald. The names might be reversed, but the same pair dominated. There was a problem, however. Parliamentary law then required that ministers stand for re-election. This was a vestige of the eighteenth-century theory that, strictly speaking, legislative and executive should be separate; if legislators were going to take money from the executive and apply the laws they had helped make, then, it was argued, their constituents should have the chance to approve or disapprove their new status in an election. Cartier and Macdonald and the rest of the ministers dared not risk an election, however; nor did they dare to be out of the House when crucial votes would be taken. Accordingly, they used a legal loophole that permitted a minister transferring from one portfolio to another within 30 days of being sworn in to the post to avoid re-election. The ministers were sworn in to one set of offices, and promptly exchanged them for another. The "double shuffle" was denounced, and gave rise to lawsuits, but the government survived. However, the whole sorry business convinced many that Canada was ungovernable, and that some radical change would have to come. What form could that change take? The only well developed alternative was that hammered out in 1859 at the Toronto Convention of the Reform (that is, the Brown-tamed Clear Grit) Party. There the elected delegates had agreed on the need to break up the union and replace it with a federation of the two Canadas; in this way Canada West would in effect win "rep by pop." However, when in 1860 Brown moved in the Canadian parliament a motion along these lines he was defeated easily. Canada East was profoundly suspicious of Brown, and even the *Rouges* voted for the union or else abstained. As Cartier's *Bleu* newspaper *La Minerve* put it, Brown's schemes would mean "no more grants to our religious bodies, no more priests in charge of education; the secret societies would be given legal status; divorce freed from its bonds; and the French language persecuted anew."

It was a hopeless situation. Deadlock prevailed.

# — 2. Expansive Pressures —

The political situation in Canada, above all, demanded change. That impetus may be described as negative, in that it was the sheer impossibility of the existing arrangements that cried out to be remedied: nothing in them suggested a course of action that would solve the problem. After Brown's abortive intervention in 1860 the only proposal was the impossible one of the Clear Grit, William McDougall, who in an assembly speech in 1861 warned that

> The Anglo-Saxon race [of Canada West] would not rest quiet. They would resort to some other plan. There were relations of an intimate kind with people on the other side of the border, and it was natural to suppose that they would look in that direction for the remedy that they were unable to obtain elsewhere.

The speech provoked the taunt from Macdonald that rebellion was being threatened.

Even while such echoes of annexation and of 1837 were being heard, there were positive forces at work, lines of development that not only proclaimed the necessity of change but that also foreshadowed the shape of things to come. Throughout British North America the realization was growing that the colonies were vulnerable. In Nova Scotia the leader of the opposition moved in the assembly "that the union or confederation of the British North American Provinces, on just principles, while calculated to perpetuate their annexion with the parent state, will promote their advancement and prosperity, increase their strength and influence, and elevate their position." Behind the high-minded phrases of the politician — but hinted at in the reference to "strength" — lay a feeling that absorption into the United States

311

was possible; that motion was made in 1854, the year of reciprocity. Experience was to show that the danger had been exaggerated, but other threats took its place. The Crimean War drew attention to Russia's possession of Alaska; if Russia lost badly, what would happen to its colony? Would the United States somehow take possession (as it did by purchase in 1867)? In very recent memory, the British claim to what is now Oregon had been sacrificed in the face of superior American determination to claim the territory; in 1846 Kingston had been fortified to withstand American aggression, but the Oregon Treaty had nonetheless been an American victory. In 1859 came a foretaste of worse to come. The French emperor, Napoleon III, had visions of reviving French influence in the New World. One step in his program was to reestablish the French maritime presence in the North Atlantic; for a basis he had the French Shore of Newfoundland, privileges granted to French fishermen in 1714 and 1783. A minor war-scare blew up over the possible French escalation of their demands in the area. The total dependence of the Atlantic region on Britain was revealed, as was the shocking fact that the militia was in no shape to contribute to imperial defence. The same was true of Canada. The episode raised awkward questions, and made many consider whether an expansion of authority, by merging some if not all the colonies into a single entity, might not be necessary.

Two years later the shock was delivered with redoubled force. In 1861 the American Civil War broke out. The South sent two emissaries to Britain on board HMS *Trent*. A Northern commander intercepted the *Trent*, boarded her, and took off the Southerners. Britain, coming close to war, rushed no less than 14 000 troops to British North America. Once again colonial vulnerability had been demonstrated. More disturbingly, it was clear that nothing effective had been done to remedy the militia defects of 1859. Sentiment in Britain was rapidly growing that military disengagement from North America (except for the naval base at Halifax) should proceed as rapidly as was consistent with preserving face; but to withdraw would mean putting the colonies into a state in which they could defend themselves. Some larger organization was indicated.

The events of 1861 had a second impact. Since the troops were rushed out in winter, an ice-free port in the St. Lawrence was not possible, and in the nature of the exercise the use of Portland, Maine, was equally impossible. There was no alternative but to disembark the troops at Saint John and have them taken over winter roads by sleigh to Quebec. In this they were repeating in comfort what the New Brunswick regiment had done in the War of 1812 — but they had been colonials and it was before the days of steam; the final dash contrasted cruelly with the nine-day crossing of the Atlantic, and everyone was aware that if the Intercolonial had been built none of this would have been necessary. Accordingly, expansion through railways was added to that by colonial integration. The peculiar situation in Canada also meant that the railway question assumed an especial importance in bringing a wider union into the realm of possibility.

Canada had obvious reasons for wanting to take up the Intercolonial again. Politicians loved railways, for the patronage possibilities were enormous. In this they were no different from their counterparts in Nova Scotia and New Brunswick, who were equally eager to resume building. In Canada's case, however, the dependence upon Portland, Maine, was worrying. Americans, not happy with the Galt tariff of 1859, were talking of retaliation, and the end of the bonding privileges by the repeal of the Drawbank Acts of 1845 and 1846 was being rumoured. Canadians were increasingly feeling the need of a British ice-free port.

There was a further reason, which overshadowed the others, for Canadian interest in the Intercolonial. It had to do with Canadian designs on the far west. The land that lay west of Fort William was obsessing many Canadians. The trading and manufacturing interests, with Toronto to the fore, lusted after the new hinterland. Agricultural Canada was also interested; the good land had been taken up, and mined to exhaustion, and outmigration had set in among the farming population. Some were making for the States, but some were moving onto the prairies west of Red River. The *Globe*, which nicely fused Grit agrarianism and Toronto metropolitanism, urged a forward policy with respect to the northwest, and a Reformer-Grit convention in 1857 went so far as to demand its annexation to Canada. Nor was Montreal to be left out. That city, headquarters of the Grand Trunk and committed to expanding railways to service its growing industry, was vitally interested. There was, then, widespread support for the expedition sent in 1857 under Henry Youle Hind to explore the west and report on the potential for settlement.

These "push" factors were accompanied by "pulls" from the west itself. The Pacific coast had been brought to Canadian attention after the Oregon crisis. The Hudson's Bay Company, determined not to lose any further territory, set up a settlement on its own initiative at Fort Victoria, populating it directly from Britain. In 1856 gold was discovered on the Fraser River, and proved a powerful magnet. The influx of Americans, and the lawlessness endemic to a gold rush, caused the Hudson's Bay official in Victoria, James Douglas, to proclaim his authority on behalf of the Queen over the mainland diggings. It was a unilateral act for which he had no warrant, but in the event the British authorities upheld his action. A second colony, that of British Columbia, was set up on the Pacific in 1858. Until the merger of British Columbia and Vancouver Island in 1866 there were two additional and very attractive prizes in the west.

A second "pull" was the fact that the Hudson's Bay Company's hold over the west was imperfect. The watershed of the Bay had been granted by charter, and assuming that to be valid the company had no need to worry about its claim to that region. However, its title to the remainder rested on a licence, granted in 1821 and due to expire in 1859. A hearing into the conduct of the company was necessary before any concession of a new licence, and it was clear that the affairs of the company would be very carefully scrutinized. The more forward of the Canadian expansionists even believed that the charter itself might be put aside, and there was widespread support for the idea that Canada, heir to French claims to the area, be represented by an observer at the London hearings in 1857.

Canadian "pushes" together with western "pulls" made a powerful combination, so it was no surprise that many elements of Canadian society were turning avidly to the northwest. There was one major exception, however. Canada East (Montreal apart, of course) was hostile to expansion. It was clear that any move to incorporate the northwest into Canada would mean an increase in Canada West's influence, further tipping a balance that was already unfavourable to Canada East. In debate Brown accused Cartier, the spokesman for French Canada, of being opposed to expansion, and although Cartier denied having used the words complained of and although Brown accepted the denial, the belief persisted that leading *Bleus* could not afford to identify with the northwest.

This was where the Intercolonial came in. A Grand Trunk extension in the west might be offset by one in the east. In this way *Bleu* politicians could downplay the aggrandizement of Canada West and disguise the force of what threatened. It helped that Cartier, so crucial a figure in swaying French-Canadian opinion, was deeply involved with the Grand Trunk and desperate to see the railway pulled out of its slough of indebtedness with extensions of lines and traffic. (Nor did it do any harm that control of the Grand Trunk had by now passed to British investors with headquarters in the City of London, and that the Grand Trunk's real master was Edward Watkin, for Watkin had the ear of the colonial office and could convince them of the need for railway expansion and, perhaps, political expansion.) At the same time, Cartier could urge that an expanded political culture that included a greater Canada West might be balanced by a greater sea-based bloc. It could be professed that the Atlantic colonies and Canada East would discover mutual interests in the face of Canada West's continentalism, and that in a new equilibrium French-Canadian *survivance* would be assured. For a while it seemed that the Intercolonial would go ahead. A meeting in London in 1862 to seek imperial guarantees seemed to be going well, but at the last minute the Canadian delegates jibbed at the terms and abandoned the negotiations. The line hung fire, and with it any likelihood of a union.

Plans for some recombination of the elements of British North America had long been in the air by the 1860s. When in 1863 the governor of New Brunswick, Arthur Gordon, suggested Maritime union he was answered by the colonial secretary in crushing terms that "the measure . . . has been constantly agitated for more than ten years, and more than once has appeared quite as near being accomplished as it does now." Each new deadlock, however, was one more straw added to the camel's back. If the right catalyst appeared, perhaps the recasting of the pieces might be possible.

## — 3. The Enactment of Confederation —

The catalyst was the American Civil War. Today it requires an act of imagination to realize how massive an impact that war had. With the passage of time its horrors have been supplanted by those of even more terrible conflicts, and the "chivalric" side of that war has been allowed to bulk too large. In fact, the American Civil War was the first of the modern wars: no fewer than four million men fought in it, 617 000 of them dying, and the mobility conferred by railways and the killing power of improved weaponry made a profound impression on all who observed it. The impact of the war on British North America has already been referred to, and will again be noted in the coming section. Here its part in helping to bring about Confederation will be emphasized.

The continuing slaughter revealed, in a way that earlier incidents such as the *Trent* affair never could, how British North America might become the *occasion* for war with America. British and colonial sentiment had been strongly pro-Confederacy, and understandably the North's feelings towards a traditional enemy had been hostile. This hostility was increased when commerce raiders were built for the South in British yards and preyed on Union shipping. The most notorious example was the *Alabama*. It became clear that the North, if victorious, would seek compensation for the losses suffered, arguing that Britain's action in aiding rebels had not only caused direct damage but had also prolonged the war. It was equally clear that a demand for colonial territory might be the form of compensation sought. As it happened, the case went to international arbitration, and Britain paid monetary damages. Nevertheless, an American invasion to make good its claims was always a possibility.

The threat of invasion took a particular twist at war's end. To the standing threat of having a victorious army complete its version of "manifest destiny" by adding British North America to its conquests was added the more limited, but in one sense more likely, danger from one section of the Union. The Irish were, by 1865, a significant factor in American life. For generations they had been migrating to the United States in large numbers, exiles from their own land and passionate haters of all things British. More recently their numbers had been swelled, and their hatred inflamed, by the famine. In 1858 the Fenian Society, an ancestor of today's I.R.A., had been established to win Ireland's independence by violent means. The Fenians saw the chance to weaken Britain by attacking it through its North American colonies. There were many Irish soldiers being discharged, men inured to killing and looking for employment.

In April 1866 a Fenian force attacked an island off New Brunswick. In June a force of about one thousand crossed into Canada from Buffalo and a skirmish at Ridgeway ensued: nine Canadians were killed before the invaders withdrew. In a military sense, then, these raids amounted to very little, and politically they were equally futile. The Fenian slogans were out of touch with colonial thinking, and an assertion that "Republican institutions have become a necessity to the peace and prosperity of your Province" had an out-of-date ring about it. Indeed, the claim that "English policy represented in the obnoxious policy of Confederation, is making its last efforts to bind you in effete forms of monarchism" was counterproductive; the *Globe* was more accurate when it commented, "the longer these alarms continue on our borders, the more will this feeling of blended indignation and patriotism be awakened, till Canada's diversified people be, through the fire of outward assault, thoroughly and unmistakably fused into one." It was, in fact, the impact on British thinking that was decisive, and there the effect was to intensify that wish to disengage from North America.

Civil War developments also revealed how British North America could become the *cause* of war with America. In the past it had always been argued that the only war possible between the United States and British North America would be an imperial one — for instance, the Fenian attacks, which were directed against Britain and not against the colonies as such. Thus, Britain could feel that it retained control over the situation: maintain good relations with the United States and the border could indeed remain undefended. In 1864, however, the complete falsity of this belief was exposed. In October a group of Confederates organized from Canadian soil an attack on the banks of St. Albans in Vermont. They got away with $200 000, but killed an American in their flight back to Canada. Northern demands for action against Canada were heated, and they became even more burning when the examining magistrate ordered the release of the raiders on a technicality. The United States gave notice that the Rush-Bagot Treaty of 1817 (that demilitarized the Great Lakes) would be abrogated, and that the Reciprocity Treaty would be allowed to run out. In the end, cooler heads prevailed, but for a while war appeared inevitable. Britain was aghast; here was a quarrel not of its own doing, but it was going to be dragged into it willy-nilly.

British eagerness to withdraw was now painful in its intensity. For a while it appeared that the American Republic would break up, and that the Southern Confederacy would balance the Northern Union and so give a leeway to British North America; but now that possibility was fading, and the colonies would have to confront a colossus. An imperial emissary, Colonel W.F. Jervois, had been sent to report on colonial defence in North America. His findings were gloomy indeed, for he recognized that western Canada was virtually indefensible and that to hold on to Montreal and Quebec would require expensive fortifications. Would imperial assistance be forthcoming? It did not seem likely. At Westminster, the younger Liberals, tightfisted proponents of retrenchment and colonial abandonment, were coming to the fore, and the chancellor of the exchequer, W.E. Gladstone, was not going to waste money on fortifications. His grant, a mere 50 000 pounds, was so niggardly that the Canadian politicians gave it out that a zero had inadvertently been omitted. It had not.

Britain, then, was prepared to use great pressure to bring about a new polity that could look after itself and permit an imperial disengagement. For those British North Americans who favoured Confederation, British determination was just as well, for, as events were to prove, the colonials, when left to their own devices, were incapable of building a union.

The serious Canadian initiative took place in 1864. Yet another ministerial crisis blew up, but this time, instead of the usual musical chairs being played by the leading politicians, an untoward development took place. The leading reformer, George Brown, let it be known that he was willing to enter a coalition in a desperate attempt to cut through the dreary round of compromise and find a new plane on which solutions might be found. This action by Brown was a noble one, for it would mean working intimately with Macdonald, with whom he had carried on a bitter personal feud for years. It made possible a "Great Coalition" far wider than even the broad centrist group had been able to mount, and it made possible a new beginning.

Brown and two other reformers were to come into the cabinet. The Intercolonial would be taken up again, and an attempt at the federation of all British North America would be made. Failing that, the Canadian union would be broken up and a federation of its two sections carried out. The coalition cabinet quickly drafted plans, and looked about for the next step.

Meanwhile, the Maritime provinces were turning over a scheme of their own. They had been furious with Canada for reneging on the Intercolonial in 1862, and in the following year they had sullenly taken up the old idea of a legislative union for the Maritimes. This was the initiative that had so captivated Gordon, and had brought him a rebuke from his superior. The colonial secretary was right. There was no enthusiasm for Maritime union, but rather apathy. Still, something seemed to be necessary, and it was in this mood that they undertook to hold a conference in 1864.

It is hard to conceive of anything constructive coming out of such a conference. There was no great urge to meet, and certainly no agenda. Indeed, not even the time and place for the conference had been fixed. Nevertheless, the Canadians were keen to precipitate matters, and when they wrote asking to be invited to what was supposed to be a discussion of Maritime union they in effect captured the initiative. Charlottetown, 1 September 1864, was agreed upon, and from the start the Canadians took charge of the proceedings. The more limited objective was pushed to one side, and the conference unfolded as a Canadian presentation of the federation of all British North America.

Charlottetown was not so much a constitutional conference as an exercise in good feelings. Not a single resolution was adopted. Spacious comments were made, and such was the magic of the occasion that most delegates appreciated the vision of a transcontinental empire. A glimpse of boundless possibilities was caught, an escape from the confines of too small a provincial theatre. Charles Tupper of Nova Scotia poured scorn on the idea of his province's being a "nation by itself." J.M. Gray, premier of Prince Edward Island, was to challenge his constituents, "shall we form part of a nation extending from Halifax to Vancouver, as citizens of which our sons will reach distinction and carve out for themselves fame and fortune?" He dared them to "record your votes among those who are content to vegetate like dormice." Charlottetown was, in a sense, a public relations exercise — except there was no public as yet. As a Prince Edward Island reporter complained, "a band of conspirators could not observe more secrecy than they have done." Perhaps the delegates were their own public, and what took place was self-hypnosis. Whatever it was, it was powerful enough to encourage them to repeat the experience, this time to hammer out specific resolutions. In October the conference was resumed at the capital of Canada, Quebec City.

There the mood held up surprisingly well. The first of the *Seventy-two Resolutions* adopted declared "the best interests and present and future prosperity of British North America will be promoted by a Federal Union under the Crown of Great Britain, provided such Union can be effected on principles just to the several Provinces"; it had been moved by Macdonald and Samuel Tilley, premier of New Brunswick. On that basis the remainder went on to spell out the broad outlines of a federation, not forgetting the stipulation that "the General Government shall secure, without delay, the completion of the Intercolonial Railway from Rivière-du-Loup through New Brunswick to Truro, in Nova Scotia," and providing that "the Sanction of the Imperial and Local Parliaments shall be sought for the Union of the Provinces, on the principles adopted by the Conference." After their three weeks of concentrated work, the Quebec delegates could congratulate themselves on an impressive achievement, and look forward to implementing Confederation sometime in 1865.

It was not to be. Opening the debate beyond the ranks of the inner few was to invite failure. One by one the Atlantic colonies discovered obstacles in the way. Newfoundland, of course, had always been peripheral to the movement, excluded even from Maritime union. Its setting, in the Atlantic, gave it an eastward not a westward orientation. Newfoundland merchants feared the high Canadian tariff, a fear shared by the Maritimers. The Irish Roman Catholic population, a majority, saw Canada West as another "Protestant Ascendancy," essentially similar to that they had fled in Ireland. Newfoundland had not been at the Charlottetown Conference, and of the two who represented it at Quebec, neither was a member of the government. The lack of interest was demonstrated when the Newfoundland papers reported on the Quebec Resolutions three weeks after papers elsewhere had carried the details. A lack of concern persisted: elections were not fought on the issue, which simply passed Newfoundland by.

The response of the other island colony was similar. Prince Edward Island also had a well developed sense of its own, withdrawn, identity. Long years of common struggle against absentee landlords had given the people a sense of cohesion, and a dread of outside domination. Premier Gray might glory in the potentialities of size, but he was answered by an assemblyman: "We might belong to Russia with her vast territories, but would that make us great?" As a newspaper editor put it, "We are content to live on our oat and barley meal, our herring and potatoes. We are not very rich, but are comfortable, and can pay our debts." It was clear that these opinions were more representative of the Island than was Gray's. He recognized the fact, and resigned; his successor, J.C. Pope, remarked that "ninety-nine out of every one hundred of the people are against Confederation" and he was not challenged. When the question of union was put before the assembly, it was defeated 23-5.

In Nova Scotia anti-Confederation feeling was pronounced. Joseph Howe, piqued that his earlier proposals along similar lines had been overlooked and that the plaudits were now going to his rival Tupper, came out against the plan. The government, fearing defeat, declined to put the issue before the people in an election, and even held off in the House; only later, using the backlash of the Fenian raids, did it obtain the vote to go ahead and request action at Westminster. Even then, the motion was merely to accept union in principle, nothing being said about the Quebec Resolutions. That Tupper was wise not to risk an election was amply borne out in 1867. In that year, Nova Scotian pride in its autonomy, together with the old elite's wish to stick by *laissez-faire* trade and commerce and avoid the protectionism sensed in Canadian tendencies, worked to return 36 out of 38 provincial members pledged to secession from Confederation, and 18 of 19 federally.

The greatest rebuff to Confederation, however, came in New Brunswick. If any one province was essential to the scheme, it was New Brunswick. In the initial geography of Confederation that was the "keystone" province. Early in 1865 Tilley had the assembly dissolved and an election called. He was opposed by the Roman Catholic bishop of Saint John, who, like his coreligionists in Newfoundland, feared a Protestant-dominated union. There was also opposition from the southwest portion of the province, which was more interested in railway ties with New England than in those with Canada. Tilley went down to defeat, his pro-Confederate party winning only 11 seats to his opponents' 30.

With the Atlantic region so inclined, it mattered little that Canada had carried a vote for Confederation 91-33. The proposal was dead. The colonial initiative was dead.

The realities of North America, especially the post-Civil War realities, now took a hand. As the *Times* was to remark when Confederation had at last been carried, "We look to Confederation as a means of saving this country from much expense and much embarrassment. . . . A people of four millions ought to be able to keep up their own defences." Westminster showed that it was prepared to use considerable pressure to get the Atlantic colonies to reconsider. Sometimes the methods were petty: for instance, the salary of the governor of Prince Edward Island was paid from imperial funds, and it was threatened to be discontinued; when that colony asked for and received imperial troops to maintain order during the 1865 Tenant Riots (the perennial question of absentee landlords and escheat again), it was billed for their cost. There were also more effective methods. Nova Scotia's governor had not been an enthusiast for Confederation; he was moved on and his place taken by the soldier hero, the defender of Kars against the Czar's hordes, Sir William Fenwick Williams. Gordon in New Brunswick had likewise been less than fully committed to Confederation; he was given a dressing down and made to put into writing his determination to do all he could to bring it about. Gordon acted with energy, and soon was reporting that "I am convinced I can make (or buy) a union majority in the legislature."

Now that the British government was making its wishes so clearly known, it was difficult to withstand the pressure. After all, was not New Brunswick the loyalist province? The vote in 1865 had been much closer than the party standings indicated, and one estimate put it at 15 949 anti-confederate to 15 556 pro-confederate. With work, that majority could be turned about. In 1866 Gordon provoked the government's resignation. In the election appreciable sums were spent, including Canadian money. The Roman Catholic vote this time round was delivered for Confederation. Coupled with the failure of the railway extension to New England, this was enough to win Tilley a majority. The vote for union (like Nova Scotia's, in principle only) was carried 33-8.

Belatedly, the way had been cleared. Late in 1866 delegates from Canada, Nova Scotia and New Brunswick gathered in London. It was unfortunate that the two island colonies were missing, but they were not vital to the exercise. On the basis of the Quebec Resolutions the British North America Act was worked out, and early in the 1867 session put through the British Parliament. Confederation was to go into effect 1 July 1867.

# — 4. The Character of Confederation —

The British North America Act that established the new Dominion, confusingly known as Canada, was designed for a giant. In many ways the

## Map 18.1: Canada, 1867–1873

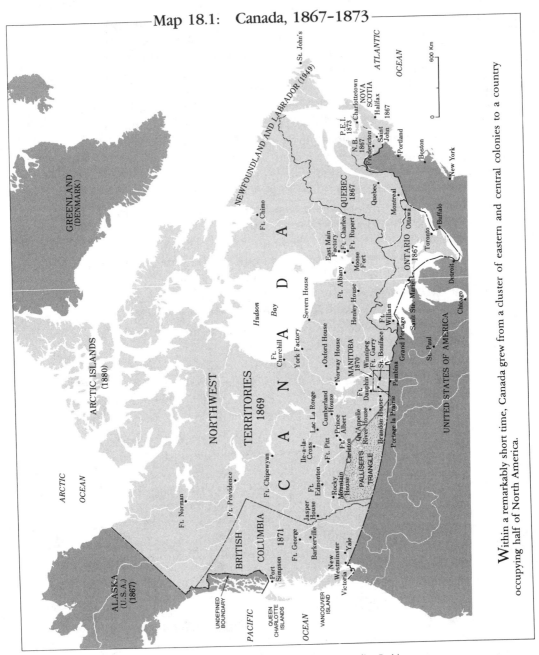

Within a remarkable short time, Canada grew from a cluster of eastern and central colonies to a country occupying half of North America.

SOURCES: Kerr, *Historical Atlas of Canada* (1975), pp. 41, 55; G. Friesen, *The Canadian Prairies: A History* (Lincoln, NE: University of Nebraska Press; 1985).

Dominion at its birth belied this description. It consisted of four provinces only, Nova Scotia, New Brunswick, and the old Canada, now split into its historical components, and renamed Quebec and Ontario. The population was small, numbering (in 1871 and in round terms) 3.5 million; of these some 1.6 million were in Ontario, 1.2 million in Quebec, with 357 000 in Nova Scotia and 285 000 in New Brunswick. When compared with the United States' 40 million it was puny indeed. Yet it was assumed that the infant would soon grow to lusty adulthood. Newfoundland and Prince Edward Island could surely not remain outside Confederation for long. There were ambitious plans for the inclusion of Red River, the North West, and the recently united British Columbia. Expansion both east and west would round out a truly transcontinental nation, and who knew what promises the north held?

A country such as Canada, even as an infant, had the problems of a giant. Although only the trunk of what was intended, Canada was still a vast land. Communication had much improved of late, for what canals had done earlier for bulk goods, the railway and telegraph were now doing for people and ideas. Even so, the obstacles to an easy union remained daunting. The country was still marked by high diversity. There were the provincial identities, strong enough to seek to undo the work of Confederation in Nova Scotia. Within provinces, striking discrepancies existed between maturing centres and the outback, where raw frontier conditions might still be found; the contrast between metropolis and hinterland could be stark. There was also religious pluralism. The Protestants were split into many denominations, and even subdivided: in 1867 the Methodists were organized in five distinct bodies, the Presbyterians in four. Catholics, in an age when they were still looked upon with grave suspicion in Britain and the United States, were 40 percent of the population and moving aggressively into high positions; this advanced standing prompted Archbishop Connolly to urge Confederation in 1866 in New Brunswick, contrasting Catholic progress in British North America with that in the United States. This is not to suggest, however, that Canada was free from Protestant-Catholic animosity — far from it, as events were to show. Also, there were ethnic divisions. At first sight it might appear that there were only two groups, French Canadians (about 30 percent) and British Canadians (about 60 percent). The others, so important in the twentieth century, were then less than 10 percent, though in local concentrations they could have a significance. On closer inspection, however, the two major groups dissolve into their components. There were United Empire Loyalists, whose ancestors had been Americans for generations, to set against Britons fresh from England. Scots were different again, and had further to be distinguished as Lowland and Highland; within this last category there was a fundamental difference of Catholic and Protestant. The Irish were quite distinct as well, whether they were Orange Protestants or Green Catholics. Even the French Canadians were split to some extent, for alongside those of Quebec was an Acadian group in New Brunswick growing in numbers and in self-consciousness; in 1881 Maritime Acadians were to meet in a "national" convention at Memramcook. With all this diversity the overworked term "mosaic" simply has to be used — though it is a term whose precise meaning should be remembered.

Aware of the mosaic, the Fathers of Confederation had to settle for a Confederation. Only in that way could the very real differences be adequately represented. However, if British North America dictated that model, another North American reality dictated caution. Once more, the American Civil War was exerting its influence.

The war has previously been mentioned for its military impact. Now its moral effect must also be noted. There had been a long history of British American dislike of things American, indeed scorn and contempt would not be too strong terms to apply. Large bodies of colonial opinion derided the Americans for their lack of restraint, of taste, for their espousal of a levelling democracy, for their political and commercial corruption — in short, for just about everything. Thomas D'Arcy McGee, a Father of Confederation, lumped the United States in with all the Latin American republics and claimed

> On the fate of so many republics we may surely be allowed to reason. . . . And what has been their invariable experience? Is there one, a single one, which can be cited as an example of a "model Republic". . . ? . . . If stability be essential to good government, they have not had stability, and therefore their description of government cannot be good either for themselves or for others.

Hector Langevin, another Father of Confederation and successor to Cartier as spokesman for Quebec, argued the case for Confederation by saying it was that or annexation to the United States, "the most materialistic, the most immoral of modern nations." Now the Civil War seemed to prove everything Canadians had been saying about American degeneracy. In particular, the war pinpointed a basic flaw in the founding of that nation: too great a scope had been allowed to local rights at the expense of the central government. Many spoke to this analysis, but Macdonald probably put it as well as anyone:

> Ever since the [American] Union was formed the difficulty of what is called

"State Rights" has existed, and this has had much to do in bringing on the present unhappy war in the United States. They commenced, in fact, at the wrong end. They declared by their constitution that each state was a sovereignty in itself, and that all the powers incidental to a sovereignty belonged to each state, except those powers which, by the Constitution, were conferred upon the general government and Congress. Here we have adopted a different system. We have strengthened the general government.

In discussion and even in drafts of the British North America Act the consequences of this approach were given free rein; at one stage it was proposed to reduce the provinces to "municipalities of larger growth," and to have their chief executive officers called "superintendents" and their legislation "ordinances." If in the end the wish to strike an elevated tone kept the terms "lieutenant-governor" and "laws," care was taken to have the former appointed by the governor-general in council, that is, by the federal government, and the latter disallowable by the central government. The balance was tipped so strongly in favour of a legislative union that A.A. Dorion, the *Rouge* critic of the Quebec Resolutions, declared, "it is no Confederation that they are proposing for us, but quite simply a legislative union disguised beneath the name of Confederation."

Dorion went too far. The British North America Act was a compromise. In the division of powers as between federal and provincial authorities this was to be seen. Section 91 stated

> It shall be lawful for the Queen, by and with the Advice and consent of the Senate and House of Commons, to make Laws for the Peace, Order, and good Government of Canada, in relation to all Matters not coming within the Classes of Subjects by this Act assigned exclusively to the Legislatures of the Provinces.

Unfortunately, it then went on to specify 27 such areas of federal concern, and although it was expressly stated that the listing was "not . . . to restrict the Generality of the foregoing Terms of this Section," it has sometimes seemed that the provinces were given everything not so listed. That was not the case, however; the following Section 92 gave the provinces an enumerated list, the last of which specifies their nature — "Generally all Matters of a merely local or private Nature in the Province." The intention becomes crystal clear when the continuation of Macdonald's speech given above is added:

> We have given the general legislature all the great subjects of legislation. We have conferred on them, not specifically and in detail all the powers which are

incidental to sovereignty, but we have expressly declared that all subjects of general interest not distinctly and exclusively conferred upon the local government and local legislatures, shall be conferred upon the general government and legislature. We have thus avoided that great source of weakness which has been the cause of the disruption of the United States.

To modern ears there seems something paradoxical, not to say illogical, about the thinking here. On the one hand important subjects are left to the federal authority, but on the other the "merely local or private" matters include the vital one of education about which Quebec was so concerned and which was to cause so much conflict. To mid-nineteenth century Victorians, however, the paradox did not exist in the same way. In their view the real concern of a citizen was making a living, and that conceived of in the narrowest of terms. The federal government was to arrange matters so that the greatest number of citizens had the greatest facility for making that living. To say that other ends, such as religion or education or reformed spelling, were private was not to say that they were unimportant, but rather to say that they belonged to a realm different from that of the public, money-getting one. Bear in mind, too, that mid-Victorians had only an incomplete understanding of the need for change and adjustment. They sensed that the economic world demanded ceaseless vigilance, but a school system was something to be implemented once and for all — the community had a consensus on it and could be trusted to put it into place. Cartier, so deeply connected with the Grand Trunk and yet a *Bleu* spokesman for traditional values, made a nice distinction between a "political nationality" and a cultural one. Today, the distinction does not make sense, but then it did.

A second compromise lay in the institutional arrangements. To satisfy those who wanted to see a vigorous government able to use politics to foster economic development, "rep by pop" was to be employed in electing the lower house (as part of the elevation in tone it was to become the House of Commons). Quebec was to be granted 65 seats, and the other provinces seats in proportion, a census being taken every ten years. It was this proposal that had affronted the delegates from Prince Edward Island at the Quebec Conference, for under the scheme as then applied the island would have received only 5 seats in a House of 194. As it turned out, in 1867 Ontario got 82, Nova Scotia 19, and New Brunswick 15, for a total of 181. To satisfy those who feared giving too much power to a large and densely populated area, and those who were opposed to a too populist approach, an upper house (the Senate) was to be composed on a regional basis. At Quebec City it was agreed that there be three regions with equal representation, Ontario, Quebec, and the Maritimes. Each was to have 24 senators, with Nova Scotia and New Brunswick having ten apiece and Prince Edward Island four. When the last declined to enter Confederation, its seats were equally shared between the remaining Maritime provinces. The regional representation was a face-saving device. It was not intended that the Senate cause problems by vetoing Commons legislation, and at London special imperial intervention occurred to find a formula by which additional senators might be appointed in order to break a deadlock. That the senators were appointed by the governor-general, that is, in effect, by the federal government, further exposed the sham of senatorial power.

Since the Fathers of Confederation so clearly repressed their first love, a legislative union, in favour of the compromise of Confederation, it has been claimed that what really took place in 1866-67 was the cementing of a pact between the provinces. The form, it is said, might have been the imposition of an imperial act, but the reality was colonial agreement that used a British rubber stamp to approve what had been done and give it legal sanction. Those who argue this way place great store by such statements of Macdonald in the old Canadian Assembly that "the scheme . . . should be dealt with as a treaty," or of Cartier that "it is the same as any other treaty," or of McGee that "[the Quebec Resolutions] we speak of here [form] a treaty." Even Lord Carnarvon, who piloted the bill through the House of Lords, can be found referring to "a treaty of union."

From this starting point two elaborations of the compact theory have been advanced. The first claims that since the British North America Act was the result of provincial treaty, it can be amended only by the unanimous consent of all the provinces (later additions to the original four are deemed to have equal standing with them). In other words, each province has veto power over constitutional change — a view, incidentally, that the absence from the British North America Act of any amending formula makes additionally attractive to some. The second elaboration is a special case of the first, and argues that Confederation was a compact between two founding races, the French Canadians and the British Canadians, and that implicit in Confederation was a commitment to bilingualism and biculturalism throughout the widening Dominion. If no evidence of this could be found in the already established English-speaking regions of Canada, yet it is claimed federal attitudes towards the just forming west support this theory.

The basis of both these arguments is defective. The terms "treaty," "pact," and so on were used, but overwhelmingly by Canadians in Canadian assembly debates, and understandably so. Proponents of the Quebec Resolutions faced telling attacks from the *Rouges* and independents who felt that the experiment was too dangerous, that Brown was not to be trusted, that once inside Confederation the English would renege on their undertakings towards the *Canadiens*. To still such accusations it was necessary for the pro-Confederates to insist upon the inviolability of agreements made at Quebec, but once away from Canada, they could acknowledge the truth. Indeed, they had to, for the Nova Scotians and New Brunswickers had never agreed to the Quebec Resolutions and openly said so. When confronted in London by this fact Macdonald had to take refuge in a typically gnomic utterance: "We are quite free," he said, "to discuss points as if they were open, although we may be bound to the Quebec scheme." It was vintage Macdonald, and if it has any meaning at all it would seem that the first "we" refers to the participants of the London Conference and the second to the Canadian delegates. Moreover, it is difficult to support the notion of contracting parties: first, any contract was presumably embodied in the Quebec Resolutions, but the final form differed from the Resolutions; second, no province — not even Canada, which had approved the Resolutions — subsequently approved the Act. Most worrying to compact theorists, however, is the following admission from Macdonald, a supposed upholder of "compact," in a letter to Tilley:

> Canada is bound by the address to the Queen praying her to submit a measure to Parliament based on the Quebec resolutions. Nova Scotia and New Brunswick require modifications to that scheme. How are we to arrive at a satisfactory solution of the difficulty? . . . It appears to us to be important that the Bill should not be finally settled until just before the meeting of the British Parliament. The measure must be carried *per saltem*, and no echo of it must reverberate through the British provinces until it becomes law.

However, he concluded cynically, "The Act once passed and beyond remedy, the people would soon learn to be reconciled to it." Finally, it may be pointed out that when in power as prime minister of the federal government, Macdonald acted and voted in opposition to explicit statements of the compact theory.

From start to finish Confederation had been marked by secrecy and less than honest maneuvering. The resurrection in 1863 of Maritime union, the peg on which Canadian Confederation was hung, had been managed by four men: the colonial secretary, the governor of New Brunswick, and the premiers of Nova Scotia and New Brunswick. When the debate was widened, it met with apathy when not with hostility. Strong external pressure had to be brought to win even the most general of approval for the London Conference. Canadian debate was fuller and more committed, but in the end that openness was sacrificed. When it was finally legislated, Confederation was not submitted to the people for their reaction. For the birth of a nation, it was less than heroic, and if Canadians have agonized over their identity it may be largely due to the manner of their parting from the parent.

## — 5. Dominion from Sea to Sea —

The rounding out of Canada, a task that was essentially completed within the next six years, gave Canadians the opportunity to show more fully the nature of the experiment they had embarked upon. One fact soon became clear: the union was to be a strictly practical affair.

Other nations springing into life have seized the chance to proclaim to the world the ideals that have animated them. The United States is an excellent example. From the Declaration of Independence sonorous statements ring forth to the effect that "all men are created equal, that they are endowed . . . with certain unalienable Rights, that among these are Life, Liberty, and the pursuit of Happiness." Even the American constitution includes the "Blessings of Liberty to ourselves and our Posterity" as an aim to set alongside the more prosaic wish to "form a more perfect Union." The British North America Act would have nothing to do with such sentiments; they are wholly lacking. What is found there instead, and in this it is surely unique, is "a declaration that the construction of the Intercolonial Railway is essential to the consolidation of the Union of British North America." It was a precedent that was to be fruitful.

In 1870 emissaries from British Columbia arrived in Canada. The province had never doubted that its future lay with the new Dominion. Its existing vulnerability was underlined by the fact that those delegates had to travel by way of San Francisco. Thus, the crux of negotiations had to be transportation. British Columbia wanted a carriage road to be built at once and a railway to be commenced within three years. The other terms, essentially the assumption of the provincial debt of about one million dollars, were not important. Cartier for the federal government overwhelmed the delegates. A railway would be begun within two years and finished in ten. As one delegate noted at the time:

> With regards to the Railway the Committee . . . were enthusiastically in favour thereof. *They do not consider they can hold the country without it.* It was a condition of

union with the provinces and they could not see any reason why if agreed on it should not be made a condition with us.

The governor of British Columbia was overjoyed and exclaimed "The terms agreed on by the Canadian Government . . . are outstandingly better . . . than what we asked for." In 1871 British Columbia entered Confederation.

Attempts to win Prince Edward Island finally succeeded in 1873. Again it was railways that did it. The Island had made a valiant attempt to go it alone, receiving an American emissary in great style in the hope of winning reciprocity with the United States. That initiative, however, was firmly stepped on by the colonial office. In a despairing attempt to maintain an independent prosperity an Island Railway was begun, but the usual sorry tale of indebtedness followed, and by 1873 the people had to contemplate a provincial debt that had increased sixteen fold since they had rejected Confederation in 1865. The Dominion undertook to rescue the railway, and sweetened the offer with a guarantee of year-round steam navigation between Island and mainland. The still-burning question of land titles and absentee proprietors was also taken a step nearer solution with the making of a special grant. Popular dislike of the necessity to enter Confederation lingered on and songs like the following made the rounds:

With dishes fine their tables shine,
They live in princely style,
They are the knaves who made us slaves
And sold Prince Edward Isle.

Railways could not be a sweetener in Nova Scotia where secessionist sentiment was strong but where lines were already adequate. However, when Howe went to London with impressive petitions for repeal, when the Imperial Commons could find 87 votes for Howe's position, and when the provincial attorney-general could say in debate that "Nova Scotia would not rebel against the Queen, but when the Queen rebelled against nova Scotia and abdicated her authority over Nova Scotia, Nova Scotians were released from their allegiance," then the Canadian government had to do something. While they maintained a fixed determination to stand on the legality of 1867 — agreeing with the British government's view that "no legal ground of objection to the Confederation Act exists . . . [and] that the Imperial legislation only took place in accordance with the expressed desire of the people of all the Provinces expressed in the only known constitutional mode — through their respective legislatures" — they could be more forthcoming in financial directions. Better terms were granted, essentially an extra $20 000 a year, and with that Nova Scotia had to be content. The problems of a loyalist people in the face of an intransigent mother-country were great, the attorney-general notwithstanding, and Howe recognized the reality. In 1869 he entered the federal cabinet and the danger of Nova Scotian withdrawal was ended for the time being.

In these three instances, the task of rounding out Confederation and smoothing away resistances was a relatively easy matter. A pragmatic approach came readily to those involved, and it paid dividends. When it came to the vast western interior, however, it was a very different story.

Much of what had to be done was carried out in the practical way just noted. It was recognized that the speedy and successful incorporation of the territory was vital. Elements in the United States had not given up hope of annexing the area. The necessity of a contiguous approach to British Columbia was plain. The productive capacity of the land had to be unlocked as soon as possible to offset the vast costs that would be involved. Settlers would have to be attracted and retained. The first step was acquiring title to the millions of hectares held by the Hudson's Bay Company. Canada and Britain together negotiated expeditiously for the transfer. For $300 000 and one twentieth of the land in the fertile belt the bargain was struck, to go into effect 1 December 1869. Soon afterwards, in 1872, a Dominion Lands Act was passed. Surveyors had been dispatched to Red River even before the transfer was to take place, and now the act made simple the actual settling on the land from a legal point of view. Law and order were the concern of the central government, and in 1873 the North West Mounted Police was established. This was an impressive beginning, but when it came to the political arrangements the sure hand of pragmatism faltered.

During 1869 the government had prepared a Temporary Act for the administration of Rupert's Land. A governor and council were to rule until, as the character of the new colony became clearer, more permanent arrangements could be made in keeping with the wishes of the settlers. Then, and it was assumed that it would be off in some distant future, the colony would be able to enter Confederation as a province. Nothing in the Temporary Act itself would necessarily antagonize the people of Red River, but the way in which matters were being arranged was insulting. Not enough was done to assure the thousands already established about Fort Garry that their rights and aspirations would be taken into account. There was not even a token appeal to local opinion, such as had happened in Nova Scotia. The majority of

Red River settlers were Métis, offspring in the main of Indian mothers and fur traders, Selkirk settlers, and varied Europeans who had worked through the area. There were English-speaking Métis, but French predominated. A few were Protestant, but most were Catholic. They had developed a sense of themselves as a new nation, and were extremely sensitive to slights real and fancied. The arrogance of Canadians, especially of Ontarioans who looked upon Métis land as a mere extension of their own province, was galling to them — as were the pretensions to superiority. They were a people in need of reassurance, but instead the government further antagonized them by appointing as lieutenant-governor William McDougall. He was an ex-colleague of Brown (with all that implied for Quebec) and had a record as a harsh negotiator ever since his dealings with the Indians of Manitoulin Island in 1862.

Métis resentment became open when McDougall attempted to cross into Red River before 1 December. He was stopped and ordered to withdraw. The Métis went on to take control of Fort Garry, the settlement's capital. A provisional government emerged under the leadership of Louis Riel, a young man of a prominent Red River family who had been educated in Quebec. Quickly he revealed charismatic qualities and was able to impose his ideas on the people. Above all he was able to work with the French-Canadian clergy and identify his conception of the new nation with the French and Catholic forces. Confronted by a dangerous situation that threatened to reopen the old sectionalism of pre-Confederation days, Macdonald and his cabinet had to tread warily. They agreed to negotiate with the Red River authorities, and a delegation left for Ottawa for that purpose. In its main aim, the delegation was successful. Instead of Red River coming into Confederation as a colony of Canada, it entered as a province, Manitoba. To accommodate the province's duality — French and English-speaking, Protestant and Catholic — its constitution was patterned on that of Quebec. There the duality had led to stipulations in the British North America Act that there would be equality of language in legislature and courts. The same was guaranteed in the Manitoba Act. Education rights were written in. It was also done with the Manitoba Act. Quebec was also given a bicameral legislature, whereas Ontario's was unicameral. The Manitoba Act gave diminutive Red River an upper house, a recognized check to cultural totalitarianism.

It is important to grasp that the Manitoba Act was wrung from a reluctant government. Without Riel's intervention it would have been able to follow a more leisurely policy of wait and see — exactly Macdonald's style. That the province was something of an aberration is revealed by the incredibly small size of the original province; before its extension, Manitoba was known as the "postage stamp" province, and in debate on the Manitoba Act the jest was made that the government should put a fence round it and whitewash it. Naturally the dominion preferred to keep the territories, where its railway was to run, as free as possible from provincial contamination, but that alone cannot explain the determination to keep Manitoba so small. For as first moved, Manitoba would not even have included the two hundred-odd families at Portage, not 80 kilometres from Fort Garry. In explaining this exclusion Macdonald said that Portage should be preserved "as the nucleus of a new Province altogether British." When later he agreed to modify his position he let the cat out of the bag with the *"qui s'excuse, s'accuse"* statement that the government had no intention "of making Manitoba a kind of French Canadian reserve."

Whenever the mosaic analogy is brought forward it would be well to follow through and consider it carefully. A mosaic obtains its effect of shimmering, blending totality by the use of hard edged, monochrome building blocks. That was how biculturalism was viewed in 1867-73, not a merging of cultures at all levels and in all areas, but a juxtaposition of enclaves. Thus, in 1871 the New Brunswick schools question blew up: the Roman Catholics in that Province appealed the denial of what they thought had been guaranteed them under the British North America Act. The federal Commons voted on whether to get involved in upholding a national conception of biculturalism; on a free vote they voted against by 176-34. In 1873 a new Parliament required a speaker. The old Canadian practice had been to alternate English- and French-speaking. Macdonald reappointed an anglophone. In keeping with this viewpoint, Quebec and Manitoba were to be islands of French culture. They might have been called ghettos.

Manitoba had, by its sheer existence, affronted Ontario, but that was not all. It had inflamed one particular aspect of Ontario's psyche, that known as Canada First. This group, centering about the poet-publicist Charles Mair and the lawyer-militarist G.T. Denison, had come together in 1868 to celebrate the birth of Canada and to champion the claims of the "Northmen of the New World." They venerated the memory of D'Arcy McGee, the one mythologist among the Fathers of Confederation, and when he was assassinated early in 1868 they resolved to immortalize his name by continuing his crusade. Canada First deplored the lack of patriotism in a country that preferred "to crawl into existence in a humdrum, commonplace, matter-of-fact way"; they wanted trial by "fiery ordeals." The Red River rebellion, as they chose to see it, appeared to provide the ideal excuse for that "rattling war" necessary to true patriotism, and all the more so when news of the murder of Thomas

Scott inflamed Ontario. Scott was an Orangeman. He had caused trouble, and to uphold the authority of his government Riel thought he had to die when condemned for striking a guard. It was a terrible mistake on the Métis' part, and played right into the hands of Canada First. British regulars under Colonel Wolseley were sent to Red River, and a militia accompanied them. The Ontarioans among them saw their mission as punitive, and their lawlessness in the settlement exacerbated the already bad relations. Meanwhile, the Ontario Liberal premier, Edward Blake, offered $5 000 for the arrest of Scott's murderers. Canada First whipped up such a storm of protest that the federal government did not dare honour its promise of amnesty for those involved in the Red River resistance. So although Riel escaped from Fort Garry, and no bloodbath ensued, the aftermath was one of bitterness.

The limits of pragmatism had been set forth. To borrow Cartier's terminology, it was to apply to the political nationality but not to the cultural. As Canada marked a crucial stage in its evolution from colonialism to independence it had reason to feel proud of the material progress that had been made, but fearful of the tensions that loomed behind the façade.

## Suggested Reading

The two dominant personalities of this period have found excellent biographers: J.M.S. Careless, *Brown of the Globe* (1959-63), and D.G. Creighton, *John A. Macdonald* (1952-55). The other Canadian leaders of the period are treated by Careless in *The Pre-Confederation Premiers: Ontario Government Leaders, 1840-1867* (1980). See also, A. Sweeney, *George-Étienne Cartier* (1976). For Nova Scotian leaders, the older E.M. Saunders, *Three Premiers of Nova Scotia: Johnston, Howe, Tupper* (1909), has the advantage of convenience. On Tilley there is J.W. Langley's, *Sir Leonard Tilley* (1926).

Overviews of Confederation will be found in P.B. Waite, *The Life and Times of Confederation* (1962), and D.G. Creighton, *The Road to Confederation* (1964). Taken together with the Morton cited in the previous chapter, they provide a balanced view from different perspectives. For a very different approach, see S.B. Ryerson, *Unequal Union: Confederation and the Roots of Conflict, 1815-73* (1975).

More specialized treatments include: R. Cook (ed.), *Confederation* (1967); K. Pryke, *Nova Scotia and Confederation, 1864-77* (1979); F.W.P. Bolger, *Prince*

*Edward Island and Confederation, 1863-1873* (1964); J.K. Hiller, "Confederation Defeated: The Newfoundland Election of 1869," in J.K. Hiller and P. Neary, (eds.), *Newfoundland in the Nineteenth and Twentieth Centuries* (1980); A.G. Bailey, *Culture & Nationality* (1972), has two chapters dealing with New Brunswick's experience. Also to be noted is W.L. White *et al.*, *The Canadian Confederation: A Decision-Making Analysis* (1979).

The wider context is treated in R. Winks, *Canada & the United States: The Civil War Years* (1960); O.A. Kinchen, *Confederate Operations in Canada & the North* (1970); H. Senior, *The Fenians and Canada* (1978).

Canada West's interest in the prairies is described in D. Gagan, "Land, Population, and Social Change: The Initial Years in Rural Canada West," *Canadian Historical Review* (1978), and D. Owram, *Promise of Eden: The Canadian Expansionist Movement and the Idea of the West, 1856-1900* (1980). For Manitoba, W.L. Morton's *Birth of a Province* (1965) must be used with care since there are misleading omissions in this collection of documents; see also G.F.G. Stanley, *The Birth of Western Canada* (1960). The Far West is treated in M. Ormsby, *British Columbia: A History* (1958), and W.G. Sheldon (ed.), *British Columbia and Confederation* (1967).

# Index

*68 finding*